BEYOND RUST

POLITICS AND CULTURE IN MODERN AMERICA

Series Editors: Margot Canaday, Glenda Gilmore,
Michael Kazin, Stephen Pitti, Thomas J. Sugrue

Volumes in the series narrate and analyze political and social change in the broadest dimensions from 1865 to the present, including ideas about the ways people have sought and wielded power in the public sphere and the language and institutions of politics at all levels—local, national, and transnational. The series is motivated by a desire to reverse the fragmentation of modern U.S. history and to encourage synthetic perspectives on social movements and the state, on gender, race, and labor, and on intellectual history and popular culture.

BEYOND RUST

Metropolitan Pittsburgh
and the Fate of Industrial America

Allen Dieterich-Ward

UNIVERSITY OF PENNSYLVANIA PRESS

PHILADELPHIA

Copyright © 2016 University of Pennsylvania Press

All rights reserved. Except for brief quotations used for purposes of review or scholarly citation, none of this book may be reproduced in any form by any means without written permission from the publisher.

Published by
University of Pennsylvania Press
Philadelphia, Pennsylvania 19104-4112
www.upenn.edu/pennpress

Printed in the United States of America
on acid-free paper

10 9 8 7 6 5 4 3 2 1

Library of Congress Cataloging-in-Publication Data

Dieterich-Ward, Allen, author.
   Beyond rust : metropolitan Pittsburgh and the fate of industrial America / Allen Dieterich-Ward.
     pages   cm — (Politics and culture in modern America)
   Includes bibliographical references and index.
   ISBN 978-0-8122-4767-1 (alk. paper)
   1. Urban renewal—Pennsylvania—Pittsburgh—20th century. 2. Pittsburgh (Pa.)—Economic conditions—20th century. 3. Pittsburgh Metropolitan Area (Pa.)—Economic conditions—20th century. 4. Community development—Pennsylvania—Pittsburgh. 5. Urban renewal—United States—Case studies. 6. Community development, Urban—United States—Case studies. I. Title. II. Series: Politics and culture in modern America.
HT177.P5D54   2016
307.3′4160974886—dc23   2015017684

CONTENTS

Prologue   vii

Introduction. The City and Its Region   1

PART I. THE STEEL VALLEY   19

Chapter 1. Building the Region   27

Chapter 2. Mines and Mills   46

Chapter 3. The Pittsburgh Story   67

PART II. A REGION OF CONTRASTS   91

Chapter 4. Live on the Hills and Work in the City   99

Chapter 5. We're Appalachia, But We Don't Need to Be   124

Chapter 6. The New Metropolis of the Plateau   149

Chapter 7. No Development Beyond This Point   172

PART III. POST-INDUSTRIAL PITTSBURGH   199

Chapter 8. Rust Belt and Roboburgh   205

Chapter 9. Burbs of the 'Burgh   231

Chapter 10. Rivers of Steel	255
Epilogue	283
Sources	291
Notes	295
Index	335
Acknowledgments	345

PROLOGUE

This book is about a working landscape and its people, in which more than a century of hard use has eroded the distinction between the natural and the man-made. It began as an attempt to reconcile two competing visions from my childhood on the edge of metropolitan Pittsburgh. I often heard stories from my paternal grandparents about Egypt Valley, a nearby farming hamlet in the rolling hills of southeastern Ohio where they were raised. Their memories of bountiful harvests and social ties forged through the local church, school, and Grange Hall stood in sharp contrast to the area I knew from the 1980s, which had been largely abandoned by its inhabitants and deeply scarred by Consolidation Coal Company (Consol)'s enormous Egypt Valley Mine that opened there in the mid-1960s. This was now a landscape of cliff-like highwalls that rose more than a hundred feet above scrub-grass plains; of spoil banks and strip pits interspersed with the ghostly remnants of crumbling farmhouses, rusting machinery, and a hilltop cemetery around which former residents still gathered for yearly reunions.

I found out later that the fate of Egypt Valley was bound up with that of Pittsburgh, where Consol was headquartered, and that the city and its suburbs had their own landscapes to interpret. In fact, at the same time the mining company was rearranging Egypt Valley's social and physical topography, some of its executives and largest shareholders were partnering with civic leaders to do the same thing downtown. In place of the messy, mixed-use, and increasingly shabby neighborhoods that had emerged over the previous century, the region's economic and political elite envisioned a modern, rational, and productive environment that could compete with other regions. As in the countryside, the urban and suburban architecture, infrastructure, and, yes, the rivers, air and ground itself revealed the political struggles over community control, of changes in technology and transportation systems, of shifting national and international economics, and of the vagaries of natural processes. It was clear that, whether viewed from the center city looking out or from the countryside looking in, telling the story of metropolitan Pittsburgh required embracing the full panorama.

As the title *Beyond Rust* suggests, this book begins with the origins of metropolitan Pittsburgh as the world's most important industrial center and ends by extending the story past hulking ruins of steel mills, mine tipples, and abandoned rail lines that formed the backdrop of my childhood. Working landscapes and the communities they nurture, after all, seldom simply disappear either in the face of environmental degradation or job losses, and the residents of metropolitan Pittsburgh have a particularly strong attachment to their region. I came across many heroes in my travels throughout this area, but even after dozens of oral histories and many years spent in the archives, I have found few clear-cut villains. This is not to say I agreed with all of the ideas espoused by the figures in the following pages, not by a long shot. But my personal and professional background has perhaps made me more sympathetic to a wider range of perspectives than might be the norm. In order to finance his dream of owning a farm, my father went to work as a coal miner, which provided the economic base on which I, an ardent environmentalist, went to college. For their part, my grandparents enjoyed a comfortable retirement after selling the coal rights to their property in the 1980s, which they were able to continue farming thanks to more stringent reclamation laws passed, in part, due to the public outcry over the Egypt Valley mine. The histories of urban renewal and suburban expansion require a similar level of nuance; for every project completed or thwarted, those on both sides were often full of good intentions.

Introduction. The City and Its Region

When I was a kid growing up on a southeastern Ohio farm, I remember most about the hour and a half drive to downtown Pittsburgh the moment when our family car burst from the darkness of the Fort Pitt Tunnel into the sunlight dazzling off the swath of skyscrapers suddenly spread before us near the point where the Monongahela and Allegheny Rivers meet. As I now travel west on the turnpike from my home in central Pennsylvania, the city reveals itself more gradually. The first billboards promoting "Pittsburgh and Its Countryside" begin to appear at about the point where the highway merges with Interstate 70 for the rugged journey through the Allegheny Mountains. If I am driving in winter, the forecast may well be "Seasonable with a 100% chance of fun," a prediction highlighting the ski resorts of the Laurel Highlands just ahead. A little farther along, it's "Exit 91 for Whitewater Fun!" at Ohiopyle State Park during the summer, while signs for the Carnegie Science Center **robo**world™ exhibit assert the city's status as a high-tech hub.

The route we are traveling is itself a lingering testament to Pittsburgh's industrial power, originally blasted through the mountains by Andrew Carnegie, Henry Clay Frick and Cornelius Vanderbilt in their war with the mighty Pennsylvania Railroad. Heading up the miles-long ascent to the Eastern Continental Divide, a roadside sign just before the entrance to the Allegheny Mountain Tunnel marks the boundary between the Chesapeake Bay and Ohio River watersheds. Shortly after this geographical transition, I know for certain I have arrived on the edge of metropolitan Pittsburgh when the six enormous wind turbines of the Somerset Wind Farm come into view along the southern ridge. As a symbol of the region's vaunted economic transformation, however, this vision of a "clean energy future" set in verdant pasture land is complete only when it includes the defiant billboard placed deliberately in the foreground, which declares that "Wind Dies. Sun Sets. You Need Reliable, Affordable, Clean Coal Electricity."[1]

Understanding the evolution of this quintessential manufacturing region is essential for unraveling national debates on topics ranging from energy and the environment to highways and heritage development. Pittsburgh's contemporary situation is, of course, mirrored in other metropolitan areas. All central cities have intense and complicated relationships with their hinterlands, but the particular nature of the Steel City's rapid rise to industrial preeminence, unusually severe decline during the middle part of the century, and uneven revival since the 1970s lays bare the structural limitations imposed by localities and residents left unaccounted for in a "post-industrial" society.[2] During its heyday between 1880 and 1920, a regional community emerged in the Upper Ohio River Valley out of an environmental and social ethic intimately connected to the vertically integrated industrial corporation. Steel mills and coal mines reshaped the topography, communities turned their backs on polluted rivers, and the air was filled with smoke that became a clichéd signature of economic prosperity. In this metropolitan region, which I will call the Steel Valley, industrialists and financiers bound distant nodes of production into a unified economic whole through a dense web of railroad lines as Pittsburgh rose to economic dominance over an area stretching across southeastern Ohio, northern West Virginia, and southwestern Pennsylvania. While their relationships with one another and Pittsburgh itself ebbed and flowed with the broader economic tides of the twentieth century, the fate of mill towns and small cities from Wheeling and Weirton, West Virginia, to Martins Ferry and Steubenville, Ohio, to Homestead, McKeesport, and Washington, Pennsylvania, was bound to that of the broader Steel Valley.[3]

On the other hand, the area's rugged topography and multi-state nature coupled with the ethnic diversity of hundreds of thousands of new blue-collar residents and the ability of corporations to manipulate municipal boundaries resulted in an early twentieth century political configuration that was as fractured as the economy was integrated. This community fragmentation, though certainly not unique, was particularly pronounced in the Steel Valley, which makes Pittsburgh's second act as the American archetype of a successful public-private partnership all the more remarkable. Following World War II, the Republican business elite and Democratic

FIGURE 1. The Pittsburgh Metropolitan Region.

political leaders developed an ambitious program of pollution control and infrastructure development aimed at overcoming regional industrial stagnation and maintaining the central city's status as a corporate headquarters. In addition to implementing pollution control measures that cleared the notoriously smoky skies, a collaboration between the business-backed Allegheny Conference on Community Development and the administration of Mayor David Lawrence made possible the razing and rebuilding of the central business district's "Golden Triangle," which became a national model for downtown revitalization in the 1950s and 1960s.

The growth coalition behind the "Pittsburgh Renaissance," as advocates branded it, pursued nothing less than the selective erasure of the existing social and physical environment in favor of a modernist, functionally divided landscape: a conceptual goal other aging cities widely copied. Emboldened by new downtown skyscrapers, hilltop commuter suburbs and highways blasted through rough terrain, the Allegheny Conference and its local, state and federal allies also sought to refashion the broader region into a form they felt would be more attractive to corporate investment and white-collar workers. By the 1970s, the Renaissance partnership increasingly touted universities, hospitals, corporate research campuses and suburban industrial parks as the foundation for a more diversified economy. *Beyond Rust* thus scales the story of urban renewal up to the regional level where it becomes clear that the political and economic capital necessary to clear mixed-use urban areas for industrial projects, institutional expansion and modernist high-rise housing had parallels in the far-flung construction of enormous flood control reservoirs, coal surface mines, and public parks on the rural periphery.

However, the social and physical landscapes of the industrial age formed an integrated framework that proved impossible for political leaders and business executives to fully overcome on a regional level. This failure owed both to the sheer difficulty of the task and the internal tensions in a public-private partnership that sought to encourage new economic growth while maintaining the profitability of existing heavy industries. Unable to fully offset overall economic declines, the Renaissance elite instead superimposed their vision on the Steel Valley's still-stagnating mill towns and rural mining areas: an uneven transformation that laid the foundation for the social bifurcations still evident in metropolitan Pittsburgh today. Between 1960 and 1980, limited employment opportunities resulted in a nearly 4 percent drop in the region's population during a period when the nation grew by a quarter and metropolitan areas increased more than 40 percent. Out-migration was particularly pronounced from the region's smaller urban centers, which were largely unable to match the powerful public-private partnerships and enormous outside investment required to repeat downtown Pittsburgh's transformation into a center of service sector employment.[4]

The inherent instability of this region of contrasts resulted in a series of challenges to the Renaissance partnership that both drew from broader social movements and helped shape public policy debates on the state and national levels. Beginning in the early 1960s, African American and other community activists contested an urban renewal order based on the wholesale removal of existing neighborhoods and rejected the voluntarist model of environmental protection that seemed to privilege industrial production over clean air and water.[5] Universities and other nonprofit organizations in Pittsburgh demanded a larger voice in decision-making at the Allegheny Conference, suburban residents battled over highways and regional planning initiatives, and in the countryside conservationists and others faced off against coal companies and their supporters over the issue of surface mining. The catastrophic collapse of basic industry in the 1980s brought these tensions to a head, as residents, many of whom looked with hope to possibilities for re-industrialization, battled over how best to reclaim huge swaths of riverfront land opened up by mill closures for the first time in more than century. A reinvigorated public-private partnership in the central city set out to infill suburban-style commercial parks by clearing these "brownfield" sites, even as new highway construction allowed dilapidated river towns to reimagine themselves as burbs of the 'Burgh.[6]

While this expanded Renaissance coalition sought once again to impose a new order on an unruly landscape, proponents of riverfront revitalization, the conversion of abandoned rail corridors into bicycle trails, and the historic preservation of buildings began to articulate an alternative vision for economic development forged by adapting rather than erasing or ignoring the built and natural environment. From their perspective, community renewal would emerge from nurturing a sense of authenticity that could attract new residents even as it empowered neighborhoods left devastated by industrial decline. This is the Steel Valley as it entered the twenty-first century, with industrial, modernist, and what we might call postmodernist identities all jostling for control of a shared geography. At each stage of its development, Pittsburgh served as a model for other metropolitan regions—it was first among large industrial cities, first to face economic collapse, and, perhaps, first to emerge from its obsolescence into a vibrant new form. In the end, its history can help us better understand the tensions in our contemporary world as they have played out on the scale of everyday life.

* * *

This is the story of an iconic American landscape told from a regional vantage midway between the local neighborhood and the national polity. The intensity, complexity, and endurance of Pittsburgh's relationship with its hinterland requires an approach that synthesizes neighborhood-focused histories with a broader regional model that has largely been the province of geographers. Key studies of the nineteenth century emphasize that urban growth manifested not only as changes within the city or in the expansion of residential landscapes but also in far ranging linkages between metropolitan centers and rural peripheries. The rise of industrial cities could only happen as residents from throughout expanding economic regions used urban capital to exploit rural areas even as they *centralized* control of those natural and human resources into city centers. On the other hand, narratives of the twentieth century have focused largely on the *decentralization* of resources, population, and political power from the central cities to suburbs. Recent studies adopting this intellectual framework have carefully examined the transformation of urban and suburban communities, while paying close attention to the interaction between battles over the control of local spaces and federal policies that have reshaped class and racial boundaries since World War II. The push and pull of these broad centrifugal and centripetal forces provide the structural stage upon which the drama of the "metropolitan region" is acted—leave out either one and the story is necessarily incomplete.[7]

This book provides a new model for writing about metropolitan regions that combines the scope and analytical framework of existing regional studies with the emphasis on metropolitan political economy, social movements, and spatial inequality that has defined urban and suburban history since the 1980s. There are important practical and theoretical reasons why historians have avoided writing this type of community study set on a regional level. Few archival repositories include materials from throughout metropolitan regions, census divisions and state boundaries often do not line up with less tangible borders, and conceptions of regional communities vary widely over time and among local residents and institutions. Furthermore, the tensions between community bonds and the cultural, geographic, and political boundaries dividing an area require a flexible concept of the metropolitan region that is both historically and analytically contingent. In this story of metropolitan Pittsburgh, for example, I have chosen to emphasize the city's smaller neighbors downriver, particularly the Steubenville, Ohio-Weirton, West Virginia and Wheeling, West Virginia-Martins Ferry,

Ohio areas, not only because of their significant historical linkages but also in order to explore the evolving limits of those regional bonds imposed by state boundaries. Similarly, case studies of the Egypt Valley Mine and Ohiopyle State Park on the region's southwestern and southeastern fringes, respectively, reveal a common set of decision-makers, institutions, networks of capital, and assumptions about the uses of rural space that inextricably link the sites to each other and to the drama of the central city.[8]

While broadly representative of manufacturing areas more generally, from the 1890s to the 1980s the Steel Valley featured two distinctive attributes—a high degree of specialization in basic manufacturing and the domination of a few very large, multidivisional industrial corporations—that together set the stage for its meteoric rise and subsequently hampered efforts at economic diversification. Paralleling work on other North American manufacturing areas, Pittsburgh scholars have charted the expansion of this industrial region in southwestern Pennsylvania. *Beyond Rust* pushes this framework both forward in time, as economic bonds began to loosen in the mid-twentieth century, and across state boundaries to incorporate a regional hinterland that formed a continuation of the heavy industrial concentration upstream. Pittsburgh was the closest big city to Wheeling and Steubenville, which were not able to support the same range of universities, theaters, professional sports teams, and business services found in their larger neighbor. Retail, wholesale, and other sales districts generally extended throughout the area, while mail delivery and the number of telephone calls from the Ohio Valley to Pittsburgh far surpassed the volume to any other city. At the Steel Valley's industrial peak, residents from throughout the metropolitan region shared a common culture, experienced a similar environment, participated in the same labor pool, and relied on a single set of economic advantages irrespective of political and administrative boundaries.[9]

The unraveling of the coal, steel, and rail nexus at the Steel Valley's economic heart holds the key to understanding the origins of America's industrial crisis. Pittsburgh reached its economic peak relative to the rest of the nation just after World War I, long before concerns materialized about foreign competition, the New International Division of Labor, robots on the assembly line, or the ossification of labor-management relations. Over subsequent decades, metropolitan population growth slowed as manufacturing and mining employment stagnated and began to decline. This deceleration reflected national trends, such as the substitution of petroleum and natural gas for the area's bituminous coal, the shifting of capital to Detroit and other newer industrial centers, and the substitution of machines for human labor. At the same time, Pittsburgh lost the advantages of location and natural resources that undergirded its rise to dominance. The region continued for decades as an important supplier of coal, plate glass, metals and other basic goods, but its population maxed out in the early 1960s—well before the cataclysmic collapse of the steel industry beginning in the late 1970s. This early decline in overall population stood in marked contrast to other large urban districts where postwar losses in the central city were more than offset by suburban growth, a fact that made the Steel Valley an important bellwether for other North American industrial regions.[10]

As a result, the story of Pittsburgh and its hinterland provides a model for a more nuanced analysis of "deindustrialization" and its geographical auxiliary, the Rust Belt. Political and civic leaders increasingly saw gains in the service sector, including education and health care, as a way to offset stagnating employment in the area's traditional heavy industrial base. By the 1970s, a new set of regional bonds had gradually emerged connecting the Golden Triangle's skyscrapers and Pittsburgh's universities to highway-oriented research and industrial parks that looked a lot like the high-tech growth areas associated with Boston's Route 128 Corridor as well as the so-called "Sun Belt" that stretched from the Research Triangle of North Carolina to the aerospace complexes of Texas to California's Silicon Valley. However, these processes never fully compensated for the continuing loss of industrial jobs, nor were employment gains distributed equally throughout the region. Consequently, older cities and towns, especially in the river valleys and on the rural periphery, became increasingly isolated from areas of suburban growth. This was especially the case for the Ohio and West Virginia communities on the western edge of the Steel Valley, where a lack of postwar highway construction resulted in the partial severing of transportation links with the metropolitan core.[11]

Reframing economic development at the scale of the metropolitan region reveals a great deal of agency at the local level that simply cannot be explained away by a simplistic Rust Belt/Sun Belt divide. The obvious economic distress of blue-collar mill towns in the Monongahela, Allegheny, Beaver, and Ohio River Valleys hastened calls in the 1980s for connecting areas of high unemployment to suburban growth centers through worker retraining and the construction of new roads. This suburban strategy, which also included the transformation of abandoned riverfront mill sites into highway-oriented industrial parks, required a shift that was as much about identity as it was about infrastructure. During the 1990s, highway improvements and the completion of a new bridge across the Ohio River, for example, allowed Steubenville to re-imagine itself as a "Burb of the 'Burgh" in much the same way local boosters had branded themselves in the industrial era—a small town with easy access to big city amenities—even as the community remained a junior partner in the process and residents largely abandoned its original downtown. Exploring post-steel development strategies in the nation's most iconic industrial region thus provides an essential case study for interpreting larger trends whereby struggling communities throughout North America sought places for themselves within a new economic and spatial order.[12]

* * *

The Pittsburgh Renaissance was the prototype for a public-private partnership transforming a city from a manufacturing to a service base; understanding its successes and failures is essential for explaining the broader narrative of postwar urban renewal as well as the evolving constellation of market-oriented public policies scholars have dubbed "neoliberal urbanism."[13] "The Pittsburgh Story," as boosters described it, began with an exposition of the Steel Valley's political incapacity, physical degradation, and economic decline in the 1930s. Following World War II, David Lawrence, the local boss of the Democratic Party, partnered with the Allegheny Conference, backed by financier Richard King Mellon, in implementing an ambitious renewal program. While business leaders touted the Golden Triangle as a privately financed venture, beginning in the mid-1950s the Keynesian expansion of federal funding underwrote both urban revitalization and suburban growth. Eventually opposition grew from neighborhood residents threatened by the advance of the city's Urban Redevelopment Authority, especially in the largely African American Hill District, and the political coalition behind the Renaissance unraveled in the late 1960s. As in other cities that copied Pittsburgh's model, postwar revitalization left an ambiguous legacy of demolished neighborhoods, modernist superblocks incompatible with inner-city densities, and a general distrust of the power of eminent domain wielded by aggressive municipal officials.[14]

Narratives of urban renewal, like this one, can be oddly placeless—set in a spatial vacuum where the archetypal battles between neighborhood groups and city hall seem disconnected from the fate of the metropolitan areas in which they took place. This scholarly myopia is troubling, because, as in Oakland, St. Louis, Detroit, and other North American cities, the public-private partnership behind the Pittsburgh Renaissance always understood its mission as improving the overall economic competitiveness of the region. Business executives and political leaders at local, state, and federal levels pursued costly smoke and flood control efforts, highway construction, a system of rural parks, and urban renewal projects, including the corporate skyscrapers of the Golden Triangle, within an overall framework of attracting and maintaining population and business investment. However, to an extent unmatched among American cities, efforts to encourage economic transformation took place against a backdrop of extreme political fragmentation, with Allegheny County alone containing nearly 130 independent municipalities. Even when the Renaissance partnership managed to coordinate among the handful of Pennsylvania counties surrounding Pittsburgh, such as in the promotion of highway construction and regional park creation, the political and cultural barriers to including the communities of Ohio and West Virginia in a shared regional vision proved virtually impossible to surmount.[15]

Turning our attention to Pittsburgh's regional hinterland underscores the fact that, as in the rest of the nation, the residents of the Steel Valley's smaller cities were not merely passive victims of Rust Belt deindustrialization. During the early 1950s, organizations modeled on the Renaissance partnership began cropping up throughout the region, including the Wheeling Area Conference on Community Development, which launched local infrastructure development programs with varying degrees of success. However, Pittsburgh had advantages in terms of administrative capacity, political connections to state and federal agencies, and economic power that the smaller cities in the region could not duplicate. Time and again, hinterland communities developed ambitious proposals for their own little Renaissances, only to fail either from lack of political will or from the inability to attract new employers downtown. From Steubenville, Ohio, to Monessen, Pennsylvania, all the Steel Valley's older cities ended the 1970s with deteriorating downtowns, continued dependence on a handful of large industrial employers, and increasingly elderly and poor populations. In turn, impoverishment in and outmigration from peripheral areas placed structural limitations on the overall economic transformation envisioned by the Allegheny Conference even as residents in neighborhoods slated for clearance questioned the benefits of urban renewal in Pittsburgh itself.[16]

This expanded view of the Renaissance also provides an avenue for exploring the public policy decisions that laid the foundations for the nation's "technoburbs" emerging most famously in Northern California's Silicon Valley, Boston's Route 128 Corridor, and North Carolina's Research Triangle. Initially, Pittsburgh's public-private partnership conceived of the suburbs in primarily residential terms complementing jobs-oriented urban renewal projects. However, beginning with the 1949 opening of the Bettis Atomic Research Laboratory, run jointly by the federal government and Westinghouse Electric Corporation, and the Pittsburgh International Airport in 1952, the development of a series of corporate research campuses and publicly subsidized industrial parks over the next two decades provided a springboard for the growth of high-tech and service sector employment in the suburbs. Back in the city, the Lawrence administration's support for urban renewal allowed several major campus expansions at the University of Pittsburgh (Pitt); affiliation with the state in 1966 led to a massive expansion of its size and the scope of its research activities. Over the next three decades, the connection between and among the city's high-tech suburbs, Pitt, and Carnegie Mellon University became an increasingly important component of the public policy response to industrial decline, culminating in the creation of high profile, publicly funded research and development centers in the early 1980s.[17]

Following the collapse of the Renaissance partnership in the early 1970s, the struggle of business leaders, executives at non-profit organizations, and municipal officials to deal with changing local, state, and federal attitudes toward urban renewal made Pittsburgh an important laboratory for public policy innovation. Between his election as the city's mayor in 1969 and his selection as deputy attorney general by President Carter in 1977, Peter Flaherty severed institutional connections with the Allegheny Conference, scaled back urban renewal projects, and directed a larger portion of municipal spending away from downtown. Faced with dramatic cuts to federal spending on aid to cities, Flaherty set the standard for a new wave of fiscal populism among liberal Democratic mayors through cost-saving measures, the elimination of public sector jobs, the reduction of some city services, and an increased reliance on community-based organizations that would play a pivotal role in subsequent urban development. Outside city government, a partnership between conservative philanthropist Richard Mellon Scaife and the nonprofit Pittsburgh History and Landmarks Foundation led to the creation of Station Square, a festival marketplace designed to showcase the economic viability of a privately financed, heritage-based commercial district.[18]

Out of this context, a revived public-private coalition gradually emerged, based on a pragmatic model for growth that adapted the earlier Mellon-Lawrence partnership to fit the changing political landscape of the 1980s and 1990s. In his last year in office before leaving for Washington, D.C., Flaherty's stance toward the Allegheny Conference softened considerably as his staff sought ways to encourage the expansion of university-related employment and cautiously advocated the selective use of eminent domain to assemble land for commercial uses. The subsequent administration of Richard Caliguiri (1977–1988) embraced these priorities and launched a major downtown revitalization program dubbed Renaissance II. Unlike the top-down decision-making of the postwar era, however, fiscal constraints on both the government and corporate sides forced the inclusion of a broader range of voices and required that the city's primary role in urban development be in arranging incentives, such as tax increment financing, to private investors. The success of Station Square and its symbolic inclusion in Renaissance II also highlighted the increasing role of foundations and community development corporations (CDCs) not only in funding projects but also in conceiving and nurturing new approaches to urban development that relied less on direct government oversight, overt public financing, and the use of eminent domain.[19]

Beyond Rust thus places the ideas that scholars associate with the emergence of the "neoliberal city" since the 1970s, such as the privatization and dismantling of public services, the increasing use of tax credits and other novel financing instruments, and the expanded role of public-private partnerships within a longer historical trajectory as well as a broader metropolitan framework.[20] Certainly, the decline of federal funding for urban development coupled with the collapse of the steel industry in the 1980s forced the region's political leaders to embrace market-driven solutions that often did little to address the problems of inner city poverty. However, many of the features urbanists ascribe to the rise of neoliberalism in the 1970s had long been part of the Renaissance model. The Allegheny Conference and local politicians created many of the key institutional players involved in Pittsburgh's reinvention of the 1980s and 1990s, including the city's Urban Redevelopment Authority, decades earlier. Similarly, the successes of newly formed CDCs could be traced to the basic pattern of public-private cooperation established during the redevelopment of the Golden Triangle and modified during the community backlash of the late 1960s. By contrast, the region's smaller cities, such as Wheeling, West Virginia, where a public referendum abolished the city's Urban Renewal Authority in 1973, again struggled to assemble the political and economic capital necessary to forge effective public-private partnerships in the even more complicated context of rapid deindustrialization. The Steel Valley thus provides a key opportunity to explore the etiology and divergent outcomes of neoliberal urbanism as it developed in an older industrial region attempting to stimulate new growth.

* * *

Metropolitan Pittsburgh's strong sense of regional identity emerged during the late nineteenth and early twentieth centuries from the deep interconnections between natural and built environments. The rugged, mountainous topography separated and distinguished the Steel Valley from other areas, while the Ohio River and its tributaries were a constant presence whether commuters were on bridges, miners were loading coal onto barges, residents were dealing with water pollution, or boaters were enjoying a sunny day on the water. On the other hand, there was nothing natural or fundamental linking the communities of the Upper Ohio Valley—the mountains and rivers, after all, served equally well as barriers to regional unification depending on the time, place, and context. Instead, each stage in the area's social and political evolution required a cultural reimagining of the relationships between and among humans and their surroundings, which, in turn, produced a range of material changes. Over time, the imprint of these land use patterns never fully disappeared, but instead existed as layers in the landscape that constrained and directed the region's subsequent evolution.[21]

Whether on the scale of the nation-state or the metropolitan region, a strong case can be made for adopting an environmental history approach in understanding the formation of "imagined" communities.[22] Pittsburgh's rise to prominence was based on the rationalization of natural resources into a production process that sought to eliminate waste and create efficiencies of scale. Even as residents celebrated the image of the shirtless, blue-collar laborer that defined civic identity, the massive assertion of power over the physical landscape went hand-in-hand with ubiquitous and sometimes violent efforts to control workers. Corporate executives proved adept at securing employee loyalty on the shop floor and in communities, eliminating or coopting political opposition, and weakening industrial unions, especially after the failure of an infamous 1892 strike in the mill town of Homestead.[23] On the other hand, air, rivers, mountains, and natural processes presented a host of formidable challenges that raised costs, hindered institution building, and constrained development. The region's bituminous coal, which formed one of the foundations of its industrial growth, also created notoriously smoky skies and those with means attempted to escape the problem by establishing wealthy enclaves upwind from the factories. By the early twentieth century, Steel Valley communities that had once begun at the water's edge increasingly turned their backs on rivers that became ever more unappealing, unsanitary, and inaccessible to residents.[24]

Pittsburgh's story allows us to push this exploration of social and environmental history forward in time to examine the complex connections between urban renewal regimes, suburban highway construction, and rural resource extraction in the countryside during the latter half of the twentieth century. As environmental costs mounted and the industrial base failed to keep pace with population growth, the public-private partnership behind the Pittsburgh Renaissance presented the revitalized Golden Triangle as a symbolic and material hub. Gleaming skyscrapers connected to new suburban residential areas by modern highways rose above a new state park that replaced a congested rail yard and tenement houses with a scene of bucolic tranquility. This symbolic erasure of the nineteenth century landscape echoed in the development of both large coal surface mines and public recreational areas on the rural periphery. Strip mines and parks, while seemingly on opposite ends of the environmental spectrum, shared important structural similarities, including the consolidation of enormous tracts of land, the application of massive amounts of outside capital to local communities, and the blurring of lines between nature and artifice. They also provided necessary ingredients for the Renaissance: profit for corporations, employment for workers, and leisure activities seen as necessary for attracting and retaining middle class residents. As with urban renewal, residents of rural "sacrifice zones," areas that shouldered a disproportionate burden of negative environmental effects so that other communities could prosper, divided in complicated ways among supporters and opponents of local projects that became flashpoints in state and national battles.[25]

By the mid-1980s, an increasing number of residents and community leaders saw in the Steel Valley's industrial heritage and newly cleared riverfront brownfields an organizing framework for revitalizing communities devastated by urban decentralization and the collapse of heavy industries. Unlike the long-standing Renaissance vision of razing the messy urban/industrial landscape in order to build a modernist cityscape, historically themed sites, heritage-based building rehabilitation, and riverfront trails sought to nurture a sense of community identity, revitalize "authentic" neighborhoods, and enhance the area's reputation among the highly educated professionals that Richard Florida later called the "creative class." Pittsburgh mayor Tom Murphy (1994–2006) reimagined most fully the nineteenth-century city as an economic development tool, championing the conversion of abandoned rail lines into recreational trails, pouring municipal resources into the remediation of polluted brownfield sites, and advocating for new office buildings, museums, theaters, and sports stadiums that embraced rather than ignored the rivers. Drawing inspiration from Pittsburgh, local officials and preservationists in Homestead and Wheeling secured designation as National Heritage Areas and achieved some success in remaking their declining downtowns.[26]

Metropolitan Pittsburgh's evolution into a national model for postindustrial transformation thus emerged, in part, out of neighborhood and environmental activism that sought to adapt and reuse rather than erase or ignore the region's working landscape. As a result, its story provides important lessons on the uses of public history for community revitalization. As Murphy found out during his sometimes heavy-handed attempts to foster economic development, the very neoliberal municipal politics he rode to electoral victory meant that elected officials seeking to reorganize the urban fabric had to contend with a wide variety of preservationist, community development, and environmental organizations with their own visions for the future. During the 1990s, activists, politicians, and business leaders throughout the region worked to control not only economic and political resources but also the sites and symbols of public memory. With the skies cleared, the rivers cleaned, and many of the mills demolished, the process of interpreting, reenacting, and symbolically consuming the "Steel Valley" helped forge new connections between communities and among residents. At the same time, however, the obvious inequities of celebrating a lost blue-collar world through participation in a service-driven economy called into question the sustainability of a post-industrial Pittsburgh.[27]

When employees first erected the Homestead Works' mammoth 12,000-ton forging press in 1903, they stood at the heart of the world's greatest steel-producing area. Though built upon an earlier foundation of riverine cities including Pittsburgh, Wheeling, and Steubenville, by the early twentieth century heavy industry formed the core of the region's civic, cultural, and political life. After being rebuilt in 1944, U.S. Steel's 12,000-ton press went on to produce armor plates for the great shipbuilding program of World War II and later for the conflicts in Korea and Vietnam. During the 1950s, however, the fortunes of Pittsburgh's steel industry had already begun to decline, and in the late 1980s Cleveland-based Park Corporation began demolishing the once fabled Homestead Works and selling its equipment for scrap.

In 1991, the press, still standing in the same spot, was left exposed to the elements, presiding over the economic and environmental problems left in the wake of steel's collapse. But this is not solely a tale of decline. In 1997 a private development corporation announced plans to remake the site along the Monongahela into an upscale riverfront shopping mall. The Waterfront, as its developers dubbed the site, catered to metropolitan Pittsburgh's middle-class consumers, many of whom worked in universities, hospitals, and other service sector industries. By the end of the century, the refurbished 12,000-ton press had once again assumed a position of prominence, with its hulking mass and freshly painted exterior serving as a backdrop of industrial heritage for the shoppers milling at its base.[28]

This story of rust and renaissance is an apt metaphor for the broader transformation of metropolitan Pittsburgh during the course of the last century. Mills *and* malls both became integral parts of the area's social and physical environment, though continuing tensions over competing land uses reveal the simultaneous existence of multiple regional identities and geographies. At its core, then, *Beyond Rust* is about understanding the ways in which Americans interpreted common social and physical landscapes, mobilized local and nonlocal resources to reshape their regional environments, and conceptualized themselves in spatial and historical terms. At the beginning of the twenty-first century, Homestead's press no longer stood at the center of the nation's steel industry, but its presence continued to provide meaning, whether for the tourist snapping a photograph, the former steel worker toiling at a retail job in its shadow, or the software engineer bicycling by on her way home from work.

PART I
The Steel Valley

IN THE SPRING of 1894, four "pilgrims"—historian Reuben Gold Thwaites, his ten-year-old son Frederick, his wife Jessie, and his brother-in-law William Turvill—set off from Brownsville, Pennsylvania, on a 1,000 mile journey down the Monongahela and Ohio Rivers. Thwaites said he "wished to know the great waterway intimately in its various phases [and] to see with my own eyes what the borderers saw; in imagination, to redress the pioneer stage, and repeople it."[1] Through Thwaites's 1898 memoir, we, too, can recapture the past and a vision of a region in transition. By the turn of the nineteenth century, the Upper Ohio Valley had already passed through at least two distinct phases since its time as a colonial frontier in the 1700s—a "Gateway to the West" superseded by a riverine culture of steamboats and mercantile exchange—and it remained in the throes of an industrial revolution, the signs of which were ever-present from the travelers' riverfront vantage.

Thwaites and his companions deliberately eschewed the comforts of the steamboat ("there are too many modern distractions about such a mode of progress") for camping and travel by raft "alert to the whisperings of Nature." As a result, one can learn a great deal about turn-of-the-century Pittsburgh's landscape from the published account of their journey, *Afloat on the Ohio*, even as the natural and cultural often blurred together in the descriptions. The Monongahela "comes down gaily enough from the West Virginia hills," they reported of their launch from historic Redstone Creek at the western terminus of Braddock's Road, until it was converted into a mere millpond at Brownsville by the four navigation dams between there and Pittsburgh. Henceforth the stream, Thwaites declared, was lined with mill towns that were "literally abutting one upon the other all of the way down to Pittsburg." "Often," he concluded, "four or five full-fledged cities are at once in view from our boat, the air is thick with sooty smoke belched from hundreds of stacks, the ear is almost deafened with the whirr and bang of milling industries."

As the *Pilgrim* (the name chosen for their skiff) made its way downstream, the visitors frequently bore witness to the changing industrial landscape of the region. The transformation of the Upper Ohio Valley into the Steel Valley had been so rapid in the closing decades of the nineteenth century that "both banks of the [Monongahela] river were lined with village after village, city after city . . . not recorded on our map, which bears the date of 1882." Indeed, while the purpose of the voyage may have been to recreate the past, much of their account focused on the process of steel making, railroad building, and coal mining at the heart of the new regional economy. By 1894 "the iron horse has almost eclipsed . . . the steamboat," Thwaites journaled early in the voyage; "Either bank is lined with railways, in sight of which we shall almost continually float." Similarly, "tipples of bituminous coal-shafts are ever in sight," lining the riverbanks to fill the waiting trains and river barges headed to towns and cities downstream. At the other end of the line, "factories and mills . . . sewer-pipe and vitrified-brick works, and iron and steel plants abound on the narrow bottoms."

One can also get a sense, flavored by the travelers' particular class and ethnic background, of the region's culture, communities, and residents. In the spring of 1894, the fledgling United Mine Workers union had just called for a walkout, and Thwaites duly noted the "miners loafing out the duration of a strike" when they set out on May 4. Less than two weeks later, company guards near Uniontown, only fifteen miles from Brownsville, armed with carbines and machine guns, held off an attack by an "Army of Intimidation" composed of 1,500 strikers, killing five.[2] At Homestead he contrasted "the famous great bank of ugly slag at the base of the steel mills, where the barges housing the Pinkerton guards were burned by the mob" less than two years earlier, with his views of "the electric cars, following either side of the stream as far down as Pittsburg, crowded to suffocation with gaily-attired folk . . . enjoying their Sunday afternoon outing." On the other end of the spectrum, west of the city (and thus upwind of the factory smoke) where "the hills are lower, less precipitous, more graceful," the city's merchants' and manufacturers' "beautiful villas occupy commanding situations on hillsides and hilltops [with] spires and cupolas . . . peeping above the trees; and now and then a pretty suburban railway station."

Perhaps most fascinating about *Afloat on the Ohio* was the way the multiple stages of metropolitan Pittsburgh's history existed simultaneously as part of the region's social and physical landscape. For all their attention to the urban-industrial development, the travelers also observed "small rustic towns in plenty." Despite the decline in importance of the rivers as transportation arteries, the cities all had broad wharfs with "steamers . . . closely packed," while they frequently met fishermen "setting their nets," as well as "houseboats, dozens of which we see daily." That said, the ability to use the rivers as anything other than industrial canals and urban sinks was rapidly fading due to "the appalling havoc which ... industries are making with the once beautiful banks of the river." "Fifty years hence," Thwaites predicted, if these enterprises multiplied, "the Upper Ohio will roll between continuous banks of clay and iron offal, down to Wheeling and beyond." This dire vision of a region crippled by the environmental consequences of an extractive economy was already foreshadowed in 1894 in the form of the deserted mining villages the pilgrims passed on their journey—"the shaft having been worked out, or an unquenchable fire left to smolder in neglect. Here the tipple has fallen into creaking decrepitude; the cabins are without windows or doors, while the black offal of the pit, covering deep the original beauty of the once green slope, is in turn being veiled with climbing weeds—such is Nature's haste, when untrammeled, to heal the scars wrought by man."

As *Afloat on the Ohio* suggests, the transformation of the Upper Ohio Valley into the Steel Valley resulted in an economy based on a nexus of coal, steel and rail that linked Pittsburgh, Steubenville, Wheeling and their hinterlands in a process of natural resource extraction. Industrial entrepreneurs pioneered the development of the vertically integrated corporation, creating an interconnected system of mammoth steel mills, coking plants, and mines extending from the heavily industrialized river valleys to the mining camps of the region's mountainous interior. Residents had a common culture shaped by the topography and grounded in a celebration of industrial triumph over nature. The logic of industrial capital reshaped the natural landscape, but so too did the region's rivers, mineral deposits, and rugged topography structure growth patterns in ways that were unique among the nation's great manufacturing areas. As a result, each stage in the social evolution of metropolitan Pittsburgh required a cultural reimagining of the relationship between humans and the natural world.

By 1900 competition for control of the Ohio headwaters had given way to a regional community, with Steubenville and Wheeling on the periphery of the metropolitan core in southwestern Pennsylvania. At the heart of this framework were the mines and mills themselves, which bound together distant areas in a sophisticated production process that resulted both in finished goods and the social inequalities observed by Thwaites. Expanding communities and industrial sites placed heavy demands on the environment, which decreased standards of living even as social reformers faced a fractious administrative and political system often dominated by large industrial corporations. By World War II, a social crisis rooted in increasing economic and environmental problems eventually resulted in a new public-private partnership in Pittsburgh that sought to remake the region both physically and symbolically. Taking the full measure of Pittsburgh's "Renaissance" first requires exploring the complicated ways in which the economic and political realignments that created the Steel Valley set in place patterns of land use, social interactions, and cultural assumptions that proved difficult to change.

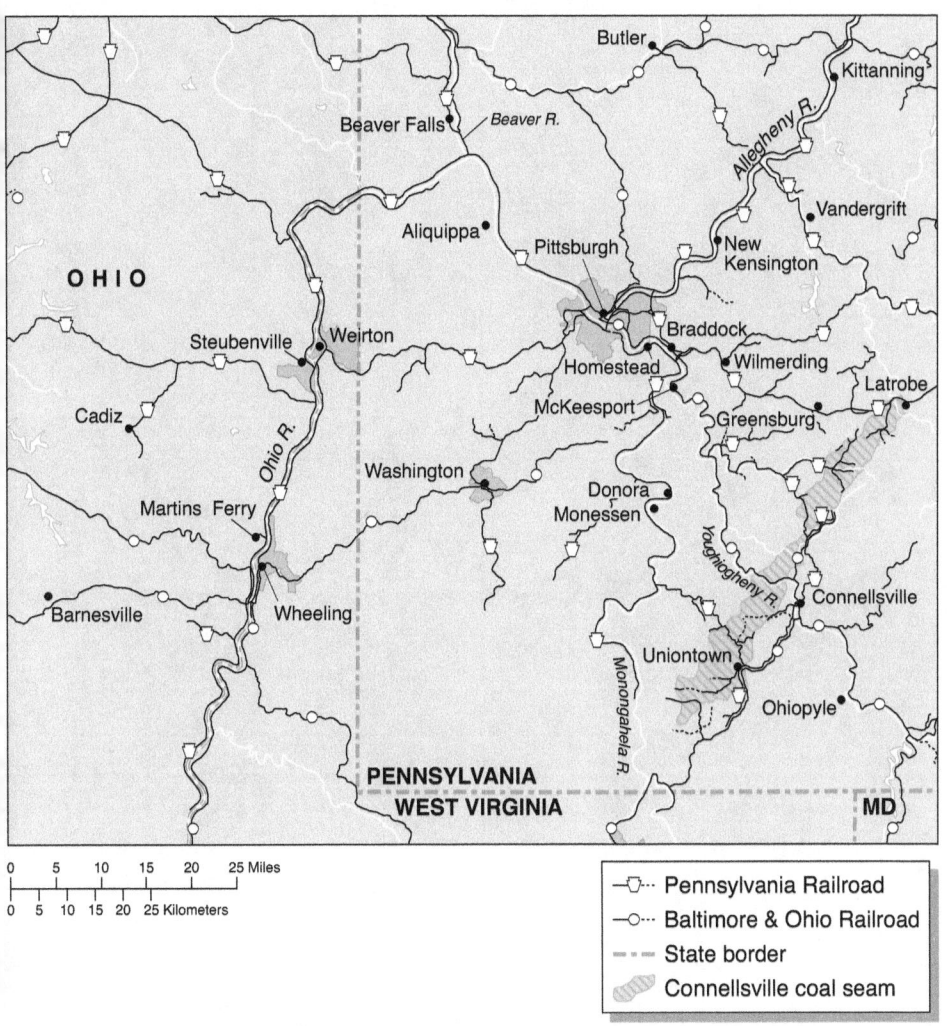

FIGURE 2. Metropolitan Pittsburgh: the Steel Valley.

CHAPTER 1

Building the Region

A cacophony of strange lights, sounds, and smells confronted wide-eyed Valentine "Val" Reuther in 1899 when he stepped off the train in Wheeling, West Virginia. Greeted by his brother Jake at the station, the eighteen-year-old German émigré had just made the trip from his family's farm in Illinois to seek his fortune in the city. Turn-of-the-century Wheeling, like the rest of the Pittsburgh metropolitan region, was bursting with vitality and Val quickly found quarters in a "very proletarian" boarding house in South Wheeling, an area full of "Germans, Poles, Scandinavians, Yugoslavs, and Irishmen." He soon started as a laborer at the Riverside Ironworks, located in a nearby industrial suburb, where he worked seventy-two hours a week for $1.50 a day. Through hard work and a personal relationship with the foreman, Reuther climbed his way up the labor ladder, eventually landing a job as a "heater" in the rolling mill and earning ten to twelve dollars for the same twelve-hour shift.[1]

In 1899, it had been more than 125 years since the Zane family first settled the east bank of the Ohio River as an outpost of the British Empire. Merchants in Pittsburgh, Wheeling, and Steubenville prospered as western markets expanded, using the river and its tributaries to gather produce and distribute manufactured goods from Europe and the Atlantic seaboard. The railroad had superseded the river as a mode of transportation by the end of the century, but industrial infrastructure merged with the natural landscape and vestiges of a riverine society to foster a common culture shared by residents throughout the region. "The mine, the mills, and the river made a fascinating setting for exploring boys," recalled Valentine's son Victor of his youth on the banks of the Ohio. "Calliope organs resounding from the river drew us to the banks to watch the steamers go by, creating great waves with their side or rear paddle wheels. We fished and swam; it was a rite of adolescence for each boy to make it all the way to the other side of the water."[2]

Reuther's story provides an important reminder that the fraught conversion to a post-industrial society that would take place a century later was not the region's first challenging transition. From the late eighteenth to the mid-nineteenth centuries, the Upper Ohio Valley's strategic position at the headwaters of the vast Ohio-Mississippi river system made it politically significant and provided access to the economic markets of the western frontier. On the one hand, we can see the beginning of a regional community defined by its rough topography, distance from other metropolitan regions, and orientation to its rivers. On the other hand, Steubenville, Wheeling, and Pittsburgh each vied for control of the headwaters with local boosters touting the advantages of their respective cities in terms of location and access to mineral resources, especially coal. In a pattern that would reemerge, especially after World War II, the success of local communities during this earlier era depended to a large extent on the ability to harness resources on the state level: a factor that further underscores the ways tensions between intra-regional bonds and barriers will matter to the subsequent story.

The expansion of the railroads lessened the area's importance as a transportation node, but trains also sparked a new industrial phase and eventually attracted investment in manufacturing, especially iron and steel making. By the end of the nineteenth century, the region had evolved into the Steel Valley, which formed the center of heavy industrial manufacturing in the United States. An extensive web of railroads connected the densely settled mill towns of the narrow river valleys with mining camps and villages in the surrounding mountainous countryside. In addition to these economic bonds, residents shared a regional culture shaped by the topography and grounded in a celebration of industrial triumph over nature. This shift had cultural, social and material ramifications as heavy industry replaced a riverine society and Pittsburgh increasingly served as the hub of a complex metropolitan landscape. While Steubenville and Wheeling were drawn into Pittsburgh's orbit as economic satellites, however, the creation of the Ohio River as a state boundary ensured that political rivalries would also play a key role in circumscribing regional development.[3]

Controlling the Headwaters

The difficulty in crossing the rugged Appalachians was a key factor in establishing the regional connections between communities in the Upper Ohio Valley, a theme that would remain centrally important throughout the nineteenth and twentieth centuries as well. The area lies in the northwestern part of Appalachia, the mountainous region stretching from southern Quebec to central Alabama. The landscape ranges from the steep hillsides of the Allegheny Mountains in southwestern Pennsylvania and northern West Virginia to the gently rolling hills of the Appalachian Plateau in southeastern Ohio. Numerous rivers and streams punctuate the terrain with the two largest, the Monongahela and Allegheny, merging in what is now Pittsburgh to form the Ohio River. Unlike the Chesapeake colonies, where the major east-west river system passed through deep gorges, the Susquehanna River from Baltimore through Harrisburg was easily traversed. From there British soldiers and settlers followed a Native American trail, the Allegheny Path, along the ridge tops farther and farther westward.[4]

On the other hand, even after the defeat of the French in the Seven Years' War, competition continued between Virginia and Pennsylvania for control of the headwaters and by 1776 rival trans-Appalachia routes ran to the Ohio River at Pittsburgh (Forbes Road) and northwestern Virginia near Wheeling (Braddock Road). The victory over the British Army by American colonists in the 1780s hastened a massive influx of white residents and land speculators that continued as the new federal government opened the Northwest Territory for settlement. Continuing a colonial rivalry that had been simmering for decades, Pennsylvania authorities frequently clashed with Virginian settlers and land speculators over the exact location of the state boundary line. Though one contingent to the Continental Congress proposed resolving the territorial dispute by creating a new state of "Westsylvania," an acknowledgement of the diverging regional interests of both Richmond and Philadelphia elites from residents of the western Appalachians, the southwestern edge of Pennsylvania was finally established in 1784. A year later, the passage of the Land Ordinance of 1785 defined how the lands across the Ohio would be surveyed and sold to settlers.[5]

As a result, while Pittsburgh remained part of the state of Pennsylvania, by the turn of the eighteenth century it was separated politically from its hinterlands to the south and west. By 1820, the city's population had topped 7,200, making it second in size only to Cincinnati along the length of the Ohio. Wheeling scored an important coup in 1818 when it became the western terminus of a new National Road that connected the port of Baltimore with the Ohio River. Anglo-American settlers laid out the village of Steubenville, Ohio, in 1797 near a fort established to protect surveyors. Twenty years later the community boasted three thousand residents and a variety of manufacturers. Town lots for smaller communities also began appearing on local tax assessment records. The southwestern Pennsylvania community of Falls City, later renamed Ohiopyle, was founded adjacent to a series of rapids along the Youghiogheny River, a tributary of the Monongahela, shortly after the American Revolution by residents attracted by the availability of water power for mills. Ohiopyle's population then slowly expanded after construction of the National Road in 1811 provided easier access to the markets of the east. Over the next century, residents were involved in the farming, mining and timber industries particularly after the arrival of the Baltimore & Ohio Railroad in 1871.[6]

This relationship between geography, market conditions and transportation technology drove metropolitan development within the region. While the Upper Ohio Valley had a temperate climate and relatively fertile soils replenished by seasonal flooding, the hilly landscape limited areas suitable for intensive agriculture and placed a premium on the level lands of the river and stream valleys. On reaching the flatter, fertile area just west of the Ohio River escarpment after weeks in the mountains, one early traveler on the National Road from Wheeling reportedly declared "This must be the land of Egypt," a name that stuck to the small farming community of Egypt Valley in southeastern Ohio. The early market towns and river cities followed a development pattern of expansion outward on the relatively narrow flatlands between the riverbanks and the steep escarpment of the surrounding hills. These small towns served a number of important functions in frontier society, clustering together a variety of skills, professional services, and economic opportunities for the region's residents. Even by 1790, Washington, Pennsylvania, located west of the Braddock Road between Pittsburgh and Wheeling, boasted sixteen retailers, thirty merchants and more than ninety-three other artisans and tradesmen, including such new trades as Windsor chair makers and coppersmiths.[7]

By the 1830s, the regional identity binding the trans-Appalachian West was overshadowed by an increasing identification along state lines. This transition was due in part to the decline in the importance of the rivers for inter-regional transportation and marketing in the face of road and canal construction. The arrival of the National Road in 1818 held out the possibility that Wheeling might challenge Pittsburgh's supremacy, but the city struggled to attract investment when infrastructure development funds from Richmond were not forthcoming. President Andrew Jackson's veto of the federal Maysville Road proposal in 1830 further heightened the role of individual states in determining the route of new transportation corridors, thus shifting the emphasis away from intra-regional improvements. "By 1835 the change wrought on Wheeling business [was] perceptible," concluded historian F. F. Crall, and advertisements in Wheeling papers suggest the increasing penetration of the market by Pittsburgh merchants.[8]

Pittsburgh, which looked largely to Philadelphia as a partner in commerce, had an advantage compared to Wheeling, for whom out-of-state Baltimore was the key Atlantic port. The opening of a canal between Pittsburgh and Philadelphia in 1834 reversed Wheeling's advantages and caused the beginning of the city's commercial subordination to its upriver rival. "We exceedingly regret that we cannot live at peace with our neighbors 'at the head of navigation,'" one Pittsburgh editor mockingly declared. "We want to see our 'little sister' thrive and prosper. But she cannot let us alone. Like a half-starved, ill-natured mangy cur, she is constantly snarling and snapping at our heels." Wheeling boosters struck back arguing that while Pittsburgh was above Wheeling, the seasonal lowness of the water and the five shoals between the two cities meant that only small boats could reach Pittsburgh—"little wet-tailed dinky boats that a cart load of rock would sink in their best days."[9]

The commercial tension between Pittsburgh and Wheeling during the early nineteenth century manifested as a battle over each city's claim to be the "head of navigation" on the Ohio-Mississippi system. This rivalry became particularly bitter during the infamous Bridge War of the 1840s and 1850s. Bridges had special significance as a triumph over nature in both Europe and the United States. Described as "one of the proudest monuments of enterprise of our citizens," the completion of the first bridge across the Ohio River in 1849 at Wheeling was hailed as one of the great marvels of its time, a triumph of human engineering over the forces of nature. For residents of Pittsburgh as well as Steubenville, however, the bridge was "an inconvenience and delay," "an unreasonable obstruction to navigation" that impeded the passage of ships upstream. A series of cases that worked their way to the Supreme Court exposed the rivalry between state and local boosters in Virginia and Pennsylvania as well as the competing merits of land versus water transportation.[10]

Even as this rivalry intensified, the relative decline of the Ohio River as an inter-regional transportation artery marked the beginning of the end for Pittsburgh and Wheeling as chief cities of the trans-Appalachian West. The growth of Cincinnati especially, which developed a direct connection to the Great Lakes via the Miami and Erie Canal, cut off markets to the south and west. While Pittsburgh's population trailed Cincinnati's by only 2,400 in 1820, by 1850 the "Queen City" had twice as many residents as its upriver rival. On the other hand, new railroad links coupled with a common geography, culture, and perceived economic interests created a strong Unionist movement in northwestern Virginia. In a series of conventions between 1861 and 1863, the first held with Union troops gathered across the river within sight of the meeting place, Wheeling residents formally ratified ties to their regional neighbors in Pennsylvania and Ohio and the new state of West Virginia took its place in the Union on June 20, 1863.[11]

Making Steel

As in the rest of the nation, railroads were key to the industrial revolution of the late nineteenth century. The 1854 completion of the Pennsylvania Railroad to Pittsburgh spurred more rapid economic and population growth, pushing new manufacturing firms up the Allegheny and Monongahela floodplains and across the water. In Wheeling, over five hundred "excursionists," including the governors of Maryland and Virginia, members of the two state legislatures, and municipal officials traveled all night from Baltimore to the opening celebration of the Baltimore and Ohio Railroad (B&O) in "handsomely decorated" railroad cars complete with "bands of music." The ceremony itself included major banquets as well as speeches by railroad president Thomas Swann and other luminaries including the Latrobe brothers and Baltimore financier George Brown. By the early twentieth century, Pittsburgh alone had six major trunk lines, sixteen industrial and switching railroads, fifteen inclines, and dozens of streetcar and feeder lines that honeycombed throughout its area.[12]

In addition to providing a faster, more direct, and more reliable means of transporting goods, the development of railroads created a vast market for iron and steel products as well as for coal. Here again, the region's location, coupled with easy access to natural resources, made Upper Ohio Valley communities ideal for supporting the industry. "The commercial advantages possessed by Steubenville are not confined simply to excellent transportation facilities by land and water," proclaimed an 1888 report, "but underlying the city and surrounding country veins of coal are easily accessible to market." In 1840 Pittsburgh produced more coal-fired steam horsepower than any other city in the United States; Wheeling was in second place. Between 1845 and 1855, coal mine production in Belmont County, Ohio, just across the river from Wheeling, exploded from less than 8,000 to 133,000 tons annually. Notably, production doubled from 40,000 to 80,000 tons in 1854, the year after the B&O crossed the river from Wheeling. Similarly, coal production around Steubenville doubled in 1854 with the arrival of the first railroad and then leaped to more than 200,000 tons in the late 1860s after the completion of the Steubenville Railroad Bridge.[13]

The expansion of the region's industrial capacity between 1850 and 1870 was largely an extension of previous patterns of production. The foundries and mills that made Wheeling "Nail City" in the 1860s, for example, had been established in 1832. The area's iron, glass, pottery, and other industries also had their roots in the older riverine economy. However, government contracts during the Civil War brought "unprecedented activity and wealth" to local manufacturers. "Vast armies had been mustered out and adventurous young Americans were scattering themselves out over the face of their half-developed country, following the railroads West across the prairies, building new homes by the million," explained one historian. "Nails were in demand and the black smoke rolled in clouds from the chimneys of Wheeling's mills." Around 1860, Wheeling manufacturers began developing the capacity to create their own pig iron, a raw material that they formerly had to have shipped from Pittsburgh. By 1885, the Wheeling district hosted over two hundred puddling furnaces, 1,400 nail machines, and an annual capacity of approximately 140,000 tons of nails.[14]

The most successful iron producer in the Upper Ohio Valley through the 1870s was Jones and Laughlin (J&L), a Pittsburgh firm founded in 1851 by two merchants and a skilled iron maker. Manufacturing facilities remained generally small affairs with the stages of production taking place in separate, often independently owned operations. Iron ore was first smelted into pig iron in an open-air furnace, generally near the source of the mine and the large amounts of wood needed to make the charcoal used as fuel. This was then shipped to forges and rolling mills, where it was converted into bars and slabs that formed the raw material for rails, nails, plates, and sheets. Still other factories produced the finished goods and tools that finally made their way to consumers. In order to address the inefficiencies in the iron production system, J&L founders B. F. Jones and James Laughlin began to introduce new labor saving technologies and to combine various parts of the production process within one firm. In 1860, J&L began work on blast furnaces on the north bank of the Monongahela that could use coking coal from nearby Connellsville to produce pig iron for existing rolling mills across the river.[15]

Jones and Laughlin's construction of the Eliza Furnaces was part of a larger trend whereby industrialists in Pittsburgh and Wheeling slowly expanded and integrated their facilities. By 1870 innovations in management structure at the nation's major railroads and radical advances in information technology began to be carried over into iron and steel production with dramatic repercussions. A new generation of managers and engineers spurred by an expansionist national policy and the political power to unite the two left an indelible mark on the social and physical landscape of the late nineteenth century. Railroads, especially the Pennsylvania Railroad, pioneered the use of new technologies, such as the telegraph, as well as a massively expanded corporate bureaucracy, because they had to. In terms of infrastructure, complexity of operation and technology, number of employees, and finances, the railroads quickly dwarfed their industrial predecessors, the New England textile mills. Unlike even the textile mills, the nature of long-distance transportation meant that railroad executives could not hope to personally observe all the workings of their company in a single day. Consequently, corporate managers had to develop systematic methods to run trains safely and on time, to ensure proper and timely maintenance, to track the thousands of shipments and millions of dollars that passed through the hands of countless employees.[16]

Perhaps no one was more responsible for transferring the management techniques of the railroads to manufacturing than Pittsburgh's Andrew Carnegie. After rising to senior management at the Pennsylvania Railroad, Carnegie left in 1872 and formed his own company to manufacture steel using the new Bessemer process, facilitating the mass production of steel from molten pig iron. While Pittsburgh had solidified its position as the Iron City by 1850, this notoriously backward industry, with its primitive accounting and segmented production system, seemed an unlikely candidate for the type of managerial and technological innovation seen at the Pennsylvania Railroad. Indeed, of the thirty-eight iron and steel plants in and around Pittsburgh, not one used the more advanced Bessemer process.

The largest of these, J&L's American Iron Works, consisted of seventy-five smaller puddling furnaces and had an output of 50,000 tons of iron annually, an amount that would be dwarfed by a new generation of mills in less than a decade. Carnegie designed the firm that would form the nucleus of Carnegie Steel to take advantage of two opportunities for enormous profits he perceived while at the railroad—the vast market for steel rails and the ability to control costs by applying new financial accounting and management techniques.[17]

Vertical integration, the combination of various stages of the production process in one facility, grew out the desire to lower unit costs by producing more goods per investment dollar and cutting labor expenses. While J&L, Wheeling's LaBelle Company, and other manufacturers had begun this process in a piecemeal fashion, Carnegie used systematic analysis to lower expenditures both within manufacturing components and in the intervals between parts of the overall process. Carnegie's first fully integrated steel mill, the Edgar Thomson Works (ET), was a key example of this process in action. Located twelve miles south of Pittsburgh along the Monongahela River and designed by Andrew Holley, one of the foremost experts on the Bessemer process, ET was the most modern steel mill in the world at the time. As opposed to the traditional separation of processes in the existing iron industry, the plans for ET combined the making of steel using the Bessemer process with the fabrication of steel rails in an integrated method based on cost-data analysis. When it opened in 1875, ET featured a plant with two 5-ton Bessemer converters and a mill capable of producing 225 tons of steel rails daily, an amount that increased to three thousand tons later in the century. The mill was initially supplied with pig iron from Carnegie's nearby Lucy and Isabella Furnaces, but a blast furnace was added in 1880 that made it possible to transform raw iron ore and coke (processed coal) into finished steel rails all at one facility.[18]

Between 1872 and 1901, when he sold the company to financier J.P. Morgan, Carnegie created a vast steel empire, centered in Pittsburgh, with an enormous array of iron and coal mines, railroad links, furnaces and rolling mills that allowed for the transformation of raw materials into finished products by all Carnegie-controlled companies. The secret to his success was high volume/low cost manufacturing—the application of the Pennsy's formula of "big trains, loaded full, and run fast" to the mass production of steel. The purchase of the Homestead Works (1883) and Duquesne Works (1891), following capital shortages and labor strife among the previous owners, allowed Carnegie the capacity to dominate the manufacture of steel rails and he also began moving into rolled steel and other goods. Through precise accounting and careful analysis of costs, Carnegie was able to drive down dramatically the price per ton of steel produced forcing his rivals to consolidate, move into niche markets, or fold altogether. Shrewd deal making, political intrigue and his increasing economies of scale also allowed Carnegie to negotiate shipping costs and access to natural resources at advantageous rates. By the end of the century, Carnegie Steel controlled the largest and richest deposits of coking coal and iron ore then known. Its Pittsburgh area plants were the most modern in the world, with an annual output 700,000 tons more than that of Great Britain and a profit in 1900 of $40 million.[19]

In addition to the purely economic explanation for Carnegie's success in transforming American manufacturing in the late nineteenth century, it is essential to consider the epistemological shifts in the relationship between humans and nature underpinning this transition. By 1870, as manufacturing—once perceived as an art, controlled, at least in part, by its practitioners on the foundry floor—evolved into an applied science, manipulated and overseen by professional managers, engineers, and scientists, business leaders increasingly saw the economic potential of applying chemistry and metallurgy to the production process. Carnegie looked for profits at every stage of steel-making and inculcated in his managers the need for constantly updating equipment that might be out-of-date though not outworn. Soon after the opening of ET, for example, its Bessemer converters became outdated when Sidney Gilchrist-Thomas discovered a new way to use iron ore with a higher phosphorous content. Carnegie immediately recognized the value of this discovery and obtained the rights to the process, which proved to be more effective in open-hearth furnaces. With substantial gains to be made at high volumes, he was prepared to scrap all his Bessemer converters despite the hundreds of thousands of dollars invested in them. Responding to objections from British iron workers that his methods created waste and recklessly destroyed equipment, Carnegie famously declared, "Most British equipment is in use twenty years after it should have been scrapped. It is because you keep this used-up machinery that the United States is making you a back number."[20]

The repercussions of Andrew Carnegie's steel empire spread throughout the Upper Ohio Valley, pulling in new residents, reshaping community bonds, and transforming the physical landscape—in effect creating a new

"Steel Valley" region that superseded even if it did not fully displace earlier regional connections. The period witnessed the creation of many works of art celebrating the triumph of mass production, while the negative environmental effects of smoke, slag, and other forms of industrial pollution were often ignored or interpreted as positive signs of economic growth. Existing industrial employers modernized their works, and new innovators, such as George Westinghouse who arrived in 1873, also contributed to the region's rapid economic growth. Between 1860 and 1890, Pittsburgh's population again surpassed that of Cincinnati, more than tripling from fewer than 180,000 to nearly 552,000 residents. This population increase corresponded to a growth in manufacturing employment from 20,500 in 1860 to 97,600 in 1890, compared to a growth from 30,208 to 103,010 in Cincinnati. The importance of the vertically integrated industrial firm in driving this growth is clearly visible as Pittsburgh dramatically outpaced its downriver rival in the size of manufacturers, with an average plant of forty employees in 1890, compared to only eleven per factory in Cincinnati.[21]

Other communities also reoriented their economies away from agriculture and small-scale craft industries toward heavy industrial manufacturing and the extraction of natural resources. Wheeling and Steubenville emerged as important subsidiary centers of heavy industry with their own steel and iron producers, railroad links, and burgeoning workforce. Wheeling carved a niche for itself as a supplier of nails and by 1880 had thirteen iron and steel works, the most prominent of which were the LaBelle Iron Works and the Riverside Iron Works where Valentine Reuther began his career. As with Carnegie Steel, after reorganizing in 1875 the LaBelle Works controlled costs through vertical integration by acquiring a stake in iron ore mines in Minnesota, coal mines and coke ovens in Pennsylvania, furnaces and mills in Steubenville, and a host of other operations connected by railroad to its sprawling facility in Wheeling. However, Carnegie's ability to access credit during the critical period surrounding the Panic of 1873 provided an opening for ET and Pittsburgh more generally that entrepreneurs in Steubenville and Wheeling could not match.[22]

As a result, despite Wheeling's success it was soon clear that it had been thoroughly outclassed by its upriver rival. The eight iron works in the city itself had a combined capitalization in 1880 of $2,274,425 with more than 2,600 employees and an output valued at $4,416,567. This compared to the 8,000 employed in 1885 at the Homestead Works alone. The 1900 census reported just over 11,000 manufacturing employees in Ohio and Marshall

Counties (Wheeling), while Allegheny County (Pittsburgh) had risen to a whopping 128,000 workers. Relatively speaking, the percentage of workers employed in manufacturing was about the same, 15 percent for Wheeling and 16.5 percent for Pittsburgh, but the dramatic overall growth in the latter was directly attributable to the "capital, transportation, business facilities and successful management which could not be equaled" in the smaller city. Even the most successful of Wheeling's iron producers, LaBelle, maintained a management structure that was more akin to the network of merchant families and artisanal ironman than the professional managers and scientists of Carnegie Steel. The company was founded by a small group of ex-Pittsburgh ironworkers who saw the potential of the community's access to coal deposits and river transportation as well as the rail connection of the B&O. There were no capitalists in the partnership and through the 1920s, when it was reincorporated as the Wheeling Steel Corporation with more than four thousand employees, was striking in its continued reliance on management still "in the hands of descendants of the founders, many of the officials and directors being connected by blood or marriage."[23]

By the end of the nineteenth century, the region that had once been a colonial frontier and later a gateway to western settlement and markets had become the Steel Valley—the world's greatest steel-producing region with a new economic system based on the large vertically integrated corporation. Between 1870 and 1890, metropolitan Pittsburgh emerged as the nation's most powerful industrial area due in large part to the successful application of new scientific and management strategies in the process of steel making. While Wheeling and Steubenville also steadily added to their industrial capacity, the overwhelming growth of their larger neighbor drew them into the metropolitan region as satellite communities. A 1902 history of the Upper Ohio Valley made clear this transition, when it stated that Wheeling's modest success as a manufacturing center was due not only to "the cheapness of fuel" but also to the city's very "proximity [to] the Pittsburg (Pennsylvania) district."[24]

Mountains of Fire

By 1907 capitalists and corporate managers as well as entrepreneurs and local residents looking to participate in the heavy industrial economy had dramatically reshaped the social and physical landscape of the Upper Ohio

Valley in ways that would have long-lasting repercussions. In that year the newly organized Russell Sage Foundation financed an extensive analysis of the nation's most important industrial area, resulting in a landmark six-volume study, entitled *The Pittsburgh Survey*. The project's scope was regional by design, an attempt to methodically examine workers and communities in the new system of urban factories, mill towns, and mining camps built on top of a pre-existing framework of agricultural settlements, market towns, and river-oriented cities. Survey director Paul Kellogg explained this vision of the area as an integrated unit, a complex totality that inextricably linked society and culture, humans and the natural world. "Pipe lines that carry oil and gas, waterways that float an acreage of coal barges, four track rails worn bright with weighty ore cars, wires surcharged with a ruthless voltage or delicately sensitive to speech and codes," Kellogg declared, "bind here a district of vast natural resources into one organic whole."[25]

Despite this recognition of the importance of understanding the Steel Valley as an interconnected "locality," the survey itself reveals some of the thornier issues in conceptualizing the region as a "definite geographical area." Part of the problem was that growth in metropolitan Pittsburgh was quite decentralized compared to other areas in the nation, a factor further complicated by the state boundaries dividing Pittsburgh from its hinterland in the south and west. Development in the older cities, such as Steubenville and Wheeling, was largely limited to the narrow floodplains between the rivers and the steep surrounding mountains. Employers looking for flat space on which to locate their enormous integrated mills and factories had little choice but to expand beyond city limits. The accompanying need for access to river and rail transportation networks resulted in a dense, ribbon-like pattern of industrialized urban development extending upstream along the Allegheny and Monongahela Rivers from Pittsburgh and downstream to Wheeling. The relationship between market town and agricultural hinterland was also remade during the period with rural mining camps forming an integral part of the region's new industrial paradigm.[26]

Everything in the Steel Valley's older communities began at the water. Prior to the arrival of the railroad in the 1850s, the region's rivers were the primary means of getting goods and people in and out of urban areas. Consequently, urban development spread away from the banks with wharfs and merchant warehouses giving way to retail establishments and central business districts and finally residential neighborhoods, which often spread to the lower slopes of the surrounding hills. Despite the region's rough topography, city founders in Steubenville, Wheeling, and Pittsburgh each adopted a grid pattern of development, making for a haphazard patchwork of steep, often impassable streets climbing up hills and down into ravines as builders attempted to master the landscape. The broken topography of mountains and river valleys tended to concentrate the population in the narrow flatlands as well as foster the growth of numerous, politically independent communities divided by breaks in the terrain. Despite enormous population growth after 1860, for example, Pittsburgh did not begin to consolidate its political power in the region and spread across its rivers until it annexed the small towns of the South Side in 1872 and its commercial rival Allegheny City in 1907.[27]

The examples of Wheeling and Steubenville suggest that the development of metropolitan regions, a process that historians have often viewed simply as industrial decentralization, also involved the incorporation and enhancement of existing local production systems. The rise of the railroads and expansion of manufacturing strengthened the connections between areas within the Steel Valley region that had previously been largely autonomous. Beginning in the 1870s, the transformation from small craft-based industries to enormous integrated mills requiring river and rail access increasingly pushed companies to search for outlying sites for new facilities. This trend was accelerated by land speculation and a desire for more control over workers as well as the region's rugged topography and the spatial distribution of its mineral wealth. As new mills and mines sprang up throughout the rapidly urbanizing river valleys and the rural countryside, manufacturers, political leaders, and engineers developed an extensive railroad system spreading throughout the region. Trunk lines and regional carriers connected the major cities, while inter-urban lines and streetcars enabled speedy movement within communities and out to their growing hinterlands. By the late nineteenth century, a trip from Pittsburgh to Wheeling that had once been counted in days by steamboat or wagon road (if the season permitted the journey at all) could now be accomplished in a matter of hours, no matter what the weather.[28]

In addition to expansion within existing municipalities, corporate managers laid out entirely new mill-oriented communities, such as Homestead (1881), Monessen (1896), Follansbee (1905), and Weirton (1909). Industrialists built dozens of enormous mills and factories that hugged the narrow flatlands up the Monongahela and Allegheny Rivers from Pittsburgh and down the Ohio Valley through Steubenville and Wheeling. The concentrated growth of mill towns in the river valleys exacerbated the issue of air pollution, leaving a legacy of environmental degradation and spawning some of the region's earliest anti-pollution legislation. By the early twentieth century, a thick smoky haze that deepened with winter's cold air blanketed many Steel Valley communities. According to local lore, smoke from the city's stoves and furnaces so fouled the air that business executives would often have to change shirts at lunch due to the grime. "I remember," recalled Wheeling resident John Hunter II, when "you drove downtown in the mornings, you'd have to turn on your headlights at ten or eleven o'clock in the morning because of the smoke."[29]

As with the region's cities, the growth of smaller Steel Valley communities during the mid-nineteenth century depended in large part on their location in relation to existing transportation systems, the vagaries of the local landscape, and the productivity of the soil. Kittanning, Pennsylvania, founded in the late eighteenth century, developed in a pattern similar to that of Pittsburgh, its neighbor down the Allegheny River. Washington, Pennsylvania, the site of the 1791 Whiskey Rebellion, was located along the Braddock Road, a major east-west route across the Appalachian Mountains. Smaller communities such as Ohiopyle on the falls of the Youghiogheny River and Barnesville, Ohio, west of Wheeling were both founded in the early nineteenth century as agricultural market towns in close proximity to the National Road. Unlike settlements in the steeper and rockier terrain of southwestern Pennsylvania and West Virginia, the gently rolling hills and fertile soils of eastern Ohio made family farming a more profitable proposition through the late nineteenth century. These small towns were hubs of regional activity, drawing local farmers weekly to downtown markets, hosting small craft-based manufacturing and artisans' shops, and serving as centers for county government.[30]

The rapid industrialization of the late nineteenth century built on this preexisting system of hinterland seats and crossroads villages that served as collection points for agricultural goods and trading centers for the region's farmers. Beginning in the 1850s, as the superiority of the Midwest for field crops and livestock became increasingly apparent, ambitious farmers in metropolitan Pittsburgh began to specialize and modernize. Agricultural entrepreneurs made the transition to truck gardens, commercial orchards, and dairy farms to supply the region's growing cities as well as rural mining and lumbering operations. Southwestern Pennsylvanians began to specialize in sheep and wool production and influenced their neighbors in West Virginia and Ohio to do the same. By 1860, Ohio had the nation's highest density of sheep; Harrison County just west of Steubenville boasted more than 150 sheep per square mile, a feat directly attributable to the construction of the first woolen mill west of the Alleghenies in the city in 1812. By the 1860s, transporting wool to the markets of Pittsburgh and the Atlantic seaboard was not difficult because railroad expansion had left few parts of the region more than ten miles from a rail line.[31]

Rather than a clear break between farming and manufacturing economies, urban capitalists and industrialists in the Steel Valley soon joined forces with local farmers and entrepreneurs to produce the large quantities of minerals, coal, oil, and natural gas necessary to feed the ravenous appetites of the region's industrial revolution. This industrialized countryside existed side-by-side with earlier agricultural modes of production. Indeed, the relationship between the two was often complementary, with local farmers tending their livestock and lands during the summer and producing a supplemental winter income by working coal seams on their own property or traveling to nearby mines. The arrival of the railroads between 1840 and 1870 fostered the growth of larger factories, provided a better outlet for locally grown produce, and allowed quicker connections with the region's cities for both work and leisure. During the 1880s and 1890s, John D. Rockefeller brought much of the chaotic landscape of individual "wildcatters" and small-time speculators under the control of his mammoth Standard Oil conglomerate. Similarly, by the end of the century, most of the hundreds of small mines dotted throughout the region producing coal for home heating, steel production, and the railroads were gradually consolidated into a handful of conglomerations generally controlled by railroad or steel interests.[32]

As mines in the Steel Valley grew larger and more numerous, they quickly outstripped the local labor capacity, necessitating the increased importation of immigrants to meet greater industrial demand. Unlike the situation in the region's more urbanized areas with pre-existing housing, these new residents often settled in shoddily constructed company towns where they were subject to the will of their employers. "At each tipple is a miner's hamlet," observed Thwaites of the hastily constructed communities, "a row of cottages or huts, cast in a common mold, either unpainted, or bedaubed with that cheap, ugly red with which one is familiar in railway bridges and rural barns." This settlement pattern also had a spatial element, with the older agricultural communities occupying the flatter uplands and newer mining camps in the river and creek valleys. These "patch" towns were often ruled with an iron fist and, when coupled with the demands of a dirty, dangerous and debilitating workplace, were the site of some of the most violent labor wars of the late nineteenth and early twentieth centuries.[33]

If Andrew Carnegie's transformation of the moribund iron industry through the creation of the vertically integrated corporation symbolized the rise of Pittsburgh as the world's greatest steel producing region, his partnership with coal baron Henry Clay Frick symbolized the new relationship between city and countryside. Born on a farm near Connellsville fifty miles up the Youghiogheny River from Pittsburgh, Frick represented the generation of Upper Ohio Valley natives who transitioned away from the region's riverine roots toward its industrial future. His grandfather, Abraham Overholt, made a fortune distilling Old Overholt whiskey, a staple of the trans-Appalachian trade. The Connellsville region was particularly appealing to mine and mill operators because of the high-quality coal, Connellsville Coke, used in the steel-making process, and because of the ease of transporting large amounts of coal by river to mills in and around Pittsburgh. Frick obtained a loan for $10,000 from Pittsburgh financier Thomas Mellon to begin mining local coal, and by 1873 he was selling all he could produce. A decade later, Frick was a millionaire with a thousand coking ovens and three thousand acres of land under his control.[34]

At the same time, Carnegie was rapidly expanding his vertically integrated steel operations even as his takeover of the Homestead Works represented his first horizontal acquisition. However, the increased production capacity of the new mill created a need for greater access to coking coal, a problem he solved with the purchase of a controlling interest in the Frick Coke Company in 1883. The industrialization of the countryside had a profound effect on the physical landscape of the Steel Valley. At its peak in 1910, over 40,000 "beehive" coking ovens in the Connellsville region produced 18 million tons of coke annually, 60 percent of the nation's total. Most of this tonnage went directly to feed the blast furnaces of J&L Steel, Carnegie Steel, and smaller competitors. In addition to the creation of dozens of mining camps throughout the area, the small cities of Connellsville, Uniontown, and Greensburg also grew dramatically during the period as local foundries and machine shops sprang up to produce and repair mining equipment and service and equip the railroad spur lines built in the late 1870s.[35]

The rural hinterland became an integral part of the heavy industrial economy as the Steel Valley's rugged hillsides were thus transformed into "mountains of fire." Nearly thirty miles separated the closest portion of the Connellsville district from the Pittsburgh iron market at the time of its initial exploitation by Frick in 1871. By World War I, a dense network of railroads, capital and labor links, and heavy industrial plants along the Monongahela River knit the two areas tightly together, both spatially and functionally. Even at the end of the twentieth century, abandoned structures relating to the oil and coal booms remained scattered throughout the region. As mining progressed, huge heaps of wastes accumulated near the mine entrances, looming over nearby housing. Silt from the piles clogged nearby streams as acid mine drainage turned the water orange and coated the hillsides in rivulets. Subsidence from underground mining was a frequent occurrence and the increased use of surface mining during World War I left enormous scars on the landscape itself, eventually prompting outcries by some local residents that their "country would be better fit for farming." In her 1947 book, *Cloud by Day*, Muriel Earley Sheppard described the landscape of the Connellsville district as "a country of extremes, ugly by day with banks of coke ovens, tipples, sidings, and fields gnawed to the rock with strip-coal operations; luridly beautiful by night when the glare of the ovens paints the sky . . . a place of wealth and great poverty, with too much smoke, too much violence, and far too many people."[36]

"I do not intend to beg for the city, nor to advise you how to dispose of your money," opened an 1899 letter from Wheeling attorney Nelson Hubbard to Andrew Carnegie, "and if the mere suggestion I am making is unwelcome to you I hope you will take no further thought of it." Hubbard went on to urge the Pittsburgh industrialist to consider locating one of his new libraries in the smaller city. "Had the prosperity continued which Wheeling had in the iron business three and two decades ago," the writer explained, "we might have had a considerable class of people with money . . . who could supply our need themselves. But Pittsburg overshadowed Wheeling and took the profit out of the iron and steel business here." Hubbard continued, "Pittsburg concerns had capital, transportation, business facilities and successful management, which could not be equaled here;

and when Pittsburg's real growth began, Wheeling died." He concluded, "Should you ever care to interest yourself in the city, the appreciation and gratitude of a minority will be correspondingly strong."[37]

Even as German immigrant Val Reuther began work in Wheeling as a skilled iron heater, the changing dynamics of industrial manufacturing meant that employers were increasingly substituting capital in the form of new labor saving technologies that made artisanal iron production obsolete. As Hubbard's letter suggests, when the communities of Wheeling, Pittsburgh, and Steubenville shifted from a riverine to an industrial economy during the latter half of the nineteenth century, the boundaries of the region's economic and cultural influence contracted even as Pittsburgh rose to dominate its smaller neighbors. By the early twentieth century, enormous firms with names such as U.S. Steel, Westinghouse, Pittsburgh Consolidation Coal, and Weirton Steel had remade the Upper Ohio Valley into the center of the nation's heavy industrial production—the Steel Valley.

This regional makeover owed as much to the evolution of new forms of management by Pittsburgh industrialists as it did to either a fortuitous location or available natural resources. During the 1870s, captains of industry such as Thomas Scott, Andrew Carnegie, and Henry Frick pioneered the development of a new way of managing railroads, rolling steel, and mining coal—the large, vertically integrated, industrial corporation. A high degree of specialization in basic manufacturing and the domination of a few very large, multi-divisional industrial corporations set the stage for the Steel Valley's meteoric rise and subsequently hampered efforts at economic diversification. Between 1880 and 1920, the full ramifications of this transformation would become clear as new immigrants, new social relationships, and a remanufactured landscape created a distinct regional culture intimately tied to the success, sites, and process of steel production.

CHAPTER 2

Mines and Mills

In 1909, Pittsburgh industrialist Ernest T. Weir purchased 105 acres of West Virginia farmland overlooking the Ohio River across from Steubenville, thirty-five miles west of Pittsburgh and thirty miles north of Wheeling. Weir was the son of immigrants from Northern Ireland and, before striking out on his own, had worked his way up to general manager of U.S. Steel's tin plate mill in Monessen. The new mill site was at the intersection of river and rail transportation with good connections to Pittsburgh and national markets. It also featured a ready supply of cheap land and cheap fuel from nearby coal mines and oil wells. Proximity to Steubenville via a new bridge provided Weir with a pool of workers, while the older city also allowed access to goods and services, functioning as a downtown marketplace for the new factory town. "As we were walking over the vacant fields and looking over the land," Weir declared of his first visit to the site, "it was already a settled matter that we would build a completely integrated steel plant." The company's first facility was in operation before the end of 1909 and consisted of ten mills. Within a few years the Weirton Steel Company had fifty mills and was second only to U.S. Steel in production of tin plate.[1]

During its heyday between 1880 and 1920, the Steel Valley developed a set of social and environmental patterns that, while similar to other industrial areas, yielded unique challenges that require a nuanced analysis in order to understand subsequent attempts at regional economic restructuring. Just as with the Ford Motor Company's River Rouge plant in Detroit or the Googleplex in the San Francisco Bay Area, Weirton's mills existed as nodes in a larger district where companies both competed over and shared a common labor force, natural resources, management expertise, and technical innovations. While cities with flatter topography like Chicago and St. Louis developed rings of manufacturing suburbs extending out from the central city, the dearth of flat land in the Upper Ohio Valley resulted in dense urban-industrial areas that snaked along the narrow riverbanks leaving large parts of the higher elevations relatively unpopulated. Further, Pittsburgh's status as both a manufacturing center and an energy capital meant that metropolitan development included an industrialized countryside with pockets of urban-like densities occurring around company-controlled mine sites. Exploring the process of steel making from mine to mill provides a clearer understanding of the ways in which the values of the Gilded Age were embedded in this landscape of production.

As the formation of Weirton suggests, dispersed industrial development, a rugged landscape, and strong kinship networks, bolstered by employment policies designed to splinter class unity along ethnic lines, encouraged the formation of small tightly knit communities divided among hundreds of separate political jurisdictions. Weak civic administrations were expected to keep taxes low and serve the needs of industry, while corporate paternalism and the repression of organized labor undercut challenges to the existing economic and political system. As late as the 1960s, outsiders remarked on the continuance of a "strange ethnonationalism" among the various immigrant communities, which made it difficult to achieve any sort of political consensus. Despite annexation campaigns and attempts at government reform during the Progressive era, understanding this history of "perpetrated factionalism that approaches total chaos" is vital for interpreting attempts at public-private coalition building in later decades. Of the region's older cities, only Pittsburgh was able to overcome this political splintering and embark on a meaningful program of urban planning and infrastructure development under the infamous political machine of Christopher Magee and William Flinn. Indeed, the creation of new public parks, and especially the expansion of the University of Pittsburgh in the hilltop civic center of Oakland, provided the first glimmer that Pittsburgh's destiny might be more than that of the "Smoky City."[2]

Coal, Steel, and Rail

The process of industrial production shaped the social and physical landscape of the Steel Valley, forming a common set of opportunities and challenges for the region's residents. A ton of steel required approximately a ton and a half of iron ore, a half ton of coke, and a quarter of a ton of limestone, not to mention a few other elements, vast quantities of water, more coal to power the railroads and barges that ferried minerals from the mines, and electricity (also produced from either coal or natural gas) to run the mills. Similar to the region's other major corporations, Carnegie Steel and its subsidiary, Frick Coke Company, owned a number of so-called captive mines that were transferred to U.S. Steel at its founding in 1901. The Leith Mine & Coke Works in the Connellsville region, for example, began operation in the 1880s to produce coke for the Joliet Steel Company near Chicago. Frick bought the mine in 1889 and upgraded operations, building the first steel tipple in the region to hoist cars loaded with coal up the shaft and lower workers into the mine. Despite some geological characteristics that made it "a hard one to manage" according to one mine inspector, the Leith mine was easily connected to Homestead and the rest of Carnegie's steel empire by both the Pennsylvania and Baltimore & Ohio Railroads. By the turn of the century, more than three hundred people worked in the mine and the adjacent coking facilities, producing nearly 120,000 tons of coke annually.[3]

As with iron and steel manufacturing, consolidation and vertical integration produced dramatic changes in the way coal was mined, particularly in large companies. Mine owners worked to replace what had been essentially underground workshops controlled by skilled miners with new management practices aimed at lowering costs and controlling the production process. Mines became much more hierarchical spaces, with individual workers forming parts of interdependent, coordinated, and carefully supervised groups. Standard practice throughout the region was to divide the actual extraction of coal among specialized workers, including cutters (operated mechanical cutting machines along the coal seam), loaders (loaded coal by shovel into mine cars), and shooters (used dynamite to blast coal from the front of the seam) as well as myriad assistants, helpers, and other subcategories. Animal or mechanically powered coal cars then hauled the coal to the mine shaft and up to the coal tipple where it was sorted and weighed by supervisors.[4]

Upon reaching the surface, coking coal, such as that produced at the Leith Mine, was processed in one of the "beehive" ovens dotting the area. Over 40,000 such ovens produced 18 million tons annually; this amounted to 60 percent of the nation's coke produced in a region only fifty miles long and five miles wide. Workers loaded the coal and processed coke onto train cars and shipped them to blast furnaces that created raw or "pig" iron. For the Homestead Works, this initial process occurred in the Carrie Furnaces, across the Monongahela River in the mill town of Rankin, "a small bleak place," according to one observer. Each day three hundred railroad cars of coal and coke, limestone, iron ore from the Mesabi Range in northern Minnesota, and other materials passed through the Carrie complex, which was dominated by the furnaces themselves—four steel behemoths more than two hundred feet high—each with the capacity to turn out sixty-five hundred tons of iron a day. Once there, the ore, coke, and limestone were hoisted to the top of the brick lined towers, while enormous stoves used coal to heat air to three thousand degrees and then blasted it into the bottom of the stacks. The downward movement of the ore, coke, and limestone, and the upward movement of hot gases refined the iron through a series of chemical reactions. Every three or four hours, workers extracted the molten iron from the furnace, as well as the heating process residue called slag.[5]

Even by the turn of the century, the dearth of flat land that forced both railroad lines and enormous mills to be located in the narrow river valleys required expensive and novel infrastructure to adapt the landscape to the needs of industry. From the Carrie Furnaces, for example, the molten iron was poured into huge cigar-shaped cars and went back across the river to the Homestead Works on a "hot metal bridge" that opened on New Year's Eve, 1900. Once inside the mill, the iron was transferred to steel ladles and transported by enormous cranes to the open-hearth furnaces where it cooked in intense gas heat and hot air with a mixture of limestone and steel scrap. The men who worked at the tapping hole, where the steel flowed from the hearth into a giant ladle, wore thick protective coats, dark goggles, and heavy leather boots for protection from the intense heat. After the mixture had cooked for eight to ten hours depending on the type of steel needed, the skilled melter overseeing the process ordered a sample to be taken. If the molten metal was judged ready, workers used a long steel lance with a dynamite charge on the end to blow out the tapping hole and release the red hot metal. The slag floating on the surface was siphoned away leaving pure steel that was then poured into molds, where it solidified into ingots the size of a house.[6]

Once the raw steel cooled, workers reheated it until malleable and sent it to the primary mills where the ingots were rolled into semi-finished forms or to the forge division where they were crushed into shape by enormous presses on the way to becoming gun turrets, railroad axles, ship propeller shafts, and other finished products. From the primary mills, the steel shapes were taken to the finishing mills and rolled into plates, beams, pilings, or railroad wheels and sheared to the desired lengths. Workers then loaded finished products onto railroad cars or barges that traveled to consumers around the world. While it was only one of dozens of mills throughout the region, by the end of World War II the Homestead Works alone could churn out annually 2 million tons of pig iron; 4 million tons of steel ingots; 1 million tons of blooms; 2.7 million tons of slabs; 1 million tons of beams, pilings, and other structural products; 1.75 million tons of plates; 10,000 tons of forgings; 75,000 tons of wheels and other circular sections; 50,000 tons of axles; and 40,000 tons of fabricated products.[7]

Each step of the production process also produced solid, liquid, and airborne wastes that quickly found their way into the natural environment, including the bodies of workers and nearby residents. At the base of the production process, coal is composed of water, carbon, and smaller amounts of other materials, including hydrogen, nitrogen, and sulfur. When mining disrupts natural groundwater systems, the interaction of water and air with coal generates sulfuric acid that is carried off through gravity drainage or pumped out of shafts. Because the Ohio River watershed is naturally alkaline, the region's streams diluted pollution from early mining operations. As coal production increased in the late nineteenth century, however, the self-purification capacity of streams and major rivers was overwhelmed. Changes in water color revealed the first signs of acid degradation as streams became deep red or brown from the iron oxide. By 1900, several Ohio River tributaries, including the Monongahela and Youghiogheny that flowed near the Leith Mine were "usually acidic" and increasingly endangered aquatic life.[8]

But the most visible byproduct of the mining process in the Connellsville region was the smoke from the coke ovens. "It takes a fine summer morning to see what the . . . valley is like," reported one resident. "Uniontown [is] sprawled in the flat in the foreground, Leith ovens smoking busily in the fields to the right . . . and the long ranks of Continental No. 1 ovens far away in the middle."[9] Coke production was a dirty business, with the frequent moving and handling of coal dispersing large amounts of dust. Furthermore, even a well-built beehive oven converted only 70 percent of each ton of coal into coke. This meant that the other 30 percent of suspended carbon particles, tars, hydrocarbons, carbon monoxide, methane, and sulfur dioxide escaped from the ovens in the form of smoke and noxious fumes. When workers doused the baked coal with water to stop the chemical process, the resulting steam lifted tiny coke particles into the air, while the used water containing coke residue, ammonia, and phenol drained into nearby streams. After World War I, as coke production moved from beehive ovens at the mine mouth to by-product ovens at the mills, the environmental effects of coke production moved from the rural periphery to the industrialized river valleys and U.S. Steel's Clairton Coke Works earned a reputation as one of the largest contributors to the region's air pollution problems. "All that is left is this desolation," declared Duquesne University biologist Emmanuel Sillman while standing on a barren hillside overlooking Clairton in 1971. "The killer is sulfur dioxide."[10]

As imposing a presence as mines and mills were on the Steel Valley's landscape, the railroad had an even more widespread, immediate, and intimate impact on the region's residents. Transportation infrastructure was omnipresent, particularly in the narrow confines of the river valleys and central cities. "The railroads blanketed the city," explained one recent study, "tunneling through the hills, bridging the rivers and ravines and usurping the riverbanks." The Pennsylvania Railroad, for example, was four-tracked throughout much of the region, combined with massive and strategically located freight and switching yards, roundhouses, and repair shops that employed many thousands of workers. Railroad exhaust was a major contributor to air pollution, particularly in those urban areas where trains idled for loading and unloading. This dense, acrid smoke helped create the "shabby, dirty and altogether unsightly" hillsides above many of the region's communities that, according to Frederick Law Olmsted, Jr., were contributing largely to the "slatternly conditions" in which so many of Pittsburgh's working people were "compelled to live."[11]

The lack of any sort of environmental regulation during the heyday of the Steel Valley meant that companies were largely free to dispose of industrial wastes as they saw fit, which created a legacy of environmental contamination extending throughout the region. As the introduction of byproduct ovens suggests, managers made decisions according to cost principles and, when corporations found it profitable, materials were recycled. Executives at Carnegie Steel were legendary for engineering waste disposal systems that maximized the use of each product. In one famous example at the Edgar Thomson Works, executive Henry Phipps found that flue-cinder and the tiny pieces of high-grade steel that were scoured off by rolling machines could be reused at another point in the iron-making process. In both cases, he ordered the "waste" to be recycled and purchased the unwanted material from competitors at a discount. On the other hand, when waste recovery was not economically valuable, plant managers allowed particulates, slag and gases to follow their natural course into the river, slag heap, or atmosphere. Of the total industrial waste produced by the mills, only a small portion went into landfills on company property as smokestacks and pipes dispersed pollution beyond the mill's borders into the community's air and water. Even offloading materials from barges and trains created vast amounts of dust around the huge stockpiles of coal and iron. When managers attempted to control the dust problem by wetting the piles, particles suspended in the water passed untreated into the environment.[12]

Those most affected by industrial pollution were the workers themselves. Laborers encountered a wide range of work environments inside mines and mills: dust almost inevitably led to breathing problems and a lifespan often shortened by the dreaded black lung; coke workers faced blasts of thick smoke and fumes when they opened the doors to insert or remove materials; and mill hands in open-hearth furnaces sometimes had to fasten themselves together with rope to navigate their way through clouds of particulates. Whether through constant exposure to environmental hazards or tending "the monstrous crucibles of molten iron and steel, the fast-moving cranes, the great cutting machines, the locomotives and railroad cars," industrial employment "was a natural place for injury and death." In an age before occupational safety requirements, workers' compensation laws, and social security benefits, employment in the region's mills, mines, and railroads crystallized the relationship between social and environmental inequalities for contemporary social reformers. "Often I was told by workmen of forty and forty-five that they had been at their best at thirty years of age, and that at thirty-five they had begun to feel a perceptible decline in strength," explained sociologist John Fitch in 1910. "The superintendents and foremen are alert to detecting weakness of any sort, and if a man fails appreciably, he expects discharge."[13]

The integrated system of coal, steel, and rail that formed the basis of the region's economic life thus imperiled the lives of its inhabitants even as it generated enormous wealth. Boosters and industrialists, labor leaders and politicians, locals and visitors alike built layer by layer a cultural framework of human triumph over nature that paralleled the physical processes transforming minerals into finished goods and industrial pollution. The body of the "Man of Steel" as well as the numerous sites of production were symbolically recreated time and again, "held motionless," in the words of one commentator, "while those who wished to understand Pittsburgh ... charted its strengths and weaknesses." This dynamic was captured perfectly by Reuben Gold Thwaites who found the essence of the region in the "whirr and bang of milling industries," "black offal of the pit," "sooty smoke belched from hundreds of stacks," and amid it all "a ninety-cent [per hour] man working in a place ... nearer to the mediaeval notions of hell ... than anything imagined by Dante." It was from this foundation that residents forged their individual and community identities even as the area's natural and built landscapes constrained development in ways that would later complicate the region's economic transition.[14]

Forging Community

The transformation of the Upper Ohio Valley into the Steel Valley reshaped the daily rhythms, identities, and demographics of the region's residents, embedding the social structure of the Gilded Age in the region's politics, economy, and environment. While corresponding in general to the sequence of city building in other communities, Pittsburgh had important differences that affected the timing and complicated the process of metropolitan development. At the same time, industrialists effectively wielded the power to shape the material and social environments in ways that limited the ability of workers to organize collectively and made many communities dependent on corporate benefaction for basic services. Following a long period of bitter labor strife, this unequal relationship resulted in deeply entrenched social inequalities and increased calls for political reform. If James Parton's 1868 description of the region as "Hell with the lid taken off" was meant to evoke the technological sublime, its use by muckraker Lincoln Steffens in his 1904 *Shame of the Cities* reflected the struggles of an "angry and ashamed [community] that has tried to be free and failed."[15]

The process of industrialization produced a range of social changes embedded in the natural and built infrastructure, but the region's topography itself presented a host of formidable challenges that raised costs, hindered institution building, and constrained development. Landscape architect and planner Frederick Law Olmsted, Jr., observed in 1911 that "no city of equal size in America or perhaps the world, is compelled to adapt its growth to such difficult conditions of high ridges, deep valleys and precipitous slopes." The ruggedness of the landscape also lent itself to the creation of neighborhoods with strong, often ethnic-based, identities and boundaries. Whether in a new mill town or a more established neighborhood, the spatial layout of housing increasingly reflected the hierarchy of the workplace, with unskilled workers occupying the dirtiest, noisiest, and cheapest housing in the river valleys, followed by skilled workers, foremen, and finally executives in their hillside mansions. As the pace of industrialization accelerated, new types of immigrants, including southern and eastern Europeans, Christian Syrians, and Maronites (Christian Lebanese), as well as smaller numbers of African Americans poured into the cities. Wheeling nearly tripled its 1870 population, peaking at around 62,000 in 1930, while Allegheny County (Pittsburgh) grew from 262,000 to more than 1.3 million during the same period.[16]

In addition to personnel policies that pitted various ethnic groups against one another, industrialists used political tools to more effectively control their workforces beyond the factory gates. From the 1860s to the 1890s, ironworkers and coal miners developed some of the nation's most powerful labor unions, including the Sons of Vulcan (1858), the Knights of Labor (1869), the Amalgamated Association of Iron and Steel Workers (1876), and the United Mine Workers (1890). Skilled workers, such as iron puddlers, heaters, and rollers, enjoyed considerable autonomy, and their unions followed a craft model that often broke down along racial and ethnic lines as well as skill level. As Andrew Carnegie, B. F. Jones and the Steel Valley's other industrialists tightened their control of workplace processes, however, the integration of coal, iron, and steel production in increasingly large mines and mills presented challenges that union organizers were able to overcome only by expanding their notions of solidarity.[17]

The introduction of new technologies, such as the Bessemer converter, lessened the importance of workers whose expertise had been acquired through years of workplace training. Without the need for artisanal labor, during strikes employers were able to introduce new workers, often of different ethnic or racial backgrounds, who were frequently either excluded from or uninterested in joining the existing unions. Even when unionists responded by building broader organizations, solidarity still had its limits for workers who defined their shared interest as often in terms of ethnic or racial prejudices as along class lines. Notwithstanding the Amalgamated's emphasis on inter-craft solidarity, for example, the organization did not allow blacks to join segregated lodges until 1881, nor did they allow common laborers admittance until 1889. Indeed, it was in the mines and not the mills where labor organizers enjoyed the most success in building a true industrial union; the United Mine Workers organized all underground workers regardless of specialty. Despite the challenges posed by technological change and ethnic prejudice, in 1882 a strike by the Amalgamated Union at the newly built Homestead Works forced the Pittsburgh Bessemer Steel Company to sign a contract with the union. A year later, the bankrupt company sold the mill to Andrew Carnegie, which prompted a decade of simmering labor tension even as production skyrocketed.[18]

The ascendance of the region's large industrial corporations also resulted in close ties between executives and politicians on the local and state levels. Among the numerous benefits of generous financial support for members of the Pennsylvania General Assembly was the creation of the infamous Coal and Iron Police, which allowed companies to create their own private security forces. In 1888 and 1889, the deputization of hundreds of armed guards allowed Carnegie to introduce replacements and break the union at the Edgar Thomson Works. However, Amalgamated Union workers at Homestead had enough support from local politicians to resist such tactics until 1892. During a final attempt to break the union, on July 5, Henry Frick, Carnegie Steel's chairman, attempted to land three hundred armed guards from the Pinkerton Detective Agency on the shore of the Monongahela to protect plant access for replacement laborers. Locked-out workers and residents resisted, which resulted in a firefight that ended with bystanders killing several guards after they had surrendered. In the aftermath, the Pennsylvania governor sent in the entire state militia to support management, effectively breaking the strike and eventually the union.[19]

The battle at Homestead quickly became a "quasi-mythical epic," in the words of one historian, captured for the world by at least 135 journalists that covered the story. Despite attempts by union organizers to halt the violence, most accounts focused on what Reuben Gold Thwaites described as "the attendant horrors [of] the mob." This negative representation of workers provided the political cover employers needed to finally eliminate organized labor in Pittsburgh's iron and steel industry. Over the next forty years, company officials and their allies in state and local government systematically rooted out union activity in mills, employed company spies to prevent worker organization, and undermined pro-labor candidates in local government. Anti-union sentiment among employers was especially strong in southwestern Pennsylvania and extended beyond the steel mills, with only one union, a carpenter's local, remaining intact throughout the entire period. While few statistics are available, one scholar discovered that officials at six Carnegie mills fired at least 700 workers between 1896 and 1910 as a result of company spy reports.[20]

A nuanced analysis of manufacturing in the Steel Valley also reveals intra-regional patterns that would later have significant ramifications for metropolitan development. On the one hand, Wheeling iron-makers, too, began vertical integration during the 1880s and adopted Bessemer converters, thereby eliminating some skilled occupations and placing more control over production in the hands of managers. Unable to match their better capitalized rivals in terms of basic steel and with a declining market for cut nails, however, the largest Wheeling firms diversified their operations into the production of pipes, tin plate, and other finished goods. The creation of the American Tin Plate Company in 1898 resulted in the acquisition of the tin milling operations of most of the large companies in Wheeling and Steubenville, with other area mills becoming parts of American Steel and Wire, American Steel Hoop Company, and National Tube Company. The 1901 creation of U.S. Steel from the merger of Carnegie's empire with Federal Steel, National Steel, and a host of smaller companies marked the high point of this wave of consolidation. The new conglomeration also included eight plants on the Ohio River in and around Wheeling and Steubenville, marking the functional consolidation of operations throughout the entire Steel Valley.[21]

Because the production of tin plate remained a relatively skilled operation, mill workers in Wheeling and Steubenville remained unionized well after the industrial unions had been crushed in southwestern Pennsylvania. After Homestead, the Amalgamated Union essentially gave up trying to organize basic steel and focused their efforts on the less technologically advanced finishing mills. However, the creation of U.S. Steel resulted in a protracted industry-wide strike, with workers shutting down all eight plants along the Ohio that had been included in the new conglomeration. Strikers had a great deal of public support in local communities, with Mingo Junction, Ohio, Mayor W. J. O'Donnell stating flatly that he was "with the Amalgamated Association men in this fight to the end." In spite of this support, the strike was in disarray by September as managers hurriedly trained new workers to take the place of skilled workers and the escalation of violence turned public opinion against organizers. In the years following the strike, the number of local union lodges in the Wheeling district fell from eighteen to about six, though this was still relatively more than along the Monongahela and other areas around the country.[22]

The complex relationship between politics, union activity, and corporate growth set the stage for increasing community dependence on companies for a wide variety of municipal services, as industrial employers matched their anti-union activities at the workplace with a positive campaign to win the hearts and minds of the area's residents. Many corporations instituted corporate welfare programs aimed at encouraging workers to identify with company interests. Beginning in 1903, U.S. Steel instituted a profit-sharing stock purchase program for employees and joined other large employers in instituting modest pension and accident benefits programs. A wave of steel strikes following World War I prompted further expansion of corporate welfare activities. "Good will is not a sentiment that trickles down from above," declared Homestead Works superintendent L.C. Gardner. "It comes into existence at the bottom of the social structure. The place to cultivate good will is where it grows naturally—in the community, in the neighborhood, where people meet as folks." Corporations held huge picnics and organized excursions to local amusement parks, such as Kennywood near Homestead and the White Palace in Wheeling, designed to cement the relationship between employees and management. Many companies fielded sports teams, with the Edgar Thomson Works fielding baseball, track and field, basketball, and boxing teams. Company coffers paid for playgrounds, community centers, government buildings, pools, libraries, and hospitals. Throughout the Steel Valley, local politicians said that if they needed something, they simply went to the mill superintendent or plant supervisor and asked for it.[23]

Industrialists also used the process of municipal incorporation to limit their tax liability, exert additional control over workers, and maintain wealthy enclaves in which to enjoy the fruits of their investments. The mill site along the Ohio River across from Steubenville, for example, appealed to Ernest T. Weir not only for its accessibility and low cost, but also for its relative isolation from older urban centers. "We had something else in mind besides building an integrated plant," Weir explained in 1955. Weirton was "deliberately selected and consciously planned as the location for both a steel plant and a community." Cities, Weir believed, "if not breeders, were certainly magnifiers of discontent among workers." "In a small town," he continued, workers and management were friendly, and residents were often "relatives or close friends." Weirton employees owned homes or rented private residences, but the company provided water and other services, paid for the police, controlled access to jobs, and dominated the local culture as well as the economy. In exchange for this paternalism, Weirton Steel employees remained steadfastly nonunion even after the great organizing drive of the CIO in the 1930s. By 1920, the area already counted 9,500 residents, and in 1940 its population of approximately 25,000 made it the largest unincorporated town in the nation.[24]

In ways similar to Weirton Steel's domination of its mill town, the famous libraries donated by Andrew Carnegie illustrate the community structure of the Steel Valley at its peak as well as the political discord that often simmered just below the surface. The Pittsburgh industrialist used the 1898 dedication ceremony for the Homestead Library to outline his program for the institution that was, in his words, "the gift of one workingman to other workingmen." "May it indeed be between capital and labor," he concluded, "an emblem of peace, reconciliation, confidence, harmony and union."[25] Local boosters throughout the region supported construction of Carnegie libraries both as needed investments in their communities and also in recognition of the financial power wielded by corporate interests. Wheeling attorney Nelson Hubbard, whose father was a state representative and later U.S. Congressman, wrote the steel magnate explaining how his "distinctly . . . labor city" desperately needed "a permanent establishment which would be a constant power in building up [its] deficiencies." On the eve of a referendum to raise the required 10 percent local contribution, the *Daily Intelligencer* also warned, "Mr. Carnegie is so situated that any affront to him at this time might in the end prove very disastrous to the physical welfare of Wheeling." The editor then cited all the steel mills in the vicinity as evidence of the city's dependence on heavy industry, concluding, "We desire Mr. Carnegie's good will. He deserves our good will."[26]

Others, however, were less enthusiastic about the new cultural jewels scattered throughout metropolitan Pittsburgh. Despite Carnegie's stated desire to bury "all regretful thoughts, all unpleasant memories," Wheeling unionists, such as Valentine Reuther whose sons later helped start the United Auto Workers, denounced any facility provided by the villain of the Homestead Massacre, who had "blood on his hands." Wheeling's funding issue failed by a slim 201 votes after members of the local Carpenters' and Joiners' Union declared they wanted a library that would be Wheeling's own, "not a Carnegie monument where a large portion of our citizens could only enter with repugnance and servility." Wheeling's failed attempt to obtain a Carnegie library also reveals the weakness of local governments in metropolitan Pittsburgh and their reliance on corporate largesse for infrastructure that elsewhere would have been a service of municipal authorities. "Wheeling needs a good library sadly," Hubbard lamented. "The city is scarcely able to provide one, and is by no means willing to do what it can and should do in that direction. For the latter reason, especially, we shall probably do without the library until someone from outside thinks best to offer substantial help."[27]

Politics of Production

The political systems forged in the late nineteenth century largely stymied attempts at dealing effectively with the environmental and social consequences of the Steel Valley's industrial economy. As in the earlier era, the relationship between local leaders and state politics in Harrisburg, Charleston, and Columbus continued to be of major importance in determining the fortunes of the region's communities. Despite Wheeling's increased influence in West Virginia politics during a period of Republican ascendance between 1895 and 1931, for instance, the ability of the community to attract investment from state government remained limited. West Virginia's taxation structure remained heavily weighted in favor of the large coal and timber companies who controlled the sparsely settled counties that made up much of the state. Lacking a sufficient source of development funds, civic administration in Wheeling remained more like a nineteenth-century frontier town than a community with aspirations to become a modern metropolis. Because of the lack of taxing authority, fees charged for liquor licenses were so important to municipal coffers that it was virtually impossible to place any limitations on saloonkeepers, some of whom served as unofficial political bosses in the shifting alliances of the period. Wheeling gained a reputation as being "wide-open" for organized crime with "Big" Bill Lias and other gangsters controlling prostitution, gambling, and later bootlegged alcohol.[28]

Things were even worse in Steubenville, which continued to decline in importance compared to other parts of Ohio even as the expansion of heavy industry brought with it the same social and environmental problems affecting other areas of the region. "Millmen are notoriously free spenders," observed a local Protestant minister, who blamed the "new tide of immigration [that] infiltrated Steubenville: Italians, Slavs, Greeks, Ukrainians [for] the jaws of vice [that] closed upon the city." Unlike Weirton and other communities dominated by a single company, civic elites in Steubenville had no effective means of imposing social control, particularly as municipal politics became increasingly fragmented along ethnic and class lines. "Other than a 40 percent Italian dominance, no other group has produced a leader capable of solidifying the sub-cultures into a cohesive community," reported a later observer. "Although the area is economically above the Ohio median income level, sociologically they respond as fractionated lower-middle class isolates. Consequently, the dynamic necessary to coalesce the diverse interests into a unified progress effort, for all intent and purpose, does not exist."[29]

Political leaders in wealthier and more populous Pittsburgh, on the other hand, established strong ties to the state government, which generally obliged with enabling legislation whenever necessary. They also built a relatively stable municipal administration that, while machine-driven and corrupt, was able to effectively deliver services to constituents. Political rings organized a fragmented, neighborhood-controlled municipal government by means of a centralized, boss-dominated system that could tame tumultuous city councils and provide basic services from rudimentary street paving and lighting to park construction and the laying of sanitary sewer and water lines. Republican operative Christopher Magee and state legislator William Flinn created this type of boss system using patronage, payoffs, and political maneuvering to enrich themselves and their followers. After 1879, those seeking to do business with the city or to bank its assets paid a premium to the machine, while Flinn's contracting business, Booth and Flinn, Ltd., received millions in padded contracts for roads and other public improvements as the lowest "responsible" bidder. The organization allied itself with the Mellon family and other bankers holding the city's funds, owners of traction (streetcar) companies with city contracts, and railroad powers such as the Pennsylvania Railroad, as well as liquor and vice interests who could depend on city hall to turn a blind eye once the proper bribes were paid.[30]

Under the reign of Magee and Flinn, Pittsburgh undertook a massive program of public improvements that far outstripped anything attempted in the Steel Valley's other urban centers. The Magee-Flinn machine pursued a pro-growth agenda focused on delivering services to those middle and upper class neighborhoods most able to pay. They were supported in this endeavor by the Pennsylvania legislature, which created a new city charter in 1887 (denounced by the Democratic *Pittsburgh Post* as the "Mageesburgh" charter) that placed appointing power for municipal departments in the hands of the machine-controlled city council. The legislature then passed a bill authorizing Pittsburgh to provide for street improvements, sewers, sidewalks, and other public works that created a bonanza of lucrative projects ripe for patronage. While public works served a political function in providing the graft that oiled the cogs of the political machine, celebrated Public Works director Edward Bigelow (who was also Magee's cousin) insisted on efficient administration of projects, resulting in the laying of 190 miles of new sewers, the grading of 94 miles of city streets, and the repairing of an additional 75 miles with asphalt or block stone between 1888 and 1899 alone.[31]

Despite these successes, ring-led development was inherently limited and provided services in such an uneven way that they actually tended to increase the social and environmental inequalities separating the middle and working classes. During the 1880s and 1890s, many new office and retail buildings rose in the region's downtown areas as Henry Phipps, Andrew Mellon, Henry Frick and others competed to build the most distinctive and opulent buildings as symbols of their growing fortunes. Similarly, Union Deposit Bank president Dorhman Sinclair built a ten-story steel-and-concrete structure in 1915 hailed as "Steubenville's First Skyscraper." Middle- and upper-class neighborhoods in the cities as well as exclusive areas in the upper reaches of mill towns and railroad commuter suburbs benefitted the most from infrastructure development initiatives. In Pittsburgh, the burgeoning East End neighborhoods of Shadyside, Oakland, Homewood, and Highland Park were protected by their topography from the grit and soot of the industrialized river valleys and were the first to enjoy paved streets, municipal water and other benefits. "The old wards of our city," explained Edward Bigelow in 1890, "are very rapidly being turned into manufacturing sites and thereby forcing the residents thereof to locate in the East End in outer wards. Having once established their homes there, they very naturally and very properly ask [for] such streets and sewer improvements as well as water supplies that will make their lives accessible and healthful."[32]

Early on, some labor leaders and others began advocating for reform of the political boss system. Not all residents of the river valleys could move, of course, and industrial expansion meant increasing crowding of working-class neighborhoods where political leaders could more easily placate residents with jobs and other personal favors. "Here was wealth beyond computation, almost beyond imagination," wrote newspaper columnist H. L. Mencken of Pittsburgh in its industrial heyday, "and here were human habitations so abominable that they would have disgraced a race of alley cats." Until the 1890s, organized labor had a powerful presence throughout the Steel Valley, and just as skilled workers continued to exercise critical control over work processes in the mills so too did union leaders, both Republican and Democrat, who often served as town burgesses and other key officials. Labor leaders also teamed up with civic officials to push for improvements to the quality of life of working-class residents through public works spending. This was particularly notable in Wheeling, where Valentine Reuther and the Ohio Valley Trades and Labor Assembly helped lead a decades long push for a municipal filtration system that would provide "water fit to drink [and] a city fit to live in." Political bosses, however, proved adept at co-opting union officials with the promise of patronage positions, a practice that effectively turned labor leaders into party hacks. Combined with blacklisting, lock-outs, and other tactics employed by industrialists as well as corporate welfare programs, the rise of political machines subverted union solidarity, effectively co-opted the role of unions in shaping a working-class identity, and undercut attempts at an independent labor politics.[33]

Middle-class reformers, too, highlighted the inefficiencies of the boss-system and blamed political corruption for the increasing inequalities in the Steel Valley. The paternalism of civic elites combined with the pro-development agenda of Magee and Flinn resulted in many high-profile public works projects in Pittsburgh, most notably in the new hilltop civic center of Oakland. However, the Pittsburgh Survey emphasized the rapid decline of living conditions for working-class residents as well as high rates of communicable diseases and rising concerns about the negative effects of air and water pollution. Kellogg and his investigators blamed the region's serious social problems and environmental degradation on the "production of wealth on a vast scale," "inequity in distribution," "and the inadequacies of municipal governments" that could "be overcome rapidly" if the community really wanted to do so. At the same time, Pittsburgh reformers seemed to hit their stride with the 1906 mayoral election of George Guthrie, a Progressive bitterly opposed to the Magee-Flinn machine. The new mayor created a Division of Smoke Inspection in the Bureau of Health, which itself was elevated to a full municipal department in 1909 in order to better regulate tenements and improve sanitary conditions. Guthrie also partnered with business leaders, who were concerned about economic threats to the city in the wake of a disastrous flood and a national financial panic, to create a new Civic Commission tasked "to plan and promote improvements in civic and industrial conditions." In turn, the group of eighteen business and professional leaders hired pioneer city planner Frederick Law Olmstead, Jr., to prepare a plan for the city. When completed in 1911, Olmsted's *Pittsburgh: Main Thoroughfares and the Downtown District* established a comprehensive framework for remaking Pittsburgh as a modern metropolis.[34]

Ethnic fragmentation, a rugged landscape, and the desire of industrialists to control the levers of political power in the area around their plants meant that vertical integration of the economy was not matched by centralized municipal administrations. Civic boosters in both Pittsburgh and Wheeling expressed a mixture of pride and annoyance at the relatively small percentage of population the central city contained in relation to that of their dependent regions. In the eyes of Progressive reformers, the region's fragmented political system created a plethora of inefficient minor municipalities that duplicated services, prevented comprehensive planning, weakened civic administrations, and lent themselves to control by corrupt interests. "Pittsburgh is dwarfed and made small in comparison with other cities, where outlying but dependent suburbs have been merged into one municipal organization," declared George Anderson of the Chamber of Commerce in 1902. "Civic pride . . . should demand that this, the acknowledged industrial center of America, should occupy her proper place among other great cities of the nation."[35] Similarly, a decade later a booster publication sponsored by the Wheeling Corrugating Company bemoaned the fact that "the census cannot go beyond legal boundaries and so Wheeling does not get credit for her real extent and true proportions."[36]

As regional elites began to see their competitive advantages slip in the early decades of the twentieth century, corporate leaders and some politicians, such as Pittsburgh Mayor William A. Magee, who replaced Guthrie in 1909, joined Progressives in their belief that "some form of centralized administration" was necessary. Similarly, proponents of a "Greater Wheeling Charter" authorized by the West Virginia Legislature after nearly a decade of campaigning cited the need for a larger water reservoir and regional sewer authority as well as the need to avoid "much embarrassment" and "great humiliation" at a time when many other cities were annexing adjacent territories. As a result of these initiatives, Pittsburgh, which had already incorporated its East End and the South Side communities across the Monongahela River during the 1860s and 1870s, forcibly annexed the separate City of Allegheny across the Allegheny River in 1906. In 1919, Wheeling, too, consolidated its control over the eight adjacent municipalities including Fulton, Woodsdale, and Elm Grove.[37]

Despite the successful campaigns of the early twentieth century, Progressive reforms as a whole largely failed to alter the Steel Valley's underlying political and social structure. Though William Magee adopted some of the proposals put in place by the Guthrie administration, the pragmatism required by machine politics ensured a watering down of more "inspiring ideals" for slum improvement, smoke control, sanitation regulation, and comprehensive planning. When the Olmsted plan appeared in 1911, local officials observed that while "there is no doubt that Mr. Olmsted is an expert engineer and a fine gentleman," his plans were not "practical." In Wheeling, city politics remained chaotic with effective municipal programs and public works spending limited by lackluster support on the state level. Indeed, the lack of alternative means of funding led many officials to conclude that, despite their illegality, it was better to regulate rather than eliminate "the vices of gambling, prostitution, etc., for revenue, and that this was really required by the financial customs of the city." Such open acceptance of and financial dependence on criminal activity for the basic functioning of the region's communities did not bode well for reformers interested in creating modern cities capable of attracting outside investment.[38]

The early twentieth century also represented the high point of annexation campaigns, particularly in Wheeling, where boosters were limited not only by municipal boundaries, a wide river and rough terrain, but also by a state line dividing the city from its hinterland in Ohio. Neither Pittsburgh nor Wheeling proved effective in further consolidating their authority in the face of a metropolitan backlash that continued into the postwar period and through the end of the century. While the 1906 referendum on Pittsburgh's proposal to annex Allegheny City passed easily, nearly two-thirds of voters in the smaller community opposed consolidation. Anger over this type of forced annexation prompted other municipalities to organize in 1911 the League of Boroughs, Townships and Cities of the Third Class of

Allegheny County to fight further consolidation. Wheeling, of course, as one booster publication pointed out, would never be able to "be made legally one [with] our strong and aggressive neighbors in Ohio" in the same way Pittsburgh was able to merge with its satellite communities across the Allegheny and Monongahela Rivers. That said, following the 1919 annexation in which all but one of the smaller communities opposed consolidation, Wheeling had no better luck than Pittsburgh in expanding substantially its southern, eastern or northern borders despite periodic attempts. As a result, metropolitan Pittsburgh remained one of the nation's most fragmented regions, ensuring that the underlying political framework established during its period of industrial growth would not be seriously challenged even as the economic conditions that gave rise to the Steel Valley began to shift in favor of areas to the south and west.[39]

The infrastructure superimposed on the natural landscape formed the prism through which residents and visitors alike crafted a regional identity for the Steel Valley. Profits from the mills were at the core of the region's prosperity; however, their products should be measured not only by the metric ton of steel produced, but also in ways equally important to understanding the region. "The pulsating whang of steel-making plants and rolling-mills" was ever-present, observed Rueben Gold Thwaites on his epic voyage down the Ohio River, making even "the air tremble." Workers carried in their bodies the burden of working in difficult conditions, where a decade of hard labor left men "only fit for the boneyard." Of course, waste from the mills manifested itself in many ways—flowing into the water or creating an atmosphere thick with smoke. By the 1890s, Thwaites declared, the region's riverbanks were already primarily used as the dumping ground for cinders, slag, and "rubbish of every degree of foulness." "Sometimes for nearly a mile in length," he concluded, "the natural bank is deep buried out of sight; and we have from our canoe naught but a dismal wall of rubbish, crowding upon the river to the uttermost limit."[40]

Taken together, the cultural, social, and physical development of the region created an integrated framework that resisted change even as residents faced a series of economic and environmental problems rooted in the very fabric of community life. Even by the beginning of the twentieth century, the Steel Valley exhibited a host of environmental and social problems, which extended from the sewage filled rivers that gave Pittsburgh the nation's highest rate of typhoid fever to the smoke-belching furnaces that kept many of the region's communities engulfed in a perpetual twilight. Indeed, the role of heavy industrial corporations in metropolitan Pittsburgh's economic and political life actually grew after World War I as glass, pottery, cigar making, and other traditional employers began to decline. Whether in the mill towns dominated by large industrial employers, small cities such as Wheeling or Steubenville that proved incapable of overcoming ethnic and class differences, or Pittsburgh of the Magee-Flinn era, however, regional politics generally impeded collective action to remediate these problems. It was not until after the jarring dislocations of the 1930s that a new public-private partnership emerged that held out the promise of urban and regional revitalization.[41]

CHAPTER 3

The Pittsburgh Story

In late October 1948, an incident in Donora, Pennsylvania, twenty-five miles up the Monongahela River from Pittsburgh, crystalized all that was wrong with the environmental, economic, and political framework that had held sway in the Steel Valley over the previous half century. The massive industrialization and urbanization of the river valleys combined with the steep surrounding escarpments to trap particulates, sulfur dioxide, and other chemicals from burning coal, particularly when cold air prevented the smoke from rising. Donora frequently had problems due to U.S. Steel's Donora Zinc Works, its American Steel and Wire Plant, and other smaller sources, but the 1948 incident was quite severe—lasting five days, killing twenty residents, and sickening thousands more. "You couldn't see to step off the curb or to the end of your hand," recalled Charles Stacey, who was an equipment manager for Donora's football team in 1948. During the game that week, people and players were sent home from the field early. "One of the players, Stan Sawa, went home and found that his father had died." For its part, U.S. Steel never acknowledged responsibility for the incident, calling it a "freak weather condition" that trapped "all of the smog coming from the homes, railroads, the steamboats, and the exhaust from automobiles, as well as the effluents from its plants."[1]

Despite an illusion of industrial dominance promulgated by business leaders and residents alike, few mills opened or expanded in the Steel Valley after 1920, while dismally smoky skies and a devastating flood in 1936 contributed to the growing sense of unease. In Pittsburgh itself, the Republican dynasty that had dominated municipal and county politics since the nineteenth century collapsed during the mid-1930s to be replaced by Democratic leadership under David Lawrence. At the same time, real estate assessments in the city declined by more than $250 million between 1938 and 1944 alone. Few corporations, it seemed, were willing to invest in the region's aging infrastructure, particularly in the growing sectors of chemical production, electronics, automobiles, and consumer goods manufacturing. "At worried board meetings," reported one magazine article, "there was more and more talk of 'leaving Pittsburgh,' and no plans for postwar expansion lay on executive desks."[2]

As a result, the Donora Smog, as it became known, was a moment of truth for civic and political leaders who sought to attract new investment by changing the industrial imagery of the "Smoky City" into that of a modernist "Renaissance City." Pittsburgh seemed an unlikely candidate for revitalization on such a grand scale, but by the late 1940s a powerful pro-growth consensus had emerged between the Lawrence administration and the Allegheny Conference on Community Development, which was backed by financier Richard "R. K." Mellon. The city's new public-private partnership combined an effective leadership structure with an attention to public relations that made it a national model for postwar urban renewal. At the heart of the Pittsburgh Renaissance was a regional vision for a modernist, functionally divided, and thoroughly engineered landscape that combined air pollution controls, a series of massive dams, and new parks with the construction of a modern highway system, the encouragement of residential suburbs, and the transformation of Pittsburgh's mixed-use central business district into the high-rise skyscrapers of the Golden Triangle.

Indeed, thanks to the implementation of its landmark smoke control law, by 1948 the city easily weathered the conditions the caused the Donora Smog without even having to "turn on its downtown streetlights in the daytime." The real legacy of the Renaissance, however, was more complicated and in key ways reflected a continuation of earlier patterns of political economy and ecology rather than the clean break from the past described by the region's boosters. After all, the same executives at U.S. Steel and the region's other industrial corporations who celebrated the blue skies now visible from their offices in the Golden Triangle also depended on profits gained from the ongoing pollution of mill towns like Donora. Similarly, the construction of dams and rural parks relied on the projection of urban political power in much the same way that urban capital had already rearranged rural landscapes in the form of mines and coking ovens. Nevertheless, the clear successes of Pittsburgh's public-private partnership established a new framework for metropolitan development in the 1950s and 1960s that helped compensate for the continued stagnation of the Steel Valley's industrial economy even as it privileged new commuter suburbs and select urban neighborhoods.[3]

Steel Valley in Crisis

The economic forces that had drawn German immigrant Valentine Reuther to the Steel Valley were shifting even by the 1920s to growing industrial centers in other areas. When Reuther's son Walter left for Detroit in 1927, he was making forty-two cents an hour at the Wheeling Corrugating Company. Walter and his friend Leo Hores reached Detroit on the last Saturday in February 1927 and were met by family friends, his brother Victor later recalled. On Sunday they found a boarding house and on Monday afternoon they were hired at Briggs Body Works in Highland Park. Within a few months Walter secured a job as a tool and die maker at Ford Motor Company making $1.05 an hour by using the skills he had gained as an apprentice in Wheeling. While his parents, older brother Ted, and younger sister Christine remained in Wheeling for the rest of their lives, Walter's two younger brothers soon followed him to Detroit, where they were instrumental in the formation and rise of the United Auto Workers union.[4]

The decision of the three Reuther brothers to leave Wheeling highlighted the region's growing economic and environmental problems. Production in the mills did not falter during the 1920s, but the rate of growth in the heavy manufacturing sector, both nationally and in Pittsburgh, slowed following the boom period of the early twentieth century. There are multiple reasons for the region's decline from industrial preeminence, including technological change that lessened geographical advantages, increased competition from other areas, and reduced demand for the types of products in which local firms increasingly specialized. The production of steel ingots and castings in southwestern Pennsylvania, for example, rose by over 450 percent between 1890 and 1910, but this rate of increase slowed to only 17 percent during the subsequent two decades. As a percentage of total national production, steel ingot capacity in the four-county Pittsburgh Industrial Area declined from 24.1 to 20.8 percent between 1920 and 1940, while its share of plate glass production collapsed from 54.9 percent in 1928 to 27.2 percent in 1940. One indicator of this loss of competitive advantage during the 1920s was the low growth rate for the total product value added by Pittsburgh manufacturers (6.6 percent) compared to the national average (27.1 percent), the total increase in the 33 largest industrial cities (29.6 percent), and the increases for Cleveland (27.2), Detroit (28.6), and Chicago (52.6). While the expansion of other industries such as window glass, electrical equipment, and food production offset losses in basic manufacturing to an extent, the Steel Valley was clearly losing ground to competitors.[5]

The region's over-specialization in a relatively few heavy industrial products and a concentration of the labor force in large mills distinguished it from other areas of the country. Because of the lack of flat land amid the rugged terrain, it also contained some of the nation's most extensively developed factory sites, with many examples of continuous occupancy, even by a single firm, for several generations. In short, this meant that a disproportionate number of workers in the region were employed by a relatively small number of corporations operating increasingly aged facilities. This was not necessarily a problem in and of itself. Weirton Steel, for example, aggressively adopted new technology, moved into new product lines, and increased employment even as new records in ingot production kept it among the nation's most important heavy industrial firms. At the much larger U.S. Steel, however, management's business model focused on maintaining stable and fixed prices on steel through monopolistic practices, such as pools and a "gentlemen's agreement" to respect competitors' territory. When chairman Elbert Gary forced out president Charles Schwab, formerly one of Carnegie's top lieutenants, U.S. Steel lost an important connection to its roots in Pittsburgh even as the company broke ground in 1905 on an enormous new integrated mill near Chicago that would soon bear Gary's name. Population figures for the metropolitan core paralleled this loss of relative industrial power during the 1920s and 1930s, as Allegheny County expanded by a meager 19 percent compared to 33 percent in Cook (Chicago), 71 percent in Wayne (Detroit), and 197 percent in Los Angeles counties.[6]

Rural communities in the Steel Valley, too, faced serious economic problems that were also intimately related to environmental degradation. The region's mines encountered increasing competition from oil and natural gas as well as the development of new coalfields in southern West Virginia and Kentucky. Broader changes in agriculture made already precarious small farms increasingly untenable, even as mining companies systematically replaced humans with machines allowing higher output with fewer miners. Between 1904 and 1944, Joseph Joy, founder of Pittsburgh-based Joy Mining Machinery, filed 106 patents on various types of mining equipment, from cutting and loading machines to drills and conveyers. As a consequence, mining employment in southwestern Pennsylvania dropped from a high of 82,000 in 1914 to only 46,000 in 1940. The decline in the need for workers also came from the rising use of surface mining, with technological advances in excavating equipment that dramatically increased the ability to reach deeper coal seams even as they left behind overturned and unproductive fields, enormous cliffs known as high walls, and a variety of other environmental problems. The United Electric Coal Company began using two electric power shovels in a mine near Steubenville in 1913, and five years later six surface mines were operating near the city. The world's largest electric shovel began mining in the area in 1935, and between 1921 and 1945 coal stripping in twenty-two eastern Ohio counties affected nearly thirty thousand acres.[7]

The Great Depression was longer and harsher in the Steel Valley than in other regions as falling demand and the economies of scale on which the coal and steel industries depended produced a glut in the national market. The nation's steel mills ran at only one-third capacity by 1933, with the result that U.S. Steel did not have a single full-time employee anywhere in the country. When companies idled workers and scaled back corporate welfare programs, the uneasy peace between labor and management that had dominated industrial relations since the 1890s began to falter. The election of Progressive Republican Gifford Pinchot as Pennsylvania governor in 1931 and President Franklin Roosevelt in 1932 further diminished the ability of employers to completely dominate the social landscape. The United Mine Workers (UMW) under John L. Lewis, whom Roosevelt appointed to his Labor Advisory Board in 1933, was the first to take advantage of the new situation. The union gambled on a massive membership drive with the slogan, "The President wants you to join the UMW!" and regained nearly 300,000 members within a few months.[8]

This rebirth of a unionization movement that had been severely weakened on the local level since the failure of the Homestead Strike and then devastated by the Great Steel Strike of 1919 had major ramifications for both labor and municipal politics. When the Steel Workers Organizing Committee of the new Congress of Industrial Organizations (CIO) arrived in the Steel Valley in 1936, the ground had already been prepared by three years of organizing activity in the region. Despite nationwide resistance by employers, the CIO soon demonstrated its ability to halt production at a major corporation with a sit-down strike at General Motors in Flint led by Wheeling natives Walter and Victor Reuther. U.S. Steel president Myron Taylor invited Lewis, who was also head of the CIO, to begin secret negotiations in January 1937—a process that initiated a top down approach to organizing that would define the subsequent relationship between the company and union leaders. The formal pact between U.S. Steel and its workers was signed on March 17, 1937, and led directly to a host of other labor agreements in the steel industry that continued without serious challenge for the next forty years.[9]

On the other hand, Ernest Weir's ability to control both the community and the company that bore his name demonstrated the continuation of the earlier pattern of industrial relations into the postwar period. As many as 10,000 Weirton Steel workers also struck in fall 1933, but Weir countered the threat of unionization with the same combination of corporate benevolence and violence against organizers used during the strike wave of 1919. When laborers at U.S. Steel and other companies "were happy . . . if you would get two or three days pay in two weeks," Weir raised his wage scale by 15 percent and the company continued to produce at nearly full capacity. A "Security League" was created in 1935 to reinforce the company-controlled Employee Representation Plan (ERP), support management, and oppose the CIO, even as Weir increased wages to five dollars a day in 1937 to match similar rates in U.S. Steel's new contract. Members of the Security League fostered community support through a series of parades designed "as an open protest against outside interference" by labor organizers who also faced continuous red-baiting. "WE DON'T WANT LEWIS OR HIS CIO," proclaimed league-distributed placards. "WE ARE STEELMEN NOT MINERS. WE ARE SATISFIED AND SECURE. LET US ALONE." Weir's success in thwarting the union movement demonstrates the power of corporations to dominate the local political economy in the multitude of mill towns where they were the largest landowners, taxpayers, and employers.[10]

Conversely, the relative success of labor unions in the 1930s came in tandem with the collapse of the Republican power structure in Pittsburgh. Democratic politicians had long reconciled themselves to minority party status in much of the region, even agreeing to deliver votes for Republican candidates in exchange for a share of the patronage spoils. The 1920s were a low point for the city's Democrats and their chairman David Lawrence, with defeat following defeat in local elections. The trauma of the Great Depression, however, shook workers' faith in the city's machine politicians, as Father James Cox of Pittsburgh's Old St. Patrick's Church led an "army" of the unemployed on a march to Washington, D.C., in January 1932 seeking unemployment assistance. Political infighting among the Republican candidates as well as federal patronage garnered after Roosevelt's victory later that year allowed Democrats to win the city's mayoral race as well as all five open positions on the city council. Republicans carried only seven wards—their worst defeat ever and an embarrassment from which the party would not recover. Lawrence, who played an important role in Roosevelt's nomination, later had a meteoric rise in the party, serving as mayor from 1946 to 1959 and Pennsylvania governor from 1959 to 1963. "For Pittsburgh's Republicans," historian Bruce Stave concluded, "the advent of the New Deal signified 'the Last Hurrah'; for the city's Democrats it sounded the first Hallelujah."[11]

World War II was a boom time for Steel Valley communities, but as residents began to make their plans for the future, the troubling trends of the late 1920s and 1930s appeared set to continue into the postwar period. Despite a wartime industrial resurgence, between 1940 and 1960, a period when the nation as a whole grew by 35 percent, Allegheny County (Pittsburgh) and Jefferson County (Steubenville) gained only 15 percent and 1 percent respectively, while Ohio County (Wheeling) actually lost more than 6 percent of its population. In confronting these problems, the nascent coalition between Pittsburgh's Republican businessmen and Democratic politicians was part of a broader trend toward community planning that emerged from Progressive-era attempts to scientifically manage the urban environment. Frederick Law Olmsted, Jr., for example, saw in his 1910 redevelopment proposal, *Pittsburgh Main Thoroughfares and the Down Town District*, an opportunity to demonstrate "practical city planning" in a community that would be divided efficiently into "healthful ... residence districts" connected by "ample streets" to separate "districts for retail and wholesale trade, manufacture and commerce." This modernist framework designed for the automobile was also the defining characteristic of New York engineering czar Robert Moses's 1939 *Arterial Plan for Pittsburgh*. Moses's proposal, funded by Howard Heinz, Ernest Weir, R. K. Mellon, and the region's other elite planning enthusiasts, went so far as to advocate scrapping the city's iconic trolleys in favor of buses and urged that "traffic science—not emotion or aesthetics should govern improvement decisions." Taken together the two reports formed the guiding framework for the Pittsburgh Regional Planning Association (PRPA), a group headed by financier Mellon that subsequently served as the planning arm of the Allegheny Conference on Community Development.[12]

The shock of the Great Depression and concerns about the postwar transition to a peacetime economy forced some among the conservative economic elite to rethink their opposition to direct government involvement in urban redevelopment. On the state level, the Pennsylvania legislature followed New York and Massachusetts by creating a Post-War Planning Commission in 1943 to coordinate the transition from war to peacetime among the various state departments. That May, PRPA director Wallace K. Richards and Robert E. Doherty, president of the Carnegie Institute of Technology, sponsored a "Citizens Conference on the Postwar Situation for Allegheny County" aimed at fostering a successful transition to a peacetime economy and "the resuscitation of a devitalized and deteriorating metropolitan area" through comprehensive, coordinated planning. Soon renamed the Allegheny Conference on Community Development, the group received the backing of Mellon, who served as Pittsburgh's spokesperson on the state commission. In December 1945, Mellon's support in turn enabled the Allegheny Conference to secure recognition as the primary voice of the private sector in public policy formulation for southwestern Pennsylvania.[13]

Earlier business-sponsored civic organizations in the Steel Valley had a narrow view of the role of government, but the industrialists and financiers at the helm of the Allegheny Conference shifted to a limited endorsement of public sector intervention. This position reflected a growing acceptance among business groups nationally of government's role in areas traditionally viewed as the private domain. In St. Louis, for example, a new generation of corporate executives joined urban politicians, civic organizations, and construction unions in a program to stem industrial flight from the city through expanded use of eminent domain to clear "blighted areas," implementation of smoke control legislation, and increased public works spending on highways and physical infrastructure. Pittsburgh attorney Arthur Van Buskirk, who served as deputy administrator of the Lend Lease program during World War II, was typical of this new generation of civic-minded business leaders. "A Republican, he was nonetheless in Pittsburgh and Pennsylvania, a liberal," recalled Leland Hazard, an attorney and a fellow member of the Allegheny Conference's executive committee. Buskirk "could live with the New Deal when others in his era spent their time in futile fulmination."[14]

The success of the Pittsburgh Renaissance was due to the nature of the city's economic and political structure, a strong partnership between business elites and municipal officials, and the ability to present the group's program as serving the public interest. By the end of the 1940s, the Conference's executive committee included the presidents and chief executive officers of the region's major commercial, financial, and manufacturing interests. Members reached decisions by consensus, with the result that policies, when decided upon, had the backing of the bulk of the business community. Between 1943 and 1947, the group developed a program, endorsed by the region's largest corporations that focused mainly on rebuilding and stimulating investment in downtown Pittsburgh. Public officials agreed with this approach, believing that the corporate offices and other business in the "Golden Triangle" furnished a tax base that supported the remainder of the city and anchored the region's manufacturing interests. Before urban infrastructure redevelopment of any kind could take place, however, both the Lawrence administration and the leaders of the Allegheny Conference had to face the environmental consequences of industrialization in a city with a dismal national reputation and little record of successful coordinated action. Indeed, when noted architect Frank Lloyd Wright surveyed Pittsburgh in 1935 while at work on Edgar Kaufmann's iconic Fallingwater, he declared caustically "This is a disappearing city; it would be cheaper to abandon it." In short, as Lawrence later put it, "the city's rescue was a close thing."[15]

Smoke and Water

The new public-private partnership, symbolized by the pragmatic relationship between R. K. Mellon and David Lawrence, united a strong political base behind many of the environmental initiatives first proposed decades earlier. As early as 1907, Pittsburgh's Chamber of Commerce had appointed a Flood Commission that urged "the expenditure of no less than $20,000,000 in the construction of [storage] reservoirs in as near a future as possible," only to face thirty years of disappointment. Five years later, another report found that the smoke problem was "the greatest single obstacle to progress." But it was not until 1941 that the city passed a meaningful abatement law, only to have it put in abeyance by the onset of World War II. Clearing the skies and damming the rivers became powerful markers of the region's commitment to postwar revitalization and important tools for mobilizing residents behind subsequent public policy decisions. Without addressing these issues, Lawrence explained, "it was clear that the economic revival of the city could not be accomplished."[16]

It has become a cliché that the dominant interpretation of smoke in industrial America was, as James Parton put it, "a blessing" that indicated economic vitality. However, for a brief period in the late nineteenth century, natural gas overtook bituminous coal as Pittsburgh's main fuel source and many residents bemoaned the return of smoky skies when the local gas supply ran out in the early 1890s. Over time, skilled workers voiced republican demands for smoke reduction as a benefit of their position, while some professionals, retail merchants, and other property owners complained of the negative effects of smoke on property values and urban consumer culture. In the wake of the landmark 1912 Pittsburgh Survey, reform-minded businessmen and women's club members often accepted the need for environmental cleanup even as they reacted defensively against working-class demands for better hours, wages, and conditions by focusing on the effects of smoke on the health of women and children.[17]

Even by the 1890s, the city of Pittsburgh began to specialize in corporate administration, financial services, higher education, and other economic sectors that, while intimately related to heavy industry, provided an economic foundation separate from the production process itself. Though the elite Mellon family invested early in Frick's coke empire and controlled the Pittsburgh Coal Company, for example, they also oversaw oil, aluminum, and banking interests that extended far beyond the Steel Valley. This partial detachment from the region's iron and steel industries, coupled with the family's investments in downtown real estate, meant that the Mellons had a financial stake in pursuing smoke abatement. As a consequence, the family was among the region's most important advocates for smoke control through their sponsorship of the University of Pittsburgh Mellon Institute Smoke Investigation (MISI) beginning in 1911. In the twenties and thirties smoke actually became somewhat less of a concern in Pittsburgh, owing in part to the industrial contraction of the Great Depression, with relative gains compared to St. Louis and Cincinnati. But the pollution problem roared back with the buildup to World War II, and in 1941, the year smoke control legislation finally passed, Pittsburgh received only one-third as much sunshine as nearby areas and had the highest rate of pneumonia of any city in the nation.[18]

Much of the smoke problem in the city itself came not from industry but from domestic sources, and so the major problem confronting the postwar public-private partnership was how to force changes in individual fuel use behavior in the name of the greater public good. Despite the support of Mellon and the Allegheny Conference, Lawrence thus took a major political risk when he agreed to support an ordinance requiring the substitution of "smokeless" coal and furnaces for domestic use beginning in October 1947 due to the potential hardships it imposed on low-income families. The implementation of smoke control regulations set the model for the city's future public-private partnerships, with an emphasis on volunteerism and cooperation, and arrests "kept to a minimum." Despite these measures, Lawrence recalled a dramatic scene from the 1949 mayoral primary, when his challenger "told the voters that I had become too friendly with the Mellon interests, too neutral in labor matters and that I was pressing the smoke program on them and that it was going to be expensive." "It was a close shave," Lawrence concluded, and if he had lost, "the political constellation which had developed the new Pittsburgh would never have become a reality."[19]

The support for regulation by politicians and industrialists was based on the assumption that smoke abatement would not exact significant costs to businesses and would, in fact, provide further economic opportunities. Between 1946 and 1955, smoke in the city was reduced by nearly 90 percent. "Statistics and the shirt collar both proved that Pittsburgh had become as clean as the average American city," Lawrence proclaimed. "The victory over smoke [was] the signal for a concentrated attack on the entire range of community problems. It was Pittsburgh's breakthrough from the landing beaches; the other triumphs came in an accelerating rush." However, there are limits to this triumphal narrative. First, coal operators and miners based their support for smoke control on projections that new technologies for creating smokeless coal would actually expand markets for bituminous coal. Backers of the smoke ordinance were thus able to gain the acquiescence of both Pittsburgh Consolidation Coal and local UMW president Patrick Fagan. In reality, low priced natural gas piped in from the American Southwest increasingly became the dominant fuel for domestic use even as emissions regulations hastened the ongoing switch to diesel

FIGURE 3. View of Downtown Pittsburgh, c. 1945. The South Side is on the far right and the North Side on the far left. The University of Pittsburgh Cathedral of Learning is visible at the center top, separated from downtown by the Hill District. Smoke Control Lantern Slide Collection, ca. 1940–1950, AIS.1978.22, Archives Service Center, University of Pittsburgh.

engines by the railroads. Consequently, smoke control actually contributed to the severing of Pittsburgh's economy from that of its rural hinterland, and, theoretically, exacerbated unemployment in the region's bituminous coal mines.[20]

The debate over extension of smoke control laws to Allegheny County suggested that the economic calculus that facilitated broad support for regulation within Pittsburgh did not necessarily extend to the Steel Valley as a whole. While regulating domestic users had been the primary concern in the city, controlling industrial polluters was the key in the rest of the region.

The railroads were the largest consumers of bituminous coal in the region and the Steel Valley's trains hauled more tons of coal than any other product. The largest rail lines were transitioning to more efficient and less polluting diesel engines, but the attempt to create enabling legislation for a countywide ordinance raised objections from the Pennsylvania Railroad, which had a strong voice in state politics. Delaying actions by the railroad's lobbyist in Harrisburg threatened legislative authorization for a county smoke control ordinance and required the direct intervention of R. K. Mellon, a Pennsylvania Railroad director, and U.S. Steel president Benjamin Fairless. While the railroad eventually backed down and allowed state authorization for county smoke regulation to pass, the episode foreshadowed decades of conflict over air pollution in the region.[21]

In short, the political economy that allowed Pittsburgh elites to mobilize successfully around a vision of regional prosperity based on clean skies in the metropolitan core was in part dependent on continued pollution in the regional periphery. Outside downtown Pittsburgh, industrialists were more concerned about keeping production costs low than about real estate values and quality of life issues. Wheeling residents, for example, were unable to muster the political will to tackle the smoke problem in even a preliminary way until the mid-1950s. As public concern about air pollution gradually extended beyond mere smoke control in the wake of the Donora Smog and other events, the volunteerist model favored by the public-private partnerships of the Pittsburgh Renaissance broke down in favor of a stricter regulatory framework that depended less on the argument that clean air was actually good for the economy. By the early 1970s, citizens groups, often indirectly associated with Pittsburgh's universities and hospitals, aggressively sued industrial polluters in southwestern Pennsylvania to force emissions cuts. At the same time, Steubenville gained a national reputation as "America's Dirtiest City" as its steel corporations and coal-fired electrical power producers lobbied forcefully on the state level to prevent the implementation of stricter national standards.[22]

If air pollution was the Steel Valley's most pervasive problem on the eve of World War II, periodic flooding constituted its most potentially devastating environmental concern. The Pittsburgh Renaissance and especially the redevelopment of the downtown Golden Triangle could not have happened without the confidence of investors that urban real estate would be protected from flooding. As with smoke, it is important to understand for whom floods were a problem and how those groups mobilized in a way that made effective flood control possible. The region's first recorded inundation occurred in 1762, with 115 additional significant floods between then and 1936. Nevertheless, the principal concern over the region's rivers remained making the Allegheny, Monongahela and Ohio navigable at Pittsburgh. It was not until three major floods in 1907–1908, which caused $6.5 million in losses, that the Chamber of Commerce created a flood commission with industrialist H. J. Heinz as president. The commission, closely associated with the city's elite-led reform organizations, eventually recommended construction of seventeen reservoirs above the city on the Monongahela, the Allegheny, and their major tributaries, without which "the relief from the destruction caused by floods would be only partial and local."[23]

Flood control required a massive exertion of political control by urban interests to reshape the environment of rural areas far from the cities themselves. Between 1936 and 1953, the Army Corps of Engineers completed eighteen flood control reservoirs on the tributaries of the Ohio River that reduced peak flood levels by more than ten feet. The building of the Youghiogheny Dam south of Ohiopyle, for example, started in 1939 with five hundred men working around the clock, though the project stalled after U.S. entry into World War II. The main purpose of the dam was flood control, but the Corps of Engineers listed the added benefits of "discharge regulation for industrial and domestic water supply and for pollution abatement," a clear acknowledgment of the serious problem of acid mine drainage. The same prominent voices that lined up behind smoke control also lent their support for dam construction. One type of public works was a "must" on any construction program, proclaimed the *Pittsburgh Press* in a 1943 editorial that shared the page with a column on the economic benefits of smoke control. "Build These Dams!" When workers completed the Youghiogheny Dam later that year, the *Press* declared, "Today the great dam stands as a monument to the ingenuity of Army engineers."[24]

The development of federal and state flood control programs had major repercussions in the rural communities in which they were built. As with surface mining, justifications for dam construction often emphasized the low value of the Steel Valley's steep hillsides for agricultural production. The construction of the Youghiogheny Dam resulted in the seizure and complete destruction of a local landscape, including farms, the river itself, and two small towns, Somerfield (population 142) and Selbysport (population 150), to serve the distant interests of urban capital. While prices paid for properties were relatively low ($55 to $100 an acre for farmland, $35 for woodland, and $600 for town lots), the financial exigencies of the Great Depression meant that many residents quickly sold out and left. On the other side of the region, the creation of Piedmont Dam north of Barnesville, Ohio, in 1936 was the first big blow to the farming hamlet of Egypt Valley, which later was subsumed by an enormous surface mine. Unlike the Youghiogheny Dam, however, there is evidence of resistance to the forced eviction of Egypt Valley residents, perhaps due to the higher quality of local agricultural land. Emma Major was nicknamed "The Lady of the Lake" because of her strident opposition to the forced abandonment of her farm in the Piedmont flood area, for which she was offered only $1.97. Though many rural residents fought the sale of their homes, with the waters lapping at their door, they had little choice but to leave. "They drowned me out," Major's son John later recalled. "You couldn't live in the water. In there were people farming. They had raised corn you know and had it cut up in shocks and the first thing I remember [was] that water coming up in their shocks of corn. They were floating on top of the water."[25]

As with smoke abatement, dam construction revealed the environmental control over distant rural areas required as the basis for the Pittsburgh Renaissance. The twin problems of smoke and water had long been concerns of the civic elites that would form the nucleus of the Allegheny Conference. It was only after the Great Depression and World War II that a broad consensus emerged about the particular mechanisms by which these issues would be addressed. The construction of dams could only occur because of the expansion of government authority and the public-private partnerships that also made possible smoke control and the urban redevelopment of the Golden Triangle. Just as corporations needed the natural resources of the metropolitan hinterland in order to supply their massive mills, so too did the urbanized river valleys need to control natural processes originating far from their borders in order to strengthen the overall regional economy and provide the stability necessary for remaking the urban core. With regional plans in place, Pittsburgh's public-private partnership turned to revitalizing the metropolitan core and remaking the city's image as a grimy mill town.

The Golden Triangle

The heart of Pittsburgh's postwar Renaissance was the redevelopment of the tongue of land at the confluence of the Monongahela and Allegheny

Rivers, known as the Point, into a state park and collection of office towers dubbed the "Golden Triangle." Originally the spot of French Fort Duquesne and British Fort Pitt, by the early twentieth century the area was a densely developed, bustling area crisscrossed by dozens of railroad tracks and packed with aging and crowded tenements. As early as 1911 Frederick Law Olmsted, Jr., called for revitalizing the "forgotten and disregarded" downtown riverfronts by establishing "a landscape area to be known as Point Park." "It is here" Olmsted declared, "that all the most inspiring aspirations of the city are chiefly concentrated. Poetically, this spot, at the meeting of the rivers, stands for Pittsburgh." However, the political wrangling that had hampered public works improvements throughout the first half of the twentieth century also prevented any movement on the redevelopment of the area through end of World War II. The Point, as historian Robert Alberts put it, "was blessed by the fortunate failures of those who had sought to develop it in decades past." For better or worse, it was a blank slate on which the city's public-private partnership was "free to attempt to design and build the most beautiful of city parks."[26]

The razing and recreation of the Point, spearheaded by the Allegheny Conference and the Lawrence administration, required radical rethinking of an urban landscape that had developed over the course of nearly two hundred years. For decades, proposals to remake the area ran into conflicts between engineers concerned with the flow of vehicular traffic over two heavily traveled bridges, historians who wanted to reconstruct the original forts, and government officials mainly concerned with public buildings. The only solution that the planning team commissioned by the Allegheny Conference deemed appropriate was to move the bridges farther from the tip of the Point, a prohibitively expensive proposition that would also require the demolition of numerous commercial buildings and the relocation of miles of railroad track. Pennsylvania's Republican governor agreed to the plan and in October 1945 Secretary of Forests and Waters James Kell wired Allegheny Conference chairman Robert Doherty asking the group to "take steps to carry forward Governor Martin's program for Point Park development." The project overcame its final political hurdle when, in a surprise announcement, Lawrence also declared his support shortly before winning election as mayor with a margin of only 14,000 votes.[27]

The development of the Golden Triangle prompted an institutionalization of the relationship between government and business that blurred the line between public and private interests. The state government, which controlled Point Park and the adjacent highway, shared responsibility with the Allegheny Conference and municipal officials, who partnered in creating a nearby cluster of high-rise corporate offices. Local boosters soon secured an agreement with the Equitable Life Insurance Company to construct the twenty-three-acre Gateway Center on land that would be cleared by eminent domain. This was made possible by the establishment of the Urban Redevelopment Authority of Pittsburgh with David Lawrence as chairman, the Allegheny Conference's Arthur Van Buskirk as vice chairman, and Lawrence's secretary John P. Robin as executive director. The official recognition afforded the Allegheny Conference by state and local governments provided a vehicle to harness private funds behind a unified urban and economic development program, while Lawrence ensured the necessary political clout to ensure cooperation from elected officials and local constituencies.[28]

The rise of the Golden Triangle in the 1950s went hand in hand with a concerted effort to sell the Pittsburgh Renaissance to a national and international audience as well as to the region's residents. Work on the redevelopment program began in 1946, with some sixty major new structures built in the area by 1967. John J. Grove, the Allegheny Conference's assistant director, worked to cultivate and maintain public support, a project he undertook in collaboration with members of the local press, such as *Pittsburgh Press* editor Edward T. Leech, who ensured generally favorable reporting of redevelopment projects. Conference and municipal officials traveled widely selling "The Pittsburgh Story," as they called it, and hosted dozens of out of town delegations, with the result that the city gained a reputation as a model for urban redevelopment with a host of conscious imitators, including the Wheeling Area Conference on Community Development, the Greater Philadelphia Movement and St. Louis's Civic Progress, Inc. Conference leaders were careful also to maintain elected officials as the face of their partnership with the city and state in order to defuse potential criticisms of using government authority in the service of private interests. Deflecting this opposition was an ever-present concern of the conference and municipal officials who faced a series of court challenges during the late 1940s and 1950s over the use of eminent domain to transfer property from one private landowner to another. "David Lawrence took his political life in his hands when he collaborated with the mostly Republican establishment in urban renewal," explained Leland Hazard, a member of the Conference's executive committee. "But he was clever. He always took the credit and R. K. Mellon, who disliked publicity, was happy for him to have it."[29]

The razing and redevelopment of the Golden Triangle literally erased the previous century of industrialization in favor of the symbolism of a nostalgic frontier (in the form of a partly reconstructed Fort Pitt) and of the modern metropolis (the gleaming skyscrapers of Gateway Center). Reversing the imagery and infrastructure of the Smoky City was also the key to a planned Center for the Arts that would replace a hundred acres of "blighted" housing east of the Golden Triangle with a civic arena, auditorium, theaters, offices, and luxury apartments. Local officials originally considered building a new municipal arena in the upscale Highland Park area, but abandoned the project in the face of opposition from neighborhood residents, including R. K. Mellon's uncle Robert King. Planners then turned their attention to the Hill District, a mixed-use neighborhood with a lively nightclub scene, high poverty rate, deteriorating buildings and a high percentage of the city's black residents. Allegheny Conference officials and the Lawrence administration envisioned recreating the social and economic makeup of the area between the Golden Triangle and the university community of Oakland into a "cultural acropolis" that would dispel "the lingering conception of Pittsburgh as a 'milltown' that is bereft of any beauty and grace" and form "the true regional capital of the Pittsburgh metropolitan area." The centerpiece of the Lower Hill development was the colossal, $22 million Civic Arena that opened in 1961. Celebratory articles portrayed the structure, with its distinctive retractable roof, as a symbol of industry in the service of culture and an indicator of the city's improved quality of life. "Can you spot the men on the scaffolding?" asked a 1960 ad for U.S. Steel. "They're putting a stainless steel skin on the retractable roof covering Pittsburgh's new civic area—one of the new engineering wonders of the world."[30]

The construction of the Civic Arena highlights the symbolic metamorphosis of the Pittsburgh Renaissance as well as the compartmentalization of land use at the core of its regional vision. The passage of state and federal housing laws in 1949 paved the way for demolition of the Lower Hill by subsidizing more than two thirds of the cost of property purchase and clearance. "I think you will agree that no greater service to slum clearance could be provided anywhere in the United States than in the redevelopment of the lower Hill," declared the Urban Redevelopment Authority's John Robin in 1950. "Nor, could the State's funds be used anywhere in the

Commonwealth to greater advantage for decent housing, improved living standards, and better public health and morals." In reality, low-cost housing was never an important factor in the Lower Hill's redevelopment or in the Renaissance as a whole. By 1966, more than five thousand families had been displaced by urban renewal in Pittsburgh, while less than two thousand new dwelling units (mostly high rent) were built or under construction. "The Lower Hill district . . . was an area of dense slum with the worst housing in the city," Lawrence explained. "Now it's gone. That the community was willing to spend so much for recreation and amusement is as sharp a break with its past as pure air and clean rivers."[31]

In the Renaissance vision, a revitalized downtown would serve as the region's economic, cultural and government core, which the Urban Redevelopment Authority emphasized, "helped stabilize the City's supply of jobs, particularly in managerial, administrative, professional and skilled industrial occupations." On the other hand, Conference officials acknowledged and even encouraged the migration of other urban functions, especially housing, to the periphery, where there was "enough land so that housing objectives may be realized, and every family live within easy commuting distance of the heart of the city." To support this vision of the city as an office park staffed by middle class suburban commuters, Pittsburgh's public-private partnership also focused on the development of a series of highways, bridges, and tunnels radiating out from the Golden Triangle and cutting through the region's hilly landscape. The most important of these projects, the Penn-Lincoln Parkway, provided a non-toll limited access link between downtown, the new Greater Pittsburgh International Airport in western Allegheny County and the Pennsylvania Turnpike in the east. Corporate leaders, too, used the city's growing residential suburbs to entice middle-class professionals to the region. In addition to "high pay, advancement, pleasant associations [and] sickness and accident insurance," a 1951 Westinghouse ad proclaimed, employees could live in "splendid conditions" in Pittsburgh's South Hills with "pleasant suburban, residential and rural sections" and "excellent schools, summer camps, hunting, fishing nearby."[32]

Rural areas, too, had a role to play in the Pittsburgh Story. The creation of Point State Park reflected a growing consensus about the importance of natural areas not only as symbols of the Steel Valley's postwar environmental and cultural transformation, but also in providing recreation opportunities for urban and suburban residents. Park creation was an important component of the comprehensive planning movement, and, since the Progressive era, states and especially the federal government had stepped up funding support for recreation. The National Park Service funded a large Recreational Demonstration Area between Pittsburgh and Steubenville during the 1930s, and the Pennsylvania Post-War Planning Commission recommended establishing a new system of state parks "for urban populations within reasonable travel distance" of the state's metropolitan areas. Dr. Maurice Goddard, who was named secretary of the Pennsylvania Department of Forests and Waters in 1954, enthusiastically embraced the recommendations of the Post-War Planning Commission and committed his agency to developing a "park or forest recreation facility within twenty-five miles of most Pennsylvanians."[33]

Local advocacy matched this state support, with the Allegheny County Sportsmen's League, local garden clubs, and other urban and suburban groups pressuring leaders to develop public recreation areas "where our children can go [but] they don't have to go many miles away from home." In response to this perceived need, members of the Recreation, Conservation, and Parks Council, an affiliate created by the Allegheny Conference, began discussions in 1950 with civic and political leaders to establish "a close working relationship with regard to the acquisition of strategic land parcels" on Pittsburgh's rural periphery. Conference leaders soon negotiated an agreement with the largely moribund Greater Pittsburgh Parks Association to merge the latter into a new more regionally oriented organization to address concerns about "deficiencies in recreational areas which exist in Allegheny, Beaver and Washington Counties." As part of this reorganization, directors of the Greater Pittsburgh Parks Association agreed to a name change that would no longer "connote the paternalism of Pittsburgh and would therefore be more likely to enlist support from the surrounding counties."[34]

The formation and organizational structure of the Western Pennsylvania Conservancy, as the new group was known, mirrored the public-private partnerships formed to redevelop the city. The Allegheny Conference provided the overall strategic planning, political clout, financing, and leadership necessary to accomplish massive public works programs while delegating day-to-day responsibility for individual projects to special purpose organizations often directly spun off from conference committees. The Conservancy quickly incorporated representatives from outside of the city to "decrease concerns about urban control of the countryside," but Conference members, such as Charles F. Chubb, B. F. Jones, III, and retail magnate Edgar Kaufmann retained positions of authority within the Conservancy, and the group relied on these members for funding. The Mellon Trusts, for example, overseen by Allegheny Conference executive committee member Adolph Schmidt, provided grants at strategic moments in the Conservancy's evolution, including its founding in 1950 and reorganization as a dues paying organization in 1958.

The activities of the Western Pennsylvania Conservancy thus served as a vehicle for metropolitan Pittsburgh's political and civic elite to extend the Renaissance vision of a modern, functionally divided landscape from the gleaming downtown skyscrapers to the commuter suburbs along the Penn-Lincoln Parkway to the new parks on the metropolitan periphery. By 1953 the group had already purchased nearly four thousand acres in rural Lawrence, Butler, and Fayette Counties using funds donated by individuals, civic clubs, and nonprofit foundations. The organization entered a new phase of its public-private partnership the following year by conveying its property at McConnell's Mill to the Pennsylvania government at cost for use as a state park. By 1967 it had acquired 29,000 acres for five more state parks, as well as a handful of recreation areas and nature preserves. We were "caught up in the excitement of accomplishment," recalled H. Graham Netting, a scientist at the Carnegie Museum of Natural History active in both the Allegheny Conference and Western Pennsylvania Conservancy. "Great parks and great highways to get to them were not distant goals but immediate concerns."[35]

As with urban renewal, the Allegheny Conference and its allies touted the symbolism of a bucolic countryside resurrected from the ravages of nineteenth century industrialization by enlightened leadership. "The Ohiopyle region was a classic example of the tragedy which comes from areas which depend upon the extractive industries," proclaimed Western Pennsylvania Conservancy leaders in 1967, shortly after the group had conveyed 10,000 acres to the state as part of the new Ohiopyle State Park. "The coal had gone; the forests had been cut; . . . the population was scarcely a third of what it had been a half century ago; many buildings along the waterfront were vacant, doors flapping in the wind." In place of this decay, boosters promised a metropolitan "neighborhood" where children could "watch Slippery Rock Creek roar between snow-capped boulders," while their parents' employer took advantage of "an unlimited supply of professional, skilled and semiskilled workers." "Look around," declared one advertisement sponsored by the Conference. "You'll find parks that were once strip mines," as well as lakes and ski slopes, that are all within an easy drive of the big city amenities of "a rebuilt downtown Pittsburgh with its bustling new nightlife."[36]

In December 1964 advertisements began appearing in national publications for a "deluxe book" showing how Pittsburgh "has grown and how it became what it is today." Edited by filmmaker and photojournalist Stefan Lorant, *Pittsburgh: The Story of an American City* included essays by noted historians on the region's colonial origins and industrial expansion. But Lorant reserved the final chapter, dramatically entitled "Rebirth," for David Lawrence, the mayor who had presided over the city's postwar renewal program. "The town took pleasure in the swing of the headache ball and the crash of the falling brick," Lawrence declared. "Pittsburgh, after all the grim years, was proud and self-confident." The Allegheny Conference used the book as part of its broader public relations campaign aimed at maintaining community support for urban renewal and establishing the city as a national model for a successful public-private partnership. Conference-sponsored broadsides described *Pittsburgh* as "a major work of American history" that traced the city's evolution through its "dramatic rebirth following World War II as the nation's prototype for urban redevelopment." Sales of the first two editions exceeded 100,000 copies as the book captured Pittsburgh's changing identity for the nation and an entire generation of residents. Writer and native Kristin Kovacic recalled that while growing up in the Steel City her neighbors all "had two books in the house, the Bible and *Pittsburgh*."[37]

Pittsburgh and other booster publications touted the Renaissance as the exemplar of what was possible in a capitalist system with enlightened civic and political leadership. However, the region's industries and labor force remained tied to the coal-steel-rail nexus of its late nineteenth-century heyday. This fact helps explain how corporate executives such as Consolidation Coal's George H. Love could support urban renewal in Pittsburgh while opposing strip mine regulation, and U.S. Steel's Benjamin Fairless could pressure the Pennsylvania Railroad to accept smoke control while disavowing responsibility for the Donora Smog. Even as some urban neighborhoods and highway-oriented suburban communities benefited from enormous public expenditures and began to diversify into growing economic sectors, the remainder of the region continued to face chronic unemployment and outmigration. This was particularly true for residents of Steubenville, Wheeling, and older river valley communities who lacked the political organization and connection to state and federal agencies necessary to effectively maintain their own urban redevelopment programs. This material and symbolic disconnect between Pittsburgh and its hinterlands continued to increase, which resulted in a "region of contrasts" by the 1970s that challenged the social and cultural bonds that had united the Steel Valley.[38]

PART II
A Region of Contrasts

ON A LATE November evening in 1973, the crème of Pittsburgh's civic elite streamed into the beautiful surroundings of Oakland's Carnegie Music Hall for the annual meeting of the Allegheny Conference on Community Development. As they walked through the grand foyer with its crystal chandeliers and elaborately carved pillars, the university presidents, industrialists, financiers, labor leaders, and politicians gathered there had reason to be proud of their accomplishments in smoke control and flood abatement as well as the success of urban redevelopment symbolized by the downtown Golden Triangle. That night's speaker, former Appalachian Regional Commission (ARC) executive director Ralph Widner, congratulated the audience on their achievements, but cautioned that the city's Renaissance could not be sustained in isolation from broader regional decline. In his speech, "The Regional City: An Approach to Planning Our Future Growth," Widner warned that the close interdependence between the "metropolis and its hinterland" had broken down. Retaining Pittsburgh's role as a city of national significance required that many parts be put together from individual neighborhoods up to the metropolitan level. "The future of the region," he concluded, "rests as much with what can be initiated in the outlying area as with what can be done downtown."[1]

Like *Afloat on the Ohio* nearly a century earlier, "The Regional City" provided a narrative tour of a region in transition. The shift from rivers to railroads defined the rise of the Steel Valley for Reuben Gold Thwaites, but by the 1970s highways largely served as the transportation arteries binding metropolitan Pittsburgh. Widner began with an overview of the changing structure of American cities that emphasized the postwar evolution of the "industrial city" into "the metropolis," where, thanks to the automobile, "the broad masses of men and women [could] live in one part of the city, work in another, shop in another, and find recreation and entertainment in still another." "These commuting fields," he continued, were "really regional cities, because no matter how isolated a family's home within one of those fields, the benefits and services of urban life are nearby." In this vision of the modern metropolis, highways served as the framework for urban and economic growth on which officials could develop "new communities, service complexes, [and] industrial parks."

The outer limits of the commuting fields that defined metropolitan regions, or "urban areas" as he called them, were "constantly changing" due to economic competition, fluctuating population levels, and evolving patterns of transportation infrastructure, especially new highways. Within this framework, central cities served as "regional capitals," which were political and administrative centers for large surrounding areas. Despite its size, however, Pittsburgh had not realized its full potential, with its postwar influence "restricted primarily to Southwestern Pennsylvania with a piece of downriver West Virginia and Ohio." In part, this had to do with a location midway between New York and Chicago, along with strong competition to the northwest from Cleveland that limited its potential reach. On the other hand, the Steel Valley's over-specialization in economic sectors experiencing slow or no growth meant that the region had comparatively little to attract new residents. "Pittsburgh is the greatest metropolis in Appalachia," Widner cautioned, "but it has not been a target for people leaving rural Appalachia for urban employment. They have gone elsewhere."

Within this overall pattern of decline, however, there were winners and losers among the region's various communities. In the 1950s and 1960s, the Allegheny Conference and its political allies invested enormous resources in building roads that linked the Golden Triangle east to the Pennsylvania Turnpike and west to the new Pittsburgh International Airport, which was also funded as part of the Renaissance. As a result, highway-oriented suburbs, often built on the higher elevation of the Appalachian plateau, were "beginning to look like newer versions of the old city," with clusters of factories, office complexes, and shopping centers scattered around the metropolitan area. Widner also praised Pittsburgh's public-private partnership for its focus on developing the city's universities "into centers of innovation and excellence" as a step toward achieving the "ferment and entrepreneurship that helped preserve Boston from final decline." Highway-oriented growth outside of the city was intimately tied to this effort, with, in the words of one influential study, "a virtually unanimous preference of postwar research centers for suburban locations."[2]

On the other hand, Widner cautioned, the industrialized river valleys continued to decline even as the "new metropolis of the plateau" grew in terms of both jobs and population, which had created a spatially bifurcated "region of contrasts."³ By the mid-1960s, the Steel Valley's older communities were losing many of their traditional retail, service, and administrative functions, and becoming "social welfare agencies" that housed the "poor, ill-educated, unemployed, aged and generally disadvantaged."⁴ In response to these obvious problems, some communities, such as Martins Ferry, Ohio, and Wheeling, mobilized behind ambitious urban revitalization campaigns that attempted to leverage federal funds to recreate the success of the Renaissance. Other municipalities, such as Weirton and Homestead, took a more corporate-driven approach in which the needs of industrial capital remained paramount. Throughout the area, local leaders adopted the Pittsburgh model of clearing older riverfront areas for commercial use and encouraging development of hilltop residential areas. "It seems quite clear," Widner concluded, that the future would ultimately rest on the ability to develop "a new urban region while minimizing the transitional pains of the older areas."

As the former head of the ARC, Widner also underscored the connections between the metropolitan core and the fate of the surrounding countryside. Once essential to industrial production, mine closures during the 1950s cast adrift many rural communities with population levels that could not be sustained by the local economy. This was a common experience throughout the broader Appalachian region in which the Steel Valley was entirely contained. Adopting the dominant model guiding the ARC's highway construction program, he argued that the "integration of once isolated rural areas with nearby metropolitan regions" through highway construction, offered the best opportunity to "improve access to quality urban services and employment." On the other hand, new highways enhanced connections to rural amenities for urban and suburban residents, which increased the overall quality of life for the middle-class and created the potential for a growing tourist economy. "The mountains of Pennsylvania and northern West Virginia," he declared, have vast potential for the region "recreationally, scenically, and residentially." However, "major mistakes in transportation planning" had left ties with outlying areas "quite weak." As a result, many rural areas became more dependent on remaining mining and manufacturing jobs even as formerly distant communities along highways closer to the city were reborn as commuter suburbs.

Widner concluded his remarks by again emphasizing "the close interdependence between a metropolis and its hinterland." Outlying communities declined as "mines mechanized and old industries disappeared," while "very poor and inconvenient highway access" meant that the city's businesses suffered from limited economic opportunities "for a metropolis its size." On the other hand, the future of these peripheral areas depended on choices made in the Golden Triangle, as the relative advantages that allowed Pittsburgh to grow into the world's steel center continued to diminish. "No region of the country," he declared, "faces graver issues in terms of its future development than this one." Yet, "we are as fragmented and fractured as ever, pretending the 20th century has never arrived." Thus, the ultimate test for "The Regional City" would "continue to be—as it has been the last two and a half decades—how well the metropolis can capitalize on its still considerable advantages to overcome its weaknesses."

FIGURE 4. Metropolitan Pittsburgh: a region of contrasts.

CHAPTER 4

Live on the Hills and Work in the City

Fourteen years before Ralph Widner's speech to the Allegheny Conference, a group of Wheeling businessmen and politicians traveled to Pittsburgh with the hope of recreating the success of the Renaissance in their own community. In a November 1959 letter to Edward Magee, the conference's executive director, Wheeling retailer Robert Levenson expressed his "gratitude for the wonderful cooperation and inspiration you provided," and declared that "the trip to Pittsburgh has galvanized our city government into action in support of the urban renewal program." Civic reformers in Wheeling had also pushed through smoke abatement laws, issued calls for new highway construction, and were about to establish their own urban renewal authority. These efforts coalesced into a unified program following the 1953 formation of the Wheeling Area Conference on Community Development, a group that was explicitly patterned on Pittsburgh's public-private partnership. Soon after its founding, the Wheeling Conference commissioned a study by urban planner Francis Dodd McHugh in order to "build scientifically for the future so that the final results will all dovetail and assure us of an orderly arrangement of all civic facilities."[1]

Wheeling was not alone in its postwar attempts to counter the Steel Valley's economic and environmental problems, and McHugh's recommendations could have served as a development roadmap for many of the region's riverfront communities. Embodied in the Wheeling Planning Commission's slogan, "live on the hills and work in the city," the 1957 report envisioned a properly designed and redeveloped downtown that would allow "Wheeling and its environs to become a more attractive and desirable urban community for working and living." His proposal included improving highway access to the central business district, flood protection, razing of older residential areas for industrial use, home construction on the hillsides surrounding the downtown, and the modernization of apartment buildings and existing housing. By the end of the decade, the Wheeling Conference president could confidently declare that the goals they had set out "at the beginning of this venture" were far exceeded in many cases, which resulted in "widespread public approval of our aims. We are now looking forward with hopes for an even greater success in the future."[2]

However, unlike the Allegheny Conference, whose unified and influential leadership worked closely with a powerful city administration, smaller groups such as the Wheeling Conference found themselves maneuvering between various political factions, some of which flatly denied the existence of the region's mounting urban and economic crisis. Nevertheless, while no single community was able to alter the larger pattern of decline, local urban and economic development projects had varying and sometimes notable successes. Across the river in Martins Ferry, Ohio, Mayor John Laslo forged a powerful partnership with state and federal officials, enabling the community to build a new riverfront highway and attract millions in federal investment through the War on Poverty and Model Cities programs. Much of downtown Weirton, in contrast, was demolished in the early 1970s to make way for an advanced "Mill of the Future," with displaced residents finding new homes in the city's suburban-like residential areas. Whether driven by public or private investment, these three trends—the desire to stimulate investment in the aging downtowns, the focus on expanding highway connections, and the shift of housing from the crowded river valleys to the surrounding highlands—serve as the common starting point for understanding postwar urban change in the region.

Remaking the Urban Landscape

The complex social, environmental and political landscapes of the Steel Valley shaped development in ways that made it particularly difficult for individual communities to respond to the burgeoning urban and economic crisis of the postwar period. Unlike many of the nation's metropolitan areas, the Steel Valley as a whole began to lose population during the late 1950s due to stagnating employment in the steel mills and coal mines. This trend was particularly pronounced to the west along the Ohio River (Upper

Ohio Valley), where the combined Wheeling-Steubenville district was one of only six metropolitan areas in the United States that lost population between 1940 and 1970. Declining employment in the region resulted partly from broader issues of automation and the industrial migration away from the Northeast and Midwest, but metropolitan Pittsburgh's rough terrain, population characteristics, and economic structure made it especially unattractive for the nation's fastest growing industries.[3]

Within this framework of overall decline, changing patterns of production and consumption hastened the deterioration of some neighborhoods and communities within the Steel Valley, while privileging others. Since the late nineteenth century, a traditional pattern of urban development had emerged in communities up and down the region's rivers and their tributaries, with manufacturing occupying the space closest to the water. Downtown shopping areas came next with residential areas spreading to the surrounding hilltops. Each successive wave of transportation innovation allowed for the development of new areas away from the increasingly crowded and polluted rivers. Because of the rugged terrain, developers and municipal officials focused their attention during the 1950s on conquering the landscape through the building of new bridges, the construction of highways, the digging of tunnels, and the grading of hillsides to make undeveloped areas more accessible. In a report to Wheeling city council calling for the creation of a new residential area on the city's north side, for example, city engineer Walter Nickerson, Jr., noted that the "topography of the City of Wheeling restricts any further extensive development unless hilltop areas in and adjacent to the city can be developed. Before this could be done, however, these areas must be made accessible by providing adequate roadways."[4]

The decline of the railroads in favor of the automobile meant that highway construction proved to be a key determinant of the success of individual communities in the Steel Valley as well as a limiting factor in the economic success of the region as a whole. The construction of east-west Interstate 70 and north-south Interstate 79 provided basic connections between metropolitan Pittsburgh and national markets, but a few highways could not replicate the dense web of trolleys and interurban lines that had knit the region together. Further, the exorbitant cost of building new roads through both the rugged terrain and the densely packed river valleys required a high degree of cooperation among business and political leaders in order to muster the necessary political capital to get projects off the drawing board. The Allegheny Conference's strong leadership in highway planning ended at the Pennsylvania state line, while ethnic fragmentation, the proliferation of small political units, and the continued reliance on private companies for municipal services meant that local politicians lacked experience in coordinating among neighboring villages let alone across the state boundary of the Ohio River. As a result, only after the passage of the Federal Aid Highway Act of 1962 did local political leaders grudgingly implement even a rudimentary system for cooperative planning.[5]

The specifics varied from community to community across the Steel Valley, but during the 1950s political officials and business leaders turned their attention to improving conditions in the business and residential areas of smaller cities. Pent up demand for housing stock, along with new federal subsidies for mortgages, for example, provided new incentives to develop the steep hillsides scattered throughout the region. In Wheeling, developer Jack Waterhouse won an award for site design from the National Association of Homebuilders for building new homes and the community's first strip mall, the Elm Terrace Plaza, on the city's east end, despite a slope that sometimes exceeded 30 percent. Meanwhile, interstate highway construction through the central business district caused the first major alteration to the city's nineteenth-century urban infrastructure. While only 14.5 miles long, the stretch of Interstate 70 through the West Virginia Panhandle took more than a decade to complete and required a new bridge across the Ohio River, a tunnel through Wheeling Hill, and a complicated series of interchanges to accommodate the city's rugged topography. The development of Elm Terrace and other residential areas east of Wheeling Hill were generally enhanced by the highway's construction, but the effects on other parts of the city were mixed. "By today's standards, it was a brutal eviction," recalled Frank Joanou, whose family home was in the path of the highway. "There was no effort to help you relocate, there were no moving expenses, or anything like that. You just had to get out and on your way, you know, or fight it in the courts."[6]

For civic boosters interested in improving the urbanized river valleys, new highway access to their communities was often high on their list of priorities. However, they also understood that new firms and jobs "would not automatically distribute themselves in proportion to the present distribution of facilities and employment"; rather the trend was "toward locations away from existing industrial centers." "In order to be industrially well-balanced," explained the Allegheny Conference's F. D. Hollinshead in

1946, the region's basic industries needed to be supplemented with "the production of consumer goods." Developers wanted "a modern, attractive building all on one floor" located on a "flat parcel of land of at least ten acres on 'a main highway' with plenty of light and clean surroundings." The region's rugged topography and the dense development of the narrow flats along the rivers meant that very few sites fitting this description remained. Just as in Pittsburgh, the region's smaller communities also had to deal with the problems of smoky air, flood-prone and polluted rivers, and deteriorating building stock that made their downtowns unappealing places to live or work.[7]

The Pittsburgh Renaissance provided a model for uniting business and political interests behind the goal of remaking the Steel Valley's urban landscapes. By 1957, McKeesport, the region's second largest city, had also established a planning commission, created a comprehensive plan, boasted an active redevelopment authority, and provided leadership in the Allegheny Conference-inspired Mon-Yough Conference on Community Planning. However, a vacuum of civic and political leadership typical of the Steel Valley's smaller communities complicated the type of public-private partnerships that made the full-scale transformation of the Pittsburgh Renaissance possible. Steubenville especially had a reputation for fractured and graft-ridden local politics, while urban planning itself had a very limited history. "A serious impediment to progress" in the city, reported one state development official, derived from the strong ties European immigrants and their children retained to their native region. This "melting pot that didn't melt," as he put it, "perpetrated factionalism that approaches total chaos."[8]

A key example of this factionalism can be seen in the relationship between Steubenville's powerful Catholic bishop John King Mussio and Protestant community leaders. In 1946, a group of local pastors launched a high-profile campaign to "keep the city clean of all forms of vice," especially gambling. When they approached Mussio, however, he responded with an editorial letter in the Steubenville *Herald-Star*, which was directed to be read in area churches, decrying "any attempt by anyone to legislate false morals for our people." Francis Brown, a Catholic priest who served at the time as acting chancellor of the diocese, later recalled "I find it amazing not only that I did not have a personal acquaintance with a single one of those 12 ministers but also that my personal perception of those men was that they were the enemy." These types of community tensions continued throughout the postwar period on issues from school board elections to public housing to a lack of cooperation between the Catholic and public hospitals. As a result, even when various civic leaders attempted urban revitalization projects in the city, they did so without the ability to unite their constituencies behind a single revitalization program. "Mussio didn't speak much, but when he spoke people listened," recalled Nicholas Kaschak, an urban planner in Steubenville. Diocesan projects such as the new hospital, school, and civic arena had an important impact, "but they were not done in concert with the locals, the civic officials."[9]

Urban redevelopment in Wheeling, on the other hand, had a more promising start with the creation of the Wheeling Conference, an organization that was dedicated to "breaking the logjam which in the past has held up many worthwhile and needed projects." As with the Allegheny Conference, the Wheeling group had a primary membership of local business executives, a project-oriented committee structure, an emphasis on comprehensive planning, and a series of spinoff organizations with interlocking leaderships. Also like its larger neighbor, the Wheeling Conference made smoke abatement the "number one project" it tackled. Successful lobbying for a municipal ordinance resulted in the installation of more than $400,000 in pollution control equipment by the end of 1956. James Martin, the city's director of air pollution control, signed the first arrest warrant under the new ordinance against the local superintendent of the Baltimore & Ohio Railroad after observing cinders from a locomotive firebox, causing "more pollution than any citizen of Wheeling should be subjected to." Along with smoke control, Conference members developed an ambitious package of proposals for slum clearance, downtown parking, infrastructure development and city beautification. Three years after its founding, chairman and local retail magnate Wilbur S. Jones could point with pride to tangible successes such as the construction of the new 900-car Wharf Parking Garage along Wheeling's waterfront as well as the secondary roles filled by conference committees, which "studied exhaustively" the building, zoning, highway, and housing problems, and "prepared legislation for consideration by the proper public bodies."[10]

The Wheeling Conference never achieved the level of quasi-governmental power granted by local and state authorities to the Allegheny Conference in the Golden Triangle, nor did the West Virginia legislature provide the type of financial support invested by Pennsylvania in the development of Point State Park. Nevertheless, conference supporters in the

West Virginia legislature spearheaded a drive for legislation granting cities the power to establish urban renewal authorities. Within the city, the public-private partnership of the new Urban Renewal Authority of Wheeling mirrored that of Pittsburgh's Urban Redevelopment Authority, with retail magnate Robert Levenson serving as chair of both the authority and the Wheeling Conference's Community Improvement Committee. Levenson was joined on the authority by city councilman Albert Howe, as well as fellow Wheeling Conference member and newspaper editor Harry Hamm. This pattern also appeared in other new oversight groups such as the Wharf Parking Garage Board (an outgrowth of the Conference's Parking and Traffic Committee) and the Wheeling Planning Commission, whose chairman publicly stated his "willingness to cooperate fully with the Conference in city improvement projects." The reactivation of the Wheeling Planning Commission itself was a condition of the Conference underwriting of a master plan for the city, which it unveiled in early 1957.[11]

In accordance with the booster vision for "expanded residential neighborhoods in the hilltop areas" and "light industrial development" along the Ohio River, the Urban Renewal Authority submitted a plan to the Federal Housing and Home Finance Agency to redevelop a portion of Center Wheeling, an area known for its ethnic neighborhoods, brothels, and organized crime. Nearly half the families in the area were African American in a county that was 97 percent white. The authority reported "that the land is ideally suited for industrial development" and a survey of the area found numerous examples of "blight" including many structures "lacking proper sanitary facilities" as well as high rates of tuberculosis, infant mortality, juvenile delinquency, and arrests. "If the project is carried out," Levenson declared, "Wheeling will be in a position for the first time to attract satellite industries within its city limits." In September 1958, the federal government authorized a little over a million dollars for the project and the city council scheduled a November referendum on a special three-year levy to pay the local share of the project.[12]

Faced with a similar referendum a decade earlier, Pittsburgh residents voted 2-1 in support of $34,000,000 in bonds for highway and other projects related to the Pittsburgh Renaissance. The Wheeling Conference was able to overcome some of the ethnic and religious tensions that hampered coordinated development efforts in other communities, with Wheeling College president, Father William F. Troy, selected to head the group in the early 1960s, for example. However, the city's political and business

FIGURE 5. View of the recently built Wharf Parking Garage in Wheeling, May 1959. Downtown Wheeling is visible to the left and Center Wheeling is near the middle. The photograph was taken during the filming of *Wheels to Progress*, a promotional video sponsored by the Wheeling Conference. Photograph by Ellis Dungan. Courtesy of Christopher Bowie and the Ohio County Public Library.

leadership never formed the same deep partnership as developed between Mayor David Lawrence and R. K. Mellon. Consequently, Wheeling politicians were unable or unwilling to deliver the popular support necessary to fully fund urban renewal in the city; thus ballot initiatives on the Center Wheeling redevelopment project failed to garner the required 60 percent to pass in November 1958 and again in March 1959. While the reasons for this failure are not entirely clear, Conference leaders blamed "public lethargy [and] the attitude of the community itself," and declared "our big task is creating public understanding of the necessity for things which must be done."[13]

Faced with insufficient votes for a property tax increase, a new conference affiliate, the Downtown Wheeling Associates, approached the city council with a proposal to increase the gross sales tax in order to meet the local obligations for urban renewal. The formation of the association by a group of downtown merchants, including Robert Levenson of the Wheeling Conference and Urban Renewal Authority, suggested the important role of downtown retailers in guiding conference activities, and its support allowed for the authority to finally begin work in Center Wheeling. By the end of 1963, land in the project area, scaled down to 9.6 acres, was almost fully acquired and 50 percent demolished. At the same time, redevelopment officials began work on a second nearby project to acquire land for the expansion of Ohio Valley General Hospital. The hospital was "one of the oldest institutions in this community," explained Frank Joanou, who served as the authority's executive director in the late 1960s. "Without urban renewal I doubt if we would have in Center Wheeling the medical complex that is now there."[14]

As the 1960s began, there was reason to be optimistic about the ability of the Steel Valley's smaller cities to replicate the successes of the Pittsburgh Renaissance. Civic leaders encouraged the development of new residential areas away from the older neighborhoods in the river valleys, which improved the "possibility of attracting small industry by releasing our bottom lands from use for housing." Social tensions, manifesting as both widespread public apathy and political rancor, continually threatened to derail urban renewal programs, but Wheeling Conference members remained optimistic at their ability to translate the Allegheny Conference's public-private model into a workable program for their city. In language clearly paralleling that of the "Pittsburgh Story," *Wheeling News-Register* editor and Wheeling Conference member Harry Hamm declared that when the smoke control ordinance was enacted, "a new day dawned in this city." "It has been a gradual, steady face-lifting which does not excite big headlines and dramatic hoopla such as marked the rebirth of downtown sectors in some other cities," he continued, "yet there is hardly a block in what is known as the business district that has escaped the handiwork of the architect and the builder." Today, Hamm concluded, "merchants and businessmen are pooling their resources in a unanimous effort to maintain Downtown Wheeling's front running position in the upper Ohio Valley."[15]

"The Pride of the Valley"

Even as the Urban Renewal Authority finally began to make headway on its Center Wheeling Project, a devastating 1962 profile of the region in *Life* magazine helped galvanize community support for an expansive revitalization program just across the river in Martins Ferry, Ohio. "Each autumn on a 35-mile stretch of the Ohio River from Steubenville and Weirton to Bellaire and Wheeling," the article's authors reported, "44 teams of youngsters" mobilized to "rattle and crack each other." In between florid descriptions of the rough-and-tumble style of football played in the region, the essay's authors depicted local mill towns in apocryphal terms—simply "depressing . . . where men missing fingers or arms or legs wander the streets." Communities seemed on the verge of social disintegration, rife with "gambling, one of the Valley's most controversial if *sub rosa* industries" and barely restrained violence. Within a decade the Pittsburgh Pirates would host the 1971 World Series in a brand new, $55 million ballpark, but the article's stark images revealed Martins Ferry's "locker room [as] a shed under the stadium [with] wire clothesbaskets taken from an abandoned coal mine." Under such circumstances, sports served as an escape of sorts both for athletes on college scholarships and "their poor but enormously proud parents," who filled the "smoky, riverfront stadiums."[16]

When the *Life* article appeared, Martins Ferry seemed an unlikely candidate for urban renewal, with a city government that was in such tight fiscal constraints that local merchants would not extend credit to municipal employees. Donald Myers, who later became the city's development director, recalled that "the children started to move away and the workforce started to get older. Older people do not have children [and] deaths started to exceed births. It just took your breath away." Nevertheless, under the leadership of Mayor John Laslo, the city of less than 13,000 managed to attract millions of dollars in federal and state development funds. Just as in Wheeling and Steubenville, Laslo envisioned using the funds to create better housing often through hillside development and clearing blighted areas along the riverfront in order to promote new industrial development. By 1970 Martins Ferry had earned a reputation as the "Pride of the Valley," with an active program of urban and economic renewal and an energetic municipal leadership at the forefront of the national War on Poverty.

Martins Ferry exhibited a set of issues related to the social and physical landscapes typical of the Steel Valley's mill towns. The city was crowded into a 3-mile ribbon, seldom wider than half a mile, between the Ohio River and a steep escarpment on the west. The community's close proximity to Wheeling meant that it never really developed much of a downtown, while "the narrow river valley tended to discourage other than coal resource using industries here." The decline of many of the city's smaller businesses meant that by the early 1960s a single employer, Wheeling-Pittsburgh Steel, accounted for 34 percent of the city's workforce as younger and better-educated residents increasingly left the area entirely.[17]

Life's depiction of the western portion of the Steel Valley stands in contrast to a more celebratory article published at about the same time in *Reader's Digest.* "The Ohio River," declared roving editor David Reed, "is emerging as one of the world's great centers of heavy industry." Giant power stations, aluminum mills and chemical plants "have risen in a region that until recently had scarcely changed since grandfather's day."[18] As Don Myers, who later took over as city development director, explained, "in the 60s if you had employment, if you were fortunate enough to work in a mine or a mill or a glass factory, that was the higher grade of employment, and you could take care of your family." It was "very difficult to get ahead, but as long as no accidents occurred, as long as dad never got killed in a mining accident or a mill accident, you survived and you ate and you were clothed and you went to school." These confused messages, of social problems occurring even as some economic sectors achieved modest growth, made it difficult to craft a workable plan to confront the city's problems.[19]

As in other communities, Martins Ferry officials attempted to encourage the development of new hilltop residential areas, in part to free up the flat land along the river for industrial development. However, the steep bluff on the western bank of the Ohio made this process even more difficult and expensive than for its larger neighbor, Wheeling. As a result, "when you made it in Martins Ferry, you moved to St. Clairsville," the seat of county government ten miles west of the city along Interstate 70, "where it was a paradise on the hilltop" according to the slogan of a local realtor. In addition to sapping the city of its tax base, this process also left poor and often elderly residents stuck in the dilapidated housing along the river. The community also suffered from insufficient highway connections, a factor complicated by the expense of building new roads over the hills or through the densely packed river valley. Finally, numerous observers identified "community attitude" as one of the major causes of Martins Ferry problems. Ethnic and religious divides made it difficult to craft consensus around particular public policies, while a fragmented administrative structure made cooperation among the area's dozens of small communities virtually impossible.[20]

The city's turnaround began in 1960, with the mayoral election of John Laslo, a Democrat running in a traditionally Republican area. Typical for mill towns, Laslo was closely connected to the steel industry, retiring in 1976 as safety superintendent after 43 years at Wheeling-Pittsburgh Steel. He was also an energetic, well-connected, and respected political dynamo with an ambitious agenda for social change that began long before his election to office.

Laslo brought to the mayor's office a three-part platform of obtaining new housing for the elderly, improving the city's highway access, and creating jobs by clearing space for a new riverfront industrial park. Though a staunch Democrat, Laslo gave his support to Republican governor James Rhodes, which helped to secure the cooperation of an otherwise hostile state administration. This connection proved particularly valuable in implementing the mayor's vision for urban renewal, which was prefaced upon the upgrading and relocation of Ohio Route 7 away from the riverfront in order to provide a highway connection between Martins Ferry and the new Interstate 70 a few miles to the south. The proposed highway project received key support from executives at Wheeling-Pittsburgh Steel, who needed room to expand their riverfront operations and a route upgrade to better move the company's products to national markets.[21]

In addition to serving the needs of Wheeling-Pittsburgh Steel, Laslo saw in highway construction the opportunity through eminent domain to remove dilapidated buildings along the highway's new route and replace them with a planned industrial district. "Route 7 was a four lane highway with intersections and it basically took where the early settlers lived in Martins Ferry," explained Myers. "Through urban renewal and the highway siting it moved everything north and west of the river." During his successful 1962 campaign, Rhodes had pledged to open up the Upper Ohio Valley to industry and announced approval of the highway plan a month after taking office " In response, William Steele, Wheeling-Pittsburgh's president, declared that the project was "a splendid example of cooperation of state government with private enterprise that will "give us the green light" for additional expansion.[22]

In addition to connections with Rhodes on the state level, Laslo also maintained strong ties with eastern Ohio's powerful Democratic congressman, Wayne L. Hays, chairman of the House Administration Committee. As campaign manager for Hays, Laslo delivered votes in the river communities. In return, Hays used his considerable political influence to deliver millions in federal funds to the community. At first, much of this funding came in the form of housing for poor and often elderly residents, a key issue as highway relocation and urban renewal eventually required the removal of up to 20 percent of the city's population many of whom lived in substandard, flood prone housing. "At that time it seemed like something special," explained Myers. "You get 50 and 100 and 500 units of public housing [and] relocate these people [that] had been downtrodden their whole life [and] you could put them in something that was so fresh and clean and bright and affordable." Myers recalled one resident, "a lovely black lady . . . that lived with no flooring and just a coal hod for winter heating." "I would visit that lady [in her new home in St. Myers Terrace] for the next ten years of my life just to make sure she was fine. I never remember walking into her house when she did not have newspapers laid throughout the white kitchen floor. It was just immaculate."[23]

From the outset, Laslo and his supporters viewed the relocation of Route 7 and construction of subsidized housing as necessary steps toward addressing their larger goal of economic development. As with urban renewal in Wheeling, the mayor pushed to transform dilapidated mixed use area along the riverfront into an industrial park in order to attract new employers to the city. However, crafting a local consensus capable of funding an economic development program in an area with a long history of social and political division proved just as difficult in Martins Ferry as in its neighbor across the Ohio. Laslo's popularity allowed for the election of other Democrats to city council, who were "pretty much willing to rubberstamp any of the programs that the mayor wanted." While there was not any public opposition to the programs that the mayor was suggesting, according to Charles Steele, who was hired as the city's first urban renewal director in 1964, the Chamber of Commerce "worried that government was taking too much of a role in the economy." Nevertheless, "the Chamber of Commerce and the businesses couldn't offer any alternatives either." This lukewarm local support for government-sponsored economic development meant that even as Laslo easily won reelection in 1961, voters rejected a half-mill levy introduced by the mayor to fund a development director tasked with "aiding the expansion of existing industry, the attraction of satellite industry and the creation of local venture industry."[24]

In this context, the publication of *Life*'s searing critique of the city in late 1962 added further impetus for altering the city's social and physical landscapes. "I think John Laslo had just been elected mayor," Steele explained. "I recall they actually did have bonfires in town for the *Life* magazine articles," but this outrage "helped to launch the mayor's programs even more." In the absence of strong support for local funding, Laslo increasingly relied on his political connections to attract federal money through the Johnson administration's Great Society programs. In addition to Congressman Hays, Laslo also had a key ally in Ohio University president Vernon Alden who was asked by Johnson to help develop the Job Corps program in early 1964. Beginning with an initial planning grant, by 1968 the community of fewer than 12,000 residents had received more than $11 million in federal aid for work on its riverfront industrial park, two apartment buildings, a day care center, a municipal park, and a senior center. Eventually, the influx of federal funding allowed the city administration to expand services to residents and employ a staff of more than one hundred.[25]

Federal involvement in Martins Ferry entered a new phase in 1969 when the Department of Housing and Urban Development included the community in its Model Cities program, which emphasized a "total attack" on the social, economic, and physical problems of impoverished communities. The city was the smallest in Ohio to qualify under the program, joining much larger communities such as Cleveland, Youngstown, and Dayton, and was one of the few in the nation to encompass the entire municipality rather than a specific troubled neighborhood. The Laslo administration used the Model Cities program to fund a wide variety of initiatives from the construction of a youth center, housing for the poor and elderly, and land clearance for industrial projects, to job training for young people, employment and recreation programs, and subsidized aides for local schools. City officials were particularly concerned with the community's growing elderly population, which by 1970 headed 24 percent of local households. In addition to housing in the new federally subsidized apartment buildings, city administrators also developed nationally recognized elderly employment and recreation programs, which were especially important in a region where elderly residents routinely refused government charity. "Government was a way out," recalled Myers. Municipal officials "started step by step. They crawled, they walked and then they took off running in the 70s. The front page story was Martins Ferry, Martins Ferry, all of these programs taking place."[26]

Urban renewal in Martins Ferry was based on the same set of environmental assumptions shared by the Wheeling Conference, the Allegheny

Conference, and planners throughout the Steel Valley. In contrast to the mixed-use neighborhoods that had emerged in the nineteenth century, in this framework the most desirable flat lands along the rivers were best suited for industrial or commercial uses and needed to be cleared and spatially separated from residential areas. The vision of remaking the city's social and physical landscape in order to attract new industries carried into Model Cities, where "the majority priority [was] assigned to Economic Development." Municipal officials divided the city into four sectors, beginning with the industrially zoned "Terrace I" along the river, followed by the residential and commercial "Terrace II" on the western side of Route 7, and moving up the difficult to develop "River Bluff" with slopes of at least 35 percent and to the flatter "Plateau" more than five hundred feet above the river. Because there was not "a firm consensus" about whether the community had the resources to develop the plateau, officials concentrated their efforts on providing social services and new infrastructure in the older areas of the valley.[27]

While Martins Ferry continued to attract millions of dollars in state and federal aid for another decade, by the early 1970s a flaw in the city's overall program became increasingly apparent. The Laslo administration recognized that the city's long-term viability depended on attracting new employers, and job creation informed nearly every aspect of its program from highway construction to elderly services. "The initial thrust of economic development must be providing land so that industries can be attracted to the city," administrators declared. "When these efforts are under way . . . then increased attention can be given to raising skill levels through job training and other techniques." In effect, the social programs of the Great Society and Model Cities in particular were seen as "stop gap measures," according to Steele. Because of Laslo's overarching focus on housing, industrial development, and highway construction, "all the rest of this was just other opportunities to bring money into Martins Ferry." As new space began to open along Route 7 in the late 1960s, city officials worked diligently to attract new employers. "I remember one day there was an indication that a company out of Michigan wanted to put what is called a carbon black plant down on the Ohio River somewhere," Steele recalled. Laslo "grabbed a couple of people and jumped in the car and he drove to Detroit. And he just walked in to see them and made them an offer."[28]

Part of the continued effort to attract new employers to riverfront sites also involved developing partnerships on the regional level to improve highway and other infrastructure. Following the failed 1961 campaign to raise local funds in Martins Ferry for an industrial development director, the *Wheeling Intelligencer* editorialized that "success can only be gained by the cooperative efforts of the all communities on both sides of the Ohio River." "The mayors of the largest cities," the editorial concluded, "should meet now to lay the ground-work for a united effort to bring industry to the valley." Laslo was never able to overcome barriers to cooperation across state lines, but he did have some success in uniting the communities on the Ohio side of the river behind his vision for planned industrial development. As land was cleared in Martins Ferry, Laslo mobilized his allies in Steubenville and other valley communities to push for better regional highway access. With work on north-south Route 7 underway in 1964, he began a decade-long campaign seeking to upgrade east-west highway access to the region north of Interstate 70 through the Short Creek Valley midway between his community and Steubenville. Despite repeated appeals to Rhodes and support from Hays, however, the highway project never materialized, leaving Martins Ferry and much of the western portion of the Steel Valley relatively isolated from the metropolitan core in southwestern Pennsylvania and thus at a greater disadvantage in trying to attract new investment.[29]

Though requiring tremendous effort and leadership by local officials, Martins Ferry was not alone among the Steel Valley's smaller industrial communities in putting together a political coalition that attracted highway funds and successfully cleared aging, mixed-use neighborhoods only to face difficulties in attracting new manufacturing employers. In Monessen, along the Monongahela River, an energetic mayor, Hugo Parentes, spearheaded a major attempt to restructure the city's economy and revitalize the cramped and aging downtown. Monessen's Eastgate project, completed during the mid-1960s, resulted in the clearing of "blighted" areas and the construction of a combined community and health center. The Westgate project, begun in the mid-1960s, was to be the most extensive urban renewal program ever planned for the Monongahela Valley, but it bogged down in the early 1970s and never fulfilled the mayor's vision. In a pattern common throughout the region, both cities eventually sold parts of their sites to various smaller, lower wage firms often associated with wholesale and retail distribution. Other portions remained vacant lots through the 1980s or were used by public agencies. Unless Laslo and his contemporaries could find an investor who was willing to develop the site, there was little they could do to spur economic growth. "Martins Ferry with all its success and all of its efforts, it's not an island," Steele concluded. "It had to rely on things happening from outside, and those things didn't happen."[30]

"Reading, 'Riting, and Route 2 to Weirton"

If economic and urban revitalization hinged on the spatial rearrangement of clearing riverfront land for industrial use and moving residential areas to the hilltops, then Weirton came the closest of any community in the Upper Ohio Valley. Unlike many other mill towns in the region, the postwar period was a boom time for the former company town. Weirton Steel boasted the state's largest workforce, a fact that led local residents to proclaim the 3Rs in West Virginia as "reading, 'riting, and Route 2 to Weirton." In order to make way for a new "Mill of the Future," the company demolished an increasing portion of the original downtown in the 1960s, which further established its physical dominance of the valley. This process added impetus to the construction of new suburban-style residential districts leading up the surrounding hillsides, which were included within the city limits at its incorporation. In November 1967, executives, workers, and residents alike celebrated the first 300-ton heat of top-grade steel produced in the new mill's advanced basic oxygen furnaces. Soon afterward, local developer Ralph Barone announced the creation of an enormous new shopping center and residential area on Weirton Heights. "We intend to make available homes to all persons working in the Weirton mills who would like to locate in our community," Barone declared. "The future of Weirton is still vastly unlimited."[31]

Though generally not emerging from such a clear projection of paternalism, corporate-led industrial expansion was common throughout the Steel Valley. Much of Homestead's original downtown, for example, was demolished in the mid-1940s to make room for an expansion of U.S. Steel's Homestead Works. However, the extremely close material and symbolic relationship between the company and the community in Weirton formed what sociologist Sharon Zukin described as the "archetypal industrial landscape." For conservative commentators, the town founded by Ernest Weir to house workers at his steel and tin mills was "Freedom Town U.S.A.," with citizens who "live and breathe Americanism as only the descendants of 39 nationalities know how." For others, especially those sympathetic to organized labor, Weirton was a "scab town" that consistently, forcefully, and at times violently rejected any attempts at unionization while earning a reputation for continuing normal production during nationwide strikes from the 1920s to the 1970s. This corporate domination coupled with the framework of business paternalism established by Weir himself made for a powerful combination that drove urban development during the postwar period.[32]

Weirton was formed in 1947 as a merger of three smaller communities with the unincorporated area around the mills of Weirton Steel. Building from E. T. Weir's vision of a symbiotic relationship between community and mill, municipal services had long been provided by the corporation through its Weirton Improvement Company subsidiary. The desire of residents to continue this relationship was made clear by the overwhelming election of Weirton Steel President Thomas Millsop as the city's first mayor. The company maintained its control during the postwar years by filling or controlling municipal positions, through its influence as the state's largest taxpayer, and by providing employees with the highest wages in the industry as well as excellent health and pension benefits. Millsop, for example, appointed Daniel Sweaney, a Weirton Steel department head with no experience in urban administration, as city manager. While Weirton resembled other company towns in many ways, from the beginning Weir emphasized private property and encouraged home ownership among his employees, leading to the expansion of residential areas surrounding the mill. "Because of the basic metals industry, folks were able to buy the home of their choice [and] took the vacation of their wish," explained Gary DuFour, who became Weirton city manager in the 1990s. "They were able to be very strong consumers. The company paid their holiday pay, their vacation pay, people actually went out and bought new cars."[33]

Of course, despite the clear benefits provided by the company, the city was not an island and disciplining the workforce also involved more direct actions. Weirton Steel had a long history of repressing worker activism, often through its control of the local police force. In one infamous example from 1919, local police officers under instructions from the company rounded up suspected unionists, forced them to kneel in the middle of the street, and then made them kiss the American flag before being expelled from the town. The possibility of any independent labor organization was further eliminated in October 1950, when after more than a decade of legal wrangling workers overwhelmingly voted for the local company-backed Independent Steelworkers Union rather than the national United Steelworkers. Weir's strategy of constructing a community in harmony with the company led to diminished ethnic, social, and political tensions particularly compared to the region's other cities. Beginning in 1934, Weirton Steel employees staged their first annual "Festival of Nations" program as part of the community's Labor Day celebration. Filled with conscious symbolism, the festival took place at the newly opened Weir Memorial Park on Marland Heights and featured three hundred participants performing "the dances and songs . . . of their parents." Fifteen thousand people viewed this "brilliant spectacle" that culminated in a grand finale with all national groups appearing on stage as the Weirton Steel Band played the National Anthem.[34]

During the 1950s, industrial expansion at Weirton Steel prompted a population boom in the community. While Wheeling, Steubenville, and Martins Ferry each lost nearly 10 percent of their residents during the decade, Weirton grew by more than 17 percent to over 28,000. Local boosters eagerly embraced this growth, attributing it to the free enterprise system and the labor-management partnership forming "the spirit of community that Weirton seems to have." "In many towns, a quality of leadership is lacking, [and] industry seems to exist apart from the community," Millsop declared. "This has never been true in Weirton; the leaders of Weirton Steel would not allow it to happen." Indeed, in a decade when planners were predicting the city's population to grow to 50,000 residents by 1980, the company provided millions of dollars for urban infrastructure and services, donated a large community center named for Millsop, leased the municipal building for a dollar a year, raised funds for a new hospital, and operated the community pool, country club, and police lodge.[35]

Weirton's residential development faced the same issues of topography as in other Steel Valley communities. The physical expansion of Weirton Steel's facilities as well as those of smaller manufacturing firms took place in a relatively narrow arc of flat land formed by a silted-in river meander. As industrial growth increasingly expanded into the residential areas around the original mill site, new housing development took place west (and upwind) of downtown on Marland Heights and then stretched east on Weirton Heights toward the border with Pennsylvania. Despite E. T. Weir's emphasis on creating a model community, early on few upper level managers lived in Weirton, preferring to commute from their large Victorian mansions along Steubenville's North Fourth Street. Ernest Weir always considered himself a resident of Pittsburgh. Just as more well-to-do residents in Pittsburgh, Steubenville, and Wheeling began moving uphill to more suburban style areas, in the 1920s a similar group moved to Weirton's

Marland Heights near the J. C. Williams Country Club built in 1931. Named for Weir's successor at the helm of Weirton Steel, the club became the city's informal seat of power ("Tons and tons of steel have been bought and sold there" according to one commentator) and the site of the city's first community swimming pool named for Weir's mother. In later years, both Weir and Williams lived in the Lodge, an exclusive residence adjacent to the club as did their successors Thomas Millsop and Charles Tournay.[36]

Among the "early risers" frequenting the country club every Sunday morning was Ralph Barone, who during the 1950s went on to become Weirton's largest real estate developer by expanding residential opportunities on Marland Heights to a larger portion of mill workers. Weirton boosters often trumpeted capitalism's rags-to-riches stories as the basis of their community's success and Barone's background certainly fit this mold. Arriving in Philadelphia from Italy with "only $2 in his pocket," Barone moved to Weirton in 1920 and worked in the mill while taking classes at Steubenville Business College. He started in real estate in 1923 and undertook a wide variety of residential and commercial development projects over the next fifty years, including the construction of more than 3,000 homes of which 1,500 were in Marland Heights. Throughout his life, Barone remained a vocal booster for Weirton and his vision of the American way of the life, proclaiming "we are constantly endeavoring to make available the best of housing and rental facilities so as to bring more and more people to Weirton as permanent residents."[37]

When Weirton was founded in 1947, the new city of 24,000 was only about two-thirds the population of Steubenville and less than half that of Wheeling, but it encompassed a land area extending from the Ohio River to the Pennsylvania border that was larger than either of its older neighbors. This room to grow coupled with a workforce of nearly 12,000 at Weirton Steel alone caused the city's population to swell by more than 17 percent during the 1950s. While this was modest growth compared to that of cities in the American Southwest or commuter suburbs such as Levittown, it stands in sharp contrast to the declines of Steubenville, Wheeling, and Martins Ferry. Indeed, away from the industrial areas and the relatively small downtown, Weirton increasingly looked less like the region's other mill towns and more like a typical postwar suburb with curvilinear streets, cul de sacs, and acres of detached single family homes set in neat yards. Upon announcing a new $32 million, 150-home project on Weirton Heights near a planned interchange for U.S. Route 22, which was being upgraded to

Pittsburgh, Barone proclaimed "our economic situation here is perhaps better than anywhere else in the nation. We are certain Weirton is destined for even more greatness in the future, exceeding the brilliant growth it has demonstrated in the past."[38]

In the fall of 1967, Barone Realty announced plans for an enormous new shopping and retail development near the expanded Route 22 on Weirton Heights. Barone's announcement was clearly timed to coincide with the opening of the first phase of Weirton Steel's new "Mill of the Future" in November 1967. The mill's concept first developed in the late 1950s when National Steel, formed in 1929 through the merger of Weirton Steel with Great Lakes Steel and Cleveland's M. A. Hanna Company, modernized its Detroit operations through construction of a new Basic Oxygen Process (BOP) furnace combined with a computer-controlled 80-inch hot strip mill. This was a period of growth in the nation's steel industry as government defense contracts for the escalating conflict in Vietnam spurred reopening of at least one shuttered plant in the Upper Ohio Valley and profit-fueled expansion throughout the sector. National Steel itself posted record profits in 1963 and 1964, with assets reaching $1 billion and the ability to internally finance its entire capital expansion program. Consequently, the company began to discuss a similar modernization program at its Weirton facilities that combined BOP technology with vacuum degassing and a high-tonnage continuous slab casting machine. "The program is a major undertaking in which we will penetrate some uncharted areas of steel's advancing technology," declared National Steel president (and Thomas Millsop's son-in-law) George Stinson. "But it will also yield broader market coverage and new high standards of quality as well as improved costs and modestly increased capacity."[39]

As new subdivisions expanded across the overlooking hillsides, the construction of the Mill of the Future between 1965 and 1968 thus took place even as the region's other mill towns struggled to attract new employers to their newly cleared industrial parks. In contrast to the Laslo administration's reliance on political connections to reroute Ohio Route 7 through Martins Ferry, when Weirton Steel needed a section of West Virginia Route 2 elevated to avoid a traffic bottleneck, it planned, financed, and completed the project entirely with its own funds. "If the State Road commission worked as rapidly as private enterprise," crowed the *Weirton Daily Times*, "West Virginia would have the greatest highway system in the country." As construction crews poured into the city to work on the enormous mill

FIGURE 6. View of Weirton Steel's "Mill of the Future," c. 1970. West Virginia Route 2 is visible behind the plant, and the water tanks at the center top are in the hilltop community of Weircrest. Photograph from Weirton Steel Archives. Courtesy of the Weirton Area Museum & Cultural Center.

rising from the valley floor, numerous articles and editorials pointed out the facility's new features from the "in-line" location that would ensure "maximum efficiency in the flow of materials" to the new equipment that would "forever end" air pollution problems. "Indeed, history will be made when the Weirton mill is put into operation," *Daily Times* editor Earl V. Wittpenn declared. "It should put the Weirton company into the forefront of competition the nation over. And all of this means that the economic outlook for the community, generally, will be one of excellence."[40]

However, amid all the booster rhetoric surrounding the massive new complex, one can begin to discern concerns about the ability of the mill to sustain growth in the community. Employment growth at Weirton Steel had leveled off in the 1950s and by 1966 nearly half the company's workers

(5,093) were members of the "25 Year Club." Furthermore, while the BOP furnace was slow to supplant the open hearth and Bessemer processes in the United States, by 1970 more than half the world's and 80 percent of Japan's steel output was produced in oxygen converters suggesting the technology being implemented in Weirton was not as revolutionary as it was being portrayed. Finally, the BOP and other technologies being introduced, including vacuum degassing to remove impurities and the computerized continued casting of the hot strip mill, replaced rather than added to existing facilities, and thus promised only "modestly increased capacity." Taken together, all this meant that by the late 1960s the community of Weirton could no longer rely solely on the company for future prosperity. "The new Mill of the Future of the Weirton Steel Division won't necessarily mean expanded employment," the *Weirton Daily Times* declared in 1967. "The times call for forceful leadership."[41]

Weirton's civic leaders responded to the problem of slowing industrial growth in a variety of ways. Those most closely associated with Weirton Steel joined with residents from other mill towns in calling for national legislation limiting steel imports and encouraging the buy-American Steelmark campaign launched in 1960 by the American Iron and Steel Institute. Of course, this response yielded limited returns within the community itself, and so others turned their attention to the same problems of urban deterioration experienced in other Steel Valley communities. Even as the Mill of the Future produced its first heat, Weirton City Council and the Chamber of Commerce began work on a joint program for urban renewal. "I will work hand-in-hand with our city administration, our heads of industry, our builders and developers and our merchants," declared Chamber president Richard Williamson, "to make our city worthy of our Mill of the Future and align our progress alongside that of our No. 1 industry."[42]

Instead of continued population growth, civic leaders now set their sites on the more realistic goal of creating a "city of which we can all be proud: a city with unlimited services, a city with ample cultural and recreational facilities, high educational standards, and a central business area." Even with the reduction of air pollution due to the new mill, however, Weirton struggled to attract businesses not directly related to steel production. In addition, as leaders in other communities found out, attracting the resources and political will to undertake a meaningful urban renewal program proved especially difficult as state and federal resources declined in the wake of the Great Society. New housing starts declined from approximately 300 per year in the 1950s to only about 100 by the end of the 1960s. Within the community, leaders acknowledged the discouragement "at the loss of several business enterprises in the downtown district." At the same time, the Weirton Heights Shopping Plaza "experienced considerable progress and continue[d] to add more buildings" as did Barone Realty, which in 1968 signed letters of intent for tenants at its 237,000 acre shopping center near Route 22. In a New Year's Resolution printed December 31, 1969, Ralph Barone declared his wish "To make more homes available in Weirton for the 50 percent of non-resident Weirton Steel employees." Heading into a decade of turmoil in the steel industry, it remained unclear whether Weirton's strategy of tying the community's fortunes to a single employer would be enough to ensure its future prosperity.[43]

Despite divergent paths in urban redevelopment during the 1960s, all the region's industrialized river valleys ended the 1970s with deteriorating downtowns, continued dependence on a handful of large industrial employers, and increasingly elderly and poor populations. Great Society-era programs offered unprecedented access to federal funds, but the inability of local officials and civic elites to fully utilize these opportunities came on a number of fronts: economic, political, and cultural. Even when they were able to do so, as in Martins Ferry, the regional nature of social and environmental problems demonstrated the difficulties faced by even a strong and determined local government to influence new private sector capital to move into the area. Corporate-led development fared little better, with Weirton sacrificing much of its original downtown only to have employment peak at Weirton Steel even before the opening of the Mill of the Future. Overreliance on continued paternalism for municipal services and tax receipts weakened city administrations and constrained the collective response to subsequent corporate disinvestment. At the same time, continued political marginalization and parochialism limited the development of a highway infrastructure that could compensate for the decline of railroad links. As a result, while the sharp economic decline of metropolitan Pittsburgh during the early 1980s was largely due to the collapse of the steel industry, these failures in public policy exacerbated regional economic problems and stalled subsequent recovery attempts.

Another way of interpreting the Steel Valley's trajectory during the postwar period, however, has to do with the model of economic development promoted by Pittsburgh's public-private partnership and adopted by the region's smaller communities. As with the Pittsburgh Renaissance, urban renewal advocates in Wheeling, Martins Ferry, and Weirton sought to erase the nineteenth century landscape of mixed-use development along their riverfronts in order to provide space for highways and factories. Residential areas were to be spatially separated from industrial districts and built along new roads that would finally open up the higher elevations of the Appalachian Plateau to development. The "Live on the Hills, Work in the City" framework accepted the basic premise that economic and urban revitalization required ever-larger landscapes of production serving as depopulated and polluted counterpoints to the clearer skies, modern infrastructure, and leafy pastoralism of suburban-style housing celebrated by Renaissance boosters. By the mid-1960s, tensions began to emerge in both the center city and the rural hinterland as the promise that the sacrifice of local communities would result in the economic health of the broader metropolitan region never fully materialized.

CHAPTER 5

We're Appalachia, But We Don't Need to Be

"It is the firm intention of the Dept. of Forests and Waters with the assistance of the Western Pennsylvania Conservancy, to create a great full-scale State park here at Ohiopyle—one which will be almost unmatched in natural scenic beauty anywhere in Pennsylvania." This is how Maurice Goddard, secretary of the Pennsylvania Department of Forests and Waters, marked the July 1962 dedication of the thousand-acre Keister tract, named for the Pittsburgh socialite whose family donated the land. The audience that day included more than two hundred members of the Western Pennsylvania Conservancy, the Allegheny Conference affiliate tasked with acquiring rural land for use as public parks. Goddard's speech made official the state's interest in redeveloping the struggling mining community of Ohiopyle into the centerpiece of a "new vacationland" in the rugged Laurel Highlands southeast of Pittsburgh. When the nearly 20,000 acre park opened in 1971, the Conservancy and state officials had partnered in "all the multifarious details" of the project, from helping the community prepare for "its future as a new recreational center" to building facilities that could accommodate more than 1.5 million annual visitors by the end of the decade.[1]

Less than five years after Goddard's dedication of the Keister tract, officials of Pittsburgh-based Consolidation Coal Company (Consol) invited members of the public to celebrate the opening of the Egypt Valley Mine north of Barnesville, Ohio. An estimated 25,000 people toured the colossal mining shovel, the Giant Earth Mover (GEM) of Egypt, among the nation's largest machines at more than twelve stories high. The mine encompassed 96,000 acres, bisected by Interstate 70, with the GEM operations initially focused on the north side of the highway. "It is an area that would seem to be doomed to economic oblivion," explained a brochure from the opening. "But buried beneath the surface of Egypt Valley is the means through which the region can enrich its people today, and provide for continuing jobs and income for generations to come." Even at a rate of 20,000 tons per day," concluded Ralph Hatch, an executive at Consol's Hanna Coal subsidiary, "Egypt Valley will be an active mine for many years."[2]

The case studies of Ohiopyle and Barnesville emerge from a common set of concerns over how the resources of Pittsburgh's hinterland could best be used for the good of the broader metropolitan region. Decision-making for both areas rested, at least in part, in the downtown Golden Triangle, whether by Consol executives or by the corporate leaders providing philanthropic funding for the Western Pennsylvania Conservancy. Consequently, the two sites reflected the tensions in the Pittsburgh Renaissance, which promised clean skies in the city and parks in the countryside even as the need for corporate profitability seemed to require rural "sacrifice zones" in the form of scarred, polluted, and depopulated landscapes. During the 1960s and early 1970s, both communities became battlegrounds in larger state and national fights over the regulation of surface mining as well as the extent to which locals could control the communities in which they lived and worked. Played out on the same metropolitan landscape but with a variety of outcomes, residents, business leaders, and politicians struggled to balance economic and environmental imperatives in the face of overall regional decline. "We're Appalachia, but we don't need to be," explained Milton Ronsheim, a local newspaper editor and community activist. "We have a lot of things that we could get going for us if we had the will to do them."[3]

Planning for the Periphery

As Ralph Widner made clear in "The Regional City," his 1973 speech to the Allegheny Conference, the Steel Valley suffered from both the postwar urban crisis of the industrialized Northeast and the problems of rural Appalachia, of which Pittsburgh was "the greatest metropolis." This Appalachian crisis manifested in three ways—population loss, moribund employment opportunities, and an erosion of environmental quality due in large part to coal surface mining. Until at least the 1920s, agriculture was an important economic activity in flatter parts of the region. From the late nineteenth century, however, mines and other industries gradually supplanted farms as primary profit generators. Postwar competition with western agribusiness made it increasingly difficult for small farmers to remain self-sufficient, while advances in technology dramatically reduced the manpower needs of local mines. Between the late 1940s and the mid-1960s, the area produced a steady stream of migrants, particularly of young workers and families fleeing poverty and unemployment. The dramatic increase of surface mining in many parts of the region compounded these problems, leaving unproductive and unattractive land that affected both environmental quality and the social fabric of rural communities.[4]

Farmers who remained in the region had to increase the size and efficiency of their operations and shift to products more suited to the hilly terrain, such as poultry, dairy, and beef production. From 1954 to 1969 alone, average farm size in the three counties around Barnesville grew from 132 acres to 172 acres despite limited capital available to local farmers and restrictions imposed by the landscape. Sam and Janet Smith grew corn and raised dairy cattle in the hamlet of Egypt Valley. Following a disastrous flood in 1956 that destroyed the family's entire corn crop, Sam took a job with Hanna Coal, the subsidiary that oversaw Consol's surface mines in southeastern Ohio, and Janet began teaching at a local elementary school. "I thought I was going to go broke," Mr. Smith recalled, "so I went to work for the coal company. I [earned enough] to pay for the production of corn and all the machinery costs of the farm."[5]

Coal executives predicted a prosperous future for the region's mines following World War II, but changes in consumption patterns for homes and railroads resulted in the industry's overall decline. In a 1946 speech to company management, Consol vice president James Hyslop explained his belief that "now that the war is over the coal industry can get down to normal operations and become a basis for security and stability for thousands of persons." "We expect," he concluded, "to be working in [the region] at least a half century from now." Despite this optimistic projection, between 1947 and 1961 total annual U.S. consumption of coal declined by 36 percent, with railroads alone accounting for the loss of over a hundred million tons per year. Indeed, the willingness, albeit grudging, of executives at Consol and the Pennsylvania Railroad to accept the smoke control program of the Pittsburgh Renaissance indicates the extent to which this process was already under way by 1950.[6]

The loss of these key markets and the introduction of labor saving technology, especially in surface mining, resulted in a dramatic reduction in employment during the early postwar years exacerbating the existing decline in family farming. In the Steel Valley, mining jobs declined from about 75,000 in 1940 to just 20,000 in 1960. Lower tax revenues stemming from industrial and population loss also resulted in a lack of highways, basic sewer and water systems, and social services, with overall education levels in Appalachian Ohio a full grade level behind the rest of the state. Because of the falloff in both underground mines and family farms, the opportunity to sell mining rights and even an entire property appealed to many farm families struggling to make ends meet, especially if the land owners had already moved away or were old enough to retire from full-time farming. Kenneth Ward, who grew up in Egypt Valley, recalled opposing his father's decision to sell mining rights to the family farm at the prices being offered. "Well, I'd come home on furlough [from the army in 1945]. When I went back, the first thing I said to my mother was don't let [dad] sell that coal. And then the first letter I got back from her, he'd sold it. That's all there is to it."[7]

While some among Pittsburgh's political and economic elite recognized the importance of developing the rural periphery, during the 1950s the Allegheny Conference regional program was largely limited to encouraging civic and political leaders in outlying areas to develop and implement their own plans. However, beginning with the Eisenhower administration, and accelerating through the creation of the Appalachian Regional Commission (ARC) and the War on Poverty, millions of dollars of federal and state money flowed into the rural areas of the Steel Valley. Underlying assumptions about the nature of Appalachian "under development"—coupled with a mandate in the 1965 Appalachian Regional Development Act that public investments made in the region "shall be concentrated in areas where there is a significant potential for future growth"—resulted in a metropolitan-oriented planning framework that privileged urban and affluent areas such as Pittsburgh over poorer and more remote communities. Championed by Ralph Widner, who served as the ARC's first executive director, this "growth center" strategy largely ignored "the pockets of poverty and unemployment scattered in inaccessible hollows all over the area" in favor of building "a network of roads so that the poor and unemployed can get out of their inaccessible hollows and commute to new jobs in or near the cities." Speaking of the Steel Valley in particular, Widner emphasized the "integration of once isolated rural hinterland areas into nearby metropolitan regions as a realistic means to improve access to quality urban services and employment."[8]

Looking outward from the Golden Triangle, Allegheny Conference leaders also saw in the rapidly depopulating periphery an opportunity for creating recreational space to serve the needs of urban and suburban residents and provide some employment for rural communities. "Great parks and great highways to get to them," after all, were the goals of the Allegheny Conference-backed Western Pennsylvania Conservancy, which by 1964 had acquired land for three large state parks along with a handful of smaller nature preserves and historic sites, including the iconic Fallingwater estate just north of Ohiopyle. A report by the Ohio Department of Development went so far as to declare that "new jobs will not be generated by mining, farming or forestry" and recommended "a program for stimulating Recreation, Resort and Retirement development" in the southeastern portion of the state. Indeed, while the rolling landscape around Barnesville had less to attract outsiders than the whitewater and rugged scenery of Ohiopyle, by the mid-1960s Piedmont Lake near Egypt Valley hosted a modest number of vacationers including Ted Voneida, a Cleveland neurologist who later became an active opponent of surface mining. "We looked for a place on the water," Voneida later recalled. "We built a little cottage there with the help of a man named Delbert Starr who [lived] just north of the Interstate."[9]

As in the rest of Appalachia, the scope and type of rural development projects in the Steel Valley depended to a significant extent on the state boundaries dividing the region as well as particular local contexts. Decision-makers in both Harrisburg and Columbus steered funds for the ARC's signature Appalachian Development Highway away from the region, but a succession of sympathetic and relatively activist governors including David Lawrence and William Scranton ensured the Allegheny Conference a voice in crafting policy in the Pennsylvania portions of the region's rural hinterland. Recreation advocates at the Western Pennsylvania Conservancy had the backing of wealthy Pittsburgh foundations and enjoyed a very close relationship with the long-serving secretary of the state Department of Forests and Waters, Maurice Goddard. Goddard's vision of a "park or forest recreation facility within twenty-five miles of most Pennsylvanians" dovetailed perfectly with the mission of the Conservancy to create parks accessible to Pittsburgh residents. Indeed, before joining the ARC Ralph Widner served on the staff of Pennsylvania Senator Joseph Clark and along with Goddard drafted the proposal for Project 70, an enormous bond issue that funded the purchase of Ohiopyle and other state parks.[10]

On the other hand, Republican governor James Rhodes controlled state government in Ohio during the 1960s and 1970s, except for a brief but important interlude under liberal Democrat John Gilligan. Unlike Governor Scranton of Pennsylvania who enthusiastically embraced the ARC, Rhodes originally opposed his state's participation in the program, preferring state investment in highways and other improvements to federal intervention. Operating under the slogan, "profit is not a dirty word in Ohio," the Rhodes administration cut government social programs and relied heavily on limited bond issues to pay for infrastructure development projects. A study of state development programs during the period concluded that the Ohio legislature, in effect, "patted the localities on the back, handed them a set of procedural and financial tools, and wished them the best of luck." Finally, despite its proximity to the newly built Interstate 70, Barnesville's location across state lines from both Wheeling and Pittsburgh, as well as its distance from Ohio's major population centers, meant that the community remained outside the dominant "growth center" model and thus was not a high priority for economic development programs.[11]

Differences in state environmental laws also shaped the development of the far-flung parts of Pittsburgh's rural hinterland, especially before the 1977 Surface Mine Control and Reclamation Act set a uniform federal standard for the region's mines. Throughout the Steel Valley, some residents echoed newspaper editor L. Milton Ronsheim's call for tougher reclamation laws as "the only way to save our fair hills from further destruction." Bills introduced in the Ohio Legislature in 1937, 1939, and 1941 faced the determined resistance of the powerful coal lobby and never made it out of committee. Despite the passage of the state's first surface mine law in 1947, Ronsheim and other activists remained dissatisfied with its relatively weak provisions. Between 1951 and 1956, at least six bills to strengthen reclamation requirements failed, with coal executives furiously insisting that increased regulation would lead to further mine closures. Ronsheim agreed that "coal has supplanted agriculture and is providing employment," but argued that "when the stripping is completed, when the coal is exhausted, then we will have no farmers and no miners. We will have lost our natural resources and the possibility of a self-sufficient economy." On the other hand, rural poverty and out-migration meant that supporters of regulation often had a difficult time convincing legislators to require "hundreds of dollars per acre to level off spoil banks" when unmined land in the same area could be purchased "for 10 to 30 dollars per acre."[12]

Wilderness parks and large surface mines seem to be on opposite sides of the land use spectrum, but they do share some important underlying characteristics. Chief among these is the need to consolidate a large swath of depopulated land under the control of a single property owner. Significantly, while Pennsylvania only passed its first surface mine reclamation legislation in 1945, two years before Ohio's first law, state officials had already explored the possibilities for reclaiming stripped land to provide recreation opportunities within driving distance of Pittsburgh. In 1935, the National Park Service began work on reclaiming a vast surface mine between Pittsburgh and Steubenville as part of a Recreational Demonstration Area that eventually became Raccoon Creek State Park. Following the war, a coalition of conservationist groups led by the Allegheny County Sportsmen's League actively lobbied the state for stricter regulations on existing mines even as they pushed for the funding of new state parks and game preserves. Pittsburgh's sportsmen found an ally in the United Mine Workers, who had difficulty organizing surface mines and were concerned about the lower manpower requirements of surface versus underground mines. By the early 1960s, supporters of reclamation seemed poised to enact a tough new surface mining law on the state level.[13]

Motivated by both a conservationist impulse and the desire to avoid stricter state laws, many surface mine operators began highlighting their voluntary efforts to reclaim stripped land. In 1940 surface mine operators led by Hanna Coal Company created the Ohio Reclamation Association, which by 1947 planted nearly two million trees on spoil banks and launched a publicity campaign to blunt charges of environmental decline.[14] In both Ohio and Pennsylvania, mining companies highlighted potential uses for stripped areas once operations had concluded, particularly the use of stripped land as recreation space. This idea seemed to make sense, at least for those willing to ignore the broader ecological consequences, since the land had often been consolidated into large single-owner tracts and was often unsuitable for farming due to the low threshold for reclamation required by law. Further, the creation of parks from mines fit in with the dominant planning narrative of the 1960s, which saw recreation development as a potential economic generator for the rural periphery. In a town north of Barnesville, Consol provided the land for the county airport, donated funds for a new health center, and built a large park on reclaimed mine land complete with camping sites and three lakes stocked with sport fish. Similarly, the Harmon Creek Coal Company voluntarily reclaimed more than 3,500 acres west of Pittsburgh and donated it to the state for use as a park in 1969—an act of generosity that earned Harmon Creek president James Hillman an honorary lifetime membership in the Western Pennsylvania Conservancy.[15]

Despite the emphasis on highways and the tourism potential of the Steel Valley, the real economic turning point for many rural communities occurred because of a dramatic upturn in the demand for coal by electrical utilities. Beginning in the mid-1960s, the mining boom brought a new level of prosperity to some residents, decreased unemployment to below the national average for over a decade, and even prompted a small population gain in some areas. This was especially the case near Barnesville, where a dramatic drop in mining employment during the 1950s slowed and then reversed during the late 1960s when a number of new deep mines opened within commuting distance. Even as the total number of mines continued to shrink, production levels in the surrounding county grew from six million tons in 1960 to a peak of more than sixteen million tons in 1972. Higher production levels at these larger, more mechanized operations as well as a unionized workforce meant that those miners who remained were also better paid. Coupled with a rise in manufacturing employment along the Ohio River and highway construction that allowed more distant commuting, the growth of coal mining caused unemployment in the Ohio portion of the Steel Valley to fall by half to around 4.5 percent at a time when the national average was 4.9 percent.[16]

While state development officials had earlier articulated a need for economic diversification, during the late 1960s local, state, and federal administrators quickly reoriented their strategies to provide support for the coal mining industry. The "critical need for coal to meet the ever increasing demand for electrical power" quickly exhausted the local supply of workers trained in the new mechanized environment, with more than three quarters of miners working in 1973 hired after 1963. "A coal miner is the kind of worker you don't just grab in off the streets," explained a local manpower coordinator. "He has to be trained" and "we need a lot of men in a hurry." Responding to complaints from the coal industry that the lack of trained workers forced them to increasingly hire "those persons who are inexperienced in the mines" leading to high rates of turnover and absenteeism, the new ARC-financed technical college and vocational school along I-70 west of Wheeling instituted a pilot project to provide "the motivational training and emphasis on job responsibility that will provide a stable employee." Local officials also pushed federal administrators in the new Department of Housing and Urban Development to subsidize housing near mine entrances as a way to support this new economic growth.[17]

As the 1960s began, then, parallel trends emerged that would reveal the tensions in expanding the promise of the Pittsburgh Renaissance, and by extension postwar American affluence in general, to the Steel Valley's periphery. Despite the injection of public money into the region in the form of highway construction and the provision of educational and health services through the ARC and War on Poverty, increased demand for the region's coal to fuel the nation's growing appetite for electricity provided hope for many unemployed residents. Even as Consol and other mining corporations expanded their operations, however, a coalition of conservationists and outdoor enthusiasts, often from urban areas in and outside the region, lobbied for stricter environmental laws that, if enacted, would place limits on an industry just beginning to hire workers. Both mine executives and conservationists consistently sought to portray themselves as having the best interests of residents in mind even as it became clear that earlier, more localist approaches to managing the landscape would no longer suffice in a region struggling to define its postwar identity.

"A Big Woods the Public No Longer Cared to Enter"

At the ribbon cutting for the tract in Ohiopyle bearing her family's name, Pittsburgh socialite Mrs. Albert Fraser Keister bestowed on Charles Lewis, president of the Western Pennsylvania Conservancy, the title park laureate because he was "victorious in every way in bringing the park into being." With the transfer of land to state ownership marking a new chapter in the community's development, Secretary Maurice Goddard concluded his remarks by urging the public to "forget the conservancy. The park now belongs to you." However, not everyone was as sanguine as Goddard in describing Ohiopyle's transition from mining town to privately owned park to public recreation area. On July 3, just days before his speech, Ohiopyle resident Lillian McCahan had written to the secretary complaining about Conservancy officers with "large foundation money [and] their own plans how to spend it." "They have enough for a beautiful small park such as we had envisioned," she declared, but now they are "offering large prices—to make our town . . . deserted, without income or taxes." In other letters, McCahan bristled at park regulations limiting traditional local uses of the landscape and was outraged at the closure of local mines "for the sake of fish." "The Conservancy," she concluded, "imposed such drastic rules the park became just a big woods the public no longer cared to enter."[18]

Given her subsequent disenchantment with the role of urban capital in transforming her community into a recreation destination, it is perhaps surprising that the official history of Ohiopyle State Park lists McCahan as one of the three most important people in its creation along with Mrs. Keister and Pittsburgh retail magnate Edgar Kaufmann. She was described by the Conservancy's M. Graham Netting, director of the Carnegie Museum of Natural History in Pittsburgh, as a "Jenny Wren of a woman," who was "small, pert, hyperactive, extremely voluble, and fully capable of confronting opponents." Her position as a station agent for the Western Maryland Railroad gave her a direct view of the decline of the region's traditional mining and timbering industries. Beginning in the late nineteenth century, Ohiopyle and the nearby highlands of the Laurel Ridge had begun to attract a modest population of summer homes and ski lodges catering to wealthier visitors from southwestern Pennsylvania and Maryland. Kaufmann, who was a key player in the Pittsburgh Renaissance as well as an original board member of the Conservancy, developed a summer camp for employees of his department stores along Bear Run, five miles north of Ohiopyle. During the 1930s, he remade the property into a vacation home: the iconic Fallingwater designed by Frank Lloyd Wright.[19]

Soon after the war McCahan began advocating for a public park on the Ferncliff Peninsula, an ecologically unique tongue of land adjacent to the falls and just across the Youghiogheny from the town. In 1951, increased interest by developers planning to timber the site and open an amusement park prompted Netting to place the issue on the Conservancy's agenda and within weeks the organization obtained a $40,000 grant from the Edgar J. Kaufmann Charitable Trust to buy approximately one hundred acres. Through the end of the decade, the Conservancy slowly improved Ferncliff Park with Kaufmann's active involvement. Despite a lack of funds for maintenance, in 1952 the Conservancy contracted with local resident Bob

Marietta, whose parents ran the old Ohiopyle House hotel, to police the grounds, dispose of trash and collect a nominal quarter fee for visitor parking. Over the next few years, Marietta and Jesse Hall, Kaufmann's caretaker at Fallingwater, oversaw demolition of a decrepit bathhouse and two small cottages along the river, rehabilitation of a third cottage for Marietta and his family, construction of new picnic tables and stone fireplaces, and removal of various hazards.[20]

Ohiopyle's heyday as a nineteenth-century tourist destination had waned with the decline of railroad travel, and in many ways it was typical of other rural communities in the Steel Valley. At the time of Ferncliff's purchase by the Conservancy, five hundred cars still packed the park on its best Sunday, but facilities were primitive, with visitors forced to "bump over a poorly graded road," don swimwear in their cars, tolerate dismal outhouses and creaking picnic tables of "ancient vintage," and risk "tall weeds reputed to be infested with copperheads." Like most riverfronts in the region, access to Ferncliff was also made difficult by grade level railroad tracks, while West Penn Power owned much of the bank on the town side of the river. As a consequence, both McCahan and Conservancy officials grew increasingly frustrated with the "pessimism and lethargy" of a "desperately poor" rural community that was "dying because young people with drive left as soon as they finished high school."[21]

The year 1959 was a turning point in the Conservancy's vision for Ohiopyle, which grew during the next three years from preserving Ferncliff as a natural area, to protecting the Youghiogheny gorges above and below the falls, to providing a recreational park that would be the centerpiece of the larger Laurel Highlands area. According to Netting, Conservancy officials had concluded two years earlier that "the community could not, or would not, do much to help itself, not even to the extent of cleaning up the riverfront on the town side" across from Ferncliff. Shortly afterward, Allegheny Conference executive director Park Martin assigned his planning director, James McClain, to prepare a report on the possibility of enlarging the park beyond its existing boundaries. In the spring of 1958, Conservancy officials met with representatives of West Penn Power to discuss use of the company's land in the area as well as with Maurice Goddard who endorsed a larger planning study to determine the desirability of creating a state park at Ohiopyle. In 1959, events moved rapidly from planning to implementation as an inspection visit by the Allegheny Conference's Adolph Schmidt

FIGURE 7. View of Ohiopyle Falls, 2006. Ferncliff Peninsula is to the left of the Youghiogheny River, and the Borough of Ohiopyle is to the right. Note the significant portion of the town's original downtown area that was cleared to create the parkland along the riverfront. Courtesy of Ohiopyle State Park.

resulted in a $100,000 gift from the A. W. Mellon Educational and Charitable Trust to begin the purchase and demolition of "the decrepit and abandoned houses along the riverfront" in the town itself. Finally, Mrs. Keister was contacted and agreed to work on obtaining the rights to her family's land on the wooded slopes facing Ferncliff.[22]

By the end of the decade all the pieces for creating a state park at Ohiopyle were in place as regional boosters and officials in the Department of Forests and Waters began lobbying Governor Lawrence for the funds necessary to complete land purchases. However, competing visions of the nature of the local landscape had yet to be resolved, a tension that came to a head over the issue of coal surface mining. Between 1940 and 1960, the Connellsville area, which included Ohiopyle, lost nearly 16,000 mining jobs, the biggest drop of any county in the Steel Valley. However, some small operations employing about nine hundred people still operated in the district, including at least six mines in the Cucumber Run watershed across from Ferncliff. Cucumber Run itself flowed through the middle of the Keister tract and featured a signature waterfall that was one of the park's principal scenic attractions. Most of the underground works were interconnected because the area had been mined by myriad local residents since the 1880s. Coupled with the fact that no accurate mine maps existed, this created an ever-present danger of catastrophe when new tunnels intersected with flooded portions of old works. In 1960, for example, the Joseph A. Miller Company was forced to close a new operation when it was inundated by water from an abandoned portion of the adjacent Whipkey Mine.[23]

While encouraging the preservation of scenic areas, the Allegheny Conference and the wealthy patrons who provided funding for conservation initiatives remained wedded to an industrial vision of the Steel Valley. Pro-growth boosters praised improvements to air and water quality in the region, but pollution regulation and mine reclamation were seen as largely voluntary affairs designed to impose the fewest restrictions on corporate profit. The Conservancy did favor restriction of mining near "areas of such imposing beauty, history, significance, or recreational potential, that they should not be stripped" and supported efforts to stop mining near "those parks which have been created through Conservancy initiative." However, officials also made it clear that while "anxious to contribute to the eventual establishment of a system of regular and administrative enforcement," they were "not opposed to all stripping of minerals"—a position deeply influenced by Conservancy board member James Hillman. Hillman, who was also an executive committee member and later chair of the Allegheny Conference, was one of the few surface mine operators in Pennsylvania to advocate state regulation of the industry.[24]

In a stance consistent with similar Allegheny Conference policies on controversial issues related to the Pittsburgh Renaissance itself, the Conservancy's leadership resisted efforts by more militant members to "participate in protests against these stripping operations," explaining that the group had "neither the staff, nor the funds, nor the privilege, as a nonprofit organization to engage widely in public controversy. However, a disaster in the summer of 1961 forced the Conservancy into more active opposition to coal stripping near its holdings in Ohiopyle. In July, employees of the Smithfield Mining Company, which operated a nearby surface mine, accidentally cut into a flooded abandoned mine, releasing a torrent of reeking, acidic water into Cucumber Run that killed fish, stained the falls a sickly shade of orange, and drove off bathers from the Youghiogheny as far as South Connellsville, fifteen miles downstream.[25]

With the operator and state mine inspector blaming each other for the incident, and neither able to stop the flow of acidic water into the stream, Charles Lewis lamented that after all the group's hard work and investment in the area, "it made us feel sick to see this splendid bit of natural beauty ruined." In response, Conservancy officials—together with downstream water authorities and fishing groups—took their protest to the Sanitary Water Board, a commission in the state Department of Health that had limited powers to regulate acid mine drainage. In October the board's three appointed citizens and four cabinet officials, including Maurice Goddard, revoked the permit it had only recently granted Smithfield to continue operations on Cucumber Run and denied a pending application by the company to mine on nearby Jonathan Run, despite the fact that their own inspectors found the company's drainage plan met state requirements.[26]

This initial victory with the Sanitary Water Board decision served as further confirmation for McCahan and some local residents of the overbearing attitude of Pittsburgh elites toward their community. As the board considered an appeal filed by Smithfield's owner, the editorial page of the *Pittsburgh Press* joined the chorus of those opposing mining upstream from Ohiopyle. The chair of the Pennsylvania Federation of Sportsmen's Clubs, himself an employee of Westinghouse and a resident of metropolitan Pittsburgh, also used the incident to call for stronger state strip mine laws. On the other hand, in a letter to Governor Lawrence, McCahan highlighted the fact that the mine owners had complied with all the demands of the state inspectors, while bringing "employment and money to an area where it is badly needed." "Cucumber Creek," she added, "has had acid water in it for 40 years." Of even greater concern than the stripping, McCahan argued to Lawrence, were "the Conservancy's attempts to stop deep mines" including those of Whipkey and Mitchell, using the implied threat of permit denial by the Sanitary Water Board. "At a large investment of capital," she concluded, a recreational park at Ohiopyle could support only a handful of employees for a few months a year. "Meantime, the rest of us have to live."[27]

In addition to being wrapped up in the debate over state regulation of surface mining, the creation of Ohiopyle Park was also deeply intertwined with the expansion of the government's involvement in park creation and infrastructure development more broadly. The Sanitary Water Board announced its dismissal of Smithfield's appeal just days after Goddard's July 1962 speech at Ferncliff, a symbolic connection that was certainly not lost on local residents. Similarly, the decision of the Mellon Trust to begin funding the purchase and demolition of waterfront buildings within the town itself had come only after Goddard endorsed the plan. Over the next year, the secretary dedicated his considerable influence and energy to gaining approval for a $70,000,000 bond issue, dubbed Project 70, to pay for parkland acquisition. As with the federal Wilderness Act of 1964, arguments for Project 70 were couched in terms of the danger that "available land" would be "swallowed up by our great cities as they sprawl outward across the countryside." Project 70 passed a statewide referendum in 1963 with more than half the 140,000 vote margin of victory coming from Allegheny County.[28]

As Lillian McCahan pointed out in an editorial in the *Uniontown Evening Standard*, Ohiopyle was no more an unoccupied area than Cucumber Run was a pristine stream, and the creation of the state park required significant rearrangement of the existing landscape under the threat of eminent domain. Over the next decade, razing of riverfront properties and purchase of land in the surrounding hills went hand in hand with a commitment by the Conservancy and state officials to modernize the community's infrastructure in order to handle increased demands by park visitors. By 1965, the Conservancy had advanced thousands of dollars in funds for engineering studies that paved the way for more than half a million dollars in grants from the federal Economic Development Administration and the state Department of Forests and Waters to build Ohiopyle's first water and sewer system. The state then rerouted and expanded the main highway through town, razing more private buildings in the process, so as to provide a hundred yards clearance from the river—an area subsequently developed as a "natural park." By the end of the decade, the Conservancy had spent more than $750,000 in creating Ohiopyle State Park, not including land grants such as those provided by West Penn Power and the Keister family, the vast bulk of which came from large Pittsburgh foundations including the Kaufmann and Mellon Trusts and the Buhl Foundation.[29]

The Conservancy and state officials took great care to present the transformation of Ohiopyle as enjoying the strong support of the majority of community members, who "after the present period of inconvenience has passed," would "enter upon a new and fruitful life, with benefits extending through long years to come." Funding for new sewers and infrastructure development helped the Conservancy gain the backing of local officials, including the Ohiopyle Borough Council, the local congressman, and the county development office. Certainly many residents did appreciate the arrival of a buyer for dilapidated properties, while others enjoyed the prospect of living next to "an eighteen-thousand acre playground." At the July 1964 hearing that led to Governor Scranton's formal approval of using Project 70 funds for Ohiopyle, Goddard argued that "development of the tourist industry near the new parks eventually will more than offset any revenue losses in the rural communities." "Residents of the Ohiopyle area seem to realize this," Conservancy officials reported, for there were relatively few protests when Goddard explained the terms of the buyout to property owners. "He said it was the easiest series of meetings he had ever attended with property owners who will lose their land."[30]

On the other hand, the Conservancy's membership and officers were overwhelmingly from the metropolitan core, and the imposition of what was, in reality, a plan funded and implemented by Pittsburgh elites, and "designed primarily for urban citizens who need park land for recreation," was not without its critics. For some nonlocal opponents of government expansion, Ohiopyle became a symbol of "the massive take-over of private lands for the good health and well-being of Americans." Lillian McCahan, who ran unsuccessfully for borough council in the mid-1960s, cast herself as the community's defender against "city slickers" whose original plan had been enlarged to include "our few, neat, needed commercial buildings, the Baptist parsonage and a large home near the falls." The Conservancy was itself not able to compel sales, of course, but the organization's close collaboration with Goddard meant that "to some people, only hairs were split between the Pittsburgh group and the state." "You could see that the Conservancy started in Ohiopyle and kept moving out," recalled Ed Jackson, a resident of Kentuck Mountain overlooking Ferncliff, "then we got a letter from the state saying something like 'your place will be bought.'"[31]

In the end, local opposition did not, as Netting feared, cause Ferncliff itself "to be torched," but the imposition of the Conservancy's postindustrial vision of their community did result in long-lasting resentment as well as a stunning act of arson that made clear the target of local anger. When the Conservancy first purchased the Ferncliff Peninsula they also acquired the Ohiopyle House, a rundown hotel that was the last remnant of the town's nineteenth century heyday as a summer resort. In October

1958, the first official members' excursion to Ohiopyle included a luncheon at Ohiopyle House that recognized both Lillian McCahan and Allegheny Conference planner James McClain, whose land use study would lay the foundation for the community's contested future. In 1963, with plans for the state park in full swing, the Conservancy began extensive renovations to the 37-room hotel including remodeled floors, ceilings, bedrooms, furniture, and a new kitchen.[32]

Soon after the Ohiopyle House reopened in November 1964, however, the building was burned to the ground in an apparent act of arson. The cause of the fire was officially undetermined, but the obvious symbolism of the Ohiopyle House as the center of the Conservancy's authority remained a potent symbol of resistance among local residents. According to reports, the day before the blaze a Conservancy employee was threatened at the hotel, and the fire has been romanticized locally as "mountain justice" and a way to "get even" after "officials forced the people who loved their homes to sell at rock bottom prices." The destruction of the Ohiopyle House has clear parallels to the backlash emerging at the same time over the razing of urban neighborhoods at the heart of Pittsburgh's revitalization program. The involvement of Edgar Kaufmann, James Hillman, Adolph Schmidt, and other prominent Allegheny Conference members in both areas underscores the regional vision of the Renaissance as well as the tensions inherent in attempting to reshape local landscapes to serve broader economic goals.[33]

"Productive Use After the Coal Is Removed"

Even as residents of Ohiopyle were preparing for the state park's official opening in 1971, on the other side of the region, Consol announced that it would soon move its enormous GEM of Egypt shovel across Interstate 70 to begin work south of the highway. The company's announcement sparked a tense debate in Barnesville, which pitted those who supported the financial benefits of surface mining against those concerned about the environmental and economic impacts of operations near the village. Increased demand for coal used in electrical production had prompted a rebound for Consol, which by the mid-1970s owned fifty-six mines, employed 19,000 miners, and was the nation's largest coal exporter. In 1956 the company transferred the enormous *Mountaineer* coal shovel from West Virginia to its mines north of Barnesville, and then acquired an even larger shovel, the *Silver Spade*, a "sister" to the GEM, for use in its Georgetown Mine west of

Steubenville. "That's the damn'ist machine I've ever seen," remarked L. F. McCollum, chairman of Continental Oil, Consol's parent firm, on a visit to the site. In 1967, the year the Egypt Valley Mine opened, executives of the company's Hanna Coal subsidiary predicted a 100 percent output hike within four years, and by 1972 surface mine production near Barnesville climbed to nearly thirteen million tons.[34]

As with the state park in Ohiopyle, the assembly of the enormous property that made up the Egypt Valley Mine required erasure of a settlement pattern that had developed over more than a century. The majority of land purchases by Consol occurred in two waves during the mid-1940s and then again in the early 1960s. Residents "sold in different ways," explained Rex Kaiser, a former Egypt Valley resident. When the coal company first started, "they were going to buy just the coal and they wouldn't strip for years and years, they said. Later they decided they was going to strip, so they come around and bought the surface." Money obtained by selling mineral rights or through mine employment allowed some farmers in the region to modernize their operations and continue farming despite the pressures of the Appalachian crisis. "They could buy equipment," explained June Stephens. "I know dad, when they sold, he bought a tractor. But if all the young guys would have stayed on the farm, there just wouldn't have been a living for everyone." While the company did not have the power of eminent domain that state officials could use in Ohiopyle, once Consol began construction of the Egypt Valley Mine, those who had chosen not to sell were left with the difficult prospect of living in the middle of a depopulated wilderness. Consol's "sales pitch was everybody else is going to sell around you and you're gonna be setting here," Kaiser recalled. Nearly everyone did sell in the end, leaving almost 100,000 acres north of Barnesville virtually uninhabited.[35]

Consol officials also articulated the themes of reshaping the local landscape to serve the greater good of the regional community in ways that bore a striking resemblance to that of the Western Pennsylvania Conservancy. In addition to highlighting the mine's contribution to local employment and ignoring the obliteration of Egypt Valley, executives incorporated the language of reclamation into their descriptions of mining operations and emphasized the restoration of the land to "productive use after the coal is removed." As with both federal and state Appalachian development plans, this vision largely disregarded small farming as a profitable venture and focused on the possibilities of using mined-out land for attracting tourists.

FIGURE 8. View of the Grand Opening of the Egypt Valley Mine, January 1967. An estimated 25,000 visitors viewed the newly erected Giant Earth Mover (GEM) of Egypt during the two-day event. The twelve-story shovel was active until 1988 before being scrapped in 1991. Parts of the shovel were used to keep its twin, the Silver Spade, operational at a nearby mine until 2006. Hanna Coal Collection, Harrison County Historical Society. Courtesy of Dale Davis.

Consol's promotional literature described in glowing terms how postmining reclamation would transform the "small farms with worked-out soil and hilly terrain" into numerous small lakes fulfilling "the demand of sportsmen and the public for increased recreational facilities," forests fostering "the growth of game animals, and choice sites . . . so that cottages and sports lodges can be erected." A brochure handed out at the mine's opening even envisioned the use of spoil piles, the mountains of overturned topsoil and rock left over from the mining operation, to create a facility "unique in southeastern Ohio—ski runs."[36]

Consol was only one among many surface mine operators in the region, but the size, scope and visibility of its Egypt Valley Mine caused particular concern among some residents, especially after the company announced it planned to expand operations south toward Barnesville. Opposition to surface mining in the area arose from two interrelated but distinct positions. The first, which originated with Barnesville Planning Commission member Norma Schuster, pushed for a "Greenbelt" surrounding the village that would limit the amount and type of surface mining in its vicinity. Like Lillian McCahan in Ohiopyle, Schuster was not a native of Barnesville, and had recently moved to the community with her children and husband, a physician at the local hospital. With a background in urban planning, Schuster was concerned with the effects that blasting, truck traffic, noise, and other problems associated with large-scale surface mining would have on residential and commercial development. Pointing to other rural communities in the Steel Valley, especially Cadiz west of Steubenville, she expressed horror at the prospect of Barnesville surrounded on all sides by devastation with no room to expand and "without a future."[37]

Schuster quickly contacted her friend Aida Rizzi, another relatively new resident of the community and manager of a local textile mill. The two women obtained a meeting with the state's new governor, John Gilligan, then at loggerheads with coal executives over a revised and expanded Ohio Strip Mine Law pending in the Ohio legislature. The governor provided Schuster and Rizzi with a stronger bargaining position in their local negotiations with Consol even as the law's supporters used the incredible visibility of the Egypt Valley mine as an example of why better reclamation laws were necessary. Gilligan, a liberal Democrat, had temporarily replaced promining Republican James Rhodes and publicly expressed concerns over the agreement signed by his predecessor permitting Consol to move its giant coal shovels across Interstate 70. During spring 1972, state officials served as intermediaries between Schuster, Rizzi, and Consol executives in negotiating concessions that they hoped would help to decrease the impact of mining on the community.[38]

The scale of operations and proximity to one of the nation's most traveled interstate highways also made the Egypt Valley Mine a prominent rallying point for state and national opponents of surface mining. The most important individual linking local concerns with these broader issues was Cleveland neurobiologist Theodore Voneida. The Voneida family cottage on Piedmont Lake was only a few miles from Egypt Valley, providing a clear vantage from which to view the mine's progress. He recalled that his neighbor "talked to us about strip mining because their house was being rocked by the blasts" and "we started looking around. It looked like a moonscape." Voneida and his students from Case Western Reserve University in Cleveland began conducting experiments to measure water pollution caused by the mine as well as taking hundreds of photographs and videos chronicling the mine's impact. Drawing from his experience in the antiwar movement, he worked to create publicity about the mine, giving speeches and providing press releases to state and national news organizations. "We were pretty naïve," Voneida recalled. "So we started going down and taking pictures and so on, just all on our own. We weren't working with anybody. It was just us. And then I went out for publicity. I got the Cleveland *Plain Dealer* interested, and I got the *Akron Beacon Journal* interested and I got *Huntley-Brinkley*." The last of these was "a sort of a turning point," followed by steadily increasing national attention including a 1972 ABC News documentary titled *Echo of Anger*.[39]

While Voneida and his supporters worked to publicize Egypt Valley as part of a larger campaign to change state and federal laws, other local activists explored legal options for halting the I-70 crossing. Barnesville Village Council member Richard Garrett, a transplanted New Englander and local retail manager, first became involved in the anti-stripping movement after two local residents, Florence Bethel and Mary Workman, approached him about damage to their homes near the Egypt Valley Mine. "Initially I think what we were trying to do was stop the stripping," recalled Garrett. "Of course, I think we felt that perhaps we could never really do that, but we wanted to prevent the GEM of Egypt from coming across because that was all in the news at the time." He quietly established contact with the Ohio branch of Ralph Nader's Public Interest Research Group (PIRG), which had been looking for a local affiliate to join in mounting a legal challenge to the Interstate 70 crossing. In June 1971, Garrett helped form Citizens Organized to Defend the Environment (CODE) in Barnesville, and the Ohio PIRG provided the legal team through which two local residents, CODE, and Friends of the Earth filed suit to stop the crossing. "We are going to fight every one of those machines when they try to bring them across," Garrett declared.[40]

On the other hand, while there was some support for limiting surface mining and requiring reclamation, many local residents continued to support the coal industry within the broader Appalachian context of rural poverty and population loss. "The concern over the environment is real enough," explained an editorial in the Martins Ferry newspaper, "but so is the concern over what could happen locally if the coal mines close. We haven't enough other jobs to take up the slack." Conversely, statements by nonlocal activists and big city reporters often depicted Barnesville in nostalgic or paternalistic terms that overlooked the social structures binding locals to the mines and allowing many to earn relatively high wages. Columbus newspaperman, shopping mall executive, and antistripping activist Doral Chenoweth began a *New York Times* editorial, for instance, with a description of the local area as filled with "lots of timber, goats and cattle, and good corn-whiskey making." This vision was out of step with the region's long history of rural industrialization as well as the poverty, unemployment, and outmigration of the postwar period. Numerous other articles implied that local supporters of mining operations were somehow backward, misguided, and in thrall to the mining companies, suggesting they needed outside leadership to show them the error of their ways.[41]

In response, Consol executives made a compelling argument for continued mining, pointing out that the average income of area farmers in 1969 was $34 per acre. "Is it any wonder that the farmer wants to sell his land?" asked Ralph Hatch, president of Consol's Hanna Division. "He can't make a living at it." Furthermore, increases in local mining employment, especially with the opening of new deep mines, coupled with the decline of family farming meant that many Steel Valley communities actually became more dependent on mining employment during the early 1970s. "I don't like stripping or any part of it," noted Barnesville furniture storeowner John Kirk, who had recently traveled to Columbus to protest new mining regulations. "But it isn't that simple. Better than 10 percent of the work force in this county works for the mines." Bill Davies, editor of the *Barnesville Enterprise*, agreed, "Our future is definitely tied to the strip mining industry—it's more important to us than you think." "We are pretty strongly divided," declared Mayor George Fitch, "but I think the majority clearly favors the move [across the interstate]. Hanna's payroll pumps a lot into this town. We're pretty dependent on that mining."[42]

The battle over the expansion of Consol's mine toward Barnesville reached a climax in the summer of 1972. Over the previous year, local issues had been superseded to an extent by the debate over proposed amendments to state regulations that would eliminate the most egregious problems that rendered mined land unfit for most future uses. Due in part to the visibility of Egypt Valley and in the face of strong opposition, including a threat by Hatch to close all his operations in southeastern Ohio, in April legislators enacted one of the most comprehensive mine reclamation laws in the nation. The new law required regrading mining areas to the approximate original contour of the land, retention and replacement of existing topsoil, and successful reseeding of sites by the mine operator. However, despite the support of Governor Gilligan, state officials and local mining opponents were faced with the facts that Consol's operations were perfectly legal, that surface mining had support even in Barnesville itself, and that state permission to cross the highway was only a convenience for company officials who could find other ways to continue the mine's southward expansion if necessary. Furthermore, because Consol's permit for the mine had been granted prior to the new law's implementation, the company was only required to reclaim its land up to the "emasculated" 1965 standards.[43]

As a result, while seen as a defeat by more militant environmental groups, Gilligan's June announcement of an agreement permitting Consol to move large equipment, including the GEM of Egypt, across the highway contained key concessions protecting Barnesville that satisfied Norma Schuster, Aida Rizzi, and their community-oriented supporters. Most important, the company agreed to conform to the higher standards of the new law in reclaiming all its holdings south of the interstate. Hatch also agreed to fund a land use plan for the area around the village and to work with local officials to ensure that the company's operations would not violate the plan. Completed a year later, the "Greenbelt Plan—Barnesville, Ohio" prohibited new surface mining by Consol within a one mile radius of the village and imposed additional reclamation for areas leading to and from the village so as to "reduce the visual aspect of strip mining." The proposal also called for post-mining planning of key areas to provide "for the development of industrial sites and access roads." A Consol spokesman agreed to the plan, stating that the company's mining program was in "no real conflict with greenbelt goals." As a result, Shuster and Rizzi felt they had achieved their basic goal of creating space for Barnesville's economic diversification and growth after mining operations has ceased. As Rizzi put it, "We've been a sleepy little town up until now, but now the newer people in town are trying to get it going forward. We are trying to attract industry, but we need to have room to grow."[44]

Company concessions did not satisfy everyone, either in the community or among environmentalists pushing for stronger regulations or even an outright federal ban on surface mining. CODE and the Ohio PIRG appealed their lawsuit through the federal courts in order to stop the road closures required to move the GEM of Egypt across Interstate 70, a level of activism that five years later earned Garrett an invitation to the White House signing ceremony for the federal Surface Mine Control and Reclamation Act. On the other hand, the increasing anger of mining supporters at the delay was made clear at a public meeting in the summer of 1972 sponsored by CODE and covered in the ABC documentary *Echo of Anger*. Bernard Delloma, a bulldozer operator at the Egypt Valley Mine, voiced his objection to the recently filed CODE lawsuit angrily stating "If that [mine] shuts down, there are 322 of us [out of a job]. If that GEM is not able to cross the road, I'm out of a job. I'm out of a ten or twelve thousand dollar a year job." He further threatened a tactic particularly feared by small town businesses, the boycott. "The strip miners, we have organized," he declared, "and we say that if they keep the publicity up on this thing, we are going to boycott the businesses in town. If we do, there won't be no town left."[45]

The failure of the CODE lawsuit in December paved the way for Consol to expand its operations south of the interstate, but in response to all the negative publicity the company chose not to use the widely recognized GEM of Egypt and instead moved two smaller shovels. In the pre-dawn hours of January 4, 1973, the *Mountaineer* and the *Tiger* slowly made their way across one of the nation's busiest highways, closing Interstate 70 to traffic for an unprecedented twenty-four hours. Among the thousands who gathered to watch the event were several dozen protestors who staged a mock funeral for Barnesville complete with eulogies, candles, and a coffin. Among them was Bill Hunkler, a young Barnesville resident motivated by the Kent State shootings who likened surface mining to the "invention of the atomic bomb." "Many of our critics," he declared in a speech broadcast nationally on NBC, "see in our pleas to halt strip mining the same mindlessness we see in their goals of maximum profit . . . campaigning behind the façade of public interest." "The demonstration," according to a *Washington Post* reporter covering the event, "while short and peaceful, was one of the first of its kind seen in this coal oriented region."[46]

Following the successful revitalization of the Golden Triangle, there appeared to be a clear consensus among the region's civic and political elite about the need to extend the symbolic transformation of the Pittsburgh Renaissance to the broader metropolitan region. Indeed, *Pittsburgh Press* conservation editor Fred Jones was so confident in the enlightened leadership of his city's industrialists that he could declare confidently that should

Ralph Hatch be "so foolish as to carry out his threat to close all of Hanna's strip-mine operations if a strong law is passed in Ohio, it is very doubtful he would get very far," as his superiors at Consol "would see that he was corrected in short order." However, the Western Pennsylvania Conservancy's hesitation in getting involved in the surface mining debate also suggests a broader concern with maintaining the profitability of the region's extractive industries. By the mid-1970s, a series of compromises in both communities allowed for an uneasy balance between economy and environment that relied in part on the voluntary cooperation of private industries and in part on more robust regulation imposed on the state level.[47]

One of the difficulties in writing the history of rural places is that opposing ideologies are rarely brought into the open for outsiders to view. The development of Ohiopyle State Park and the Egypt Valley Mine were two such events when underlying social and cultural tensions were unearthed that, despite the forging of temporary settlements, remained unresolved and ready to emerge during future periods of economic uncertainty. Taking into account the obvious differences between a surface mine and a state park, in neither case was land use change a straightforward narrative of environmental decline or a simple story of enlightened conservation. Both environmentalists and mine executives pointed to the future benefits of tourism in local areas sacrificed for the greater good of the regional economy even as broader national trends and public policy failures left communities increasingly reliant for employment on those remaining extractive industries. In the few areas with significant public and private investment, such as Ohiopyle, a thriving tourist industry provided a legitimate, if fiercely contested, economic alternative. Even there, however, continued population loss and double digit unemployment in the surrounding county belied the idea of tourism significantly altering the rural crisis that so concerned Ralph Widner and his audience sitting in Oakland just a few months after Consol's shovels crossed Interstate 70.

CHAPTER 6

The New Metropolis of the Plateau

In 1920 the area that became Monroeville looked much like the rest of metropolitan Pittsburgh's rural periphery. Originally agricultural, the community's first real growth came from a coal boom peaking during World War I that left much of the district scarred from surface mining. "Patton Township was one of the ugliest farmlands," recalled resident Miles Span. "It was coal country. There were big hills of coal and strip." However, the subsequent construction of the Penn-Lincoln Parkway and the Pennsylvania Turnpike established Monroeville as Pittsburgh's eastern gateway and as a center for corporate research, with travel time to the Golden Triangle cut to less than thirty minutes. In 1954, the Miracle Mile, the region's first suburban shopping center, opened in Monroeville to great fanfare. "You can't imagine what it was like then," recalled Dorothy Larson of nearby Penn Hills. The Miracle Mile had "everything under the sun, like a bake shop, things we weren't used to having." When the larger Monroeville Mall opened its doors fifteen years later, it dwarfed its predecessor with over a million square feet of shopping space for 125 stores, parking for 6,500 cars, a full-size ice rink, and the other trappings of a "massive regional shopping complex." As a result, while the Steel Valley's overall population stagnated and began to decline, Monroeville boomed from less than 8,000 residents in 1950 to 33,000 by 1976.[1]

Highway-oriented suburban communities like Monroeville became increasingly important components in the regional vision espoused by the public-private partnership promoting the Pittsburgh Renaissance. The postwar relationship between the Republican business leaders of the

Allegheny Conference and Mayor David Lawrence's Democratic machine provided a means to marshal the enormous political and economic resources necessary to build the "expressways of tomorrow" through rugged terrain. With the decline of rail transit, these highways formed a key determinant of which rural areas would continue to experience the crisis of deindustrialization and which would resemble the booming suburbs associated with the Sunbelt. Suburban growth was initially conceived in residential terms, but more and more employers also chose the flatter, more spacious locations of the higher-elevation plateau, such as near the new airport west of the city, over the crowded river valleys. Even as urban renewal projects cleared mixed-use neighborhoods in the hopes of attracting new manufacturers downtown, the growth of suburban employment increasingly belied the Renaissance credo of living on the hills and working in the city.

By the early 1970s, political and civic leaders looked to highway-oriented industrial parks, such as the publicly subsidized RIDC Park West near the airport and Thorn Hill in rural Cranberry Township near the intersection of the turnpike and Interstate 79, as the best hope for regional economic revitalization. However, this "new metropolis of the plateau," as Ralph Widner called it in 1973, remained largely isolated from the "generally disadvantaged" communities of the river valleys that were "acquiring the mirror-image characteristics of contemporary suburbia." This regional bifurcation eventually led some public officials to question the suburban-oriented strategy adopted by the Allegheny Conference and its affiliates, as the stirrings of revolt in urban neighborhoods affected by both urban renewal and highway construction began to put strains on the Renaissance partnership.[2]

"Expressways of Tomorrow"

In general, metropolitan Pittsburgh's suburban development followed national trends, but the region's topography, political systems, and economic structures also shaped the process in important ways. Transportation improvements played an especially important role in urban expansion due to the region's mountainous topography, and by 1902 nearly five hundred miles of track linked Pittsburgh neighborhoods with nearby communities in Allegheny, Beaver, and Westmoreland Counties. The construction of the Liberty Bridge and Tunnels in the late 1920s subsequently paved the way for growth in the South Hills area, which, despite the collapse of the real estate market during the Great Depression and wartime housing restrictions, increased by more than 95,000 residents during the three decades after 1920. The expanding suburbs soon stretched deep into the South Hills almost to the Washington County line, east from the junction of the Allegheny and Monongahela Rivers to Westmoreland County, north over flatter terrain to Butler County, and west in an expanding corridor along the Ohio River to the existing population centers of Beaver County. "With the choice property gobbled up long ago," reported the *Pittsburgh Press*'s Edwin Beachler in 1951, "people came to look on the city as a place to make a living and the suburbs as a place to live."[3]

The same announcement by Governor George C. Martin in October 1944 setting in motion the Allegheny Conference's plan for the Golden Triangle also authorized construction of a limited access "Penn-Lincoln Parkway" from the Point to a new airport west of the city and east to the Pennsylvania Turnpike. The notion of a limited access highway forming the eastern "Gateway" to Pittsburgh actually had its roots in 1921, when the Citizens Committee on City Plan of Pittsburgh proposed upgrading Second Avenue through Nine Mile Run to Swissvale, a mill town nine miles east of the Point. While Robert Moses reiterated and expanded this recommendation in his 1939 *Arterial Plan for Pittsburgh*, it was not until the formation of the Allegheny Conference that a sufficiently strong partnership existed to see the proposal put into effect. Conference officials carefully monitored and helped mediate disputes, promoted long-range planning, and endorsed the higher taxes, increased public debt, and federal subsidies necessary for the postwar highway program.[4]

Groundbreaking for the parkway took place in 1946 and Conference officers met several times a year with state highway officials and representatives of the governor's office to keep track of progress and discuss engineering issues, public relations, and appropriations. As in the rest of the region, the construction of the highway was filled with potential political, economic, and environmental challenges, requiring multiple bridges and tunnels, expensive property acquisition, and extensive negotiations with state, county, and municipal officials over who would pay for it all. Just as construction on the segment between the Point and Oakland was about to begin in 1952, for example, the management of the Baltimore and Ohio Railroad rejected the state's compensation offer for its downtown terminal. To avert delay, the Conference stepped in and pressured the company to back down by "enlisting the biggest shippers on the railroad." After a series of Conference-brokered meetings and a visit by R. K. Mellon confidant Arthur Van Buskirk to the B&O headquarters in Baltimore, the company agreed to settle.[5]

Building limited access highways through the Steel Valley's densely settled and rugged landscape also entailed enormous costs that the rural-dominated and (until 1955) Republican controlled state legislature was wary of shouldering, particularly as it benefited an urbanized Democratic stronghold. When the Department of Highways began construction on the Parkway's Squirrel Hill Tunnel in 1948, for example, it awarded the largest contract in state history despite the funding including neither the tunnel lining and highway surface nor the ventilating building or pavement of the approaches. By the time the last section of the Parkway East was completed between the Point and Monroeville in 1959, the total project exceeded $31 million. Effective lobbying by the Allegheny Conference contacts in Harrisburg helped generate support for the region's roads, but a more appealing solution presented itself with the passage of the Federal Aid Highway Act of 1956, which offered 90 percent funding for interstate highways. While wary of interference by federal and state bureaucrats, Allegheny Conference planners began work with state officials on a broad survey of future highway needs even before Congress authorized the Interstate system. Though many of the specific details still remained to be worked out and most of the anticipated interstates remained confined to planning documents, by the end of the 1950s the basic structure of the region's new highway-oriented transportation network was in place.[6]

Unlike metropolitan regions where suburbanization took place in a more or less concentric pattern, the Steel Valley evolved erratically from a series of urbanized corridors stretching along the three major river systems. The region's rugged terrain interspersed barriers to the "continuities of block patterns and land development" and was thus not generally well-suited to the type of mass produced housing made famous by the contemporary development of Levittown. Consequently, as the new wave of suburban growth expanded to the Appalachian Plateau from the lower elevations of the river valleys in the 1950s, white-collar commuters encountered pre-existing communities that had followed the railroad lines and coal seams. As mining and agricultural employment declined, working-class residents, too, increasingly commuted to jobs throughout the region. "The travel was a pain," recalled Bill Arsehn, a resident of Shoaf, a coal "patch" town in

Fayette County, who worked at the Homestead Works in the late 1960s. "But it was a good paying job."⁷

This meant that residents with very different social, economic, and cultural perspectives at times inhabited the same geographical space, complicating notions of what the "suburbs" were and creating tensions between residents of different backgrounds and expectations. Consequently, the orderly growth of suburban communities thus became an important and contentious issue for civic leaders concerned about maximizing investment and building a positive image of a modern metropolis. "Coverdale, which closed its mines only two years ago, has painted and prettied up," reported one observer of the transition from rural mining camp to middle-class suburb in 1951. "Out-houses are gradually being replaced by inside facilities," and the community is well on the way to becoming "one of the brighter suburbs. It has made certain that coal is dead by outlawing strip mining."⁸

Beginning in the late 1940s, the Allegheny Conference and its affiliates regularly warned of the dangerous potential for unplanned growth in formerly peripheral communities that would soon be within easy commuting distance from the Golden Triangle. In Monroeville, for example, the eastern end of the Penn-Lincoln Parkway quickly "lost much of its usefulness for through traffic" due to the proliferation of "taverns, night clubs, gasoline stations, diners, etc., all of which gravitated toward the highway." Conference leaders sought to protect their vision of the region by helping guide growth through the Pittsburgh Regional Planning Association (PRPA), with which it shared an interlocking board of directors. Led by R. K. Mellon himself, the PRPA offered subsidized services to local municipalities, helping to create dozens of comprehensive plans, zoning restrictions, and building codes during the 1950s alone. "All municipalities and areas of Allegheny County are tied together in the economic and broad community sense," concluded one group of local officials. "They will pretty much 'sink or swim' together as the economic future and general livability of the county rises or falls."⁹

Nevertheless, planning for suburban growth ran into the same political and cultural roadblocks affecting local and regional planning in the rest of the Steel Valley. Despite a major annexation on the East End in the early twentieth century, for example, Pittsburgh had the smallest percentage of population within the central city of any major metropolitan region in the nation. Outside the city, the settlement pattern created a complex jumble of nearly 130 independent municipalities in Allegheny County alone. The decentralization of housing exacerbated pre-existing ethnic, economic, and social tensions as local politicians jockeyed for control over new resources, especially in the rural townships, which experienced the greatest rates of postwar growth. Smaller communities were limited in their taxing authority, and many residents eagerly sought annexations to neighboring cities and boroughs in order to obtain municipal services. But, existing political elites were often determined to retain their individual identity and bitterly resisted these attempts, as in 1946 when a group of residents clamoring for water, sewer, and other infrastructure improvements in suburbanizing Versailles Township just south of Monroeville petitioned the nearby city of McKeesport for annexation. On the morning the pro-annexation group submitted its petition, another faction led by members of the township's board of education, volunteer fire department, and board of supervisors submitted an application for incorporation as a borough. Following a protracted legal battle stretching for more than a year, the Borough of White Oak finally came into existence in June 1948.[10]

In 1952, a similar set of issues resulted in the creation of the Borough of Monroeville from the remaining unincorporated parts of Patton Township, which were steadily being annexed by the neighboring industrial communities of Turtle Creek, Wilmerding, and Pitcairn. With an area of nearly twenty square miles initially divided among fewer than 8,000 residents, completion of the Monroeville Interchange of the Pennsylvania Turnpike (1950) and the Parkway East (1954) paved the way for a doubling of the community's population from 1950 to 1958 alone. During the same period, real estate valuation jumped even more dramatically (336 percent) propelled by the growth of businesses lining the highway between the Parkway East and the turnpike interchange. The strategic value of the site soon attracted the attention of Ohio developer Don Casto, a pioneer in shopping mall construction described by commentator Paul Harvey as "the man who changed the shopping habits of the free world." "This Monroeville Community," Casto predicted, "will be one of America's great decentralized drive-in shopping centers." And, on November 1, 1954, his ten million dollar "Miracle Mile" shopping center opened with a carnival-like atmosphere featuring prizes, fireworks, and "Suicide Pete," an Evel Knieval precursor whose act included crashing through a tunnel of fire on his motorcycle.[11]

The consumerist spectacle of the Miracle Mile quickly became closely associated with the area's identity as the area along Route 22 became recognized as the "commercial core of the community." The importance of highway construction to this new development is clear as the value of properties adjacent to Route 22 increased by a whopping 526 percent between 1950 and 1958 alone, more than double that of other properties in the community. "The Turnpike was a real boon to this borough," declared local burgess Samuel Jenkins in 1952. "And from the looks of new and contemplated construction, our business district hasn't even got a good start." However, this growth created a problem for Allegheny Conference planners, as local traffic clogged the five-mile stretch from the end of the Penn-Lincoln Parkway to the Turnpike despite an upgrade of the route to four lanes in 1957. To compensate for Monroeville's rapid expansion, construction began in 1961 on an extension of the parkway that would bypass the area entirely and connect directly to the turnpike.[12]

This economic boom was tied intimately to residential growth as Monroeville's population blossomed to more than 17,000. However, only a fraction of this growth was due to the classic pattern of decentralization from the urban core, with one new subdivision being filled in roughly even proportions by residents from Pittsburgh, the rest of Allegheny County, and elsewhere in Pennsylvania and the nation. This breakdown suggests that the community's cheap land and highway provided an attractive option for office workers in the Golden Triangle as well as blue-collar workers commuting to nearby mills and factories. The ability to attract residents from other regions also stands in stark contrast to the outmigration and population loss experienced by many other communities. As with other suburban communities, the PRPA looked with dismay at the strain on urban infrastructure caused by this rapid growth and urged communities to approve comprehensive planning and zoning. After its incorporation, Monroeville, for example, adopted plumbing codes, joined the Allegheny County Sewer Authority, and established a planning commission, but initially failed to create a master plan because it was "too costly, too delaying, and too subject to change."[13]

On the other hand, Monroeville's dependence on the Penn-Lincoln Parkway underscores the importance of Pittsburgh's public-private partnership in guiding public policy decisions that directed growth to certain parts of the Steel Valley even while the region as a whole declined. In April 1955, Wanda Jennings, Mrs. America of 1954, greeted visitors at the opening of the Garden City, a 500 acre, 1,500 home residential area that offered 3 and 4 bedroom homes with contoured "flower named" streets, a community center, an elementary school, a shopping and professional center, and a large park with playgrounds, tennis courts, and a swimming pool. The community's developer, the Sampson Miller Company, had just formed in 1953, and over the next two decades went on to become one of the region's largest residential builders, with more than 8,000 homes constructed, mainly in the eastern suburbs. The Miracle Mile and the new middle-class homes "made each other successful," explained a local attorney associated with the developments.[14]

Park Martin, executive director of the Allegheny Conference, described Garden City as "the first planned and integrated unit of this size that I know of in the country. It's a big step forward and such construction as this will go far in solving our suburban problems." In addition to other services, the community included its own water and drainage system, with a $225,000 sewage treatment plant. Among other honors, the new National Housing Center in Washington, D.C., included architect Richard Benn's designs for Garden City homes in a special exhibit. The community was an immediate success, and other developments such as Turnpike Gardens (1955) and Alpine Village (1959) followed, creating neighborhoods that, in the words of one local historian, "helped transform Monroeville into a modern, middle-class suburb." A community, in other words, that was as much a part of the Renaissance vision as the Golden Triangle.[15]

"Whoosh of Jets . . . and Rumble of Bull-Dozers"

Even as Monroeville became a symbol of the region's booming highway-oriented suburbs, the rural area around the city's new airport also emerged as a hub of economic activity and the focus of significant public investment aimed at diversifying the metropolitan economy. "Out in the coal-stripped hills that form the Western pocket of Allegheny County, giant townships are stirring from a deep slumber," declared *Pittsburgh Press* journalist Edwin Beachler in 1951. "They have been awakened by the whoosh of jets at Greater Pittsburgh Airport and rumble of bull-dozers on the Penn-Lincoln Parkway West." By 1963 the Airport Corridor formed the region's second largest business center, as several large out-of-town firms chose to locate their regional branch offices along the Parkway West rather than in the downtown Golden Triangle. A decade later development officials went so far as to declare that the area offered "unlimited potential" for industrial and office development oriented to the airport. On the eve of the Steel

Valley's industrial collapse, the 1979 construction of RIDC Park West, a large planned industrial district built partly with public funds, highlighted the importance of suburban manufacturing to the changing booster vision of regional development.[16]

South of the mill towns along the Ohio River, the townships of Moon, Robinson, North Fayette, Findlay, and Colliers were primarily agricultural through the 1950s, with additional income deriving from the oil wells and coal mines exploited by nearby Pittsburgh industrialists. The 1911 completion of a bridge over the Ohio between Moon and the community of Sewickley prompted the development of several country estates by Pittsburgh industrialists and financiers, including Union National Bank (later National City) President Charles McCune, III. The next year McCune joined others with property in the area to form the Sunset Golf Club, which reorganized as the Montour Heights Country Club and expanded following World War I to take advantage of continued growth. At about the same time, new automobile-oriented residential growth began spilling over the borders of Pittsburgh's South Hills neighborhoods to the neighboring boroughs of Green Tree, Rosslyn Farms, and Carnegie along U.S. Route 22/30. Consequently, even as the area remained primarily rural through the dislocations of the Great Depression and World War II, growth slowly entered from both the northwest and southeast.[17]

This general trend of slow, transportation-oriented growth picked up dramatically during the postwar years with the decision to relocate Pittsburgh's main airport from a cramped site along the Monongahela to a former dairy farm on the border between Moon and Findlay that had been commissioned as an army airfield in 1941. The construction of Greater Pittsburgh Airport was tied explicitly to a western extension of the Penn-Lincoln Parkway, with partial funding for both coming from the landmark 1946 "People's Bond Issue" that launched the broader Pittsburgh Renaissance. Groundbreaking for both the Parkway West and the airport took place in July 1946, and within two years the Allegheny Conference's Park Martin was advocating zoning measures to control the growth of residential communities that would soon be within a short commute of both downtown and the new terminal. By 1951 Beachler declared that Green Tree Borough was in the midst of a housing boom because travelers who "paused long enough to take a good look" had "discovered the sunny, rolling hills were only a 15-minute hop from the Golden Triangle."[18]

With the opening of both the Penn-Lincoln Parkway and Greater Pittsburgh Airport in the early 1950s, corporate executives also began considering office locations along the highway corridor west of the city. The opening of the Fort Pitt Tunnels in 1960 completed this rapid highway connection, allowing travel between the downtown skyscrapers and the airport in about twenty minutes. While administrative offices outside the city remained limited, by 1960 firms with smaller personnel requirements, including the regional headquarters of Aetna Insurance and General Electric, had already chosen sites in the Airport Corridor. Similarly, even among the largest and most iconic Pittsburgh-based companies, "the virtually unanimous preference" of postwar researchers for peripheral locations was "striking." Links with downtown offices contributed to the popularity of sites on the Parkway for suburban research installations, explained one observer. Companies believed that research centers with "a campus atmosphere" of "low sprawling buildings, landscaped grounds, and extensive parking lots" served as symbols "of progressive management which will impress the company's customers and the general public." Consequently, even as the Airport Corridor grew to feature the region's second largest concentration of corporate offices, in 1953 U.S. Steel consolidated its research facilities to a new campus in Monroeville, a move copied by Westinghouse (1955), Koppers (1961), and PPG (1962).[19]

Encouraging economic growth was a key pillar of the postwar public-private partnership driving the Pittsburgh Renaissance with both the Lawrence administration and the Allegheny Conference concerned with reversing the region's underlying economic malaise. Signs at the Parkway interchanges in Monroeville soon touted the community as the "Research Center of the Nation," while the Greater Pittsburgh Airport, which had the country's largest terminal when it opened in 1952, continued its expansion with scheduled jet aircraft service (1959), expanded cargo facilities (1968), and a new International Arrivals Building (1971). However, with a few notable exceptions, such as U.S. Steel's Irvin Works (1938), manufacturing operations remained largely confined to existing industrial locations in the urbanized river valleys. "In order to be industrially well-balanced," our basic industries should be supplemented with "the production of consumer goods," explained F. D. Hollinshead, a member of the Allegheny Conference's executive committee. Developers wanted "a modern, attractive building all on one floor" located on a "flat parcel of land of at least ten acres on 'a main highway' with plenty of light and clean surroundings." Of course, metropolitan Pittsburgh's settlement pattern and rough topography

FIGURE 9. Aerial view of the Westinghouse Research and Development Center, 1956. The center, which occupied a 100-acre site ten miles east of Pittsburgh in the suburb of Churchill, would come to encompass eight major buildings, including a cafeteria, auditorium, and library. Photograph by Lou Farris. Allegheny Conference on Community Development Photographs, 1892–1981, MSP285.B021.F15.I02, Library & Archives, Senator John Heinz History Center.

limited such locations, leading Hollinshead to warn that "we have almost no well-developed plant sites that would be of interest to the manufacturer of consumer goods."[20]

As in Wheeling, during the 1950s municipal officials and business leaders in Pittsburgh sought to apply the same combination of private and public resources used in downtown revitalization to stimulate new manufacturing in nearby neighborhoods. The city's Urban Redevelopment Authority (URAP) cleared two sites for J&L Steel, for example, while the federal Model Cities program later subsidized an expansion of Westinghouse in the nearby mill town of Turtle Creek. But these expansions were limited to existing large industrial employers, and Allegheny Conference and local officials grew increasingly concerned with the decline of urban manufacturing and the concomitant shrinking of the municipal tax base. Rather than approaching companies individually, Hollinshead called for "an intelligent approach to the problems of inducing manufacturers to locate plants in Pittsburgh" based on the success of planned industrial districts in Chicago and other cities. At the initial meeting of the URAP in November 1946, David Lawrence echoed this call to build ready-made industrial sites within the city and officials soon focused on the neighborhood of Manchester across the Allegheny River from the Golden Triangle.[21]

Initially, Manchester seemed a good choice for the project and by June 1947 the Conference had already commissioned a confidential report on the feasibility of creating a "new light manufacturing area" covering a substantial part of the neighborhood. The community was situated on a flat river plain, featured good transportation connections, already had a manufacturing base, and met the criteria for a "blighted" area necessary for condemnation and clearance. However, the report also highlighted substantial obstacles, most notably the enormous cost of land acquisition which was estimated at $4 million for a property that when fully developed would sell for less than $1.5 million at market rates. The Lawrence administration subsequently dropped the Manchester proposal and focused instead on using the URAP to support the expansion of J&L Steel on the South Side and in the Hazelwood neighborhood. At the same time, Allegheny Conference and county officials began considering other alternatives for creating a planned industrial district on a site where the "cost of removing buildings and rehousing people" would be less "prohibitive."[22]

Faced with the high cost of remaking urban neighborhoods and the trend "toward locations away from existing industrial centers [for] facilities and employment," metropolitan Pittsburgh's pro-growth leadership increasingly embraced the need for coordinated action to develop new suburban manufacturing sites. Responding to the perception that industrial development increasingly required a "highly organized and coordinated approach" on the regional level, in 1955 the Allegheny Conference collaborated with politicians from Allegheny, Beaver, Washington, and Westmoreland counties to form the nonprofit Regional Industrial Development Corporation (RIDC). Sponsors charged the RIDC with fostering a healthy business climate in the area through research and education, providing employers with assistance in obtaining low-interest loans for public and private sources, and acquiring and developing sites suitable for industrial employers. The group spent the next few years studying the Steel Valley's economy, included commissioning the landmark *Economic Study of the Pittsburgh Region*. However, a variety of factors including leadership problems and the absence of a clear mandate from its various sponsors caused the organization to drift during its first few years. As a result, a series of initial planning reports, including a 1959 study, *A Community of Interest Between the Pittsburgh Metropolitan Area and the Upper Ohio Valley*, that offered a rare argument for coordinating development across state boundaries, were filed and quickly forgotten.[23]

Frustration with the underperformance of the RIDC boiled over in 1961 when the region's sluggish recovery from an economic recession sparked a bitter and public disagreement between RIDC President Robert Downie and United Steelworkers President David McDonald, a member of the organization's board. Following Downie's resignation, the group obtained a new charter and under President Robert H. Ryan devoted its energies to developing the business parks that political leaders and the Allegheny Conference felt were "needed to rejuvenate the region's economy." With the pool of financial backers extended to local governments and labor unions, the organization eagerly sought local, state, and federal incentives and coordinated local participation in federal Area Redevelopment Administration and Manpower Development and Training programs. Ryan, a graduate of Harvard Business School who left his position as vice president of the Boston Development Authority to head RIDC, made clear his goal of growing new industries, especially the kinds that "didn't even exist 10 years ago . . . with two guys out of a research lab in a garage."[24]

While Ryan held open the possibility of developing downtown sites, his model was clearly that of the Route 128 Corridor outside Boston that, between 1950 and 1957 alone, had attracted nearly $100 million in capital investment for companies often related to technology from Harvard University and MIT. With this type of highway-oriented greenfield development as the centerpiece of its regional vision, the RIDC quickly struck a deal with the Allegheny County commissioners to acquire 700 acres of county owned property in suburban O'Hara Township. Between 1963 and 1969, the corporation invested over $28 million in public and private sector funds in converting the site into a planned industrial district that featured twenty buildings with employment for four thousand workers and accounted for a nearly $4 million increase in O'Hara Township's property tax valuation, the largest increase in the county. Visiting the site in 1968, *Post-Gazette* business editor Jack Markowitz drew a sharp contrast between the grimy "row of industrial buildings stretched along a railroad track" that featured prominently in the region's mill towns and the RIDC Industrial Park with its "trees, fields, hills, ravines, curving drives" and "elbow room." "While it might not exactly beckon a man back to nature barefoot," he crowed, it "doesn't insult the word "park." And it's filling up ahead of schedule." Based on this success with its first site, in 1971 RIDC established the 925-acre Thorn Hill Industrial Park on the border between Allegheny and Butler Counties near the intersection of the Turnpike and Interstate 79. By 1979, the two RIDC sites accounted for nearly 10,000 jobs.[25]

At the same time as RIDC was developing its own industrial parks, it also embarked on an aggressive program of coordinating efforts to finance new or growing enterprises through its Industrial Development Fund (IDF). During its early years, an ideological antipathy toward seeking government "concessions or subsidies" for private development among the RIDC's sponsors meant that by 1960 Pittsburgh was alone among the nation's thirty-five largest metropolitan areas in not forming any Small Business Investment Companies and the region had received less than half a percent of federal Small Business Administration loans. Under Ryan's leadership, the organization rapidly reversed this trend and by 1970 the IDF had made 170 loans totaling $16.8 million. Drawing favorable comparisons to Boston's celebrated Route 128 Corridor, Ryan pointed out that "Pittsburgh has an economic base . . . and pattern of binding private and public efforts." "The trick," he concluded, "is to tie these things together in the field of economic development."[26]

The focus on new and emerging sectors in RIDC's suburban industrial parks, combined with the industrial targeting of the IDF, represented a significant change in direction for the Allegheny Conference and the public-private partnership seeking to improve the region's sagging economy. As in Wheeling, Weirton, and the Steel Valley's other small cities, when Pittsburgh elites spoke of the need for industrial diversification in the 1940s and 1950s, they were calling for, as F. D. Hollinshed put it, "plants that can use the products of the basic industries" already in the region. Even in 1959, RIDC's planning reports connected the establishment of offices and research centers in Monroeville and the Airport Corridor to industrial plants built because of traditional advantages, such as salt deposits, lower cost power and water transportation, available labor supply, and access to major coal deposits. However, while the region's corporate leaders remained divided on how best to address the region's economic problems, during the 1960s the RIDC itself increasingly emphasized "a form of diversification that goes beyond the conventional meaning of the term." Here, where atomic power is harnessed for military and peaceful uses, one publication announced, "there is a widening chain reaction" that was "opening up un-dreamed-of fields where these scientific break-throughs are translated into established manufacturing techniques in such opposite fields as metallurgy and medicine." Of course, the facilities housing these emerging new fields, including Westinghouse's nuclear research center, were largely in highway-oriented suburbs.[27]

Reshaping Pittsburgh's image went hand in hand with this emphasis on economic growth in new sectors and again the region's suburban office and industrial parks played a prominent symbolic role. The first half of a 1964 RIDC promotional tract, for instance, largely reiterated the traditional "Pittsburgh Story" of smoky skies, urban renewal, and the Golden Triangle, but latter pages trumpeted its "well-planned open space industrial park" that offered an "attractive and economic environment with compatible neighbors, long-term values, and an all-inclusive service." Suburban industrial parks, the pamphlet concluded, represented the metropolitan community's way of demonstrating its "strong interest and assistance in aiding the growth of new and expanding companies." In the Airport Corridor, pro-growth boosters easily made this same type of connection between economic transformation and the modernist architecture of the Greater Pittsburgh Airport itself. "The spacious and striking terminal building is virtually a little city within itself," proclaimed the Allegheny Conference in 1956. It was also a popular attraction for sightseers and "the pride of Pittsburghers" with shops, services, and conveniences of all kinds, including a "spectacular" glass-enclosed dining room and nightclub overlooking the airfield."[28]

During the 1960s and 1970s, the Airport Corridor continued to attract new residents and employers connected to the expanding Greater Pittsburgh Airport. Allegheny Airlines, which was renamed USAir in 1979, grew to become one of the region's largest employers after the Allegheny Conference and the RIDC helped to establish aircraft maintenance facilities in the mid-1960s, and the airport gained international status in 1971. In 1979,

RIDC officials opened the third of its publicly subsidized industrial parks, RIDC Park West, just south of the airport along the Parkway. According to L. R. Love, an executive at energy and environmental consulting firm National Utility Service, one of the site's first tenants, the RIDC West Park site helped "combine our activities here making them more efficient." "Our work involves a lot of air travel" and employees could reach the airport "in a few minutes." According to Frank Brooks Robinson, Sr., who would later become RIDC's president, the opening of the new facility allowed the organization to become "financially self-sufficient," a goal set in the mid-1960s by Robert Ryan. By 1982, the three RIDC industrial parks provided nearly 6.5 million square feet of space for 185 different companies employing more than 16,000 people. If the Renaissance vision had originally emphasized urban employment and suburban living, by the early 1980s it was clear that highway-oriented development in areas that had been rural just decades earlier would play a key role in the public policy response to the decline of the region's traditional industries.[29]

"Parkway North"

On September 16, 1989, Pennsylvania governor Robert Casey joined a crowd of about five hundred dignitaries, reporters, and spectators standing on the newly completed Interstate 279 near its East Street Exit on Pittsburgh's North Side, to formally open the last two-mile section of a $440 million regional parkway that city leaders first envisioned more than fifty years earlier. Casey declared that the completion of the highway, known locally as the Parkway North, "would open the door to new economic growth for the city, for Allegheny County and for all of southwestern Pennsylvania." Like the east-west connections of the Penn-Lincoln Parkway, the city's public-private partnership had originally conceived of a northern parkway linking the Golden Triangle to the industrial markets of the Great Lakes and the Northeast. However, as delays mounted, the route's completion became increasingly associated with the continued growth of the booming North Hills suburbs, including Cranberry Township near the intersection of Interstate 79 and the Turnpike, at the expense of the urban neighborhoods through which it was built. A backlash against the "arrogance and destructiveness of public decisions" regarding the parkway helped launch a revolt against the Allegheny Conference and its political allies that by the late 1980s called into question the suburban strategy of public investment.[30]

Beginning in the 1920s, the rural area north of Pittsburgh between the Allegheny and Ohio Rivers increasingly attracted residents and employers economically connected to the city. The growth in Cranberry was an extension of postwar growth in Pittsburgh's suburban North Hills communities propelled by the improvement of McKnight Road in the late 1940s, a local highway project supported by the Allegheny Conference, as well as upgrades in the early 1950s to U.S. Route 19 between Pittsburgh and Butler County and the western extension of the Pennsylvania Turnpike. Between 1920 and 1950, 75,000 new residents had moved to North Hills communities from Fox Chapel and Sewickley, exclusive playgrounds of the rich, to "the far reaches" of Pine and Richland townships "where deer and trout once ruled unchallenged."[31]

Growth in the North Hills did not go unchallenged, with clashes between suburban development and older residents often associated with the area's thriving truck farms described by one Pittsburgh observer as "the greatest garden farming spot in Pennsylvania." The relatively flatter terrain to Pittsburgh's north and west meant that agriculture remained a more prominent part of the local economy with residents "conservative by nature" and "reluctant to spend money for modern conveniences." As late as 1951, for example, only 25 percent of Reserve Township had sewers despite the fact that it shared a border with Pittsburgh itself. Complicating matters was the fact that septic tanks were not reliable in the area due to clay and shale deposits, with the result that sewage often seeped to the surface and drained onto roads.[32]

Though farther away from the city, Cranberry experienced the same general pattern of transportation-driven development as the suburban North Hills communities. During the 1950s, the widening of U.S. Route 19 and extension of the Pennsylvania Turnpike to the Ohio state line situated Cranberry at the intersection of the main east-west and north-south routes in the North Hills, a position that was solidified in the early 1970s by the completion of Interstate 79. Population growth began in earnest in 1957 when Cleveland-based Dover Company began construction of its Fernway housing development offering ranch style homes on lots for $10,495. Other new housing developments soon followed, causing Cranberry's population to more than quadruple in just a decade. By the late 1960s, an increasing proportion of commuters into the city originated in Butler County, where the availability of "highly rural" land combined with "excellent location with regard to highways, existing and proposed" made Cranberry Township "a prime area for future development."[33]

The importance of Cranberry to the regional economic transformation envisioned by the Allegheny Conference and its political allies was made clear in November 1970, when Leonard Staisey, chairman of the Allegheny County Board of Commissioners, joined with his counterpart from Butler County in breaking ground for the second of the RIDC's industrial parks. The Thorn Hill Industrial Park was situated twenty miles northwest of Pittsburgh on the border between the two counties and the near the intersection of the Turnpike and Interstate 79. Hiram Milton, RIDC's president, highlighted what he called the "unusual action" of building "a major industrial park" across multiple political boundaries as "tangible evidence of regional cooperation." Like the other RIDC locations, the Thorn Hill site featured a large block of inexpensive land along "a triple highway network, with direct access to major U.S. markets in the East, Midwest, North, and South [as well as] Canadian markets via I-79 to Erie." Not only Allegheny and Butler Counties, Milton concluded, but also the state of Pennsylvania as a whole would share in the economic benefits of the "jobs and further diversification of the region's economic base" that would "flow from orderly planned development of this kind."[34]

The opening of Thorn Hill heralded a new development phase, as light manufacturing, research laboratories, and administrative offices provided an employment base, making Cranberry a place for workers as well as families. Over the next two decades, the development of the Parkway North, which would cut travel time to the Golden Triangle to less than a half hour, became increasingly connected to this suburban growth. Calls for a new highway through Pittsburgh's crowded North Side originated in the early 1950s with a state-funded study of commuter patterns between the North Hills and the Golden Triangle, then rising across the Allegheny River. In April 1954, the Pittsburgh City Planning Commission and Pittsburgh Regional Planning Association published a call for redevelopment of the city's North Side that included plans for a "high density highway" connecting to the suburbs. The highway would require the relocation of hundreds of residents living in the narrow and densely settled East Street Valley. Over the next decade, state officials wrangled with local residents and businesses over various alignments for the project, with state officials supporting an alignment along the hillside and local officials supporting an alignment on the valley floor.[35]

The Parkway North proposal emerged out of the development model of the Pittsburgh Renaissance, with municipal officials and the Allegheny Conference anticipating a route that would link employers in the revitalized downtown with suburban residential areas and then to the national highway system. The 1954 *North Side Study* envisioned an enormous riverfront stadium along the Allegheny and a new mixed-use planned district to be known as Allegheny Center. Between 1959 and 1962, the URAP began demolishing more than 500 buildings to make way for Allegheny Center, a project trumpeted by the RIDC as "a new business community" created on some "78 blighted acres," with offices, shops, and stores as well as apartments and private dwellings in "park-like settings." In 1962, the Conference, the city of Pittsburgh, and Allegheny County reached an agreement on a location for a new sports stadium on the North Side that was occupied by deteriorating warehouses and railroad tracks as well as sixty-three families. By 1965, the URAP had used a federal urban renewal grant of $14,400,000 as well as funds from the city and county to clear the area.[36]

Even as the lower North Side neighborhoods across from the Golden Triangle were cleared to make way for Allegheny Center and Three Rivers Stadium, the city's northern suburbs continued to attract new population growth. Residents of the North Hills, especially the thousands of drivers who had to "sweat it out on East Street getting from their homes in the northern suburbs into the city," paid close attention to plans for the Parkway North. As McKnight Road and other local roads became increasingly congested, local officials increasingly saw construction of the new highway as the key to the future of their communities. "Without the expressway," Allegheny County transportation coordinator David Wooster declared, "the North Hills will not develop properly." However, in July 1963, a tumultuous public hearing on the proposed alignment for the Parkway North forced state officials to return to the drawing board, and it was not until 1967 that the lower route through the East Street Valley itself received final approval.[37]

When state officials began acquiring properties in early 1970, highway development stalled once again as North Side residents demanded higher payments than state officials offered. Then, changes to the way payments were calculated caused so much confusion that, in February 1972, Pennsylvania Governor Milton Shapp placed a year-long moratorium on local right-of-way acquisitions. Even after work resumed, the Parkway North continued to attract criticism from North Siders in the path of the highway, some of whom formed a citizens group called Highway Emergency and

Relocation Team (HEART). "Prices are very low," declared one HEART spokesman. "The average payment is about $8,000 and what the hell kind of home can you buy with that today." Residents were also concerned with the planned eight-lane expressway that when pushed through the narrow confines of the East Street Valley would not leave room for local service roads across and adjacent to the highway, effectively destroying the viability of entire neighborhoods. "We have reservations about ever taking on something like this again," confessed state highway official Fred DePasquale in 1971. "There is just no easy way to move that many people around."[38]

The election of Pete Flaherty as Pittsburgh's mayor in 1969 effectively ended the strong public-private partnership at the core of the Pittsburgh Renaissance and further complicated the development of the Parkway North. Although the city of Pittsburgh was one of the highway's chief sponsors, with state and local planners coordinating efforts throughout the 1950s and 1960s, the mayor publicly withdrew his support for the project declaring that the highway was not needed for the city's economic progress. In June 1975, Flaherty and state officials finally reached an agreement on a revised proposal for a six-lane highway with a two-lane median strip. Even with the city's backing, however, residents continued to fight state officials over compensation and road alignment, including a bitter struggle, supported by the new Pittsburgh History and Landmarks Foundation, to save the hundred-year-old St. Boniface Catholic Church. Finally, despite the "high priority" placed on the parkway, highway projects throughout the state ground to a halt in the late 1970s as Pennsylvania officials struggled to deal with a combination of inflation and the economic collapse of the steel industry.[39]

As a result, actual construction of the highway did not begin until 1982, with Pennsylvania governor Dick Thornburgh and local officials turning over the ceremonial first spades of dirt at a June ceremony attended by 2,000 people. The Pittsburgh Chamber of Commerce provided fireworks and gifts at the event, including free tickets to Pirates baseball games at Three Rivers Stadium. While the thirty-year battle raged over the highway, the East Street Valley and the lower North Side continued to lose population with highway development and renewal projects exacerbating the neighborhood deterioration prompting movement to the North Hills and other suburban areas. While remaining upbeat, Pittsburgh mayor Richard Caliguiri lamented that "we removed an entire community from the East Street Valley." Similarly Allegheny County Commissioner Tom Foerster, himself a resident of the North Side, cautioned attendees to not forget those people who suffered "the trauma of being forced to move from their homes." On the other hand, while Thornburgh's speech emphasized the intent of the highway to "create a better economic climate" and "increase job opportunities," he also acknowledged that it would "make it easier to commute in and out of Pittsburgh from the North Side and North Hills."[40]

Between the 1950s when the Parkway North project began and its completion in 1989, the focus of regional economic growth had shifted firmly from the industrialized river valleys to the hilltop suburbs opened up by new highways. Growth in the North Hills did slow during the late 1970s and early 1980s, reflecting the economic decline of metropolitan Pittsburgh as well as the entire state of Pennsylvania. While other parts of the region continued to languish following the collapse of the steel industry in the mid-1980s, however, the area underwent a new housing boom as the completion of each stage of the Parkway North provided quicker access to the city. In 1988 local officials issued nearly 850 permits for single-home construction with a value of $144 million in the North Hills and Cranberry during a year when there were only about two thousand new housing starts in all of Allegheny County. Further, the 1,247 total housing units sold in the North Hills (not including Cranberry) that year had an average value nearly twice that of the rest of the county. Ramblewood, a typical North Hills subdivision near I-79, was cleared in 1987 and soon contained a hundred homes ranging from $250,000 to $275,000.[41]

Perhaps no other outlying community benefited as much from the new highway as Cranberry. The community's population nearly doubled during the 1980s, from 11,000 to 19,000, and during the early 1990s the township recorded five times the regional average for annual home construction. "Half-acre lots which sold five years ago for $30,000 today go for $50,000," reported one builder in 1989, with a local official subsequently likening new residential construction to a "Wild West Stampede." Further, the new arrivals were among those most desired by developers and local boosters—overwhelmingly middle- and upper-middle-class whites—and raised the area's median household income by 14 percent to $40,000. "The good-life seekers, particularly young first-time home buyers and crowd-weary Pittsburghers, are flocking here for a change of life-style," gushed a 1992 article in the *New York Times*. "Tired of the traffic and long lines for tennis courts and tables at restaurants, they have discovered a retreat that is closer, cheaper and quieter than the old steel city."[42]

Businesses, too, flocked to Cranberry drawn by a combination of low taxes, available land, and excellent highway connections. When the RIDC broke ground for its Thorn Hill Industrial Park in 1971, officials argued that the suburban industrial parks generated vital new development for the region overall "at a time when no private developers were interested in the locations." By the early 1980s, the three RIDC industrial parks included 124 buildings that accounted for $250 million in capital investment and served as models for extensive private development of nearby sites. In 1984, for example, work began on the Cranberry Corporate Center, a $70 million dollar complex centered on a 42,000 square foot "warehouse/office incubator" along with residential condominiums. "We're selling Cranberry Township," declared developer Richard Hartung. "The project will be a city in itself."[43]

By the time the Parkway North opened in 1989, Pittsburgh's public-private partnership could point to booming peripheral communities, such as Monroeville, the Airport Corridor, and Cranberry, as successful examples of the highway-oriented strategy of economic transformation. Even as other parts of the Steel Valley struggled to stem economic decline and population loss, some suburban residents worried about the consequences of their community's rapid growth. Officials portrayed Monroeville's 1984 Master Plan as balancing "the continuing push for commercial growth against go-slow pleas for some peace and quiet." Similarly, as early as 1962, planners in Cranberry warned that residential and commercial growth coupled with a low-density residential pattern adopted to maintain a "spacious, semi-rural character" was creating environmental and other problems. Despite passage of zoning regulations in 1972, over the next twenty years "Cranberry" became "a shorthand reference" to everything Pittsburghers "hate about urban sprawl." Significantly, some of the township's greatest growth occurred as the region overall was hemorrhaging population in the wake of the steel industry's collapse.[44]

More significantly to the public-private partnership seeking to support Pittsburgh's overall economic recovery, suburban growth prompted a political backlash against a development model that seemed to create a region of "haves and have nots." In 1992, Tom Murphy, a Democratic state representative from the North Side, launched a series of legislative hearings focused on the RIDC's policy of using public subsidies to offer private companies land at below market rates in lucrative suburban markets. While

Frank Brooks Robinson, RIDC's president, argued that he did not try to "convince companies to relocate from one county or region in our service area to another," Murphy declared that RIDC had subsidized the move to the suburbs of companies "with no intention of leaving the region." This growing disenchantment with the suburban model of regional development grew out of a broader rebellion against the policies of the Allegheny Conference and its political allies that emerged in the mid-1960s. Murphy, who would go on to serve as Pittsburgh mayor from 1994 to 2006, got his start as a neighborhood organizer on the North Side just as the Parkway North was decimating urban neighborhoods. This revolt against the Renaissance would have wide-ranging consequences that fractured the relationships among Pittsburgh's corporate and political elite.[45]

CHAPTER 7

No Development Beyond This Point

One origin of the complex story of the neighborhood revolt against the Pittsburgh Renaissance can be found in 1960 on the hillside overlooking the $22 million Civic Arena under construction just east of the Golden Triangle. With its ultramodern design and signature retractable roof, the arena was to be the first stage of a planned "Center for the Arts" that would extend through the upper elevations of the working-class Hill District. Construction on the Hill had required destruction of 1,300 buildings and removal of 8,000 residents, mostly African American. In response to growing discontent over the project's proposed expansion, a group led by James McCoy, a civil rights officer with the United Steelworkers union who subsequently founded the United Negro Protest Committee (UNPC), and local business owner Frankie Pace, an activist with the Urban League and Pittsburgh NAACP, erected a large billboard at Centre Avenue and Crawford Street proclaiming "No Development Beyond This Point." "That billboard gave hope to those of us who had watched the demise of the Lower Hill," one local resident recalled. "We had businesses and homes and we wouldn't give them up."[1]

Opposition from black residents in the Hill District was part of a larger challenge to the Allegheny Conference's vision for the city that stalled the Renaissance program by the late 1960s. Whether in the creation of the Regional Industrial Development Corporation (RIDC) suburban industrial parks or the transformation of the Point into Gateway Center and Point State Park, metropolitan Pittsburgh's public-private partnerships focused on erasing the nineteenth-century industrial city in favor of modernist, automobile-oriented communities. Even as boosters promoted the Renaissance as a model for downtown development, the city became a particular target of critics, such as New York activist Jane Jacobs, who condemned the Golden Triangle in 1958 as a lifeless "ersatz suburb." Neighborhood groups focusing on renovation rather than demolition gained ground in the wake of increasing national criticism of large-scale urban renewal. Further, federal policies requiring local participation and feedback on a range of issues from urban renewal and highway construction to the preservation of historic structures and environmental protection complicated the closed-door decision-making that had occurred between the Allegheny Conference and its allies in municipal government. As the underlying contradictions of the Renaissance became more apparent, the strong political coalition necessary for urban renewal became increasingly difficult to maintain even as federal support for cities began to wane in the 1970s.[2]

In this context, metropolitan Pittsburgh became a laboratory for public policy experimentation that would lay the pragmatic foundations on the municipal level for what would later be termed neoliberalism. The election of Peter Flaherty as mayor in 1969 was generally seen as a retreat from the massive urban renewal of the Renaissance. Even so, the willingness of city officials to work with nonprofit organizations such as the Allegheny Council to Improve Our Neighborhoods ACTION-Housing and the Pittsburgh History and Landmarks Foundation (Landmarks) offered opportunities for new public-private partnerships based on a nascent vision of community revitalization through rehabilitation rather than the removal of existing infrastructure. On the other hand, a coalition of businessmen and community activists succeeded in saving downtown Wheeling from the wrecking ball in the early 1970s through grassroots mobilization, but they failed to develop an effective alternative vision for urban revitalization. This left the city without the institutional capacity or political will to respond in a meaningful way to the economic turmoil of the 1980s. As a result, the stage was set for an increasing divide between the trajectories of Pittsburgh and the Steel Valley's other industrial communities.

From Renaissance to Revolt

The strong public-private partnership at the heart of the Pittsburgh Renaissance proved difficult to maintain over time. In 1958, David Lawrence was elected Pennsylvania governor and soon named Park Martin, the Allegheny

Conference's executive director, as his secretary of highways. At first, these moves further strengthened ties with Harrisburg, ensuring a smooth flow of highway and urban development to the city. However, the departure of key figures combined with retirements among public officials and business leaders weakened personal relationships as the Renaissance partnership began to give way to tensions over specific policies. Chief among these was a battle over a new sports stadium planned for the North Side directly across the Allegheny River from the Golden Triangle. Following years of negotiations and the painstaking assembly of local, state, and federal development funds, in January 1963 Edward Magee, Martin's successor as the conference's executive director, unveiled a plan received enthusiastically by city officials and Pittsburgh newspapers to finance the stadium. After a week of silence, however, Allegheny County officials publicly rejected the plan, with one of the commissioners turning it into a divisive campaign issue. While Pittsburgh mayor Joseph Barr was able to salvage the project, the unexpected controversy set in motion a series of delays that left the stadium site an empty lot for nearly a decade.[3]

The proliferation of administrative boundaries, political provincialism, and a lack of business leaders with the clout and vision of an R. K. Mellon meant that coalitions were even harder to maintain outside the central city. Even as increasing federal subsidies offered new opportunities for highway construction and urban redevelopment, the involvement of new federal agencies further complicated decision-making by introducing new bureaucracies as well as mandates for regional comprehensive planning and public involvement in decision-making. Beginning in 1962, federal highway funding required states and local governments to implement a "cooperative continuing comprehensive" planning process, but "really didn't have a history of an integrated area," recalled one Steubenville official, with each municipality pushing "their own kind of agenda whenever they could." Rivalry at the state and federal levels mirrored competition among local leaders, with the result that important projects often bogged down in jurisdictional disputes between organizations seeking to maintain hegemony over the spheres of influence. In southeastern Ohio, for example, Wayne L. Hays was a notorious Democratic partisan with particular animosity toward Wheeling's Arch Moore, Jr., his Republican counterpart in the House of Representatives who was elected governor in 1968. On being informed that the joint metropolitan planning commission responsible for the area had decided to fund a highway study he previously supported,

Hays reportedly stood up, struck the table with his fist, and with the entire room staring at him, declared, "God damn they will. That organization is controlled by West Virginia and Governor Moore."[4]

In addition to conflicts among political and economic leaders, by the early 1960s new neighborhood groups from outside the region's traditional power structure began to question some of the basic assumptions that drove Allegheny Conference-backed initiatives. Public support hinged on the perception that the benefits of the Renaissance outweighed the sacrifices residents were being asked to make in the form of taxes, forced relocations, and neighborhood upheaval. The increasing danger, at least from the perspective of urban boosters, was that disaffected local groups might find common cause with nonlocal government agencies and institutions on the basis of growing nationwide movements, such as environmental protection, civil rights, or historic preservation. Smoke control, for example, was one of the earliest and greatest success stories of the Renaissance. However, residents of the industrialized river valleys who had not shared equally in the trend toward cleaner skies increasingly questioned the volunteerist model in which industrial polluters had significant input into crafting new regulations. In 1959 a grassroots organization, Allegheny County Citizens Against Air Pollution presented county commissioners more than seven hundred letters protesting the weak provisions of a proposed pollution ordinance. While the group had little impact on public policy at the time, over the next decade a series of updates to the federal Clean Air Act removed much of the power to enforce air pollution regulations from local control and thus limited the influence of industries. This change in national attitudes was reflected in Pittsburgh with the formation in 1969 of the activist organization Group Against Smog and Pollution.[5]

Even more pressing than neighborhood concerns over environmental issues, however, was the problem of housing. Despite the construction of some public housing and the beginning of overall population decline in the city, Pittsburgh's housing shortage became so critical that it imperiled the future of the Renaissance itself. In 1957, Allegheny Conference and Pittsburgh officials supported the formation of the nonprofit ACTION-Housing to sponsor new and rehabilitated homes for "minority, aged, and lower-middle-income residents" with incomes above the public housing level. "It is the class of residential property," declared one report, "which is sorely needed for relocating the families which must be moved as a result of redevelopment projects." In its first decade, ACTION-Housing developed a program for channeling funds from the Mellon Foundations and other Pittsburgh charities into sponsorship of new and rehabilitated housing, neighborhood citizen organizations, and research. Though a private organization run according to business principles, following the passage of the 1964 Economic Opportunity Act, ACTION-Housing was also contracted by the city's Mayor's Committee on Human Resources to develop a cooperative home improvement program "designed to upgrade houses of low-income families." In 1966, a pilot program launched in the Hill District was extended to other neighborhoods.[6]

While the lack of decent housing for low and moderate-income residents was an issue that transcended race, racial prejudice among both housing officials and white residents placed African Americans in a particularly vulnerable position. In 1967, for example, a white couple was quoted a price of $87 to rent a home on Steubenville's west end, recalled community activist Rose Marie Schick. But when the owner's next inquiry came from a black couple, "it had jumped to more than $200." Similarly, while more than half the 263 white families displaced by the Lower Hill Renewal purchased homes in newer residential areas on Pittsburgh's South Side or suburban South Hills, only 6 percent of the 899 black families could purchase homes, all in the increasingly black Upper Hill or East End neighborhoods. At the same time, a series of high-profile protests in Pittsburgh by the UNPC, including a landmark demonstration at Duquesne Light with some 5,000 pickets, also drew attention to job discrimination limiting both white- and blue-collar employment for black residents. Within a context of regional economic stagnation, African Americans were doubly disadvantaged as they were generally stuck in the dirtiest, most dangerous, and lowest paying industrial jobs, and often barred entirely from higher-paying service sector and management employment. Despite "definite signs of progress" for African Americans in some areas, in 1966 the Mayor's Commission on Human Relations concluded that "more Negroes are worse off educationally, economically, and socially" than they had been a decade earlier.[7]

Tensions between race and urban renewal in metropolitan Pittsburgh were, of course, linked to broader national developments. The availability of federal funds for infrastructure development increased rapidly throughout the 1960s by way of a host of War on Poverty, Great Society, and other programs including the Appalachian Regional Commission. Local leaders met the creation of urban and economic programs with a great deal of enthusiasm, and dozens of local and regional groups formed to take advantage of development funds between 1964 and 1968. As precondition for federal aid, however, civic leaders had to meet requirements for citizen participation in decision-making, a process that was increasingly at odds with the top-down approach to urban renewal adopted by the city's Renaissance partnership. Beginning in 1958, ACTION-Housing contracted with the Mayor's Committee on Human Resources—the designated Community Action Program agency under the Economic Opportunity Act—to set up citizen neighborhood councils in areas slated for urban renewal and similar groups in other areas with demographics that suggested future deterioration.[8]

While Allegheny Conference and municipal officials viewed these new neighborhood organizations as a forum for gaining support for projects they supported, the councils tapped into growing frustration over the negative consequences of urban renewal. Initially, many African Americans saw in the Renaissance an opportunity for improving deteriorating neighborhoods and providing better public housing for low-income residents. In 1960, the city's black newspaper, the *Pittsburgh Courier* praised the Renaissance for "redevelopment of the now famous Hill District" and boasted of the list of well-known performers appearing at the new Civic Arena. However, as implementation of the second phase of the planned "Center for the Arts" began in 1961, the tensions inherent in building a lavish symphony hall and luxury apartments next to a low-income African American neighborhood increasingly threatened to derail the project.[9]

Continuing discrimination and a high incidence of poverty served to create racialized ghettos in the remaining portion of the Hill District as well as other older urban areas such as East Liberty, Homewood-Brushton, and Manchester on the North Side. Through the end of the 1950s, the city's white dominated newspapers continued to advertise properties as "for colored," while real estate agents in the suburban communities touted by the Allegheny Conference as symbols of the region's progress simply refused to show homes to African Americans. Among residents displaced on the Upper Hill, 78 percent of those in private housing rented substandard or mediocre housing at "comparatively high" prices. At the same time, low-income families, thrust out of the Lower Hill, found their way to Homewood "because they were not wanted elsewhere," one report concluded in 1958. Because they could not rent houses in other areas, many of those displaced by urban renewal were forced to buy in ghettoizing neighborhoods at inflated prices with as many as four or five families "cramped into a one-family house." Others turned to new public housing projects, which, while often representing material improvement, could not replace lost communities and, over time, increased residential segregation. By 1960 Pittsburgh had the worst housing conditions for blacks among the nation's fourteen largest cities.[10]

The Renaissance vision of the Golden Triangle as the corporate and cultural centerpiece of a broader regional transformation had little room for displaced African Americans, who were prevented by racial discrimination from enjoying the economic benefits promised by the city's public-private partnership. As a result, by 1963 the *Pittsburgh Courier* was charging the city's planning department with "brainwashing" the community in an attempt to forcibly relocate residents to make room for middle and upper income apartments and townhouses. While professional planners in city government continually repeated that "the Hill District will remain residential in character," *Courier* reporter George E. Barbour declared: "Unless there's a revolutionary change in job opportunities for Negroes, you can be certain there will be few of the 55,000 people in the area remaining when renewal [is] completed." Civil rights activists and residents were particularly galled at the lack of African Americans hired to work on renewal projects taking place in what had been predominantly black neighborhoods. In August 1965 police arrested eleven civil rights pickets outside the Civic Arena on charges ranging from disorderly conduct to inciting a riot and resisting arrest. Militant residents of the Hill labeled Crawford Street "the end of the line" and a UNPC official declared, "I swear to God that you will be sorry if any more of the Lower Hill is devoted to construction of housing for the affluent society."[11]

In addition to drawing inspiration from the national drive for civil rights, the protest movement in the Hill District was also part of a broader reorientation in American municipal politics that resulted in the creation of new types of neighborhood organizations, particularly community development corporations (CDCs). As a national phenomenon, CDCs evolved out of the concern over increasing tensions in inner cities caused by urban renewal, rural-urban migration of African Americans, and efforts of many whites to segregate African Americans from their neighborhoods. Due to the Steel Valley's particular landscape and history, the region developed a pattern of particularly strong neighborhood identification; Pittsburgh, alone, contained more than ninety distinct neighborhoods. A tradition of machine politics, often organized around sporting clubs and ethnic societies, also provided the capacity for mobilizing residents around issues of neighborhood control. In the Hill District, for example, forty local groups combined in early 1963 to form the Citizens Committee for Hill District Renewal, with Walt Worthington, secretary of the Hill District Community Council, declaring, "urban renewal requires a complete new orientation between citizens and government."[12]

The increasing role of corporate and family foundations in guiding neighborhood renewal formed a key part of this policy reorientation from the top-down decision-making of the Renaissance partnership to the neoliberal urbanism that would take shape in the 1980s. Once again, Pittsburgh, where Andrew Carnegie had initiated modern philanthropy in the 1890s with his articulation of "The Gospel of Wealth," already featured an impressive array of well-financed foundations associated with the fortunes accumulated by the Mellon and Heinz families as well as other industrial age elites deeply engaged with the redevelopment programs of the Renaissance. As federal funding for urban renewal peaked under the Johnson administration's Great Society initiatives, the city provided fertile ground for experimentation in nongovernmental, not-for-profit community development. With funding from the Buhl Foundation, in 1960 ACTION-Housing undertook a pilot project in neighborhood self-help in the predominantly African American Homewood-Brushton neighborhood. A few years later, the Ford Foundation provided matching funds for a five-year demonstration program designed to connect local residents and neighborhood groups with social agencies and the technical resources of the city's universities. While the results of these early efforts remained ambiguous, by 1970 this new type of philanthropic "flexibility" that emphasized provision of seed money to leverage other public and private dollars formed an increasing part of the activities of the city's foundations. "One measure of a grant's effectiveness," wrote the Reverend Dr. Alfred W. Wishart, Jr., director of the Pittsburgh Foundation, established in 1945 along with the Renaissance itself, "is its catalytic potential."[13]

This shift in emphasis coincided with the emergence of a national movement for building rehabilitation based on the principles of historic preservation, a convergence that would have profound repercussions for the nascent partnership between Pittsburgh's neighborhood organizations and its foundations. In the face of increasing opposition to the wholesale destruction of urban neighborhoods, in 1964 city planners and Mayor Barr softened the Renaissance approach of erasing the nineteenth-century urban

FIGURE 10. Billboard at Crawford Street near intersection of Centre Avenue, Hill District, 1969. The billboard's sponsors are listed as the Citizens Committee for Hill District Renewal, the National Association for the Advancement of Colored People, the Martin Luther King-inspired Poor People's Campaign, and local organizers associated with the federal Model Cities program. Photograph by Charles "Teenie" Harris. Carnegie Museum of Art, Pittsburgh: Heinz Family Fund, 2001.35.9463.

form and began emphasizing links to new federal anti-poverty programs and opportunities for rehabilitating rather than razing existing structures. At the time, however, municipal officials and the elites of the Allegheny Conference could not come to an agreement with the neighborhood activists of the Hill District Community Council over how best to reconcile the Renaissance with these two competing visions of the community. The racialized unrest following the assassination of Martin Luther King, Jr., in April 1968, while relatively mild compared to those in other cities, nevertheless spelled the end of the Center for the Arts in the Hill District. As a herald of what was to come, the Heinz Endowments, which had been a key backer of building a new home for the Pittsburgh Symphony adjacent to the Civic Arena, instead purchased a dilapidated theater near the Golden Triangle. When the renovated and renamed Heinz Hall opened in 1971, it would serve as the foundation for a new Cultural District that linked downtown offices to the Allegheny River. On the other hand, aside from sporadic public housing construction in the Crawford-Roberts area, much of the district intended for urban renewal remained a sea of parking lots, empty land, and vacant buildings for more than three decades.[14]

Despite concessions to neighborhood groups made by the city's public-private coalition, in 1969 support from dissatisfied residents allowed "maverick" Pittsburgh council member Peter Flaherty to win election as mayor. During his tenure from 1970 to 1977, when he was named deputy attorney general by President Carter, Flaherty severed the institutional links between city hall and the Allegheny Conference, directed a larger portion of urban development funding to neighborhoods outside the Golden Triangle, and dramatically cut the municipal spending necessary to maintain a massive urban redevelopment program. While new public and private projects were certainly completed in the city during his administration, including Three Rivers Stadium (1970) and Point State Park (1974), Flaherty's program of fiscal conservatism put the brakes on a number of high profile initiatives, most notably an experimental mass transit system called Skybus that advocates hoped would serve as the basis for a new manufacturing sector. On the other hand, the Flaherty administration created a new Community Planning Division in the Planning Department and initiated budgetary changes that firmly established neighborhood organizations as pillars of city government. By taking the initiative in including not just the poor, often African American neighborhoods mandated by federal programs, Flaherty also helped moderate the resentment that had emerged among white ethnics left out of Community Action and Model Cities programs. Actions such as his (temporary) withdrawal of support for the Parkway North when North Side residents complained about their treatment at the hands of state officials angered leaders of the Renaissance partnership even as it endeared him to voters who returned him to office in 1973 as the candidate for both the Republican and Democratic tickets.[15]

Flaherty's cost-cutting measures, reduction of public sector jobs, and devolution of some municipal functions to community-based organizations set the standard for a new wave of fiscal populism among liberal Democratic mayors. The backlash against postwar urban renewal in the late 1960s that halted construction of the Center for the Arts coincided with a leveling off of federal funding as well as decreased interest in social responsibility among corporate leaders, a combination that radically altered the landscape of urban decision-making in the region. While specific issues differed across the various communities in metropolitan Pittsburgh, residents and local leaders alike were forced to confront these national trends against a backdrop of overall economic decline. For supporters of renewal projects, these broader problems added impetus to their efforts, which resulted in even more sweeping visions of raze-and-rebuild revitalization. For others, however, the price of urban renewal was too great, with resistance to increasingly wide-ranging initiatives springing up even among those who supported the overall goal of modernizing urban infrastructure. The contrasting trajectories of Pittsburgh's North Side and downtown Wheeling reflect a range of possible outcomes for Steel Valley communities struggling to make sense of the changing social and political contexts of the 1970s.

Contesting the "New Urban Order"

Casual readers of the August 1966 issue of the architectural journal *Charette* might easily confuse the volume with one of the many booster publications released at about the same time extolling the successes of the "Pittsburgh Story." The striking cover featured "the dramatic barrel vault roof" of the Allegheny Center Mall, which was slated to open in the heart of the city's North Side later that year. A host of advertisements for companies involved in the redevelopment project followed inside, along with a description of the site's advanced heating and cooling system and an announcement that its chief architect, Dahlen K. Ritchey, had just been elected a Fellow of the American Institute of Architects. The centerpiece of the issue was an essay by the journal's editor, James D. Van Trump, entitled "A Document of the New Urban Order," which provided a background of Allegheny Center renewal and praised the "classical openness and breadth" of the mall's "great central space" with "its aluminum vaults" recalling distantly the "Roman Baths of Caracalla." "As we stand on the plaza looking toward the old center of Allegheny," the article concluded, it is "as if the new city were, by means of some invisible giant, being moved in over the old."[16]

Despite an obvious wistfulness for the "old image of the Victorian city," Van Trump's article betrayed little of the emerging battle over the Pittsburgh Renaissance in which he and *Charette* publisher Arthur P. Ziegler, Jr., played a significant role. Faced with the impending demolition of much of the North Side to make way for the Parkway North, a new stadium, and other forms of urban renewal, in 1964 the two architectural enthusiasts along with their supporters formed the Pittsburgh History and Landmarks Foundation (Landmarks) to advocate for renovation rather than removal of historic structures. Indeed, an editorial by Ziegler in the same issue of *Charette* drew attention to private interests "undertaking a restoration program on the City's North Side," a clear reference to Landmarks' early projects in the Manchester and Mexican War Streets neighborhoods. In the same month as *Charette* highlighted the opening of Allegheny Center, the second issue of Landmarks' newsletter reprinted a letter to the *Pittsburgh Press* lambasting the Renaissance program for being "too much involved with tearing down, building and relegating the labor and money investment of the past to the dump heap." This vision of "blending of the old and the new" as the basis for urban renewal coupled with the creation of new institutions laid a foundation for the powerful neoliberal partnerships that would emerge on the municipal level in the 1980s.[17]

As with the rest of the region's older communities, Pittsburgh's North Side grew increasingly dilapidated during the first half of the twentieth century. While it continued to "faithfully serve" North Side residents, one report declared, the central business district's economic importance was "drastically reduced," its "physical beauty badly scarred," and its "future seriously threatened." In 1951, the Pittsburgh Regional Planning Association began discussions with the North Side Chamber of Commerce and the City Planning Commission on the need for a survey to assess conditions as a foundation for urban renewal. The resulting recommendations of the 1954 *North Side Study* followed in the same trajectory as the Golden Triangle then beginning to rise across the river, with planners calling for the razing of large swaths of the nineteenth-century urban fabric to create their vision of the modern, automobile-friendly city.[18]

The study called for a planned industrial district and expanded state highway to be cleared along the Ohio River to the west, while the Parkway North would connect the suburban North Hills to downtown providing an expanded customer base for an enclosed regional shopping center that would replace the central business district. The authors also suggested that new garden apartments should replace deteriorating residential neighborhoods and soon a large area along the Allegheny River was chosen as the site for what would later be Three Rivers Stadium. A stadium on the North Side would complement the development of Point Park and the Golden

Triangle across the Allegheny River by clearing out "rundown commercial and residential property," the *Pittsburgh Post-Gazette* declared. "Traffic would pour off the new Fort Duquesne Bridge into another redeveloped area of the city."[19]

Advocates made little progress implementing this sweeping vision of urban redevelopment until 1958, however, when the closure of the iconic Boggs & Buhl in the heart of old Allegheny City shocked political and business leaders into action. In 1908, store founders Russell Boggs and Henry Buhl had underwritten the construction of a new railroad line into Pittsburgh's northern suburbs to quickly bring both farm goods and rural residents to their North Side emporium. Fifty years later, the explosive growth of the North Hills meant an increasing loss of customers to highway-oriented suburban sites, such as the Northway Shopping Center (1953) that reopened in 1962 as the state's first indoor mall. Consequently, while the Allegheny Center proposal included plans for office and apartment buildings, its centerpiece was an enormous enclosed mall patterned on the "so-called regional suburban shopping center." Indeed, the expected continuation of population decline on the North Side meant that planners projected that most shoppers would be coming from new residential areas on the edge of the city and from the North Hills suburbs. As a result, though less than half the current customer base reached the district by car, planners sought to replace the existing neighborhood with a facility designed for patrons who "prefer to use their automobile for shopping trip transportation."[20]

Pittsburgh City Council advanced $112,500 to finance planning studies for the Allegheny Center area and, after certifying the area as blighted, the Urban Redevelopment Authority began the process of acquiring and demolishing properties in 1961. While the *North Side Study* suggested the rehabilitation of significant portions of the site, the final URAP plan called for the almost total demolition of existing properties and development of new residential and commercial facilities "in open landscaped surroundings." The suburban framework for this new urban form was emphasized in the ways in which "obsolete, inefficient and scattered" commercial buildings were to be razed and the uses relocated in "a well-balanced, integrated and esthetically attractive shopping center" with underground parking directly beneath. Similarly, the project's proposed town homes and apartment buildings were to be oriented toward upper middle income families, working in the Golden Triangle, who were "presently harassed with long drives to and from work."[21]

Even before the URAP broke ground, the publication of the *North Side Study* created a common perception among homeowners that their properties would soon be taken by eminent domain, resulting in an unwillingness to make repairs, plummeting real estate values, and, for those who could afford it, an exodus to the suburbs. All told, Allegheny Center resulted in the demolition of more than five hundred buildings and the forced relocation of over five hundred largely low-income families. As land acquisition began, city officials also had their eyes on several other redevelopment areas on the North Side. Work began in 1968 on the new Three Rivers Stadium that displaced seventy families along the Allegheny River. At the same time, state officials were clearing land and more than 1,000 families in the Manchester neighborhood for Ohio River Boulevard. Over 250 acres of mixed-use buildings west of the highway were slated for "total conversion" that would be suitable for industrial expansion as soon as "customers for the cleared land are mobilized."[22]

This was the dismal scene encountered by architectural enthusiasts Arthur Ziegler, Jr., and James Van Trump during a walk along Liverpool Street in Manchester in early 1964. Though just east of the planned industrial district and a few blocks west of Allegheny Center, the residents of Liverpool Street indicated they saw no positive connection between the adjacent urban renewal areas and the quality of their daily lives. Echoing the sentiment of protesters in the Hill District, "they unanimously and justifiably" scorned city departments they felt were ignoring their existence. The redevelopment model adopted by the Allegheny Conference and its allies in city government dismissed much of the North Side as "an unplanned conglomeration" of blighted residential and commercial buildings. But Ziegler and Van Trump argued that Liverpool Street's collection of dilapidated homes constituted, "in its own solid bourgeois way," the finest intact Victorian neighborhood remaining in Pittsburgh. "The clearing, redesigning and rebuilding of the central section of Old Allegheny," they declared, required a closer look at the "ever-widening rings of urban blight" that would surround Allegheny Center's new urban core. "The past," they concluded, "*must* have a place in the total picture of the city."[23]

In forming the Pittsburgh History and Landmarks Foundation, Ziegler and Van Trump did not dismiss entirely the dominant model of urban renewal, admitting the demolition and "redesigning of decayed urban neighborhoods" was "often mandatory if the cityscape is not to dissolve into chaos." But, they declared, buildings or areas "especially representative of the past history of the city" should be rehabilitated rather than razed to provide a sense of authentic community for citizens who were so often "shunted rapidly from one new quarter to another without any clear sense of where he is." Seen within the context of Allegheny Center, this criticism was clearly aimed at the postwar redevelopment vision of creating spatially segregated, functionally divided districts within the modern city by erasing the nineteenth-century urban form. "Civic-minded citizens of Pittsburgh," Van Trump concluded, "must come to grips with the problem of destruction or preservation in a day in which much of the city as we have known it is vanishing around us."[24]

The nascent historic preservation movement in Pittsburgh walked a fine line in criticizing the direction of large-scale urban renewal even as Landmarks sought out the support of both municipal officials and some of the region's most prominent elites, such as Helen Clay Frick, who sponsored the initial study of Liverpool Street. While not a direct outgrowth of the Allegheny Conference, the creation of Landmarks bore striking similarities to other conference-affiliated groups such as the Western Pennsylvania Conservancy. Among the foundation's incorporators can be found many of the key financial backers of the Renaissance, including Adolph Schmidt, a close associate of R. K. Mellon, Henry Hillman, Conference president, and Stanton Belfour, head of the Pittsburgh Foundation. Conservative philanthropist Richard Mellon Scaife's foundation provided the organization with a $100,000 grant in 1966 to begin purchasing historic properties. The conservative and elite nature of the organization's vision was made explicit in Landmarks president Charles Covert Arsenberg's declaration that the organization was "a charity," but did not intend to be "controversial." "We do not feed the poor or bring them a better life in the material sense," he continued. "We are not engaged in a struggle for civil or constitutional rights. We do not even focus on the future primarily. But we do see the past as a way of providing a better future for Pittsburgh."[25]

Nevertheless, Landmarks presented a powerful vision of elite-led but grassroots driven community renewal that focused attention on the houses, shops, neighborhood churches, and other "small, anonymous structures," which were "still legion in the city." Van Trump acknowledged the many difficult economic problems facing preservation of Victorian or early twentieth-century buildings often presented, but pointed out that middle-class houses lent themselves more easily to restoration "than the great mansions of the Allegheny tycoons" and "might well attract owners or tenants of today's middle class." Further, Ziegler and Van Trump worked to avoid the problems of gentrification cropping up in preservation-minded efforts in other cities by involving poorer residents "in the restoration activity rather than dislocating them." Building on its detailed study of individual homes on the street, in 1967 Landmarks completed its first restoration at 1329 Liverpool Street based on a mix of funds from private foundations, most notably the conservative Sarah Scaife Foundation and the URAP.[26]

The role of Richard Mellon Scaife, who along with his sister Cordelia inherited much of the family's wealth on the death of their mother in 1965, in financing Landmarks market-oriented rehabilitation placed Pittsburgh in the vanguard of an evolving neoliberal approach to economic development and urban renewal. As community opposition to the Renaissance program of large-scale land clearance grew, Landmarks found willing partners in new community organizations, such as the Manchester Citizen's Corporation, founded in 1965 as a neighborhood-based response to blight and abandonment, and the Mexican War Streets Society founded in 1969. Over the next decade, Landmarks and residents initiated the "Manchester Program," the first of its kind to explicitly link neighborhood redevelopment and historic preservation. The foundation began an experimental program in which it bought a two-story walkup on Monterey Street from the city housing authority, restored it, and rented it back as low-income housing, a process that used federal housing funds to subsidize restoration for the first time. Landmarks' collaboration with the URAP was soon formalized with a contract to create a preservation study of Manchester with the aim of establishing a cost-benefit analysis of restoring versus demolishing individual properties, a relationship later expanded to other neighborhoods throughout the city.[27]

By the mid-1970s, the massive renewal projects of Allegheny Center, Three Rivers Stadium, and Manchester's riverfront industrial districts were drawing to a close, but the impending construction of the Parkway North continued to cast a pall over North Side residents uncertain about the future of their neighborhoods. Even as the postwar highway and urban renewal programs had provided federal funding for large-scale demolition, however, the passage of the National Historic Preservation Act (NHPA) of 1966 and the National Environmental Policy Act (NEPA) of 1970 provided new ways for activists to mobilize in defense of their neighborhoods. Passed in direct response to the Renaissance model of erasing the nineteenth-century city, the NHPA both created a National Register of Historic Places and established a state and federal bureaucracy for identifying and protecting buildings of historical significance. While the specifics of the law were relatively limited, the passage of the act symbolically reversed the emphasis of postwar renewal on razing and rebuilding by putting a federal imprimatur on preserving a wide range of buildings of historic significance.[28]

Along with NEPA, which set up a similar review process for evaluating the environmental impact of federally funded projects, the NHPA also emphasized the role of citizen input by requiring public hearings and encouraging research on proposed development sites. At the same time that East Street Valley residents organized the Highway Emergency and Relocation Team (HEART) to advocate for better relocation services, Landmarks received a grant from federal and state officials in spring 1969 to photograph and preserve fragments from buildings scheduled for demolition. Among the structures in the path of the highway were St. Mary's (1854) and St. Boniface (1925) Roman Catholic churches. Both churches suffered from declining membership, and the Catholic diocese planned to consolidate three area parishes into one church, even before state officials acquired the properties in the early 1970s. However, as a result of the Landmarks' survey, St. Mary's Church was determined to be eligible for the newly established National Register of Historic Places, meaning that federal funds could not be used for demolition without a clear case of necessity. State officials then redesigned an interchange to avoid the property and in 1983 the church was purchased, with Landmarks aiding in the conversion of the priory into a bed-and-breakfast.[29]

On the other hand, the battle over St. Boniface exposed the fracturing of the public-private partnership that drove the Renaissance through the mid-1960s and the emergence of a new vision of heritage-based neighborhood revitalization. Initial plans for the Parkway North called for an eight-lane interstate running through the East Street Valley that would "plow through" 2,000 properties, including the "architecturally interesting" gold-domed church. During a contentious highway hearing in June 1972, Mayor Flaherty questioned the importance of the Parkway North as an economic asset and demanded the plan be amended to bypass the church. "When the time comes we may have to lie down under the bulldozers," declared one resident, "but our main purpose now is to let the public know we want to save our church." Under pressure, state officials agreed to residents' demands, but the Pittsburgh Catholic Diocese refused to keep the church open, preferring instead to construct a new building to house the remaining parishioners from the other two churches in the path of the highway. Faced with an August 1977 deadline from state officials to vacate St. Boniface, political pressure from Landmarks and its allies succeeded in forcing the Federal Highway Administration to seek a determination on whether the church qualified for the National Register of Historic Places, a first step in a process that eventually prevented federal funds from being used in the project.[30]

The Parkway North was eventually completed, but the razing of a large part of the North Side spawned a new constellation of nonprofit organizations wielding considerable power through federal laws and partnerships with neighborhood organizations, private trusts, and sympathetic municipal officials. As a result, by the time the term crept into national discourse in the early 1980s, the revolt against the Pittsburgh Renaissance had already laid the pragmatic foundation for neoliberalism on the municipal level. In part, this was a matter of the Flaherty administration making the best of a difficult situation with declining federal funding, a shrinking tax base, and skyrocketing employee costs. On the other hand, the devolution of some aspects of municipal planning to neighborhood groups and the incorporation of a wider range of constituencies into the urban renewal process reflected more widespread anger about perceived government overreach. Within this framework, Arthur Ziegler and James Van Trump represented a new breed of social entrepreneurs who combined the market-driven philosophy of their wealthy backers with a willingness to leverage public funds and partner with government agencies in order to serve community needs. While only one of many community development corporations then emerging in the city, Landmarks's assertion that old buildings could provide the base for an authentic community provided the perfect framework for partnerships that transcended existing notions of liberal or conservative.

"The Wishes of the People"

As with the broader Pittsburgh Renaissance, the early success of the Allegheny Center Mall also served as a model for urban renewal in other parts of the Steel Valley. In 1971, Wheeling's Urban Renewal Authority (URAW), too, put forward a plan to redevelop the city's aging central business into an enclosed regional shopping center. Backed by the municipal planning commission, city council, and the Chamber of Commerce (the successor to the Wheeling Area Conference on Community Development), the Fort

Henry Mall proposal followed the completion of a successful renewal project expanding Ohio Valley General Hospital in Center Wheeling. Though private entities, hospitals' nonprofit and community service status allowed for the continued razing of entire neighborhoods in both Wheeling and Pittsburgh during a time of increasing public opposition to other uses of eminent domain. This tension over the appropriate function of urban renewal complicated the actions of the URAW, which was accused of ignoring "the wishes of the people," when neighborhood opposition arose to the development of the mall. Unlike Pittsburgh, however, the revolt against Wheeling's Renaissance never coalesced around a viable alternative strategy for urban revitalization nor did new institutional partnerships emerge that could lay the foundation for community development by the 1980s.[31]

Wheeling began the 1960s with its modest Renaissance agenda focused on clearing land along the riverfront for light industry that looked a lot like Pittsburgh's original plans for a similar district in the Manchester neighborhood. In 1967, the National Planning Association projected that Wheeling's employment base would grow "substantially faster" than its hinterland due to its role as a "transportation-utilities and trade center for the neighboring areas," outpacing Charleston, Huntington, and Steubenville. However, the declining importance of manufacturing for the city can be seen in the difficulty URAW officials had in attracting employers to the 55-acre planned industrial district completed in Center Wheeling in 1962. After heroic efforts to save the project by the Wheeling Area Conference on Community Development and the Downtown Wheeling Associates, the merchants group formed by URAW chairman Robert Levenson in 1959, a lack of interest among new industrial employers resulted in parts of the site eventually being occupied by a trucking company and a new post office.[32]

As efforts to attract new manufacturing to the city stalled, the URAW looked for other ways to improve conditions in the deteriorating neighborhoods, including a partnership with the city's public hospital. The healthcare system in metropolitan Pittsburgh formed around a series of municipal and Catholic hospitals in the major urban areas, including Allegheny General, Presbyterian and Mercy (Catholic) in Pittsburgh, Wheeling (Catholic) and Ohio Valley General in Wheeling, and Gill Memorial (Catholic) and Ohio Valley in Steubenville. Federal subsidies for hospital expansion began in 1946 with the passage of the Hospital Survey and Construction (Hill-Burton) Act. In 1949, Presbyterian Hospital formally affiliated with the University of Pittsburgh and began using a combination of federal, state, and institutional funds to grow into one of the nation's premier research hospitals. Through the 1960s, however, the medical system in much of the Steel Valley remained inadequate due to its particular geographical and economic landscape. The creation of a federal health insurance program for the poor (Medicaid) and elderly (Medicare) in 1965 increased access for thousands of Steel Valley residents and further fueled changes in healthcare consumption. Those who had previously relied on charity wards or suffered without hospital treatment could now become paying customers. Medicare "started out paying on the cost," recalled Sam Nazzaro, an administrator at Wheeling Hospital, and it "was pretty good in terms of the hospital getting reimbursed."[33]

The publicly financed consolidation of the health care industry transformed hospitals into some of metropolitan Pittsburgh's largest employers and hospital executives into key players in the development of neoliberal urbanism. Federal subsidies and the new influx of patients sparked significant growth and by 1975 local administrators had expanded and updated facilities at every hospital in the region. Wheeling Hospital, a Catholic institution founded in 1850, used Hill-Burton funds to add several additional units to its cramped downtown facility before building an entirely new suburban-style campus in 1975 on a two-hundred acre site along Interstate 70. Faced with the same limits on growth in a crowded urban setting, in the early 1960s Ohio Valley General Hospital in Center Wheeling began exploring options for expanding its physical plant that was just a few blocks away from the city's planned industrial district. Hospital administrators partnered with the URAW, which used federal subsidies and the power of eminent domain to purchase and clear a large residential area around the hospital, a process completed by 1968. Unlike other renewal projects the authority attempted in the 1960s and 1970s, the expansion was completed quickly and with little public opposition, which was due in large part to the nonprofit, community service status of the hospital. "Without urban renewal I doubt if we would have in Center Wheeling the medical complex that is now there," explained Frank Joanou, an official with the URAW from 1966 to 1970. "Whereas anything else that we were involved in, we were going to be [taking] private land to then turn over to private ownership."[34]

With the successful completion of the hospital project, the city's public-private partnership turned to the more difficult task of redeveloping the community's increasingly shabby downtown. The Wheeling Conference developed initial plans in the late 1950s for the aging Market Auditorium on Market Street between Tenth and Eleventh Streets, built in 1910 on the site of the city's original market house and town hall. The longest building in Wheeling, by 1960 the auditorium had deteriorated significantly and planners eyed it for the site of a new parking garage and additional private development that would form a new "Northern Gateway" to the city. Various ideas surfaced for a rebuilt municipal auditorium, a parking garage, and space for retail shops, but public opinion finally settled on a large new civic center, an idea promoted by the Wheeling Area Conference, which had several members on the city's Municipal Auditorium Board. Local officials obtained a nearly $1.8 million federal matching grant and the auditorium was demolished in 1964. However, new construction was delayed when voter referenda in 1966 and again in 1967 failed to reach the required 60 percent majority needed to issue bonds for the local share.[35]

When members of the city's Municipal Auditorium Board, including developer Jack Waterhouse and retailer Robert Levenson, placed the civic center proposal before voters again in 1971, it had become "linked with a bold and exciting, but separate, revitalization program for downtown Wheeling." With the civic center as its western anchor and a new riverfront marina and amphitheater to the east, the heart of the proposal was a radical vision for an enclosed regional shopping center, the Fort Henry Mall. Rather than redirecting traffic around the site with parking at ground level as with Allegheny Center, URAW officials instead proposed the general maintenance of existing routes with walkways and an "extensive open air pedestrian promenade" above the streets and retail levels. Proponents hoped the new facility would help to achieve Wheeling's full potential as "a complete regional commercial center" as well as the focus for the area's "cultural, civic and recreational activities." Further, as the downtown area was transformed it would create new employment opportunities for "personnel with a variety of management, service, and administrative skills."[36]

As in Pittsburgh, the late 1960s and early 1970s were a particularly tumultuous time in Wheeling politics, making the already delicate process of urban renewal even more difficult. Irritated with the unwillingness or incapacity of city council to undertake a variety of redevelopment projects, a group of civic leaders including Ogden Nutting, publisher of the Wheeling *Intelligencer*, and Frank Haig, S.J., president of Wheeling College, backed a slate of candidates that defeated eight of the nine existing council members. After this coup, the new city council fired the city manager and then the URAW's entire board of directors resigned in protest at being shut out of decision-making. Advocates of a more forceful urban renewal program scored a victory when city council named Charles Steele as the new city manager. Steele, a Wheeling native, had extensive experience in municipal planning and served as Martins Ferry's first development director under Mayor John Laslo before joining the Ohio County Planning Commission. With council approval, Steele reconstituted the authority with a strong board led by William Doepken, president of Wheeling Corrugating Company, and Arch Riley, a politically savvy former county prosecuting attorney. "They were some of the strongest leaders in Wheeling and they absolutely had their heads on straight," Steele later recalled. "They were committed to making sure Wheeling stayed as the [area's] center city."[37]

With the appointment of George Cieply, a public relations executive with Wheeling Steel, as executive director of the URAW in January 1971, the stage appeared to be set for a radical remake of downtown Wheeling. Following a publicity campaign by Wheeling City Council, the Municipal Auditorium Board and the authority, the required 63.5 percent of county voters finally authorized the city in November to issue $900,000 in general revenue bonds to cover the local share of the civic arena. With the keystone structure for its broader central business district plan approved, the authority turned to implementing the rest of its Fort Henry Mall proposal. Wheeling qualified for annual appropriations of federal urban renewal funds, which gave the authority resources that did not require local bond issues. Further, since it controlled the site of the demolished Market Auditorium, the authority already owned a significant part of the project location. By spring 1972, the mall design was in place, additional land acquisition was under way, and officials had begun a national search for "an experienced developer" to "share in the ownership and profit of the proposed mall." Within a few months, Arlen Inner-Cities Industries agreed to oversee the project and quickly obtained commitments by retailers Sears, J.C. Penney, and Montgomery Ward to anchor the facility.[38]

The speed with which the URAW moved to implement the Fort Henry Mall project suggested that the city's public-private partnership had finally achieved the level of cooperation called for by the Wheeling Conference nearly twenty years earlier. As land purchases began, however, the project generated stiff resistance from some local merchants who believed that downtown Wheeling could retain its traditional role as the region's marketplace without the loss of autonomy implicit in an enclosed shopping center.

The Fort Henry Mall project incorporated Stone & Thomas, Inc., the largest of the locally owned retailers, into its design, but developers would demolish and replace other structures with new buildings. As a result, owners of those buildings, many of whom were in the second or third generation, were upset at the loss of property made possible by the authority's power of eminent domain. On the other hand, a number of major local retailers such as Boury Corporation and Reichart Furniture, of which Robert Levenson was president, were located outside the project area, requiring them to rent space from the mall's developer if they wished to participate. Some store owners felt that this amounted to paying for entry to a retail market they currently controlled, and for smaller retailers, renting space in the mall potentially involved a higher rental fee than they previously paid for downtown properties. Opponents also disliked the arrangement with mall developer Arlen Industries, which they believed would have an inherent bias toward national chains over local mom-and-pop establishments. From this point of view, the paucity of developable land in the cramped downtown was actually a blessing because if "there was no room for the marketplace to expand, there was no reason to allow any more national competition into the marketplace."[39]

In April 1971, a representative of the DWA denounced the proposed mall at a public hearing as "entirely unfeasible, unrealistic, and financially unsound." Mall opponents claimed that the commercial redevelopment plan was a "radical departure" from the authority's mission of slum clearance for lower- and middle-class housing and a "patent attempt" to use eminent domain to transfer property from one private owner to another, an argument that resonated with the national backlash against urban renewal. In reality, however, urban renewal in Wheeling was never focused on housing, and its activities had regularly resulted in the transfer of property from one private entity to another. While the use of eminent domain for the Ohio Valley General Hospital expansion could be interpreted as serving a quasi-public institution, Levenson had been the authority's executive director when it cleared the mixed-use neighborhood in Center Wheeling for use as an industrial park, a project supported at the time by the DWA. On the other hand, disagreements over the shape and scope of the city's Renaissance had plagued the Wheeling Conference since its inception. According to one account, the creation of the DWA itself was a result of concerns on the part of Levenson and his allies that the Conference was not paying enough attention to downtown businesses. Furthermore, the DWA played a key role in the razing of the Market Auditorium, which took place over the objections of historic preservationists. This suggests that the fight over Fort Henry Mall, at least for civic-minded businessmen like Levenson who had been actively involved in the postwar renewal program, was a struggle over decision-making control rather than ideological principles.[40]

The growing opposition to the Fort Henry Mall demonstrated the difficulty in assembling and maintaining public-private coalitions for urban redevelopment in the political and social context of the Steel Valley. Unlike Pittsburgh's strong mayor system, executive powers in Wheeling were vested in an appointed manager who could be fired at any time by a simple majority of the city council, a governing structure that hampered the type of strong public-private partnerships that made the Pittsburgh Renaissance possible. The city council itself was elected through an awkward system of representation on a nonpartisan ballot—adopted in 1935 out of a desire to eliminate patronage—making any sort of effective political coalition virtually impossible to maintain. Further, the routine failure of bond issues related to urban renewal were due to both structural impediments, such as the required 60 percent majority for approval and the general lack of support from the state, and a civic culture defined by opposition to public spending and declining tax revenues. When the URAW and its allies on city council finally attempted to move beyond relatively small-scale projects and intervene in the city's central business district in the way Pittsburgh leaders had in creating the Golden Triangle twenty years earlier, the resulting controversy revealed the unstable political foundation on which the coalition was formed.[41]

The fight over the Fort Henry Mall had all the hallmarks of a classic neighborhood revolt, including public hearings to express opposition, lawsuits to delay program implementation, and a publicity campaign complete with "Fort Henry Mall No No No" bumper stickers. Over the next two years, the DWA pursued a series of lawsuits and a publicity campaign attacking the Fort Henry Mall, the Wheeling Civic Center, and the URAW. After the county circuit court dismissed their suit in April 1973, mall opponents, who had organized as the "Save Downtown Wheeling Committee," launched a ballot initiative to force city council to either revoke the authority's 1957 charter, which would disband it entirely, or to call a public referendum on the issue. Appearing before city council, committee members Julia R. Boyd and Fred Friebertshauser, owner of a downtown beauty and barber supply business, declared that municipal officials are "obviously unwilling or unable to protect citizens from reckless Urban Renewal Authority schemes." The group subsequently acquired the 3,000 signatures necessary to force a public referendum, and in August residents voted by a two-to-one margin to scrap the Ft. Henry Mall as well as the URAW itself. While the powers of the URAW and the property it controlled technically remained with city council, Wheeling would no longer have a development agency capable of independent action.[42]

At the same time as a novel public-private coalition based on a pragmatic neoliberalism was gradually emerging in Pittsburgh, Wheeling residents, too, sought to craft a new consensus in the wake of the revolt against Fort Henry Mall. Mall opponents declared they would implement their own scaled-back version of downtown revitalization, but a "blue ribbon" advisory committee proved largely unable to enact meaningful change using purely voluntary means and local resources. The long-delayed civic center finally opened in 1977, but was moved from the site of the former Market Auditorium to a more isolated location several blocks away that did little to draw shoppers downtown. As early as August 1973, officials in Belmont County, Ohio, just across the river from Wheeling began seeking federal and state funds to prepare a site for a proposed regional shopping center seven miles to the west of Wheeling. With the failure of the Fort Henry proposal, Sears, Montgomery Ward, and J. C. Penney quickly signed agreements to anchor the new facility. The 1978 opening of the Ohio Valley Mall prompted a round of soul-searching among residents whose "hubris," in the words of one commentator, had defeated the Fort Henry Mall proposal five years earlier. "I remember I said something to Bob Levenson once," recalled John Hunter, II, a local business owner, "and he shook his head. I just forget what he said, but it was a terrible thing to do. The city died from there on for many, many years."[43]

In 1975, a second edition of *Pittsburgh: The Story of An American City* appeared to pick up the city's narrative where the first edition had left off in 1964. For the first new chapter following David Lawrence's celebratory "Rebirth" essay about the postwar Renaissance, Lorant's title "Leveling Off" is an apt descriptor for the trajectory of both the city and the region in the early 1970s. Coming just a few years after Lawrence's pronouncement that residents "took pleasure in the swing of the headache ball and the crash of the falling brick," Arthur Ziegler's 1967 response that "the crash of the headache ball, the falling stones, the crumbing brick and rotting wood discourage everyone sensitive to our architectural heritage" takes on particular significance. "But," he concluded, "the ravaging of the emblems of our past can spur us on." In Pittsburgh, the revolt against postwar urban renewal fractured the city's public-private partnership as the election of Peter Flaherty signaled an end to the close relationship between municipal officials and the Allegheny Conference. However, the city retained the URAP along with the institutional capacity to undertake significant development programs. Indeed, new partnerships emerged in the 1970s between and among city agencies, neighborhood improvement groups and non-profit organizations like ACTION-Housing and Landmarks, which would drive a more community-based reformulation of urban renewal.[44]

Unlike Ziegler and Van Trump, whose founding of Landmarks emerged from a sense of loss following the creation of the Allegheny Center Mall, Wheeling residents were able to stop the Fort Henry Mall before the URAW could complete its acquisition of downtown businesses. Wheeling residents raised many of the same objections to projects that seemed to benefit outside interests at the expense of local property as their counterparts in Pittsburgh. The early 1970s also saw a flurry of heritage preservation projects in Wheeling following the founding of the non-profit Friends of Wheeling as part of the drive to secure National Register status for West Virginia Independence Hall. Indeed, the failure of the Fort Henry Mall saved a number of historic structures later listed on the National Register as part of the East Wheeling Historic District. However, the elimination of the URAW also meant that the institutional capacity necessary for connecting heritage-based rehabilitation to neighborhood renewal in Pittsburgh did not happen in the smaller city. Consequently, while Pittsburgh had some success in crafting the neoliberal policies and partnerships that would lay the foundation for a second Renaissance beginning in the late 1970s, Wheeling remained, along with the rest of the region's smaller communities, on a trajectory that left it unprepared for the economic cataclysm of the 1980s.

PART III
Post-Industrial Pittsburgh

IN SUMMER 1987, two college students from Cleveland—a budding historian named Andrew Wiese and his artist friend Ben Parsons—set off from the North Side of Pittsburgh on a journey that would take them down the Ohio River to Wheeling. Like Reuben Gold Thwaites a century before, Wiese said that he "had read Frances Parkman," and wanted to see "what that frontier of the colonial era looked like today." "But," he added, "also I was really profoundly moved by the process of deindustrialization [in] the Ohio Valley of my childhood, which still was filled with steel and burning rivers and all of that smoke and that smell." The postwar period was a time of steady decline in this landscape of production, but in the five years before Wiese's trip the number of steel workers employed in the mills of the Monongahela Valley had dropped precipitously. U.S. Steel shuttered its operations in Rankin, Duquesne, Clairton, and McKeesport, with the iconic Homestead Works closing in 1986. "It was collapsing all around," he explained. "I wanted to put the boat in the river at Pittsburgh [and] to come down the Ohio River, and see the mills and the towns."[1]

"I guess we must have had my uncle or my mom drop us off in Pittsburgh, across from the Golden Triangle," Wiese began. "In we went, right in the area where the Ohio begins, took a bunch of pictures and kinda headed south." Much of Pittsburgh's economy and population had shifted by that point to the "metropolis of the plateau" described by Ralph Widner in his 1973 speech to the Allegheny Conference, but for Wiese and his companion, "there was a romance to the river."[2] "On the other hand," he recalled, laughing, "everybody was like, don't touch that water and certainly don't drink it." His narrative provides both an avenue for direct comparison with the landscape of Thwaites's earlier journey and a foreshadowing of the changing uses of the rivers and riverfronts following the collapse of steel. Indeed, in language reminiscent of his predecessor's, Wiese described "some of strongest memories of this trip" as "the stillness of the water in the very early morning before the wind picks up, and mist and the sound of trains." "Then," he added, "the pleasure boats came by with the people with their beer cans in their bathing suits and the tubes dragging behind them and you are back in the 1980s."

To their surprise, the travelers found that "the city was reinventing itself" and "pretty well springing back" following the job losses of the early 1980s. "The section right across from Three Rivers Stadium was undergoing a lot of gentrification," Wiese recalled. "The brass door set was now on their way in" among the nineteenth century brick row houses visible from their canoe. As they left downtown Pittsburgh, however, they came into greater contact with "the working river, the towboats and barges," which were "a little bit scary from the perspective of a canoe." "We got to Ambridge, which is not far from Pittsburgh and pulled the canoe out because the mill was closed and was right along the water," he continued. "We went into one of these big factory buildings, where they built ships, as far as I know. Here we were in the mill [and] it was sort of like touching what had been left behind. It seemed like a big thing to throw away. Not just crush a beer can and toss it in the garbage, but crush an industrial infrastructure and just leave it to rot."

The disintegration of metropolitan Pittsburgh's steel industry also had a profound effect on the communities the modern pilgrims encountered. "We had driven through Ambridge on the way down to Pittsburgh," Wiese explained, "so we had seen the town itself, which was devastated. The taverns were closed and people were selling their houses, it was a wreck at the time." The Steel Valley's overall population had declined by an average of nearly 6,000 residents annually between 1960 and 1980, but more than 20,000 people left the region every year during the 1980s.[3] Wiese recalled seeing many abandoned houses on their drive in and then along the river route. "I remember my friend took photographs through the window of this one house where it looked someone had just been evicted and the place was just being let go back to the grass." "It really was very clear to me," he concluded, "the world that had been was rapidly disappearing. Maybe that is why I wanted to go see what it looked like. It seemed to us like [the region] was dying, and we wanted to be witnesses to the death."

As with *Afloat on the Ohio*, Wiese's account is striking in its depiction of the ways the multiple stages of the region's history were embedded in the contemporary landscape. It was surprising to the young scholar that the mill towns were "turned backside to this river, which, as I was reading in the colonial history had been the lifeblood." The industrial infrastructure of "old factory complexes" as well as "bridge abutments, mine outlets, and railroads running on both sides of the Ohio" that were new in 1894 often still remained, despite the fact that much of it had long fallen into disrepair.

Wiese concluded by reflecting on "all the hopes" embodied in the names of the mill towns that had been too new to be on the 1882 map Thwaites carried.[4] "Ambridge obviously was a company town and Aliquippa, which I didn't know at the time was J&L [Steel]'s company town. And we went past Weirton, of Weirton Steel, and Steubenville. That was an exciting part of it, trying to imagine how these town names got there, how these towns got there." But, he concluded, all that history was juxtaposed against "all of the hardships and failed hopes that were reflected in what we were seeing."

While steel was still produced, coal was still mined, and railroads still operated in metropolitan Pittsburgh, Wiese's observations make it clear that the social and cultural bonds uniting the Steel Valley had snapped. At the same time, a new regional identity began to emerge with its own economy and symbols as residents sought to adapt the existing social and physical landscapes in order to create a "postindustrial renaissance."[5] Since the 1960s, economic growth had shifted spatially, to a few urban neighborhoods and the highway-oriented suburbs of the plateau, as well as functionally to service sectors and more advanced manufacturing, often associated with the city's research universities. In part this had to do with the sheer difficulty in transforming a regional environment and social structure formed around a unified process of heavy industrial production. It proved to be easier to add new social, cultural, and physical layers onto the existing landscape than to remake the older mill towns and mining villages that grew increasingly impoverished.

On the other hand, the changing composition of Pittsburgh's neighborhoods Wiese observed was due in part to the efforts of a rejuvenated Renaissance partnership, which grew to include additional stakeholders in the late 1970s, that was determined to use an emerging neoliberal public policy framework to attract businesses and residents into the city through an emphasis on combining heritage preservation with growth in the education and healthcare sectors. The abandonment of the mill sites also allowed public access to the rivers for the first time in more than a century, prompting a wave of riverfront revitalization already underway at the time of Wiese's trip. However, residents left out of this imagined community contested this post-industrial project from the outset and advocated instead a re-industrialization of the shuttered mills and reopening of the abandoned mines. Indeed, Wiese and Parsons arrived just at the moment when the competition between these two visions was at its peak.

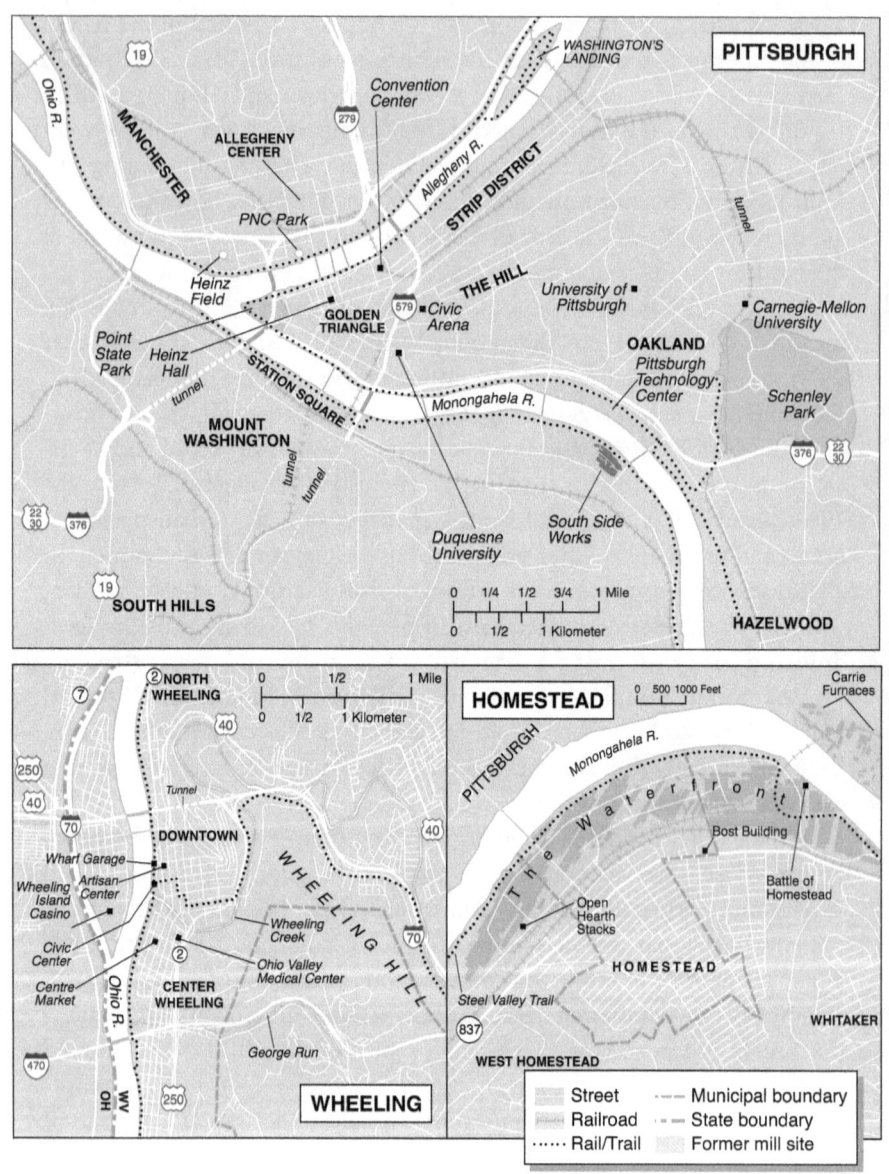

FIGURE 11. Key sites in post-industrial Pittsburgh, Wheeling, and Homestead.

CHAPTER 8

Rust Belt and Roboburgh

The closure of U.S. Steel's Homestead Works on a hot, muggy day in July 1986 symbolically ended a chapter in the Steel Valley's history that had begun in the nineteenth century and made the region the hub of the nation's heavy industrial production. The mill, which supplied steel beams for such iconic American structures as the Empire State Building and the Sears Tower, had slowly been shutting down over the previous years until only 23 workers and a few supervisors remained in a facility that had employed 20,000 during World War II and several thousand through the late 1970s. "I got 38 years in that rusty mother," declared Bob Krovocheck, a fifty-six-year-old crane operator. "It's a damn shame." Homestead's abandonment was just one step in a process of divestment for U.S. Steel and other large corporations that accelerated rapidly during the early 1980s, devastating the region's industrialized river valleys. "We come today to beg of your help," pleaded a Clairton pastor to Allegheny County officials in 1991. The mill towns have "fallen down and we can't get up."[1]

In late September 1987, just a year after the Homestead closure and only a few miles down river near Weise's starting point, the new Benedum Center for the Performing Arts opened with the debut of "Purely Pittsburgh," a musical variety show featuring local composers and performers. "What this represents is just the beginning of a lengthy program to retain artistic talent in our own community," announced Carol Brown, president of the Pittsburgh Trust for Cultural Resources, the nonprofit corporation set up by the Allegheny Conference to create a new downtown Cultural District. For the city's public-private partnership, the opening of Heinz Hall in 1971 and then the Benedum Center during the climax of the steel industry's collapse signaled not only the revitalization of a deteriorating downtown neighborhood, but also the transformation of the "Smoky City" into a post-industrial mecca for the educated, middle-class residents Pittsburgh hoped to attract. "The center represents much more than the restoration of the former Stanley Theater into one of the finest performance centers in the United States," the *Pittsburgh Post-Gazette* declared. "Pittsburgh's distinction as a center of the arts will prove a unique asset as this region competes for jobs and growth [and establishes] a level of cultural amenity that will be critical to this region's long-term prosperity."[2]

The juxtaposition of the closing Homestead Works and the Benedum Center opening highlights the deepening economic and symbolic divisions that had emerged in metropolitan Pittsburgh. For development officials as well as residents employed in the region's expanding research and service sectors, Rust Belt imagery rooted in the dirty, blue-collar mills of the industrialized river valleys increasingly became "a barrier to recruiting talent, attracting businesses, and giving the Pittsburgh market area the economic stature it deserves." Instead, Mayor Richard Caliguiri envisioned the city resurrected as a "service and retailing center, a center for health care, a city of transplants, a city of High Technology, a city of Robotics, of computer programming." However, for many blue-collar workers and their families, the region's future prosperity instead required reindustrialization through advanced manufacturing, more efficient production, and better cooperation between workers and management. These tensions came to the forefront during the economic upheaval of the 1980s when LTV (formerly J&L) Steel closed its South Side and Hazelwood Works within the city. The struggle to control the redevelopment of the two sites paralleling each other across the Monongahela River came to define the conflicting meanings of community in post-industrial Pittsburgh.[3]

"A Challenge of Transition"

Though dwindling mining jobs spurred population loss in many rural areas and helped keep unemployment rates above the national average, it was not until the recession of 1957–1958 that the Steel Valley's political and economic elite really began to worry about deeper structural challenges to prosperity. The next year, the Pittsburgh Regional Planning Association began work on an exhaustive *Economic Study of the Pittsburgh Region* that, when published in 1963, bluntly characterized the "challenge of transition" facing metropolitan Pittsburgh. First, the basic economic structure of the region had changed very little since the forging of the coal-steel-rail matrix in the late nineteenth century. Even new employers, such as the coal-by-wire power plants and chemical manufacturers sited along the Ohio River, followed the same basic pattern as Weirton Steel, J&L Steel, U.S. Steel, and other corporations that expanded their operations within well-established categories. On the other hand, despite new suburban office parks and research campuses, the service sector remained underdeveloped even compared to that of other industrial cities about the same size. In short, Pittsburgh's particular mix of slow-growth manufacturing sectors such as steel, glass, and industrial machinery coupled with a lack of faster-growing service sector jobs placed it in a disadvantageous position in comparison to other metropolitan regions.[4]

However, the *Economic Study* concluded that the unfavorable industrial mix alone could not account for the severity of the economic malaise affecting the region by the early 1960s. Indeed, the authors identified deeper problems rooted in the political, economic, and environmental landscapes of the Steel Valley itself. First, broader trends of decentralization to the South and West had eroded the regional competitive advantage exploited by Andrew Carnegie and other late nineteenth century industrialists. Pittsburgh's location on the edge of the Appalachian Mountains also meant that it remained relatively isolated from other population centers and thus unlikely to attract employers focused on regional sales. Despite a series of postwar settlements with unions that allowed attrition through automation in exchange for higher wages and job security, tense labor-management relations continued to reflect the echoes of the 1892 Homestead Strike. Similarly, the domination by several large, multidivisional firms limited opportunities for entrepreneurship and innovation outside existing corporate bureaucracies. Finally, the rugged landscape of the region coupled with the dense settlement pattern of the river valleys left relatively few sites that were suitable for the facilities that growing industries favored.[5]

Despite calls for "an all-encompassing community effort" like the one behind the Pittsburgh Renaissance, over the next two decades the Allegheny Conference did not move much past its traditional focus on physical development in the metropolitan core. In part this had to do with the sheer difficulty in transforming a regional landscape that reflected the large corporations' efforts to integrate diverse communities in a unified process of industrial production. Conversely, the dominant thrust of postwar economic development was to separate functions geographically, with the Golden Triangle and select, highway-oriented suburbs supplying the relatively flat locations needed for administrative and research activities as well as a modest number of new light industrial firms. Indeed, it was much easier and less disruptive simply to layer these new and more prosperous "greenfield" spaces onto the existing landscape than to remake the industrial brownfields of the older mill towns and mining villages, which then grew increasingly impoverished. As the authors of the economic study concluded, "it is a long step from a coal miner to an electronics technician: from an obsolete steel mill to a modern industrial park; from a giant corporation to a multitude of innovators and ambitious small entrepreneurs."[6]

The failure to fully engage in economic renewal also stemmed from the fundamentally contradictory vision of the Pittsburgh Renaissance itself. Even as the city cleaned up its skies, controlled its rivers, and tried to erase its nineteenth-century neighborhoods in favor of gleaming modern skyscrapers, its fortunes continued to depend on corporate exploitation of the surrounding mill towns and mining villages. As long as the mills and mines remained profitable, there was little incentive to invest the enormous resources necessary even to begin transforming "a Sharpsburg or a Turtle Creek to a Santa Monica." As a result, both white-collar and skilled blue-collar workers created enclaves in the new suburbs, while civic leaders increasingly relied on out-migration to dampen the rise of unemployment. Indeed, aside from a few new education-related initiatives including a campaign that resulted in the University of Pittsburgh's affiliation with the state, the Allegheny Conference primarily relied on its affiliated groups, particularly the Regional Industrial Development Corporation, to transform the regional economy.[7]

The 1961 rechartering of the Regional Industrial Development Corporation (RIDC) and selection of Robert H. Ryan, a graduate of Harvard Business School who left his position as vice president of the Boston Development Authority to serve as RIDC president, marked a new phase in Pittsburgh's public-private partnership with increasing input from state and federal agencies. While the organization's most apparent initiatives focused on the development of its suburban industrial parks, under Ryan the corporation also sought local, state, and federal incentives to finance new and growing businesses throughout the region. After the Area Redevelopment Administration designated metropolitan Pittsburgh as a "depressed area," millions of dollars of federal money flowed into the region from a host of new programs including the Manpower Development and Retraining Act (1962) and the Appalachian Regional Development Act (1965). On the state level, the Pennsylvania Industrial Development Authority (1956) and Site Development Act (1968) provided subsidized loans to encourage plant expansion and relocation. Soon after Ryan took the helm in 1962, the RIDC created Pennsylvania's first Industrial Development Fund (RIDC-IDF) to pool equity and long-term credit for companies that had difficulty obtaining bank loans.[8]

With the creation of its industrial parks and the RIDC-IDF, a new vision for transforming the Steel Valley slowly began to take shape. Compared to other areas, the *Economic Study* revealed a host of obstacles to "starting up relatively small and novel types of businesses" in a region "long wedded to mammoth enterprises." Nevertheless, Pittsburgh had many of the components necessary for this type of economic innovation: good colleges and universities, a growing medical center in Oakland, and one of the nation's largest concentrations of corporate research laboratories. Ryan made clear his goal of finding new ways to foster economic growth, especially the kinds of innovative companies that started with "two guys out of a research lab in a garage." RIDC's growing suburban industrial parks as well as increasing numbers of medical and engineering-related firms indicated that this approach had some success during the 1970s, which saw significant expansion in technology jobs. At the same time, federal support for health care and medical research spurred additional economic growth in the region's hospitals, especially the university center of Oakland.[9]

Even as state and federal involvement in economic development initiatives was reaching a peak, metropolitan Pittsburgh's public-private growth partnership re-emerged after its precipitous decline under Mayor Peter Flaherty. In 1977, City Council president Richard Caliguiri was appointed mayor after Flaherty left to become deputy attorney general in the Carter administration. Later in the year, Caliguiri, who had served as city parks director in the Lawrence administration, won a full term running on a platform of forging better relations with the business community and the Allegheny Conference in particular. Renaissance II was a program of downtown high-rise construction built on a number of key projects initiated or completed during the mid-1970s, including a new convention center and a light rail system, combined with the emphasis on neighborhood rehabilitation championed by Mayor Flaherty. City officials also encouraged a wave of new office construction downtown coupled with heritage-based rehabilitation and limited efforts at riverfront renewal.[10]

One of the key components of Renaissance II was the return to prominence of the Pittsburgh Urban Redevelopment Authority (URAP), weakened during the Flaherty administration. In addition to absorbing the duties of the city's departments of Housing and Economic Development, the revived URAP was chaired by John P. Robin, who had been a key official in the Lawrence administration and had returned to the city in 1973 as an advisor to the Allegheny Conference. Under Robin, the authority became a comprehensive tool for the land acquisition essential for economic revitalization as well as the low-interest loans and grants that made Renaissance II possible. In some cases, the URAP assisted other agencies and organizations with design and site planning, while at other times it served as the principal agent in negotiating sales and assembling entire sites. For example, the authority acquired and cleared the property adjacent to the new David Lawrence Convention Center for the Liberty Center project before selecting a private developer to which it then extended two large loans.[11]

The reinvigoration of the public-private partnership between the Caliguiri administration and the business leaders of the Allegheny Conference was immediately visible in a new wave of high-rise construction that resulted in at least five major projects downtown. The most significant of these began in 1979 when executives at PPG Industries (formerly Pittsburgh Plate Glass) announced plans for a new 5.5-acre headquarters complex centered around One PPG Place, a striking forty-story, Postmodern Gothic "crystal tower" encased in thousands of glass panels. Agreements between the city and PPG authorized the URAP to acquire remaining properties, relocate existing businesses, and prepare the site for development after it was designated as "blighted" under the eminent domain code. As with the Fort Henry Mall in Wheeling a decade earlier, however, five small businesses including a hardware store, a plumbing supply company, and a Catholic bookstore objected to the forced sale and launched a legal battle to prevent the seizure of their properties. Whereas municipal officials only supported the Wheeling Urban Renewal Authority in a limited way, however, Pittsburgh City Council quickly stepped in and formed a seven-member committee to serve as liaison between the disaffected business owners and PPG. Mayor Caliguiri pledged to provide "bigger and better" facilities for those affected, including a brand new two-story building erected "square by square," and PPG assumed all legal costs when the suit was finally dropped, allowing construction to proceed.[12]

Renaissance II took place in a context of declining federal funds and increased citizen involvement that required an evolving and pragmatic approach to the kinds of development associated with "neoliberal urbanism." As American business executives moved from an ideology of "corporate civic responsibility" to the singular focus on "shareholder value" popularized by economist Milton Friedman, philanthropic foundations and trusts increasingly served as the primary vehicles for channeling the inherited wealth of the industrial age into projects designed to foster economic growth. Furthermore, the Flaherty administration's creation of a Community Planning Division served as the basis for expanded neighborhood funding and the emergence of a prominent network of community development corporations (CDCs). Concepts like "leverage" and "revolving fund" were embedded in the lexicon of CDCs from the beginning, as both philanthropic organizations and government agencies increasingly used competition and market-based decision-making as the determinant of whether projects were funded. With support from the Pittsburgh Foundation, for example, the Oakland Planning and Development Corporation established a real estate office, built more than a hundred housing units, and attracted a developer to build a hotel, a parking garage, and a 50,000-square-foot office and commercial building. This new framework for urban and economic development was scaled up to the citywide level following the establishment of the Pittsburgh Partnership for Neighborhood Development (PPND) in 1983, with $1 million in funding from the Ford Foundation, Howard Heinz Endowment, Mellon Bank, and City of Pittsburgh. A decade later, PPND would support the activities of ten CDCs and manage a $4 million commercial and real estate development fund.[13]

The Ford Foundation would later describe the PPND as "one of the most admired networks of neighborhood-oriented community development corporations and commercial banks in the country," but Pittsburgh's success in developing an effective neoliberal growth partnership depended equally on political leadership and the administrative capacity of city agencies developed over the course of the twentieth century. Under Caliguiri's reorganization, the URAP assumed oversight for a wide variety of planning, coordinating, and loan assistance programs, including the expansion of affordable housing through rehabilitation—a function that fostered close collaboration with nonprofit organizations such as the Pittsburgh History and Landmarks Foundation (Landmarks). As early as 1970, the National Trust for Historic Places declared Pittsburgh "a preservation laboratory" that avoided "shunt[ing] off the poor to faceless projects." In 1979 the URAP launched the nation's first large-scale neighborhood renewal program based on preservation in the North Side's Manchester neighborhood, which had been designated a National Historic District in 1975. Over the next decade, nearly 280 homes on the North Side were rehabilitated using a combination of private and public funds. The Manchester Citizens Corporation, initiated by Landmarks and local residents in 1967, headed the project, with one of its leaders, Stanley Lowe, becoming director of Landmarks' Preservation Fund. This was a major turnaround for Lowe, who had initially opposed preservation programs, believing the needs of local African Americans were better served by tearing down brick townhouses and building suburban style tract houses.[14]

Arthur Ziegler, who cofounded Landmarks along with James Van Trump, famously declared that "our primary goal is not preservation as an end in itself," but rather "preservation is a tool for achieving economic vitality and a better quality of life for our citizens."[15] As a result, even as the organization and the city teamed up to demonstrate the viability of market-oriented housing rehabilitation, Ziegler, Van Trump, and some of their foundation supporters, particularly conservative business leader and philanthropist Richard Mellon Scaife, sought to apply the emerging neoliberal model to a larger commercial development without use of eminent domain or public subsidies. Despite doubts raised about the project by a market study and skepticism on the part of municipal officials, in 1976 Landmarks used a $5 million grant from Scaife's Allegheny Foundation and a $2 million investment by an outside restaurateur to purchase the old Pittsburgh and Lake Erie Railroad Terminal on the city's South Side. In line with the principles articulated a decade earlier in his critique of the Allegheny Center development, Ziegler hoped to distinguish the 52-acre, mixed-use Station Square, as the development became known, from festival marketplaces in other cities by serving the needs of "hometown folks first, with tourism extra." In 1977, the renovated Express House opened as a three-story office building, followed by the 550-seat Grand Concourse restaurant (1978), Bessemer Court (1979), the Freight House shops (1979), and Commerce Court (1982). By 1994, the year Landmarks sold the site to finance new projects, the 134 shops, offices, and restaurants overlooking the Monongahela River in Station Square's five main buildings received

FIGURE 12. View of Station Square from downtown Pittsburgh, c. 1982. The renovated Pittsburgh and Lake Erie Railroad terminal building is to the left and the Sheraton Hotel is to the right. The Commerce Court office complex is under construction on the far side of the Bessemer Court plaza. Photo by Louise Sturgess. Courtesy of Pittsburgh History & Landmarks Foundation.

more than three million visitors a year and created an estimated 3,000 jobs.[16]

What Scaife and his Allegheny Foundation were to Station Square, H. J. "Jack" Heinz II and his family's foundation were to the development of Pittsburgh's downtown Cultural District. In response to the revolt of African Americans in the Hill District against the proposed Center for the Arts and the fraying of the Renaissance partnership with the election of Peter Flaherty, Heinz and the Allegheny Conference turned their attention to the dilapidated Penn Theater a few blocks from the Golden Triangle. Following an extensive renovation funded by a $7 million grant from the Heinz Endowments, the renamed Heinz Hall opened in 1971 as the opulent new home of the Pittsburgh Symphony. While Heinz Hall stood alone in an increasingly shabby area for the next decade, a "peacock on a pile of ashes," as one observer put it, in 1979 the Allegheny Conference commissioned a report that called for the creation of a new downtown "cultural district" that would "be a positive selling point for attracting and retaining businesses for the region." Envisioned as the "antithesis" of the earlier Center for the Arts proposal, the Cultural District was designed as a "walkable riverfront neighborhood with elegant entertainment, proudly preserved architecture and housing." Heinz found partners for his vision in the Benedum Foundation, which stepped in with a $5 million grant to convert another dilapidated theater into the Benedum Center for the Performing Arts, and political leaders, including Richard Caliguiri, Senator H. John Heinz III, and the Allegheny County commissioners, who threw their political weight behind obtaining one of the last federal Urban Development Action Grants given to a major economic development project. The newly created Pittsburgh Cultural Trust, the nonprofit organization set up to oversee projects in the district, then leveraged public money and private philanthropy into a $150 million mixed-use development that included an office tower built between the two theaters. "In a few elegant strokes," a commentator later summed up the Cultural District's neoliberal framework, "the plan had wedded the arts to economic development."[17]

The development of the Cultural District and Station Square thus highlight the pragmatic evolution of new public-private partnerships, market-based financing methods, and an emphasis on using historic preservation as a development tool that distinguished the neoliberalism of Renaissance II from its postwar predecessor. "The exuberant feeling of the first Renaissance is back," Lorant declared in the 1980 edition of *Pittsburgh: The Story of An American City*. "Pittsburgh is once more on the march. Its future looks golden." While this confidence would soon be undercut by the imminent collapse of the region's steel industry, the central city's ability to weather the downturn stood in marked contrast to the deindustrializing river valleys that lacked both the resources and the political will of their larger neighbor. The efforts of the Shapp administration in the 1970s indicated the increasing willingness of the state to incentivize economic development, but Pennsylvania officials remained focused on an industrial recruitment model that produced only limited results. Under Mayor Caliguiri and Governor Thornburgh (1979–1987), civic and political leaders increasingly turned their attention to fostering new economic sectors connected to the city's universities, which in turn became vital strategic partners as the region's residents faced the full onslaught of Rust Belt deindustrialization.

"Postindustrial Renaissance"

As with postwar redevelopment, Pittsburgh's second "Renaissance" was as much about transforming the city's image as it was about changing the skyline. In 1981, the Allegheny Conference convinced twenty-one of the region's largest corporations to contribute more than $800,000 to a national advertising campaign by Penn's Southwest under the slogan, "Dynamic Pittsburgh." A series of full-page ads in the *Wall Street Journal* clearly illustrated the emergence of a post-industrial economic vision along with the cultural and environmental amenities believed necessary to attract and retain highly educated employees. Metropolitan Pittsburgh was home to 25,000 scientists and nearly two hundred research facilities with "renowned programs in robotics, medicine, science and engineering" ads sponsored by Westinghouse, National Steel, and H. H. Robertson declared. It was also a region where historic neighborhoods were renewing themselves and "classic architecture combines with contemporary living," explained Dravo Corporation in a broadside highlighting Station Square. "From rich valleys to rugged mountains, wild rivers to placid lakes," yet another ad concluded alongside an image of the Ohiopyle rapids, the region's varied topography made it "a natural for recreation."[18]

Over the next decade, a neoliberal growth-oriented coalition of business leaders, politicians, and university administrators worked to implement this vision of what U.S. senator and industrial heir H. John Heinz III described as a "postindustrial renaissance." By 1980, research and development spending by the University of Pittsburgh (Pitt) and Carnegie Mellon University (CMU) totaled nearly $100 million annually, while southwestern Pennsylvania hosted 170 private research and development laboratories, including forty major corporate facilities that employed more than 25,000 residents and had an annual expenditure of nearly $1.5 billion. As it stood, the region's research and development activities would spin off economic growth in various forms and continue to employ tens of thousands. Yet, the potential for something much greater existed, concluded a 1984 study, with Pittsburgh having the financial, corporate, and industrial base that could help "nurture the application of new technologies" on a scale that would "serve as an example to the world."[19]

As with the hospital system, colleges and universities throughout the Steel Valley benefitted from increasing public subsidies during the postwar period. Catholic-sponsored colleges founded in Steubenville (1946) and Wheeling (1955), for example, grew to be among the cities' largest employers by the 1980s, while state supported schools in more rural areas provided employment and created an educated workforce. However, Pittsburgh's two research universities alone had the combination of financial support and expertise necessary to serve as the locus for regional economic development. Originally founded in 1787, the University of Pittsburgh's rise to prominence began in 1908 when work began on an expansive campus on a hilltop east of the Golden Triangle later known as Oakland. From the 1920s to the 1950s, civic boosters hailed the development of Oakland into the city's educational and cultural "Acropolis," a symbolic and physical transformation of the Smoky City highlighted by the completion of the monumental "Cathedral of Learning" during the depths of the Great Depression. The industrial elite's philanthropy largely financed Pitt's prewar growth, but in 1957 a new Graduate School of Public Health (GSPH) Building opened on ten acres cleared by the city's Urban Redevelopment Authority. The URAP removed another thirty-one acres of "blighted and slum dwellings" around the upper campus and health center area that were transformed into a parking lot, gymnasium, and swimming pool. The most ambitious plans to convert the 75-acre Panther Hollow "wasteland" on the university's eastern border into a $250 million urban research center was a casualty of the anti-Renaissance revolt, but Pitt's decision to affiliate with the state in 1966 further solidified its importance to the city's public-private partnership.[20]

Pitt began its surge in the health sciences following the development of a polio vaccine by Dr. Jonas Salk in the early 1950s. In 1944, the Buhl Foundation had provided funds to the university to establish a Division of Research in Natural Sciences in the School of Medicine, followed two years later by a grant from the Scaife Foundation to create a virus research laboratory housed in the Municipal Hospital for Contagious Diseases. From this humble beginning, Salk, who was recruited to head the lab, became the national face of polio research and in 1954 Pittsburgh catapulted in the public mind to a major center of medical research with the announcement of a successful vaccine. Complementing the expansion of the GSPH, and under pressure from the Mellon family and the Allegheny Conference, the Medical School shifted to a more academic focus, with the local hospitals that had affiliated with the university gradually subsumed into a consolidated University Health Center of Pittsburgh (later University of Pittsburgh Medical Center or UPMC). Under the leadership of Dr. Thomas Detre, UPMC became a key player in psychiatric research in the 1970s, with federal grants increasing from an insignificant $200,000 a year to $13 million. The recruitment of Dr. William Starzl, a pioneer in organ transplantation, in 1981 paved the way for the city to earn the moniker "Transplant Capital of the World," with Detre using the revenue from organ transplantation to fund major additions, including a new comprehensive cancer center, making UPMC the city's largest employer by the mid-1980s.[21]

The city's growing reputation as an engineering powerhouse symbolized by the 1967 merger of the Carnegie Institute of Technology and the Mellon Institute of Industrial Research into CMU complemented the combination of public and private support that underlay Pitt's rise in medical research. Building on the extensive technical capability embedded in the region's industrial corporations, in 1949, the federal government and Westinghouse opened the 200-acre Bettis Atomic Research Laboratory in suburban West Mifflin. By the time the world's first nonmilitary atomic electric power plant opened west of the city in 1957, the new suburban research campuses of U.S. Steel, Gulf Oil, and especially Westinghouse had created a network of highly educated professionals that civic leaders hoped would serve as a foundation for future economic growth. In the context of escalating Cold War rhetoric, the marketing of advancements in nuclear energy, in particular, emphasized the increasing partnerships between the urban universities and suburban research enclaves, especially Monroeville. A 1956 Allegheny Conference brochure, for example, mixed images of Oakland's neoclassical academic buildings with spacious corporate campuses in the suburbs, while the text proclaimed that research was contributing significantly to Pittsburgh's growth, as "the world of tomorrow is unlocked in the laboratories of today." In 1965, grants from the Richard K. Mellon Foundation and the federal Advanced Research Projects Agency enabled CMU to launch one of the first computer science departments in the nation. After being named president in 1972, Dr. Richard Cyert parlayed this early specialty into corporate funding for a pioneering Robotics Institute in 1978 and a Magnetics Technology Center in 1982, as well as a $103 million defense contract in 1984 to build a landmark Software Engineering Institute that eventually employed a staff of 700.[22]

In his 1973 speech to the Allegheny Conference, Ralph Widner congratulated the city's leadership for its focus on developing Pitt and CMU, and urged residents to try and capture that "flavor of ferment and entrepreneurship that helped preserve Boston from final decline." Outside the two universities, responsibility for developing research-related economic development fell to the RIDC, whose hiring of Robert H. Ryan was certainly in line with Widner's sentiments. The RIDC promoted its three suburban industrial parks as places for "young and growing companies" to live, "with high quality locations at a price they can afford." To market this vision of economic transformation to a broader audience, the Allegheny Conference and its political partners created the Penn's Southwest Association. Penn's Southwest's first national advertising campaign in 1973 featured both Westinghouse chairman Donald Burnham and the University of Pittsburgh's dynamic new chancellor Wesley Posvar, who declared to *Wall Street Journal* readers that "we've got the people you need" and "cooperation between education and business is a way of life."[23]

State officials worried about the Commonwealth's inability to compete with high-tech growth areas in Massachusetts, North Carolina, and northern California as Pennsylvania lost more than 190,000 manufacturing jobs and nearly 440,000 residents during the 1970s. Earlier state and local efforts to bolster the regional economy had culminated in the successful campaign to attract German automaker Volkswagen (VW) to New Stanton, thirty miles southeast of Pittsburgh in rural Westmoreland County. Despite the commitment of nearly $100 million in public subsidies, however, the automaker failed to live up to expectations due to a declining market for compact cars, quality issues, management problems, and labor strife. The closure of the plant in 1988 as well as new evidence pointing to the role of small and new businesses in job creation led Governor Richard Thornburgh to repudiate the "smokestack chasing" that had guided state economic development programs in the 1970s in favor of encouraging growth of new industries, particularly "advanced technology enterprise." These new policies included changes to the Pennsylvania Industrial Development Authority (PIDA), resulting in a new focus on small and medium size businesses; by 1984 half of all PIDA loans went to firms with fifty or fewer employees.[24]

The changing focus of state policy significantly increased the role of Pittsburgh's research universities in regional economic development following the creation of the Ben Franklin Technology Partners (BFP). Enacted in 1983, the BFP created four regional "job incubators" that provided grants to universities with matching private sector funds to "promote new job opportunities in the advanced technology fields of the future." Pitt and CMU jointly administered the Ben Franklin Technology Center of Western Pennsylvania out of a PIDA-financed and RIDC-renovated building in Oakland chosen for its proximity to the "renowned advanced technology activities" of the two institutions. The Western Pennsylvania Advanced Technology Center, as it was initially called, focused on biomedical technologies and robotics, the two areas of specialization to which Pitt provost Posvar and CMU president Cyert had committed their respective institutions. By summer 1984, the nearly $5 million in state funds provided by the BFP was matched by more than $11.5 million in private and other funds for 65 programs extending from commercializing robots for hazardous waste disposal to developing a prototype speech prosthesis for cancer patients.[25]

Even as the BFP incorporated research universities into state economic development programs, the inclusion of Pitt and CMU into the leadership of the city's public-private partnership became a hallmark of Renaissance II. At the request of state representative Tom Murphy (D-North Side), Robert Pease, the Allegheny Conference's executive director, invited business and political leaders, including Posvar and Cyert, to develop a joint strategy to transform the regional economy as it entered the twenty-first century. Unveiled in June 1985, *Strategy 21* sought to take "maximum advantage" of the trends toward "advanced technology" in order to create a diversified economic base that included light as well as heavy manufacturing, capitalized on the region's natural resources, and promoted a new mix of large and small businesses marked by a "renewed spirit of entrepreneurship and university-linked research and development." To accomplish these goals, the authors proposed five project areas: an expansive new midfield terminal, later dubbed the "Airport of the Future," at Pittsburgh International Airport; three urban redevelopment projects along the Allegheny River near the Golden Triangle that would "transform underutilized land into riverfront attractions"; a "Metals Retention/Reuse" study of ailing manufacturing properties along the Monongahela River; new highway connections at the airport and in the Monongahela Valley; and a handful of new research centers to be operated by Pitt and CMU.[26]

While some of the projects proposed in 1985 never came to fruition and others took a decade or more to complete, *Strategy 21* provided an organizing structure for the emerging vision of a post-industrial Pittsburgh.

The coupling of high-tech economic transformation with sites on the newly cleared urban riverfront was perhaps most evident in the transformation of J&L Steel's Hazelwood Works into the Pittsburgh Technology Center. Andrew Carnegie's chief competitor in the late nineteenth century, J&L remained one of the city's largest employers for much of the twentieth century despite the company's purchase by Dallas-based Ling Temco Vought (LTV) in 1968. While its South Side mill remained active for a few more years, LTV shuttered the Eliza Furnace and its other operations on the north bank of the Monongahela in 1981. The URAP purchased the site for $3.5 million in 1983, the same year the state created Ben Franklin Technology Partners and local high-tech advocates established the Pittsburgh High Technology Council (HTC). Spearheaded by CMU provost Angel Jordan, a robotics professor, and Penn's Southwest executive director Jay Aldridge, the HTC epitomized the emerging neoliberal partnership between the public and private sectors in promoting the growth of high-tech industries. We hope to attract a "critical mass of companies that will form a real high-tech community," HTC executive director Timothy Parks declared in 1986. What is needed is a "classic juxtaposition, a dramatic symbol of change."[27]

Within this context, the URAP quickly developed plans for a technology center to house "advanced technology firms" on the former mill site with RIDC as project coordinator. Situated along the Penn-Lincoln Parkway between the Golden Triangle and Oakland, the location was ideal for demonstrating the Renaissance II partnership between business, political, and university leaders. As the URAP began clearing the land, administrators at Pitt and CMU joined as sponsors of Centers for Biotechnology and Engineering, and Advanced Manufacturing and Software Engineering, respectively. This project represented the "very real and visible transformation" of a segment of the economy from heavy industry to advanced technology, the authors of *Strategy 21* declared. By 1988 the state had contributed nearly $40 million to the project and CMU attracted matching funds from outside investors for its research center. Just a year and a half after the closure of the nearby Homestead Works, the old J&L site was cleared and construction was set to begin on the two university research centers with CMU President Richard Cyert anticipating "a beautiful place that becomes a statement of the new Pittsburgh."[28]

Following a century and a half of industrial use, the architects of *Strategy 21* confidently predicted that the high-tech center would "both beautify the riverfront and make it economically productive." Notwithstanding these aspirations and the high level of funding, a number of factors that would also plague other "brownfields" in the region slowed the project. The URAP already anticipated the need for significant environmental remediation and removed more than 420,000 gallons of waste oil and contaminated water. However, the discovery of buried cyanide caused additional delays and expenses as well as placing limits on how parts of the site could be used. This problem scared off potential investors with the result that CMU had to reduce the size of its facility and was in danger of pulling out of the project entirely. Consequently, by late 1990 ground had still not been broken on the "sore-thumb example of failed potential" despite the expenditure of more than $26 million in mostly public funds.[29]

Even as the signature conversion of the J&L site slowed to a crawl, employment growth in health, business, and educational services continued in what boosters celebrated as a "collective career change." Advocates of *Strategy 21* could also point to a number of high profile projects during the mid-1980s including the conversion of Gulf Oil's suburban research campus into the University of Pittsburgh Applied Research Center (U-Parc), a facility that soon housed 130 companies and 1,200 workers. Following the 1984 announcement of a Pentagon-financed Software Engineering Institute at CMU, advertisements by Penn's Southwest proclaimed the region to be "the nation's third largest knowledge center." Similarly, Rand McNally's decision to rank Pittsburgh as the nation's "Most Livable City" prompted the erection of a series of billboards particularly in Sunbelt cities, such as one in Atlanta that proclaimed: "Want to Live in America's No. 1 city? Move to Pittsburgh! Y'all Come."[30]

While it took nearly a decade to complete, boosters celebrated the April 1993 opening of the PTC's first building as "just the beginning of a new era for this post-industrial city." Pitt's Biotech Center was moving into a new $10.2 million home where corroding mills had previously stood, the *Post-Gazette*'s art and architecture critic crowed, with the new facility stretching along the riverfront "like a postmodern grandchild of Swiss architect Le Corbusier." The original facility was only expected to house a few dozen scientists relocated from Oakland, but high-tech advocates could point with optimism to the groundbreaking for CMU's Robotics Center and the announcement by Union Switch and Signal that it would become the site's first private tenant. The dramatic progress of the last year at the Pittsburgh Technology Center was "evidence of readiness for real growth in

FIGURE 13. One of the advertisements produced for the Penn's Southwest Association's "Dynamic Pittsburgh" campaign. More than a dozen of these full-page ads appeared in the *New York Times, Los Angeles Times, Wall Street Journal,* and other national publications in 1981 and 1982. This ad, sponsored by National Steel, the parent company of Weirton Steel, emphasized the booster vision of Pittsburgh as a hub for high technology workers. Dynamic Pittsburgh Collection, 1973–1985, acc. 2002.0093, Library & Archives, Senator John Heinz History Center. Courtesy of the Allegheny Conference on Community Development.

technology companies and jobs," boosters declared. "It is time to develop a strategy to make the Greater Pittsburgh region itself a Technology Park."[31]

"A Community Right to Industrial Property"

Despite the modest successes enjoyed by proponents of this high-tech "RoboBurgh," transforming a regional economy and culture so intimately linked to heavy industry proved extraordinarily difficult and contentious. While ostensibly setting out to change the region's image, the 1981 Dynamic Pittsburgh campaign sent mixed messages that undercut the vision of Renaissance II, which led a *Wall Street Journal* reporter to dismiss its effect in attracting new downtown businesses. The H. J. Heinz Company boldly declared that Pittsburgh was "ecology conscious" and an ad sponsored by Consolidation Coal and Joy Manufacturing highlighted research on "wind turbines, solar cells, and geothermal power," but the text was overshadowed by adjacent pictures of oil rigs, nuclear cooling towers, and a coal loading facility. The campaign's message of post-industrial dynamism became even more disjointed when seen in the light of the impending economic catastrophe that would make metropolitan Pittsburgh into part of the Rust Belt. Campaign sponsor LTV Steel would soon shut down and dismantle the Pittsburgh Works, bringing unintended poignancy to its ad depicting an imploding building making room for a new office tower.[32]

Over and above the decade-long decline of employment in the Steel Valley's mines and mills, the 1980s were breathtaking in the speed and scope of closures. Between 1981 and 1987, the number of steel workers employed in the Monongahela Valley alone plummeted from over 35,000 to fewer than 4,000 as U.S. Steel closed mills and furnaces in Rankin, Duquesne, Clairton, Homestead, and McKeesport. Dozens of smaller manufacturers, too, closed or dramatically downsized; LTV Steel (formerly Jones & Laughlin) closed its South Side, Aliquippa, and Hazelwood plants in 1985, the same year Wheeling-Pittsburgh Steel declared bankruptcy. The passage of revisions to the federal Clean Air Act in 1990 also capped a decade of turmoil in the coal industry, with mines supplying electrical power plants operating at an increasing disadvantage to low sulfur coal operations in other regions. Between 1988 and 1996, mining employment remained virtually unchanged in western states but declined by nearly 50 percent in Ohio and Pennsylvania and nearly 30 percent in West Virginia where losses in the Ohio Valley were partially offset by low-sulfur coal mined in the southern part of the state. In 1994, Robert Murray, owner of one of the largest mines remaining in the region, said the loss of purchasing orders from a key customer would force him to close his doors the following year. "We're talking about one of the highest production mines in the world," Murray proclaimed. "If we can't make it, no one in Ohio's coal industry can make it."[33]

Public policy failures and the changing regional dynamic of the previous decades meant that the Steel Valley's precipitous decline in the 1980s disproportionately affected the urbanized river valleys and the areas outside of the metropolitan core. The cities of Pittsburgh and McKeesport, which contained less than a third of Allegheny County's population, accounted for more than half of its 7.8 percent population loss during the decade. On the other hand, a 34 percent increase in Cranberry residents allowed rural Butler County to grow by just under 4 percent, the only county in the region to gain during the decade. The more diversified economy of southwestern Pennsylvania also weathered mining and manufacturing losses better overall than the Ohio and West Virginia communities along the Ohio River. There the population declined at more than double the rate of the metropolitan core—a gap that would widen during the 1990s. While thousands of residents left the region each year, the choice was often a difficult one taken after all other options were exhausted. When joblessness in Beaver County reached 23 percent in the mid-1980s, steel worker Kenny Johnston explained that long-term unemployment was something he had never dreamed of before. "Man, I've worked since I was sixteen. I've tried like hell [to find a job], there's nothing out there. With one out of every four people looking for work, there's not much to go around."[34]

Obtaining a college education formed the key to securing a good job in metropolitan Pittsburgh's new economic system, and the federal government provided increased funding for retraining to workers affected by deindustrialization, foreign trade, and environmental regulations. On Christmas Eve in 1981, Larry Prisbylla arrived at U.S. Steel's Clairton Works to find a notice posted, "No more work scheduled." After discovering that the only job he could obtain with a high school diploma was as a dishwasher at less than one-third his previous salary, Prisbylla enrolled in a subsidized nursing program at a local community college while his wife's job at a local bank paid the family's bills. "It seemed like all the technical schools were pushing computers, so I picked the health industry," he explained. "We've got all these hospitals [and] it seemed like nursing would give me lots of options."

On graduation Prisbylla accepted a position at Mercy Hospital, making a salary similar to what he had in the mill. Because of the rapid growth in the healthcare industry, hospital recruiters were anxious to attract new nurses to their facilities. "They would pump your hand and shove an application into it," recalled Prisbylla. "What a switch!" I told my wife that I would have loved to "turn down the first five or six, just to get back at all the people who turned me down, just to see how it felt."[35]

While the resurgent partnership of Renaissance II was eager to emphasize a future of "Brawn Forged into Brain" that could carry the Steel Valley beyond the ruins of deindustrialization, there remained a great deal of wishful thinking on the part of civic boosters and visiting journalists alike. One Mellon Bank vice president said that fifty people, at least a third of them ex-steelworkers, applied for every computer technician opening at the bank. This was especially the case in rural and river valley areas where the growth of nonmanufacturing sectors had only a "marginal impact" in alleviating the economic plight of residents. Race, class, and gender distinctions also shaped the distribution of wealth in post-industrial Pittsburgh as the gendered nature of the region's fastest growing industries, the need for a college education, and the glut of job-seekers limited the ability of most working-class men to obtain high-paying employment after the mills closed. Both black and white college graduates formed a lower percentage of Allegheny County's population than in the nation as a whole, but whites remained twice as likely to hold a degree as blacks. As a result, while Pittsburgh's unemployment rate fell to 6.9 percent for white men and 4.4 percent for white women during the early 1990s, it remained at 14.3 percent for black women and nearly 20 percent for black men.[36]

Median hourly wages in metropolitan Pittsburgh recovered somewhat during the 1990s, but workers still trailed the state and national average, with earnings less in real terms than they were in 1979. Beaver County residents Randy and Denise Weigel provide an important contrast to the experience of Larry Prisbylla and his wife. After Randy (27) lost his job at LTV Steel in 1988, his wife Denise (26) went back to work part-time as a graphic artist and substitute teacher. While Denise paid the bills, Randy spent his days at home watching their 2 1/2 year-old daughter, Aimee, an arrangement that created tension between the couple. "Randy gets frustrated and gets on me," Denise explained. "I've got a lot on my mind and I need that first hour or so [after work] to relax and wind down. A year ago it was the other way around." At the time of their interview in 1990, finances were tight and Randy's unemployment benefits were scheduled to expire in six weeks. Through her work, Denise had contact with residents of post-industrial Pittsburgh, whose lifestyle bore little resemblance to her own. "The people I deal with all day are the ones who are making money and spending it. They drive around in a big car, they've got a phone in it. It's like being in a different world. You know, this is the first time that Randy doesn't know what to do or where to find a job. I just wonder what's going to happen."[37]

Even as high-tech advocates began articulating their post-industrial vision during the accelerating closures of the early 1980s, many residents of the deindustrialized river valleys focused on reinvigorating the steel mills that had long sustained them. In response to National Steel's announcement in 1982 that it would close its Weirton Steel subsidiary, local management and the Independent Steel Workers Union (ISU) formed a Joint Study Committee that developed a plan to purchase the mill. Under the terms of the agreement reached with National Steel and approved by 88 percent of ISU members voting in September 1983, Weirton Steel would pay $66 million over fifteen years and assume future pension liabilities in return for the mill's physical property, patents, and trademarks. To pay for the deal, workers would be required to give up a substantial portion of their wages and benefits in exchange for profit sharing, a relationship known as an Employee Stock Ownership Plan (ESOP). The new company was immediately profitable and for much of the 1980s employment remained above 8,000.[38]

Weirton's particular political economy made possible the relatively conservative ESOP approach in ways that were impractical for other mills in the region. Unlike the privately financed ESOP, more radical activists argued that the long-standing relationship between companies and mill towns created a "community right to industrial property" in the event of a closure. The Tri-State Conference on Steel, formed in 1979, embodied this approach with organizers calling for government grants or loan guarantees, local management by workers and community representatives, and the use of "eminent domain power to acquire abandoned or under-utilized facilities." Endorsed by the United Steelworkers of America (USWA), the group led reindustrialization campaigns at Crucible Steel in Midland, Mesta Machine Company in West Homestead, and Westinghouse Air Brake, among many others. In January 1985, more than five hundred people participated in a rally to save the "Dorothy Six" blast furnace at U.S. Steel's

Duquesne Works, with speakers including USWA president Lynn Williams, Pittsburgh mayor Richard Caliguiri, and the Rev. Jesse Jackson, who declared the Monongahela Valley "the Selma of the plant shutdown movement."[39]

The most sustained and visible attempt to implement this ideology of community-led reindustrialization focused on the South Side Works, the section of the LTV site that sprawled along the Monongahela River across from what would become the Pittsburgh Technology Center. Emerging out of the fight to save the Duquesne Works, the Steel Valley Authority (SVA) led efforts to restart the facility—the last integrated steel mill in the city—after its closure in 1985. With backing from nine Monongahela Valley communities including Pittsburgh, supporters envisioned SVA as a "new political structure with the legal power to wrest control of plants from their present overseers."[40] The SVA tried to intervene in the demolition of other mills, but a 1988 steel retention study by the Allegheny County Planning Department found that the South Side Works was the only shuttered facility that represented a "realistic, potentially viable stand alone business opportunity." As a result, subsequent efforts focused on raising the $220 million necessary to restart the site's two relatively new electric arc furnaces and produce rough steel slabs for sale. "For the first time in this area," declared SVA board member and USWA activist Mike Stout, "a strong, community based-coalition is beginning to mount a serious challenge to the prerogative of corporations and banks to make all investment decisions, shut down viable plants, and otherwise do with capital what they like."[41]

SVA officials were able to delay the demolition of much of the South Side Works, but the supporters of reindustrialization faced serious economic obstacles. The SVA theoretically could assert eminent domain, float public bonds and seek government funds, but actually exercising those powers was "neither simple, quick nor cheap." While Mayor Caliguiri was a charter member of the SVA and provided $50,000 for its startup costs, for example, he insisted on restrictions in the organization's charter that effectively gave him veto power over any potential project in the city. Project director and Carlow College economist Robert Erickson complained that the South Side site was being overvalued, but the main problem was difficulty in attracting private capital at a time of slack demand for the steel slabs that could be produced at the facility. As a result, while a coalition that included state legislators from the Mon Valley and members of Pittsburgh City Council succeeded in securing public funding for the 1988 feasibility study, local and state governments proved unwilling or unable to commit the hundreds of millions needed to restart the mill without significant investment from the private sector. This lack of institutional support left the organization with "only enough money to cover its day-to-day expenses," and, according to SVA solicitor Jay Hornack, reliant "exclusively upon how much private financing we arrange."[42]

Enthusiasm for the SVA's alternate vision of public-private partnership for reindustrialization was strongest in the region's mill towns, but many Pittsburghers without direct ties to the industry questioned the desirability of restarting the mill at all. At the same time as Caliguiri was providing support for the SVA, city officials and the Allegheny Conference were emphasizing cultural and recreational opportunities on the riverfronts that were not necessarily compatible with extensive industrial activity. "If Pittsburgh and the region are looking for a source of employment," declared one analyst, "they can do better than try to resurrect that works." Furthermore, the formation in the 1960s of environmental advocacy groups alongside neighborhood organizations, most notably the Group Against Smog and Pollution (GASP), underscored the inadequacy of the voluntarist model of pollution reduction favored by the original Renaissance partnership. As with surface mining in the countryside, during the 1970s industrial corporations routinely raised the specter of job losses if environmental laws were implemented, a tactic that challenged the ability of the city's public-private partnership to craft a unified vision of the future. Indeed, up until and through the closures of the 1980s, GASP was party to a number of active lawsuits aimed at reducing emissions from U.S. Steel and LTV sites, including the South Side and Hazelwood Works. Making explicit reference to the long-running tensions in Renaissance imagery, one resident declared in 1991 that "Pittsburgh's skyline may no longer be black with soot, but those of us living downwind of LTV are still breathing polluted, unhealthy air."[43]

By the late 1980s, the two former LTV sites facing each other across the Monongahela became potent symbols of a broader struggle over metropolitan Pittsburgh's identity. "Image is terribly important [and] ours is more negative than it should be," complained one advertising executive. While post-industrial boosters insisted they "were not trying to put the knock on steel," they celebrated a narrative of "the city's steelmaking past . . . being buried under 90,000 cubic yards of dirt to prepare for a future shaped by robots and miracle drugs." Penn's Southwest's Jay Aldridge, a founder of the HTC, famously joked that the community's beloved football franchise should consider a name change to the "Pittsburgh Softwares" to emphasize this shift. On the other hand, former steelworker Angelo Georgeiano explicitly criticized the emphasis on a high-tech economy, declaring "They are going to make jobs for scientists, professors and their relatives. They are not going to make jobs for displaced steelworkers." As job losses mounted and the rhetoric of high-tech post-industrialism intensified, some activists associated with a group called Denominational Ministry Strategy undertook controversial direct action campaigns such as depositing fish in safety deposit boxes and dumping pennies in the lobbies of banks accused of divesting from steel. In response to challenges that these tactics were "keeping out the very people who might be able to bring some hope," one local minister and activist replied, "They can have their image back as soon as they deliver for the people."[44]

However, a lack of sufficient funding meant that SVA remained unable to implement its vision for the South Side Works even as Pitt's Biotech Center finally broke ground across the river. LTV initially supported reindustrialization and vowed to cooperate with local efforts, but reversed course shortly after the completion of the steel retention study and announced plans to raze the entire mill site. In a last ditch effort to save the site, the SVA attempted to partner with the Pittsburgh History and Landmarks Foundation and a local development group to create a mixed-use site where "history and development" could occur at the same place. In a controversial decision, in March 1988 Pittsburgh city council nominated the South Side Works as a historic site in an effort to stall LTV's planned demolition. The effort failed; LTV cleared a quarter of the site in 1990 and began razing the remaining buildings the next year. With little to show for preservation efforts despite an expenditure of $600,000, the *Pittsburgh Press* editorialized "it is important for all concerned to realize that the site's future does not include steelmaking, and that postponing or deferring action in hopes of saving the electric furnaces appears futile."[45]

Among the thousands of residents who witnessed the final demolition of the South Side Works and the beginning of construction on the Pittsburgh Technology Center, was Peter Miller, a journalist with *National Geographic* magazine. Miller's 1991 profile of the city, "Stronger than Steel," praised a community that "now thrives, not just because it found new ways to use old resources, but also because its traditional, strong-willed people would have it no other way." Through interviews with public and nonprofit officials, including Carol Brown of the Pittsburgh Cultural Trust, Mayor Sophie Masloff, and state legislator Tom Murphy among many others, the article captured the story of a post-industrial renaissance based on higher education, service sector employment, a cleaner environment, and quality of life amenities. While the region had lost 120,000 manufacturing jobs over the previous decade, it had gained 115,000 nonmanufacturing jobs, mostly in business services and health care. "Pittsburgh is the classic overachiever among American cities," declared University of Pittsburgh professor Franklin Toker. "It industrialized first, it became obsolescent first, and it overcame obsolescence first."[46]

Even as Pittsburgh worked to grow its research, higher education, and healthcare sectors ("eds and meds" as the approach came to be known), it is important to understand the "myths and evidence" of the region's post-industrial revitalization. While the city itself no longer contained large mills, manufacturing and heavy industry in particular remained a key part of the regional economy. Though employment dramatically declined overall, mills continued to produce steel in Weirton, Steubenville, and many other communities. In 1992, for example, U.S. Steel installed a $250 million continuous caster at its Edgar Thomson Plant, which along with a coke plant in Clairton, and a rolling mill in West Mifflin, remained part of a fully integrated Mon Valley Works. Nevertheless, the dismantling of industrial infrastructure and the clearing of large swaths of land in the river valleys left enormous voids in the region's physical and social landscapes. From the periphery to the metropolitan core, Steel Valley residents adopted a variety of strategies during the 1990s to make a place for themselves in this new economic order taking shape *Beyond Rust*.[47]

CHAPTER 9

Burbs of the 'Burgh

In spring 1998, early morning commuters along Route 22, a four-lane highway running west from Pittsburgh, woke to find a new billboard touting "Pittsburgh's New Suburb . . . in Ohio." The sign was part of an advertising campaign spearheaded by the Progress Alliance, a pro-growth coalition of local officials and business leaders formed to take advantage of the extension of the Byrd Expressway, which included a new bridge across the Ohio River. This may sound like the typical narrative of booster-driven sprawl, but the community seeking to reestablish frayed links to the metropolitan core was Steubenville, which had become a withered, polluted and poverty-stricken shell of its former prosperity. "You could let off a howitzer down on Market Street in Steubenville and not harm a soul," declared one local resident in 1994. "In fact, I'm not even sure there would be enough people there [to notice] a big bang." By the time of the "Burb of the 'Burgh" campaign, however, highway-driven metropolitan growth had already begun to reach the community, with a new upscale residential project by a Pittsburgh developer and a number of tenants in a recently built industrial park. The billboards "accomplished what we needed to do," explained city manager Gary DuFour. Pennsylvania residents and business leaders "began to think, 'Oh yeah, it isn't that far.'"[1]

Many residents in the region's smaller communities looked to new highway construction and the suburban model of greenfield development as the keys to community revitalization. While often exacerbating urban problems, highway-oriented development also provided opportunities for strengthening links between growth centers and disadvantaged parts of the region that had grown increasingly isolated. In the Monongahela Valley, for example, abandoned mill sites were converted to industrial parks under the auspices of the Regional Industrial Development Corporation (RIDC), which joined officials from throughout the area in calling for improved access through the construction of a Mon-Fayette Expressway. Similarly, the Allegheny Conference and Pittsburgh's Democratic political leadership cast development of a new "Airport of the Future" as the catalyst for growth in the western part of the region. By the mid-1990s, the highway upgrades and new bridge brought Steubenville within commuting distance of the Airport Corridor, which set the stage for the community to reinvent itself as a "Burb of the 'Burgh."

New transportation routes also had significant implications for metropolitan Pittsburgh's rural areas. The development of state parks and private resorts in Ohiopyle and the Laurel Highlands southeast of Pittsburgh, for example, highlighted possibilities for transforming abandoned rail corridors into recreational trails and developing a tourist economy in the hinterland. In addition, locations along major highways offered opportunities for residents to commute or for local officials to develop suburban-style industrial parks. Unemployment and out-migration remained high in many areas through the end of the century, however, with communities often struggling to overcome expensive legacies left over from more than a century of natural resource extraction. Furthermore, though many mines closed in the late 1980s due to market issues and new environmental regulations, by the late 1990s coal was on the upswing again, which offered new economic opportunities even as the social and environmental consequences raised questions about the trajectory of post-industrial Pittsburgh.

"Airport of the Future"

During the 1980s, a rejuvenated growth coalition that included the Allegheny Conference, a variety of nonprofit development organizations, state and local political leaders, and administrators at Pittsburgh's two research universities looked toward the construction of an enormous new Midfield Terminal at the airport as both a symbol of post-industrial progress and an economic generator for the region. For Pittsburgh, which had to transform its economy from one built by steel to one "balanced on high-technology industries, corporate offices and services industries," one observer noted, "the airport project has come to mean as much to further development and diversification as it does to area aviation." This new "Airport of the Future," which had formed a key component of *Strategy 21*, opened to tremendous fanfare in September 1992 and included a new seven-mile expressway that proponents hoped would eventually link to a new Southern Beltway running to the poverty-stricken Monongahela Valley. "Thousands of new jobs will emerge, companies will relocate here to do business, and our natural beauty will attract conventions and tourists," concluded the Allegheny County Commissioners. "In years to come, Pittsburgh international Airport will become a mighty engine of economic development for the entire tri-state district."[2]

Creating a modern airport had long been an important component of the Pittsburgh Renaissance vision for remaking metropolitan Pittsburgh's image and economy. The dedication of the Greater Pittsburgh International Airport in 1952 provided the western anchor of the Penn-Lincoln Parkway extending through Pittsburgh to the Pennsylvania Turnpike at Monroeville. The Allegheny Conference and its political allies envisioned the new airport as complementing downtown redevelopment, but during the 1950s and 1960s the Airport Corridor itself emerged as one of the region's most significant commercial centers. In addition to single-family homes, the area also increasingly played host to multi-family and condominium developments. One development, Pennbury Hills, featured the highest density in Allegheny County at fourteen thousand residents on forty-nine acres. By 1963, the Airport Corridor formed the region's second largest business center as several large out-of-town firms, including Aetna Insurance and General Electric, chose to locate their regional branch offices along the Parkway rather than downtown in the Golden Triangle.[3]

Airport Corridor development formed a key component of the regional growth strategy promoted by a revived public-private partnership in the wake of rapid declines in the region's traditional industries. In 1979, the publicly subsidized RIDC Park West opened just south of the airport, and advocates went so far as to declare that the area offered "unlimited potential" for industrial and office development. Local officials had difficulty leasing the colossal, interconnected mills abandoned in the river valleys, but the new industrial parks met the demands for the small and medium sized firms driving regional growth during the 1970s and 1980s. A 1982 industrial site survey found that purchases of existing manufacturing sites had dropped by 50 percent from the previous year but that sales of more modern facilities, found predominantly in suburban industrial parks, rose

35 percent. The 39-acre Vista Industrial Park off the Parkway West in Robinson Township had nine buildings containing more than 400,000 square feet of space, while construction of a fifteenth building in the adjacent Parkway West Industrial Park provided a total of about 540,000 square feet of industrial space. According to an executive at an energy and environmental consulting firm that was one of the site's first tenants, RIDC West helped "combine our activities here making them more efficient," especially since "we can reach the airport (Greater Pittsburgh) in a few minutes."[4]

Allegheny County commissioners began planning for an airport upgrade during the late 1960s, but political wrangling and a declining local economy stalled the project for over a decade. In January 1985, state representative Tom Murphy (D-North Side) broke the log jam over airport expansion and other economic development initiatives by persuading officials in Pittsburgh, Allegheny County, and the region's two major research universities to coordinate their requests for state funding. The *Strategy 21* report, overseen by the Allegheny Conference, argued that airport construction "would have a dramatic effect on the region's economy" by creating 18,000 jobs over the next fifteen years. It would "strengthen the region's attraction as a corporate headquarters" and "convert seriously underutilized land to diverse, new business purposes with heavy job creation potential." Of the $495 million in state funds initially requested for Strategy 21, officials earmarked $173 million for airport expansion. "The new airport," declared county commissioners, "represents our collective efforts to pull ourselves up by our economic bootstraps and prepare to assume our proper place in the emerging world economy."[5]

Residents and local officials hit hard by industrial decline in western Allegheny and nearby Washington and Beaver counties worked to tap into airport-oriented growth. Shortly after the start of terminal construction, work began on the Airport Corridor's largest project to date—Robinson Town Centre—the first stage of a mixed-use development with plans for a 435,000 square foot retail center, a super-regional shopping mall, and more than 1.5 million square feet of office space with facilities for research and development. Excellent highway access "combined with the growth projects due to construction of the new Midfield terminal" made Robinson Town Centre viable, explained developer Michael Zamagias. Similarly, by 1993 two housing projects, a golf course, and office buildings for a precision tool manufacturer, an engineering firm, and Mitsubishi's Rotary Nozzle Division had opened at the Washington County Redevelopment Authority's six hundred acre Southpointe development twelve miles southwest of the airport along Interstate 79. Beaver County's connection to the airport also increased with the opening of the Beaver Valley Expressway as a toll road in 1991. "New jobs," declared Jay Aldridge, a Beaver County native and the director of regional marketing firm Penn's Southwest, "are not from J&L like they used to be. They are from the new job generator—the airport."[6]

Steubenville's "Burb of the 'Burgh" campaign can thus best be set into a context of older industrial communities in the Steel Valley working to reshape themselves, both symbolically and physically, into a form suitable for the "post-industrial" economy. The regional bonds forged in the late nineteenth century between southwestern Pennsylvania and the Upper Ohio Valley had slowly unraveled as new highway connections across the state border did not keep pace with the decline of rail travel. Over time, outlying communities in Ohio and West Virginia lost population and grew more isolated, in relative terms, from the cultural and economic activities of the metropolis. Eventually this left residents of Steubenville and other local communities to face the collapse of heavy industry without easy access to the social and institutional resources of their larger neighbor. Indeed, the process of postwar economic decline went hand in hand with Steubenville's growing seclusion from the larger metropolitan region. You still had a two-lane road, recalled DuFour, of transportation links in the 1970s and 1980s, and "in Pittsburgh they would say, 'Oh, you're over in Weirton, West Virginia or Steubenville, Ohio. You're clear over there?'"[7]

Even before the opening of the Byrd Expressway, Steubenville residents began to mobilize in order to capitalize on their new highway link. Uniting under the Progress Alliance coalition, initially called Alliance 2000, public officials and business leaders sought to transform the image and reality of their community as a polluted, de-industrialized dead end into a progressive, post-industrial alternative to more traditional commuter suburbs. Through an advertising campaign targeting southwestern Pennsylvania residents and businesses, the Progress Alliance emphasized low taxes, opportunities for outdoor recreation, culture, and proximity to Pittsburgh, less than forty miles away. According to one Alliance member, the campaign focused on reaching out to Pittsburgh's civic and business leaders, with the message that, "Hey we're right here. We're not all this distance, two states away from you. We're just a few miles down the road."[8]

The decision to focus marketing efforts on greater Pittsburgh involved an important shift in the regional vision of local leaders. In part, political and administrative policies that deemphasized the social and cultural bonds of the Steel Valley in favor of development projects organized on the state level caused the declining relationship between outlying areas of the Ohio Valley and the metropolitan core in southwestern Pennsylvania. Consequently, from the 1960s through the 1980s public officials in Ohio and West Virginia largely looked to more distant cities such as Cleveland, Youngstown, and Charleston as potential economic partners. The 1990s, then, were a period of "rediscovery" for local residents who suddenly found themselves within easy commuting distance of the universities, hospitals, shopping malls, and industrial parks of the metropolitan core. "We do not see ourselves as raiders," declared Rick Platt, Progress Alliance executive director. "We want a strong Pittsburgh, and if it comes down to cheering for some other part of Ohio and Pittsburgh, we will cheer for Pittsburgh just like we cheer for the Steelers over the Browns."[9]

The suburban strategy of economic development complemented and reinforced the rapid growth of highway-oriented peripheral areas, with little new construction actually taking place in the old central business districts near the rivers. In Steubenville, for example, development officials focused on an expansive, county-owned industrial and commercial park just off Route 22 that offered generous tax incentives under a state program to help distressed communities. Officials in Steubenville and Weirton did "begin looking at reutilization strategies for brownfields" in the early 2000s, according to DuFour, who held a variety of positions in both cities, as a recognition "sort of evolved" that "the entire community advances, not just a piece." However, even the promise of state and federal subsidies for the removal of toxic wastes from former mill sites along the riverfront required matching private funds and a level of coordination that was very difficult, especially outside the metropolitan core. As a result, the first significant brownfield redevelopment project in the Steubenville area, a modest 7-acre site with a projected twenty jobs, was not completed until 2009.[10]

As urban poverty increased, especially among African Americans, some political leaders began to publicly question the uneven distribution of wealth inherent in the suburban development model. In 1991, a handful of high profile relocations to the RIDC Park West prompted a series of legislative hearings questioning the use of public funds to "create low-cost parks in the suburbs when so much needs to be done in the Monongahela Valley and the city." Headed by Rep. Tom Murphy, a few years before his election as Pittsburgh mayor, the Pennsylvania House hearings indicated significant

FIGURE 14. View of Veterans Memorial Bridge looking east across the Ohio River. The bridge was the final link in upgrading U.S. Route 22 to a four-lane highway from Pittsburgh across the West Virginia panhandle to Weirton and Steubenville. Courtesy of Historic Fort Steuben & Visitor Center.

tension within the *Strategy 21* public-private partnership of which he was a prominent member. "The fact of the matter is that RIDC has provided significant subsidies to companies with no intention of leaving the region," declared Murphy. There are limited funds available and "we have a responsibility to decide whether we want our public funds to be used like that."[11]

While Murphy's concerns were ostensibly about the RIDC, in private he emphasized the larger context of economic development efforts in the region that seemed to privilege suburban growth at the expense of the older downtowns. "If we had a metropolitan government with one taxing jurisdiction," he explained in a letter to an executive at a high-tech firm located in the RIDC Park in O'Hara Township, "it would make no difference where a company was located." "The fact of the matter is that we have 130 municipalities" in Allegheny County alone and "it becomes increasingly important where companies locate." In another letter to Tom Foerster, chair of the Allegheny County Commissioners and a key backer of *Strategy 21*, Murphy complained, "I am convinced that our economic development efforts are not having the effective impact they could." Linking "job creation *and* job access," Murphy cited a list of three hundred union airport employees of whom only three lived in Pittsburgh and none came from the hard hit Monongahela Valley. Without "any public transportation the Airport is too remote for many residents, and so is not a place that they would think of for a job." "I fear that only those who have the resources will get the jobs," he concluded, "and that those jobs will increasingly be away from the poor areas" of the deindustrialized river valleys.[12]

The efforts of the Progress Alliance to transform Steubenville into a "Burb of the 'Burgh" had some notable successes, including opening a major Wal-Mart distribution center in 2001. Similarly, in 1999, discount clothing chain Pennsylvania Fashions (rue21) opened an enormous warehouse at Three Springs Business Park along Route 22 on the eastern edge of Weirton. On the other hand, the low-tax strategy of luring investment actually contributed to a stall in housing and some types of commercial growth in the Airport Corridor during the late 1990s. When it came to homes in the $200,000 to $350,000 price range, you could "drive another 20 minutes" to Weirton or Steubenville and reduce your taxes by $300 to $500 a month, explained the owner of a Pennsylvania construction company. As a result, in 1999, only Moon Township, of all Airport Corridor communities, placed in the top ten of the region for number of building permits issued for housing construction. "There has been some growth there, but not what you think," added Ron Croushore, CEO of Prudential Preferred Realty. "Lots of people still come from the north and south. The malls and shopping centers are drawing from all over. The traffic has been unbelievable, but the housing has not been ahead of the other parts of the city."[13]

By the end of the twentieth century, Tom Foerster's prediction that "whole new cities will grow up around the airport" proved true to some extent, though the 18,000 jobs projected by the architects of *Strategy 21* to stem from the enormous public investment never fully materialized, due in large part to the decline of the airline industry following the September 11 attacks and the subsequent bankruptcy of US Airways. In the face of criticism that airport-driven development had not taken off, civic and political leaders in southwestern Pennsylvania doubled down on the suburban strategy of highway construction and greenfield development. Indeed, Foerster pointed out that fewer business executives said proximity to the airport was a leading factor in their decision to move to the area than those who cited highway access and overall location. Boosters called especially for creation of a new six-mile expressway, the "Findlay Connector," that would link the airport directly to Route 22 and open new areas to the south and west for development. In this effort, they found an enthusiastic partner in the Progress Alliance, which hired Tom Bayuzik, former head of economic development under Pittsburgh mayor Tom Murphy, as their new executive director. By 2006, leaders in Steubenville and Weirton had embraced their reengagement with the broader metropolitan region to such an extent that Bayuzik declared that the completion of the Findlay Connector, a toll road built entirely inside Pennsylvania, was the Upper Ohio Valley's "single most important highway project."[14]

In the end, Steubenville's efforts were part of a broader transition whereby industrial small cities struggled to find a place for themselves in a new economic and spatial reality. In general terms, the deindustrialized river valleys and especially the Ohio Valley communities separated from Pittsburgh by state lines remained junior partners in the process of metropolitan development, with little choice but to compete for the employment opportunities available as mill towns continued to lose population in the face of ongoing plant closures. However, the development of new transportation links allowed residents to sell their communities in much the same way civic boosters had cast them in the industrial era—as small towns with easy access to big city amenities. In the process, locals once again refashioned a common physical and cultural landscape into an identity that embraced the commonalities shared with their larger neighbor upriver. "If proximity is a measure of being part of the Pittsburgh area, Steubenville has it," declared William Chesson, president of the local Chamber of Commerce. "We proudly call ourselves the "Burb of the 'Burgh." Steubenville is just 10 miles from the Post-Gazette Pavilion and just 30 minutes from Pittsburgh International Airport. How much more 'Pittsburgh area' can a city be than that?"[15]

"No Longer Is This Valley a Forgotten Valley"

Pennsylvania Governor Robert F. Casey made his first state visit to Homestead the day after his inauguration in January 1987 to announce a package of plans to help the areas hardest hit by the collapse of steel. Earlier urban renewal had involved large-scale demolition of older downtowns for conversion to commercial and industrial use, but state and local officials now emphasized a two-pronged redevelopment approach largely modeled on the success of the postwar suburbs. The closure of the Monongahela Valley's mammoth steel mills opened large swaths of land and prompted calls for planned riverfront manufacturing and retail districts similar to sites sprouting up at suburban interchanges. A second and related effort involved schemes to build new highways tying aging communities in the river valleys to both Pittsburgh and new suburban growth areas, including both the Airport Corridor and Monroeville, which was less than ten miles away. Indeed, Casey had a special project in mind for revitalizing the iconic Homestead—construction of the long-delayed Mon/Fayette Expressway that would parallel the river south of Pittsburgh and, hopefully, connect to the new Airport of the Future via a southern beltway. This was another big step to help "bring businesses and jobs into the region," the governor later declared. "No longer is this valley a forgotten valley."[16]

Casey's declaration reflected a desire among many residents of the Monongahela Valley to reforge frayed regional links through a suburban strategy just like that of Steubenville. While river valley communities throughout the region suffered dramatic employment losses during the 1980s, however, the historical significance of the closure of most of U.S. Steel's massive mills made the Monongahela Valley a potent symbol that attracted enormous attention on the state and national level. In 1983, Governor Richard Thornburgh, a Republican from metropolitan Pittsburgh, initiated the Ben Franklin Partnership (BFP), which created a regional job center in Oakland administered jointly by the University of Pittsburgh and Carnegie Mellon University and provided grants to promote job opportunities in advanced technology sectors. The RIDC built and managed the facility using state funds, marking one of its first forays in managing an urban site. The initial *Strategy 21* proposal in 1985 included funds for a study of retaining the existing metals industry to gain support from legislators in the Monongahela Valley, but the overwhelming majority of funds for capital improvements went to construction of the Midfield Terminal and advanced technology projects in Pittsburgh and Monroeville.[17]

Building from the success of BFP, Casey promoted technology transfer through a new Southwestern Pennsylvania Resource Center (SPIRC). One local official declared that the program would "bring advanced technology to small and medium sized manufacturing companies to increase manufacturing productivity both for high tech and traditional manufacturers." Ray Christman, who had worked at both the Allegheny Conference and the Urban Redevelopment Authority of Pittsburgh before becoming commerce secretary in the Casey administration, believed that the combination of SPIRC with the Ben Franklin Partnership would give the state an "unparalleled one-two punch in assisting the development and transfer of new technology in manufacturing." Christman's importance in coordinating state and local economic development efforts in southwestern Pennsylvania quickly came into focus. The week he assumed his new post, Volkswagen announced it would close its New Stanton plant, idling 2,500 workers. Along with Jay Aldridge, executive director of Penn's Southwest, Christman was widely credited with persuading the Sony Corporation to select the site for a new TV-tube production facility. By the late 1990s, the Sony Technology Center—Pittsburgh employed approximately 3,000 on site and contracted with more than 1,100 local suppliers in the immediate area.[18]

In addition to statewide programs, such as the BFP and the IRCs, the Casey administration also secured additional funds to help the Monongahela and Beaver Valleys make the transition to smaller, more efficient facilities. The program to extend the economic growth of Pittsburgh's universities and middle-class suburbs to the urbanized valleys largely focused on converting the abandoned riverfront mill sites to planned industrial districts modeled on the RIDC industrial parks. Indeed, Tom Murphy's criticism of the RIDC came at a time when the organization already had shifted some of its resources to urban projects, including three University Development Centers in Oakland, CMU's Software Engineering Institute, and the Pittsburgh Technology Center on the former LTV steel site along the Monongahela River. Frank Brooks Robinson, Sr., worked for RIDC for several decades before leaving to serve in various capacities in the Thornburgh administration, including as head of the Pennsylvania Industrial Development Authority. According to Robinson, when he returned in 1981 to take over as president of RIDC, a position he would hold until 2003, Mayor Caliguiri told him "Take a look around and see what you can find in the city of Pittsburgh to do *here* what you've been doing in O'Hara and Thornhill." "The offer was a god . . . it was a giant," Robinson explained. "So, I looked throughout the city of Pittsburgh, walked a lot of sites, talked to a lot of people, looked over on the West End and places like that, and finally ended up talking to LTV."[19]

Building from its successful projects in Pittsburgh and the suburban greenfields, in 1988 the RIDC was tapped to run the Monongahela Valley sites and over the next three years purchased the 92-acre Westinghouse Plant in East Pittsburgh as well as U.S. Steel's 135-acre National Tube Works in McKeesport and the 240-acre Duquesne Works. Rechristened the Keystone Commons, Industrial Center of McKeesport, and City Center of Duquesne, respectively, the sites became the centerpieces of the state's redevelopment strategy for the post-steel era. Robinson envisioned sites in Turtle Creek and McKeesport serving as an economic development "bridge" for small businesses drawing on the expertise of skilled workers that had been employed in the mills. Instead of electricians, plumbers, and other workers moving to suburban sites, the "companies that needed the electricians would move to McKeesport in order to get their services." He was particularly excited about Keystone Commons in Turtle Creek as the site had deteriorated less than some of the other properties and the layout was more conducive to this incubator model of business development. As he walked the building with Tom Foerster at the outset of the redevelopment effort, Robinson recalled telling the Allegheny County commissioner, "When I look into this *huge* manufacturing area, I see a cross-section of a gothic cathedral. We've got this magnificent nave, and on the side aisles I've got room for small businesses, and then I've got the monk's walk that's got room for small businesses." "Foerster could see it with me," he concluded. "He understood what I was trying to do. And I think he trusted that the corporation could take it on and do it."[20]

Within a few years, officials could point to a number of successes at old plant sites such as Keystone Commons, which had grown to 48 tenants with 650 employees, a number approaching the 800 workers at the Westinghouse Plant in its last years. Mixed-use development in the three RIDC parks included a marina with room for 210 boats in McKeesport as well as a wide variety of firms from cookie makers to machine shops. "It's not like when we had 10,000 to 15,000 employees, naturally, but it's a start," Turtle Creek clothier Ben Forman declared. "It upgrades the whole area—rather than the deterioration you see in [other] communities." "Duquesne is a very pleasant place to work," agreed Eric Hoffman, president of K2T, a robotics firm founded by three CMU faculty members that leased space in the RIDC City Center facility. "This is centrally located to where our employees live. There is free parking, a 150-acre playground and wildlife"[21]

Despite the emphasis of neoliberal public policy on market-driven solutions, the reality was that brownfield redevelopment required a high level of public funding, a well-crafted and adaptable regulatory structure, and a local institutional framework capable of coordinating among a wide-range of interests. Compared to the Steel Valley communities of Ohio and West Virginia, the Monongahela Valley benefited from Pennsylvania's early leadership in brownfield redevelopment. In 1995, the General Assembly passed a package of laws establishing its Land Recycling program with uniform standards for remediation, a variety of financing options targeted to brownfield situations, and release from liability for approved cleanups. In Duquesne and McKeesport, RIDC removed 2,200 barrels of oil chemicals and other toxic liquids, disposed of asbestos-lined pipes and tanks, eliminated old PCB-laden electrical transformers, and even dug up an old railroad car. Even with state support, however, cleanup costs and the uncertainty of achieving environmental standards limited private investment, with many local banks and potential tenants opting instead for hilltop suburban sites despite significant tax breaks and other incentives designed to lure employers to the riverfronts. "I would love to have a private interest come down here, buy five acres and build a building," RIDC president Brooks Robinson explained in 1999 as he surveyed the rubble strewn field that still constituted much of the Duquesne City Center. However, "there's still a lot of butt-ugly around here."[22]

The lack of good highway access was a second major obstacle in creating suburban style industrial parks in crowded river valleys. Between the 1950s and the 1980s, the overall goal of regional highway construction in metropolitan Pittsburgh evolved from an essentially urban program—improve access *to* the downtown Golden Triangle—to a more suburban-oriented model of providing transportation *through* the crowded river valleys and then *around* the city via a proposed beltway. Political infighting and dense development meant that despite the "relentless" efforts of local leaders, the "long, hard battle to get the Mon Expressway off the drawing board and into the construction stage" yielded few results through the mid-1980s. Consequently, Governor Robert Casey's announcement in March 1987 that he would commit $40 million to resume construction on the highway was greeted with a great deal of enthusiasm. "I have made a commitment [to] revitalize the Mon Valley," the governor declared. "I have decided to proceed with a portion of the long-planned expressway [to] improve this area's access to other major commercial routes." "This is excellent news," Washington County commissioner Frank R. Mascara responded upon hearing the announcement. "I think the Governor recognizes that the long-term solution for developing the Mon Valley is good highways."[23]

This vision of economic revitalization through highway construction also led advocates to envision a grand "Southern Beltway" extending from Monroeville down the Mon-Fayette Expressway then west to Interstate 79 and finally the airport. While the initial idea for the Southern Beltway had originated in 1970, the collapse of the steel industry in the Monongahela Valley and the emphasis on the "Airport of the Future" as a spur to regional development propelled the project to the forefront in the 1990s. The coupling of the Mon-Fayette Expressway to the Southern Beltway proposal unified pro-highway advocates throughout the region, including the Progress Alliance, which agreed that economic development could best be achieved through "roads, more roads and education." Indeed, the sweeping nature of the project meant that the westernmost leg of the route, the Findlay Connector, intersected with Route 22 less than eighteen miles from Steubenville. "We stand on the threshold of economic recovery and growth," declared one group of local business leaders. We need a "highway that is a thru-way that links to other highways—highways that are easily accessible—highways that become the catalyst for transforming this area" and allow us "to finally discard the burdensome image of being a depressed and abandoned aftermath."[24]

Highway promoters achieved considerable success, including the opening of the Mon-Fayette Expressway between the West Virginia border and the enormous Century III Mall, which U.S. Steel built south of Pittsburgh on a former slag pile, as well as the Findlay Connector to the airport. Despite the increased resources brought to bear, however, the section of the Mon/Fayette Expressway north to Pittsburgh along the Monongahela River as well as the remainder of the Southern Beltway proved much more difficult and contentious. In part, this was due to the enormous expense and logistical difficulty of building a highway through such a densely developed and mountainous area. During the late 1980s, Mayor Caliguiri stunned advocates by announcing his opposition to extending the route through the city. "Over the years, the city has given up a number of neighborhoods to highway links serving suburban and regional areas. Unfortunately, these neighborhoods are never replaced or enhanced by the projects," Caliguiri explained in October 1987. "I cannot allow that pattern to continue." After his election as mayor in 1993, Tom Murphy remained equally skeptical offering only qualified support that was contingent on making sure the full route would be funded before work started and on the selection of a design that would be "the least disruptive to city neighborhoods and most supportive of economic development." Other residents along the proposed highway were even less enthusiastic. "This expressway will disrupt our lives, jobs and property," concluded a petition signed by residents of suburban West Mifflin Township. "It will not benefit anyone [and] will DIVIDE our community in half and destroy those along its path."[25]

In the end, if highway construction provided a means for again linking communities like Steubenville to the Steel Valley's metropolitan core, they were clearly less effective at solving the problems of urban decline in the deindustrialized river valleys. Throughout the 1990s, the Mon Valley/Fayette Expressway and Southern Beltway Alliance (SBA) fought a long-running campaign through the legislative process, public hearings, letters to local newspapers, and a variety of publications against environmental and community activists with alternative visions for connecting the valleys to regional prosperity. In 2002, expressway opponents, including Citizens for Pennsylvania's Future (PennFuture), the Group Against Smog and Pollution (GASP), and the Oakland Community Council, united around a "Citizens' Plan," funded by the Heinz Endowments, which proposed a combination of urban boulevards, improved surface connections, and transit investments. While Joe Kirk, executive director of the business-backed Mon Valley Progress Council and chair of the SBA, declared the expressway project as the "cornerstone for the economic revitalization of southwestern Pennsylvania," the Citizen's Plan pointed out that the "1960s-style destruction" embodied by the highway plan would emphasize "speed through the Valley over access within the Valley." Looking to the success of infrastructure rehabilitation and neighborhood-level revitalization in Pittsburgh itself, backers argued the Citizens' Plan would focus on "connections to and among brownfields, redevelopment sites, and existing urban centers, providing better incentives for economic development." After all, plan backers concluded, "the Braddocks, Duquesnes and East Pittsburghs will not be resuscitated by bulldozing a highway through their midst. But they can be revived one house, one business, one block at a time."[26]

"A Happy Medium"

"The land used to tremble under the feet of the Gem of Egypt as it worked its way across [the] landscape. Now it's quiet except for the shrieks of red-tailed hawks [and] mystical cries of other waterfowl and birds. The best part is that the land will stay this way for a long time to come." This was how outdoor writer Tony Denslow explained the 1994 opening of the Egypt Valley Wildlife Area, which was created when the Ohio Division of Wildlife purchased 14,000 acres of Consol's worked-out mine north of Barnesville. The financial support from three national conservation groups that made the project possible marked the advent in southeastern Ohio of a pattern begun by the Western Pennsylvania Conservancy forty years earlier. The area already provided excellent deer hunting opportunities" and due to the adjacent Piedmont Lake had "a tremendous potential to offer some fine waterfowl hunting opportunities, as well," explained Mike Budzik, the division's district manager. "As this wildlife area develops in the future, it will also provide a good economic boost for Belmont County."[27]

As in metropolitan Pittsburgh's cities and suburbs, rural residents struggled to refashion their common social and physical landscapes into a form that could sustain local communities. Just like in the region's former mill towns, many left the area entirely, while others moved to larger communities or commuted long-distance for work. Development officials hoped to spur economic activity by attracting new employers to highway-oriented industrial parks and regional shopping centers, or, as in the case of Barnesville, by developing recreational facilities on former industrial sites. While local conditions and a lack of facilities at Egypt Valley limited its function as an economic generator, extensive public and private investment in and around Ohiopyle accounted for 18,000 tourism jobs by the end of the 1990s. Unemployment and out-migration remained stubbornly high in many areas, however, while an upswing in coal mining by the end of the century offered new economic opportunities and called into question the very meaning of a deindustrialized countryside. As it became clear that the variety of potential land uses were not always compatible, local officials, activists, and business leaders struggled to find a "happy medium" that could balance competing environmental and economic objectives at the dawn of the twenty-first century.[28]

Rural development strategies increasingly resembled those of highway-oriented suburbs with low land price, accessibility and natural amenities combining to attract new residential and commercial development. In Fayette County, which contained Ohiopyle, the population increased for the first time since 1940, due in part to growth in communities near Interstate 76 and the Mon-Fayette Expressway. New housing developments near Ohiopyle and Laurel Ridge State Parks also accounted for significant gains, with Wharton, a mountainous township minutes away from a host of attractions, jumping by nearly 23 percent. In Belmont County, Barnesville's location near Interstate 70 also provided opportunities for commuting to jobs in other areas as well as local economic development. In 1996, the opening of a second regional shopping center near the Ohio Valley Mall boosted the county to one of the highest per capita sales rates in the nation with nine thousand jobs in the retail sector. Other developments included a residential psychiatric facility (1990), a $33 million medium-security prison (1993), Mayflower Vehicle Systems, an advanced technology auto supplier (1993), a $6 million fitness center at the local branch of Ohio University (1998), and Fox Commerce Park, a $3 million, 125-acre industrial park that opened in 2000.[29]

While many rural areas sought to reinvent themselves as far-flung burbs of the 'Burgh, Ohiopyle and other communities in the Laurel Highlands marketed themselves as a "new vacationland" built on a long history of upper-class hunting lodges and ski resorts, such as Hidden Valley and Seven Springs. By the 1980s, even as national newspapers sought out Monongahela Valley steelworkers turned nurses who could symbolize the region's post-industrial transformation, other stories pointed hopefully to rustic tourism entrepreneurs, such as Ohiopyle's Bob Marietta who worked odd jobs and cut timber before the Conservancy hired him as part-time caretaker of Ferncliff Park. In 1967 Marietta and a friend decided to "get in on this rafting" and with the purchase of a few inexpensive "suicide rafts" started a guide business called White Water Adventurers. By 1981, the company served 15,000 customers a year, had 200 rafts, employed fifteen river guides, sold thousands of t-shirts and owned a nearby campground. "I think it's a fantastic tourist area," declared Marietta's wife and company co-owner, Shirley. "It just seems like it's more popular every year."[30]

As with urban brownfields and rural surface mines, the abandonment of railroad lines provided an opportunity to adapt the Steel Valley's industrial infrastructure to serve the needs of post-industrial society. Lillian McCahan's Ohiopyle station closed in 1964 and following a merger the Western Maryland Railway discontinued operations in the early 1970s. In May 1975 a small train carrying local officials, conservation organization officers, and members of the press left Pittsburgh on a survey of the scenic corridor over the Eastern Continental Divide from Cumberland, Maryland to Connellsville. While the Conservancy hoped to preserve the entire 116-mile route as a hiking trail, state officials were only willing to acquire about fifteen miles in and adjacent to the state park itself. The first nine-mile section opened in 1986, just three years after the passage of federal "railbanking" legislation, and, according to park superintendent Larry Adams, "it became overwhelmingly popular." By 1989, more than 100,000 people used the trail each year and a series of subsequent expansions north and south of the park prompted *Leisure & Travel Magazine* to name it one of 'The World's Best Walks."[31]

The rapid expansion of rail-to-trails during the 1990s came from a series of new public- private partnerships that united a diverse group of heritage advocates, outdoor enthusiasts, and economic development officials in a shared vision of post-industrial transformation. In 1990, Tom Murphy, then a representative from Pittsburgh's North Side, helped lead an effort in the General Assembly that resulted in Pennsylvania becoming only the fourth state to provide direct support for rail-trail conversions. Eyeing the more than 100,000 visitors using the trail at Ohiopyle within two years of its opening, tourism boosters in the Laurel Highlands began acquiring the forty-two miles of right-of-way running south through Somerset County. "Everywhere these trails have been built, it's really stimulated the economy," explained Hank Parke, who served as both president of the new Somerset County Rails to Trails Association and executive director of the Somerset Chamber of Commerce. To the north, the nonprofit Allegheny, Fayette, and Westmoreland Counties created the nonprofit Regional Trail Corporation (RTC) in 1990 to transform the abandoned Pittsburgh & Lake Erie line into a route they hoped to eventually link up to the Three Rivers Heritage Trail in Pittsburgh. A similar coalition of industrial heritage and recreation-oriented organizations in the Monongahela Valley soon formed a committee, later incorporated as the Steel Valley Trail Council, to oversee the nineteen mile section of the trail from Homestead to its confluence with the Youghiogheny River in McKeesport.[32]

To unite all these disparate pieces and organizations into a grand project, representatives of the various trail councils, interested foundations, and local governments met at Hidden Valley resort in 1995 and formed the Allegheny Trail Alliance (ATA). After the decline of the railroad following

World War II, "the towns were all separate entities," recalled Eric Bugaile, who helped found the state chapter of the Rails-to-Trails Conservancy in 1989. "I think people feel in those communities now that they are part of something bigger." The Great Allegheny Passage, as the emerging trail system came to be called, reimagined the frayed steel-coal-rail nexus as the infrastructure for a new regional community. As with other riverfront and heritage-based development plans in the region, creating economic opportunity was a central tenet of trail construction and boosters anticipated that benefits would overflow into the towns along the trail. By the end of the 1990s, the Laurel Highlands region was a tourism success story with the overall industry generating $780 million and communities along the Great Allegheny Passage receiving $2.6 million to $3.8 million annually. Using a combination of private foundation grants, individual donations, and state and federal funds, over the next decade the ATA completed the entire route from McKeesport to Cumberland, Maryland, where it met the Chesapeake and Ohio Canal Towpath, with plans to finish the final connection to Pittsburgh by the city's 250th anniversary in 2009.[33]

The transformation of a mining area into a series of successful parks and an abandoned rail corridor into the Great Allegheny Passage was contingent on significant investment by federal and state governments as well as a neoliberal coalition of private trusts and nonprofit organizations. By comparison, the creation of the Egypt Valley Wildlife Area included very little investment in infrastructure and was more an acknowledgment of the denuded landscape's low value than a springboard for economic growth or community revitalization. Barnesville, too, was a stop on the railroad and had a beautiful passenger depot that was abandoned by the Chesapeake and Ohio Railway in 1983. "In these times when our small town needs the encouragement of all who love it," a website developed by the Barnesville Area Rails to Trails Committee declared, "we hope to provide another reason for people to visit and a benefit for those dwelling in Barnesville and the surrounding area." With little public land along the route, at a greater distance from a large urban area, and with Ohio's initial lack of funding for recreational trails and heritage preservation, those interested in rehabilitating the depot and creating a rail-trail were unable to forge the type of partnerships that made possible the Great Allegheny Passage.[34]

In comparison to the difficulty of coalition building in rural areas, the introduction of new mining technologies suggested a more traditional path to prosperity in many parts of the region. In 1987, Robert E. Murray, an independent coal operator who grew up near Egypt Valley, purchased the Powhatan Mine fifteen miles east of Barnesville, and over the next ten years increased annual production from 1 to 4 million tons, transforming it into the nation's fifth largest underground mine at a time when the area's high sulfur coal was at an increasing disadvantage due to the passage of amendments to the Clean Air Act intended to reduce acid rain in the Northeast. "We are value-added people," Murray later declared, "who take something that others see no potential in and apply a lot of sweat equity and capital." In 1995, Murray expanded his operations to U.S. Steel's former Maple Creek Mine near the Mon/Fayette Expressway twenty-five miles south of Pittsburgh, which had closed the previous year due to cost and environmental concerns. Expressing relief that miners can now "go on with their lives," Robert Gaydos, president of United Mine Workers Local 1248, declared "anytime we can revive a mine," especially in an area where jobs are scarce, "is a victory."[35]

In an era of increasing hostility on the national level between business groups and conservative politicians on the one hand and environmental activists and state and federal regulators on the other, the Steel Valley presented important case studies on the role of state laws in mediating between competing land uses. Acid mine drainage continued to affect the area's waterways with discharges affecting fish populations in the Casselman and Youghiogheny Rivers decreasing opportunities for recreation-based economic development. In addition, while mine supporters vehemently denounced air pollution regulations affecting coal-fired power plants along the Ohio River, during the 1980s acid rain caused by the plants' sulfur dioxide emissions further decimated trout fisheries in the Laurel Highlands and prompted the state of Pennsylvania to sue the Reagan administration for stronger controls. A highly publicized sinkhole in 1995 that closed Interstate 70 west of Barnesville and led to the preventive closure of Interstate 470 near Wheeling highlighted the issue of subsidence from abandoned mines that often made it difficult to find suitable sites for new industries.[36]

Further, the passage of the federal Surface Mining Control and Reclamation Act diminished but did not completely abrogate the problems of surface mining, especially near rural population centers. The 1973 compromise brokered by Gov. John Gilligan during the expansion of Consol's mining operations south of Interstate 70 prohibited mining within a one-mile "Greenbelt" around Barnesville. The greenbelt was outside of municipal limits, however, and no efforts to codify the concept ensued either on the local or state level, leaving enforcement dependent on the good will of the company. When the Egypt Valley Mine closed in the mid-1980s, Consol sold the remaining mineral rights to smaller companies with little incentive to abide by the Greenbelt agreement. Amid concerns about the city's water supply and physical infrastructure, in 1987 Barnesville council supported an unsuccessful petition to have the state department of natural resources declare land around the community unsuitable for mining.[37]

Throughout the 1990s, Barnesville residents continued to struggle with the continued effects of surface mining even as they sought to stem continued population loss. Some advocated heritage-themed tourism as well as a new industrial park near the interstate as potential economic opportunities. In 1997, Barnesville officials and the trustees of the surrounding township formally adopted resolutions for a one-mile greenbelt to "protect the village of Barnesville with a buffer zone between the village and coal mining operations." "We've never been about anti-mining and fully realize the benefits that industry has meant to thousands of people here in the valley," declared Roger Deal, Barnesville village administrator. However, in 2002, the director of the Ohio Department of Natural Resources again rejected the appeals of local residents and community leaders, declaring, "the Barnesville Greenbelt Plan may clearly state a preference of the community, however it lacks the authority of rule or law and therefore cannot be enforced by our agency."[38]

In addition to the expansion of surface mining, new underground mining technologies created even more strains on local communities struggling to balance competing land uses. The profitability of Robert Murray's Powhatan and Maple Creak Mines, for example, came from a combination of union acquiescence to lower wages, shrewd marketing, and the adoption of the longwall mining method, a process whereby all the coal in an area is extracted, causing the overlying rock to collapse in behind. In addition to greater economic efficiency in terms of the amount of coal produced, the introduction of longwall technology also resulted in subsidence of areas above active mines in the form of depressions, pits, or open cracks. As a result, the reopening of the Maple Creek Mine pitted local miners against the Nottingham Network of Neighbors, a group of nearby residents afraid of the effects of subsidence on surface property and water supplies. These concerns were exacerbated by Act 54, a controversial 1994 amendment to the Pennsylvania Bituminous Mine Subsidence and Land Conservation Act that eased restrictions on damage to surface structures and water supplies. "My 4-year-old son thinks that our house is going to fall in a mine hole and he will lose all of his toys," declared Debbie Bartman at a hearing on Maple Creek's plans to mine under several hundred homes. "It is awful that they have a permit to long-wall mine in this area and there doesn't seem be anything we can do about it."[39]

In southeastern Ohio, residents and political leaders also expressed concern about the consequences of longwall mining, though they did so in an economic and regulatory framework that differed substantially from their neighbors across the state line. Within a year of Murray's purchase of the Powhatan Mine, nearby residents sued, citing the potential for property damage due to subsidence; the mine also fought a long-running battle over plans to mine under an old growth forest owned by Ohio University. Local officials interested in economic diversification, however, were most concerned about Murray's plans to mine under an industrial park planned along Interstate 70 ten miles east of Egypt Valley. Spearheaded by county development director Don Myers, who began his career working for Martins Ferry mayor John Laslo, the 125-acre Fox Commerce Park capped a decade of feverish industrial recruitment and required a major investment by county officials along with more than $2 million in federal grants and no interest loans. "We looked all over for a quality piece of land [and] we got all kinds of publicity on it," Myers recalled. "Anybody that came in, you no longer have to scour the area, we'd have the site available."[40]

However, reconciling incompatible land uses proved a difficult task for county officials and business leaders concerned about angering one of the area's largest employers. Myers recalled a particularly illuminating exchange he had with a new set of Belmont County commissioners elected shortly before the park was slated to open. According to Myers, the commissioners had been invited to a meeting at which Robert Murray threatened to longwall under potential tenants at the new commerce park. After being informed of this problem, Myers said he responded to the commissioners that, according to state law, "whatever he destroys," through surface subsidence "he's gotta fix. Is he going to fix million dollar buildings?" He recalled urging officials to "contest this, like they do everywhere else." In contrast to this adamant articulation of a post-industrial vision voiced elsewhere in the region, statements by Belmont commissioners in January 2002 still revealed a lingering hope for balancing competing land uses on the rural periphery. "It is sad we must choose, but we are caught in a dilemma.

The coal jobs, which are vitally important to everyone and the Fox Commerce jobs—which were needed yesterday" one commissioner explained. "We are trying to reach a happy medium," so that "coal jobs can be preserved and new jobs created as well."[41]

While the announcement went largely unheralded, even by the Progress Alliance, in February 2013 the U.S. Census Bureau finally provided official recognition to the process of regional reunification that had begun decades earlier. By expanding the Pittsburgh Combined Statistical Area to include Weirton and Steubenville, census officials highlighted the increasing social and economic ties measured by commuting patterns that had come to define the Steel Valley in the post-steel era. Much of this connection owed directly to the suburban strategy of highway building, greenfield industrial park construction and development of the Airport of the Future that traced its roots to the formation of the RIDC and the evolution of the Renaissance vision in the 1970s and 1980s. On the other side of the partially completed Southern Beltway, however, the debate continued over extending the Mon/Fayette Expressway to Pittsburgh, with state officials caught in the crossfire refusing to either dedicate funding or officially abandon the project. As a result, some business and political leaders, including John Fetterman, Braddock's mayor, elected to move on brownfield redevelopment projects in the highway's path. "I've been lobbying them to call for the time of death for years now," Fetterman declared, adding that alleviating the threat of land seizures through eminent domain would further help resuscitate his community.[42]

If the suburban strategy represented one route to regional re-integration, then another announcement in 2013 represented a different path to reworking the bonds that had united the Steel Valley. On December 5, Robert Murray and Consol Energy CEO J. Brett Harvey announced the transfer of Consol's deep mines in northern West Virginia to the closely held Murray Energy for about $1 billion in cash and future royalties. When the deal was completed, the small town mine foreman's son who grew up in the shadow of Consol's southeastern Ohio operations became the head of the nation's largest underground coal mining company with about 7,100 miners and thirteen active mines. Boosters who articulated the vision of Pittsburgh's high-tech transformation were probably thinking more of converted rail-trails connecting white-collar workers to a bucolic countryside than a resurgent extractionist sector, but capital-intensive longwall mining was equally based on the types of technologies developed in Pittsburgh's engineering programs and research parks. "To me, this whole thing is a human issue," Murray declared of his opposition to environmental regulations designed to limit power plant emissions and protect water quality, "because I know the names of our employees here. If these mines go, these malls will be empty." In the end, Murray's perspective, shared by many in the region, underscores the continued layering pattern by which economic and cultural transitions supplanted but never fully replaced the working landscapes of the past. Scratch the surface of post-industrial Pittsburgh and you'll uncover the Steel Valley buried not far beneath. Indeed, during the 1990s a renewed push for downtown revitalization found urban residents, too, looking to the legacy of the industrial age as a way forward into the twenty-first century.[43]

CHAPTER 10

Rivers of Steel

Even as the Progress Alliance was hoping its "Burb of the 'Burgh" campaign would lure Airport Corridor commuters across the bridge to Steubenville, in the summer of 1998 local residents and public officials in Wheeling gathered on the bank of the Ohio River to mark a building demolition that symbolized a different approach to reconnecting the region. "We've taken down a decrepit garage and put in green space," declared Charles Flynn, executive director of the nonprofit organization formed to oversee the new Wheeling National Heritage Area (WNHA). "A year from now, we'll have a riverfront park with an amphitheater where we can host large riverboats and pleasure craft" as well as "festivals, fairs and concerts." The razing of the Wharf Parking Garage, which had been one of the signature achievements of the Wheeling Renaissance during the 1950s, signaled a broader rethinking of the Steel Valley's built and natural landscapes that emphasized heritage-based renovation and riverfront revitalization. In Pittsburgh, dilapidated industrial buildings, abandoned mill sites, and railroad rights of way were reimagined as loft apartments, high-tech laboratories, and recreational trails that complemented the city's transformation into a center of education, health care, and corporate services. Others envisioned the creation of an even more ambitious Rivers of Steel National Heritage Area, headquartered in Homestead, that would preserve key production sites and narrate the entire industrial process from mine to mill. The goal in each community was to create a "new kind of richly interpreted cityscape" where visitors and residents alike could find meaning through the symbolic consumption of "a shared and distinctive space."[1]

Concerned that suburban-oriented development could not reverse regional economic decline without a parallel strategy in the cities, civic leaders in metropolitan Pittsburgh looked to broader national trends as well as models within the region, especially Station Square on the South Side, in emphasizing a two-pronged approach of revitalizing deindustrialized riverfronts as sites of consumption and using heritage-based building renovation to create more attractive communities and lure visitors downtown. New office buildings, recreational trails, museums, theaters, and sports stadiums embraced the rivers, adapted industrial age infrastructure to serve the needs of post-industrial society, and sought to enhance the region's reputation among the young, middle-class professionals that urban theorist Richard Florida, then a professor at Carnegie Mellon University, described as the "creative class." "Call it Renaissance III or call it just a better place to live," the *Post-Gazette* editorialized in 1998, "this is the blueprint of a renewable city that more people will be proud to call home."[2]

While metropolitan Pittsburgh's neoliberal growth partnerships worked to create new tools for regional economic development, others saw heritage rehabilitation and the transformation of riverfronts as ways to nurture a sense of community identity, rebuild impoverished neighborhoods, and enhance opportunities for urban residents still reeling from the collapse of heavy industry. "This was all about helping communities that had been stomped on" and left "without much identity and sense of self-worth," explained one activist involved in the creation of Rivers of Steel. While the goals of economic development and community organizing frequently overlapped, the complexity of crafting public policies on the municipal level also led to clashes between and among various stakeholders, particularly when development goals came into conflict with notions of authenticity and local control. Tom Murphy, who served as a "major catalyst" for urban renewal during his tenure as Pittsburgh mayor, successfully negotiated with community organizers in the mixed-use redevelopment of LTV's South Side Works. However, the city's attempt to raze and replace the Market Square business district near the Golden Triangle with an enclosed shopping mall was ultimately defeated by a coalition that included the same types of young professionals and preservationists with whom he was often allied. Similar tensions between development and authenticity also appeared in Homestead and Wheeling, which, despite designation as National Heritage Areas, also struggled to mobilize the types of economic and political resources available in Pittsburgh.[3]

"A 12 Mile Story of Who We Are"

Rather than emerging from a coherent set of policies, Pittsburgh's neoliberal model for urban redevelopment and economic growth evolved as local residents, business people, and political leaders sought to "address urban needs and interests" in ways that preserved cities as areas that were "distinct from our suburbs." In a time of "jittery lenders," declining state aid, and withdrawal of the federal government from most urban development projects, business and political leaders looked to new types of public-private partnerships and innovative funding mechanisms, such as tax increment financing (TIF). It became clear by the early 1990s that "the industrial past" of urban communities would not "continue into another generation," especially along the riverfronts. The 1990 update of the Allegheny Conference-backed *Strategy 21* funding request abandoned even superficial support for reinforcing the region's traditional dominance of the metals industry. Of the eight projects the proposal sought to fund, nearly all were connected to riverfront revitalization and several were connected to historic-themed redevelopment, including the John Heinz History Center in the former Chautauqua Ice Company building in the Strip District, the Andy Warhol Museum in the former Frick & Lindsay plumbing supply company building on the North Side, and the Pittsburgh Cultural Trust's renovation of theaters in the expanding downtown Cultural District.[4]

As this list suggests, the conception of "downtown" expanded to include the areas across the Allegheny and Monongahela Rivers from the Golden Triangle. Beginning in the 1970s, the Pittsburgh History and Landmarks Foundation had pioneered the use of heritage redevelopment as a community revitalization tool in their transformation of an old rail yard along the Monongahela into the festival marketplace of Station Square. As with their earlier activities in the North Side's Manchester and Mexican War Streets neighborhoods, Landmarks officials also partnered with local groups in the surrounding South Side neighborhoods to provide an alternative to the bulldozers of the Urban Redevelopment Authority. The shuttering of the LTV site in the mid-1980 added a sense of urgency to this development agenda, and in 1982 Landmarks joined with the South Side Chamber of Commerce in creating the South Side Local Development Corporation (SSLDC). In 1985 the East Carson Street Historic District was selected as an urban demonstration project by the National Trust's new

Main Street program. "A region's heritage, especially in a period of radical and negative change," declared Earl James, director of preservation programs for the Pittsburgh History and Landmarks Foundation, "becomes the binding force maintaining its identity and, by drawing the community together, becomes the driving force for renewal."[5]

With this proof that focused heritage-based redevelopment driven by private investment could revitalize areas in an economically viable way, boosters turned to expanding the downtown Cultural District beyond Heinz Hall (1971) and the Benedum Center (1987). Beginning with the 1990 purchase and renovation of the Fulton Theater, the overall development program for the area was largely entrusted to the nonprofit Pittsburgh Cultural Trust, which served to channel funding from the city's corporate foundations into the neighborhood. Pittsburgh's Urban Redevelopment Authority (URAP) and the Heinz Foundation invested heavily in street and façade beautification, and, in 1987, the same year that Andrew Wiese noted the gentrification of the Cultural District's Italianate buildings from his canoe on the Allegheny River, the area was designed a National Historic District. The goal of the public-private partnership was not only to create new facilities through heritage-based revitalization but also to "change the sociology" of a neighborhood in which visitors "d[id] not feel comfortable spending time."[6]

In 1993, the Trust began work on an innovative, split-level park that would connect the Cultural District to the Allegheny River. With the exception of a few riverfront municipal parks built in the early 1980s, this focus on the riverfront as an amenity represented a marked departure even from recent projects in the city, such as the Pittsburgh Technology Center, which tended to ignore the possibility of riverfront recreation despite the fact that the rivers were much cleaner and more attractive than they had been for more than a century. Allegheny County officials even chose to locate a massive new county jail on a former railroad property overlooking the Monongahela River. However, the decline of the city's railroads coupled with the rise of state and federal rails to trails programs provided the opportunity for a new vision of the riverfronts. In December 1990, the Three Rivers Task Force, a coalition of environmental and civic groups, announced a plan to create a twelve-mile "Three Rivers Heritage Trail" along the Allegheny and Monongahela Rivers. The next year, trail advocates formed the nonprofit Friends of the Riverfront, and on Earth Day (April 5) hundreds of volunteers joined the group in beginning to clear the first section of the route.[7]

No municipal official embraced the reinvention of the riverfronts as the key to economic development more than Tom Murphy, who made the transformation of disused railroad lines into waterfront pedestrian paths one of the cornerstones of his successful campaign for Pittsburgh mayor in 1993. "If ever there was a place to unfold the history of Pittsburgh," Murphy declared, "it is along our riverfronts—a 12 mile story of who we are." A native of the North Side—active during the 1970s as a community organizer and during his time as a state legislator in the 1980s—Murphy played an instrumental role in channeling state funds to the Strategy 21 urban renewal program. An avid runner and cyclist, Murphy was a founding member of the Pennsylvania chapter of the Rails-to-Trails Conservancy as well as Friends of the Riverfront, which joined the Pittsburgh History and Landmarks Foundations and the Pittsburgh Cultural Trust in promoting urban revitalization based on riverfront and heritage renewal projects. "The recreation value of our riverfronts is obvious; the economic value for development on adjacent property is equally important and obvious," Murphy declared on Earth Day in 1991.[8]

On becoming the city's mayor in 1994, Murphy declared his intention of making Pittsburgh a "24-hour" city and laid out a plan of public works. He placed particular emphasis on the twelve mile Three Rivers Heritage Trail, the linchpin connecting diverse urban neighborhoods with both a revitalized riverfront and new cultural facilities, including the construction of two new sports stadiums on the North Side. Undertaking this robust urban development policy during a time of shrinking federal support, with a local and regional population that was still declining, and in a city with a shrinking tax base required strong partnerships with county, nonprofit, and corporate officials and new methods of financing. Murphy forged a strong relationship with Richard Stafford, the new executive director of the Allegheny Conference, and surrounded himself with a group of visionary, hard-driving municipal officials drawn from his community organizing days. Finally, in 1997 Allegheny County Commissioners Michael Dawida, a Democrat with whom Murphy had served as a state legislator, and Bob Cranmer, a Republican who split with the other Republican on the commission, formed an alliance with Murphy that made possible a number of signature projects. Over the next three years, city-county cooperation improved to such an extent that Mulugetta Birru, a close associate of Murphy, served as both head of the URAP and county development director from 1997 to 2000.[9]

The development projects of "Renaissance III" required a series of neoliberal funding mechanisms that allowed the city to leverage public and private investment in innovative ways. Murphy and his supporters made "a fundamental decision" that they needed a source of "money in a flat broke city," centralized land control and development capacity, and to "be able to make deals." In his final days as state legislator, Murphy pushed for legislation that created the Allegheny [County] Regional Asset District (RAD), which provided grants for civic, cultural, and recreational facilities as well as property tax relief in distressed communities by imposing a 1 percent sales and use tax. Formulated by Richard Stafford at the Allegheny Conference and supported by Murphy's predecessor as mayor, Sophie Masloff, the RAD was designed to shift the tax burden for regional facilities away from Pittsburgh and gave Murphy a financial platform for his program.[10] On taking office, Murphy also began diverting seven million dollars a year out of the city's operating budget to finance a $60 million Pittsburgh Development Fund that was subsequently matched by local corporations and foundations through the Allegheny Conference's new Strategic Investment Fund. Finally, city officials made extensive use of TIFs that earmarked future taxes to pay off construction loans in order to lure businesses to city properties.[11]

Murphy's aggressive approach to urban redevelopment was most successful on sites that the city could purchase outright. During his first year in office, the URAP acquired more than 500 acres of former industrial property, the largest land purchase in its history, which included U.S. Steel's infamous slag heap at Nine Mile Run and the South Side Works as well as a failed shopping center in the East Liberty neighborhood. But perhaps the best example of Pittsburgh's evolving neoliberal development model emerged following the collapse of the Steel Valley Authority plans to reindustrialize LTV (J&L) Steel's South Side Works in 1991. By the time the URAP purchased the 123-acre site from LTV in 1993, the SSLDC had a decade of experience in heritage-based revitalization and a strong record of attracting new businesses to the East Carson Street neighborhood. At first, however, Murphy and the URAP ignored ongoing local planning efforts and directly brokered a deal with New Jersey-based Hospitality Franchise Systems, which lent $10 million to purchase the site in exchange for an option on a fifty acre parcel on which the company hoped to construct a riverboat gambling and entertainment complex. After necessary changes to state gambling laws failed to materialize, the

URAP acquired full ownership and began site remediation under the guidelines of the state's innovative brownfields Land Recycling Program (Act 2).[12]

As the URAP worked to clean up the site and attract private investors, Murphy and Birru formed a strong though often contentious partnership with SSLDC executive director, Rebecca Flora, who had previously managed the URAP Washington's Landing and Pittsburgh Technology Center projects. The involvement of the SSLDC resulted in a number of tangible results for the site, including the extension of Carson Street's historic designation along the site's border and the construction of senior housing units. Even more important, the SSLDC insisted that "even though the land is available and even though it may be priced at a level comparable to that of a good suburban site," any new development had to blend in with the existing neighborhood by respecting the high-density urban grid pattern. Over the next few years, URAP partnered with the Soffer Organization, a local real estate development firm to create a TIF plan that helped lure high profile projects to the site, including sports-related facilities for the University of Pittsburgh, the regional headquarters of the FBI, several office buildings, and mixed use office retail buildings that included loft apartments.[13]

Despite these successes, the 1990s remained a difficult period in metropolitan Pittsburgh's history, and the city's experimentation with neoliberal growth strategies resulted in failures as well as successes. The proliferation of community and nonprofit groups often made it difficult to reach consensus on projects, especially when they involved eminent domain and the destruction of existing buildings, a reality illustrated by Murphy's failure to develop a downtown retail mall similar to Wheeling's earlier Fort Henry Mall proposal. In September 1997 city officials signed an agreement with Urban Retail Properties to develop a 400,000 square foot retail center, which would have replaced a mix of national and local independent shops with forty destination-oriented chain stores, between Fifth and Forbes streets just east of the Golden Triangle. As retailers Lazarus (1998) and Lord and Taylor (2000), enticed by generous public subsidies and TIF agreements, signed on over the next three years, Urban Retail Properties began to market the $400 million project despite the fact that much of the area was privately owned. "We think Pittsburgh is a terrific city with a tremendous amount of retail potential," declared an executive at Urban Retail's parent company. "If there is some deal that makes sense there, we would love to get involved with it."[14]

During the heyday of the Pittsburgh Renaissance, the city's public-private partnership could use eminent domain to transfer private property from one private owner to another with little regard for local concerns. However, the political landscape had changed by the 1990s, with opposition to the Fifth and Forbes proposal uniting a diverse group of stakeholders, including the Pittsburgh History and Landmarks Foundation, young professionals who formed an ad hoc group called the GroundZero Action Network, and local businesses suffering from an uncertain market that aligned themselves with attorneys at the free-market libertarian Institute of Justice. For Arthur Ziegler, Murphy's plan was a backsliding "demolition and rebuilding project" reminiscent of the Allegheny Center project that had horrified the founders of Landmarks in the 1960s. GroundZero, on the other hand, was an experimental "open network of doers, makers, and creative people" that emerged in 2000 focused on arts and culture projects with a particular emphasis on young, hip, "creative people." The Fifth and Forbes controversy, according to group member Pat Clark, who worked at a real estate job nearby, was "the issue that drove them to mobilization." "It was an artificial economy," he concluded. "It was just so ill-advised. It was like watching dad try to dance."[15]

Landmarks and groups like GroundZero that viewed Fifth and Forbes as part of a broader agenda allied themselves with neighborhood organizations, such as the Market Square Association (MSA), a business cooperative that marketed local retail, dining, and entertainment. As with Ziegler at Landmarks, MSA executive director Bernie Lynch was concerned that the city was making plans with national retailers behind closed doors at the expense of local business and that, in the meantime, the area slated for redevelopment was suffering from a frozen real estate market. "It wasn't blighted before," Lynch argued, "but the plan caused it to become blighted." These concerns about eminent domain and the viability of Murphy's plan were shared by the libertarian Allegheny Institute, founded by Richard Mellon Scaife in 1995, and the Institute for Justice, a Washington, D.C.-based public interest law firm that Lynch contacted for advice in the fall of 1998. Faced with the difficulty of attracting investors in the face of this opposition, Murphy eventually abandoned the proposal and agreed to work with opponents on a more collaborative effort, dubbed "Plan C" for compromise. Furthermore, within five years of opening, both Lazarus and Lord and Taylor closed their stores, costing the city up to $90 million in public subsidies and adding impetus to the search for a compromise. In the end, the URAP and other stakeholders settled on an incremental, "Main Street" approach that provided city funding for modest improvements to local property owners.[16]

Murphy's aggressive approach to urban development created an even bigger backlash in his plans for replacing the aging Three Rivers Stadium, which had long been criticized for its inaccessibility, boring architecture, and unsuitability for baseball viewing, with two new facilities designed to highlight the city's new relationship with its rivers. The opening of the Carnegie Science Center in 1991 kicked off a decade of construction and planning on the North Shore of the Allegheny River, including the relocation of Alcoa Corporation to a beautiful new headquarters. In 1996, the new co-owner of the Pittsburgh Pirates, newspaper publisher Kevin McClatchy, announced the team would leave the city unless a new park was built. While they did not threaten to leave, the Pittsburgh Steelers football franchise also requested a new facility. Facing increasing financial difficulties, Murphy negotiated a deal to establish an eleven-county Regional Renaissance Initiative, modeled on the Allegheny County RAD, which would use an additional .5 percent sales tax to fund infrastructure projects, including the two new stadiums. Despite strong support by the region's public-private partnership, in 1998 the proposal failed spectacularly, not getting the required majority of votes in any of the eleven counties, including Allegheny. Following the defeat and in spite of enormous local opposition, Murphy pushed through a "Plan B" that used TIF and other funding mechanisms to support the stadiums.[17]

Despite low unemployment and increased national attention for its new developments, the realities of governing a city with a population that continued to decline hurt Murphy's position. Furthermore, lack of the political savvy necessary to collaborate effectively with various community and non-profit stakeholders undercut his successes as a visionary in articulating a renewed emphasis on the riverfronts and as a technocrat in cobbling together the financial capacity to "make deals" with developers. "Reformers tend to be people who listen. He didn't cultivate that talent very well," explained Mike Dawida, Murphy's long-time colleague in the state legislature and frequent partner during his time as county commissioner in the late 1990s. "It got a lot worse in the mayor's office." After Murphy cruised to an easy reelection victory in 1997, growing anger at his apparent lack of respect for local desires made the 2001 campaign divisive. Although he squeaked by in the election with only six hundred more votes than his opponent, city councilman Bob O'Connor, Murphy's final term as mayor was tempered by ballooning public debt that occurred despite only a modest increase in actual public spending.[18]

The mayor's repeated attempts to "change fundamentally" the municipal taxing dynamic during the early twenty-first century by imposing commuter and use taxes and attempting to tax the nonprofit universities and hospitals that controlled a large portion of the city's real estate was stymied in an increasingly hostile state legislature. His close alliance with county commissioners was replaced by a cooler relationship with a Republican county executive elected under a new home rule charter for Allegheny County in 1999. Faced with few options, in 2003 Murphy led Pittsburgh into the state's "distressed city" program, which paradoxically allowed a state appointed overseer to impose the kinds of financial remedies Murphy could not use himself. By the time he left office in January 2006, after having chosen not to seek reelection, nearly 50 percent of residents polled gave him a grade of D or lower. Despite this loss of popularity, the city's fiscal problems, and the cloud of a federal investigation involving a sweetheart contract with the city's firefighters union, Murphy left a legacy of brownfield and riverfront development projects that his successors as mayor, Bob O'Connor, Luke Ravenstahl, and Bill Peduto, built on for the next decade. "In Pittsburgh, with a strong mayor system, you can have huge influence on the pace and quality of the development," Murphy later concluded. "That's what a mayor needs to do—imagine what we could be."[19]

"Victorian Wheeling"

As with the Renaissance of the 1950s, community leaders in the region's smaller cities sought to copy Pittsburgh's relative success in reinventing itself as a high-tech, post-industrial hub with the cultural amenities necessary to attract new residents. Since the 1950s, local business leaders had struggled to make their downtowns attractive destinations for shoppers who increasingly chose the comfort and convenience of regional shopping centers. In Wheeling, for example, the 1978 opening of the Ohio Valley Mall in a rural area seven miles east of the city prompted a round of soul-searching among residents whose "hubris," in the words of one commentator, had defeated the Fort Henry Mall proposal five years earlier. The long-delayed civic center finally opened in 1977, but it was somewhat isolated from the central business district and the relocation of several national retailers prompted the city council to launch a downtown revitalization program focused on facade improvement and the construction of a new parking garage. However, these modest improvements could do little to protect downtown from the precipitous economic and population declines of the 1980s. By 1991, council member Clyde Thomas declared that the city had "nothing to lose now. We are scraping bottom."[20]

Wheeling's heritage and riverfront development strategy in the 1990s built on two decades of preservationist work by the Friends of Wheeling (Friends), a non-profit organization formed in 1970 as part of the drive to secure national register status for West Virginia Independence Hall. The driving force behind Friends was Beverly Fluty, a Colorado native who had moved to Wheeling in 1968, and Betty "Snookie" Nutting, wife of newspaper publisher Ogden Nutting and owner of a local demolition and building rehabilitation company. Over the next decade the organization helped lead the charge for securing similar status for the 1849 Wheeling Suspension Bridge and the 1850 Centre Market. In the mid-1980s, the city council officially designated the community as "Victorian Wheeling" and the state governor proclaimed a similar designation the next year. Wheeling was also among the first in the state to gain official acceptance into the National Trust's Main Street program. By 1990, the city was an early success story for heritage projects, with an impressive renovation to the Centre Market that reopened in 1989 and housed such small businesses as the iconic Coleman's Fish Market.[21]

Preservationists found a key ally in Harry Hamm, a founding member of the Wheeling Area Conference on Community Development. While the Wheeling Conference faded as an organization, Hamm continued his booster role as editor of the Nutting-owned *Wheeling Intelligencer* newspaper and gained valuable insight into the post-industrial transformation of Pittsburgh through his position on the board of the Claude Worthington Benedum Foundation—an organization instrumental in the formation of the Pittsburgh Cultural Trust. During the late 1980s, heritage proponents turned their attention to the riverfront downtown area with the founding of the Victorian Wheeling Society. In 1987, the same year the aging Stanley Theater reopened as the Benedum Center for the Performing Arts in Pittsburgh's Cultural District, Hamm began building support for a comprehensive revitalization program based on "Wheeling's rich historic past" as well as creating "a living panorama of riverfront activity and points of interest."

This connection to the riverfront built on the successful campaign over the previous decade to light the Wheeling Suspension Bridge and build a modest amphitheater near the Wheeling entrance to the bridge, which opened in 1987 on the same spot that the Fort Henry Mall proposal had once envisioned a bandshell.[22]

Looking to Pittsburgh as a model, Wheeling's nascent growth partnership hoped that emphasizing quality of life issues would draw in new employers, particularly in the high tech and business services sectors, attracted to a combination of cheap urban land, low taxes, and access to both heritage-based and natural amenities. Advocates joined forces with the city council in adopting Hamm's proposal, *Wheeling 2000*, a clear nod to Pittsburgh's *Strategy 21*, as their roadmap, and backers hired fundraiser David E. Tork to lead their efforts. As in Pittsburgh, the key goal of *Wheeling 2000* was to use heritage preservation as an economic development tool to both "create a city attractive to tourists year round" and help provide the "cultural, educational and recreational opportunities which appeal to persons in the high-tech field." Acknowledging the long-standing difficulty in raising local public funds for development projects, Tork declared that "the most important aspect of this plan is that it will be funded entirely privately."[23]

While it was clear the Hamm and his supporters looked to Pittsburgh as a model, Wheeling had neither the private funding nor the public administrative capacity available to its larger neighbor. Despite grants from the Benedum Foundation, for example, advocates faced difficulty in raising even the modest local share for the National Trust's Main Street program. As a result, by 1990 advocates had begun lobbying for designation as a National Heritage Area, a federal program begun in 1984 that provided limited funding for local development initiatives. Local boosters partnering with the National Park Service oversaw the creation of a series of interpretive and management plans that sought to "narrate" the city's nineteenth-century history through new and renovated physical infrastructure. Following the adoption of an initial development plan, in 1994 the project's sponsors created the Wheeling National Heritage Area Corporation (WNHAC) as the nonprofit vehicle for combining public and private funds as required under federal guidelines. Charles Flynn, a former aide to New York Mayor Ed Koch and owner of a historic Pennsylvania amusement park, was hired as WNHAC's first executive director. "I think they were interested in me because I had this rather unique combination of political experience, business experience, tourism experience and an appreciation for historic preservation," Flynn later explained. "So, they decided to hire me, and that's how I got to Wheeling."[24]

From the beginning, the implementation of Hamm's vision benefited from the political patronage of West Virginia Senator Robert C. Byrd, who secured the original federal funding for the 1992 plan and regularly added funds for the project to appropriations bills for the Department of the Interior. "It was a phenomenal amount of federal money," Flynn recalled. "Senator Byrd was amazing." "That would never happen today, that kind of investment he made in Wheeling. He agreed with the vision and wanted to drive to make it happen." When Byrd left his position as Senate president pro tem in 1988 to become chair of the Appropriations Committee, he declared a goal of earmarking $1 billion for his home state. Though the city remained a Republican stronghold in a Democratic state, the senator was friends with Harry Hamm and Randy Whorls, the influential director of the Wheeling Park Commission, who served as a core member of the Wheeling National Heritage Task Force after Hamm's death in 1991. By the time he introduced legislation in August 1993 to create a National Heritage Area in Wheeling, Byrd had already secured $4.7 million dollars for development projects and earmarked $3 million more for future use. This "early Byrd" money, as supporters later dubbed it, made possible a raft of investments that carried downtown revitalization through the early twenty-first century. Building on the vision of *Wheeling 2000*, Byrd also set out to enhance the city's high-tech infrastructure through the 1991 creation of the National Technology Transfer Center housed at Wheeling Jesuit University, which also garnered an educational outreach center affiliated with NASA.[25]

Riverfront amenities played an increasing role in this calculus, with Charles Flynn declaring, "The real centerpiece of our whole effort is waterfront redevelopment." The first component of the 1992 heritage plan to be implemented was the Wheeling Heritage Trail, a 13-mile rail-trail bike and pedestrian facility on the east bank of the Ohio River that attracted strong local use. Soon afterward, work began on what would become one of the most visible parts of Wheeling's waterfront development: an open-air amphitheater, park, and marina dubbed the "Heritage Port." During the 1990s, WNHAC worked with NPS officials to develop an overall plan for the community, a program of physical redevelopment, an interpretive master plan, and an oral history database. In 1996, the city's first federally funded attraction, the $6 million Wheeling Artisan Center, opened a block from the waterfront, featuring exhibits, an arts and crafts retail shop, an art gallery, and a privately managed restaurant and brew-pub. The senator's efforts culminated in 1997 in the opening of the Robert C. Byrd Intermodal Transportation Center, a grandiose name designed to obscure what was in reality a federally funded parking garage, which housed a modest visitor center and allowed demolition of the waterfront Wharf Parking Garage to make way for the Heritage Port.[26]

Aside from the increased tourism spending from events at the Heritage Port and the Artisan Center, the public investment in heritage rehabilitation as an economic development tool paid its greatest dividends a few blocks south of downtown in the neighborhoods surrounding Centre Market. Hydie Friend, a Wheeling native with a master's degree in urban and regional planning, was hired by the city's development department in 1983 and oversaw the restoration of the historic market using a combination of private funds raised by the Friends of Wheeling and public investment from the city and federal government. The area had the advantage of being near both the Ohio Valley Medical Center, one of the city's largest employers, and West Virginia Northern Community College, which had recently moved into the beautiful 1913 Baltimore and Ohio Railroad Terminal, the renovation of which also represented a significant public investment. These public investments slowly prompted private restoration of nearby homes and commercial sites that took advantage of both state and federal tax credits for historic rehabilitation. Wheeling also developed its own local expertise in historic preservation, including the architectural firm of McKinley & Associates, founded by civil engineer David McKinley in 1981, the same year he was elected as a state legislator.[27]

This neighborhood-based approach to growth in Center Wheeling paid its most significant dividend in 2001, when community leaders recruited the San Francisco-based law firm of Orrick, Herrington & Sutcliffe to establish its global operations center in the nearby Wheeling Stamping Building, a vacant warehouse complex along the riverfront. McKinley & Associates' extensive rehabilitation of the site, which involved linking three existing buildings, required a $7 million financing package from a combination of local, state, and federal sources, including $2 million from the National Park Service through WNHAC. "We proved we had a pool of talent, the real estate costs were favorable, and we had proximity to Pittsburgh International Airport," explained Will Turani, who moved from his position as Wheeling city manager to director of Orrick's new facility. Over the next

FIGURE 15. View of the Wheeling Heritage Port built on the former site of the Wharf Parking Garage, 2002. The Robert C. Byrd Intermodal Transportation Center and the Wheeling Artisan Center are visible in the center to the left of the Wheeling Civic Center. Photograph by Jim Barnett. Courtesy of Sasaki Associates.

decade, the company expanded the center to three hundred relatively highly paid employees, which in turn prompted additional rehabilitation of other nearby buildings. Later estimates suggested that the Wheeling facility saved the company $10 million to $15 million annually, primarily as a result of lower salaries and real estate expenses than it would pay in other major metropolitan areas. "I believe that we have far surpassed our goal of simply improving client service and reducing operating costs," declared Ralph Baxter, Orrick's chief executive. "We've helped revitalize a former steel town."[28]

Despite the modest growth of the Center Wheeling neighborhood in the 1990s, sustaining the political consensus and economic resources necessary for transforming the main downtown area proved extremely difficult. In the early 1980s, city council had agreed to spend $1 million in capital improvements downtown in exchange for property owners voluntarily upgrading their properties, developing common hours of operation, and otherwise cooperating on promotions and advertising. This framework was subsequently the foundation for involvement in the National Trust's Main Street program, with the city providing initial funding and property owners expected to invest their own resources and coordinate future activities. With a city charter change in 1992 that strengthened the municipal government, Wheeling seemed poised to take advantage of the new opportunities. However, within three years supporters were unable to raise even the bare bones $40,000 annual budget from downtown merchants and the Main Street program folded. "Merchants are very difficult to grab," explained Hydie Friend, who retired from her position in the city's development department to take over as WNHAC executive director in 2001. "Even if you're in a strong Main Street program, to get them to have the same hours and common graphics and advertising and that kind of thing, they're just real independent. And then putting their money in on it was a whole other obstacle." Combined with the Steel Valley's continuing economic problems, this lack of participation meant that there was little local money available to take up the slack when a shift in national politics made it more difficult for Byrd to obtain funding earmarks.[29]

Wheeling's public-private partnership also struggled to reconcile two competing visions of the goal of downtown revitalization within the framework of a National Heritage Area. The goal of heritage-based rehabilitation in the original *Wheeling 2000* proposal was to take "the old, idle and abandoned factories and plants and create in and around them the conditions of a functioning park." Aside from looking to other urban parks, especially Lowell National Historic Park, Wheeling's 1,650-acre Oglebay Park was already a national model for a self-supporting public municipal park that also generated extensive revenue for surrounding neighborhoods. Oglebay, the summer estate of a coal, iron, and shipping magnate donated to the city in 1926, expanded following World War II to include a zoo, museum, 270-room lodge, planetarium, extensive gardens, and two championship golf courses. Under Randy Whorls, the park began the Winter Festival of Lights in 1985, an extensive display of landscape lighting that soon spread throughout the city and eventually grew into the nation's largest holiday display. Funded in part by Byrd's largesse, in 1993 Whorls also spearheaded the creation of Oglebay's Carriage House Glass Museum and Artisan Center, which combined a venue for demonstrating glass blowing and other artisanal works with a retail venue for regional arts and crafts. Along with Tamarack, an enormous West Virginia-themed artisanal center along the interstate north of Beckley, the Carriage House served as the model for the larger downtown Artisan Center with 30,000 square feet of retail that was to be an anchor for the heritage redevelopment of the entire central business district.[30]

When Charles Flynn arrived in Wheeling in 1994 as WNHAC's new executive director, he had a different vision of urban revitalization than that promoted by Whorls and his supporters. Randy was "a big believer that retail would help," Flynn explained. "But Oglebay, was a resort [and] that's a very different environment than a downtown." Afraid that the sale of crafts would not be able to cover the operating expenses of the restored wholesale grocery building that housed the Artisan Center, Flynn advocated shrinking the retail footprint and putting a brewpub on the first floor that could host events and serve the local neighborhood, including the corporate offices of Wesbanco across the street. Rather than focusing on enhancing the retail and tourist trade in the central business district, a key goal of the long-standing "Live on the Hills and Work in the City" motto that still served as a basic framework for urban revitalization in the heritage area, Flynn saw riverfront redevelopment as a key factor in encouraging people to live downtown. "Let's put it this way, I never believed that retail was the solution," he later recalled. "I was a big believer that if you could create a great place and you could strengthen the office market and strengthen the residential market then any retail market would cater to it. That's why I fought so hard [and] we sort of changed the nature of the Artisan Center."[31]

As with the contemporaneous efforts of Tom Murphy to launch a mall at Fifth and Forbes in Pittsburgh, for many in Wheeling the focus of redevelopment efforts remained on enhancing the downtown retail trade. The 1998 purchase of prominent downtown retailer, Stone & Thomas, by Elder-Beerman, Inc., and closure of the store two years later caused a major upheaval in the city's traditional retail sector. Soon after Flynn left his position at WNHAC to head Arizona's Yuma Crossing National Heritage Area in 1999, a local investment company revived the idea of a mall on approximately the same site as the ill-fated Fort Henry project. In 2001, plans for the Victorian Wheeling Outlets were included in the Wheeling National Heritage Area's revised master plan and over the next two years, WNHAC spent nearly $2 million in site studies despite concerns expressed by local business owners about losing control. "We are looking at taking the outlet malls like you see in the middle of cornfields alongside interstates," William Wilmoth, WNHAC chairman declared, "and finding out if that concept would work in a downtown."[32]

At the turn of the twenty-first century, then, several trends converged that presented both opportunities and obstacles for copying Pittsburgh's model of heritage-based rehabilitation and riverfront-oriented revitalization in Wheeling. Public investment in the restoration of Centre Market, the B&O Railroad Station, and Independence Hall as well as the earlier expansion of the Ohio Valley Medical Center gave rise to a vibrant mixed-use urban neighborhood that attracted private investment and the type of creative class entrepreneurship envisioned by *Wheeling 2000*. Other public-private partnerships paid off in the form of slowly expanding riverfront amenities and the modest success of the Artisan Center. However, these projects remained relatively scattered, as the central business district continued to reflect regional economic dislocation and an urban population that had declined to less than 30,000.[33]

The efforts of the city's public-private partnership to attract national retailers to the Victorian Outlets thus reflected a sense of both desperation and continued tension over the goals and means of stimulating urban revitalization. State officials approved a $70 million economic development grant for the outlet project, but a lawsuit over the process of awarding grants delayed release of the funds. Even as proponents of the downtown outlets attempted unsuccessfully to attract tenants without clear funding, county officials tapped the same state grant process for $35 million to finish work on the Fort Henry Industrial and Commerce Park, a publicly subsidized effort that blasted the top off of a mountain east of the city to create developable flat land along Interstate 70. In 2003, the sporting goods giant Cabela's, Inc. announced that it would create an enormous warehousing and retail complex on the site. Over the next decade, many of Wheeling's traditional retailers closed their downtown locations and moved to "The Highlands," as the enormous shopping area came to be known. "It's rather disappointing to go out this way," concluded William Gallagher, the longtime general manager at Crone's Clothiers Ltd., a landmark men's clothing store that once counted The Righteous Brothers, Dean Martin and James Stewart among its clients. "I never dreamt downtown Wheeling would fall apart the way it has."[34]

Malls and Museums

In light of their efforts to attract the stores, restaurants, and vibrant nightlife essential for remaking the downtown riverfront, Wheeling officials would have gladly changed places with Betty Esper, Homestead's mayor, at the groundbreaking ceremony for the Waterfront Town Center in October 1998. Ten years earlier, U.S. Steel had sold the shuttered Homestead Works and the Carrie Furnaces across the Monongahela River to the Park Corporation, a Cleveland-based firm known for buying abandoned industrial properties and making whatever use of them it could. Residents spent the next decade watching the Steel Valley's rusted industrial heart being cleared and sold for scrap, even as the borough itself entered the state's distressed communities program in 1993. It is no wonder, then, that the announcement the brownfield would be transformed into a $300 million, suburban-style mixed-use mall felt "like a Christmas present" to Esper. Furthermore, Continental Realty, the Waterfront developer, supported telling "the story of what Homestead was about" and agreed to incorporate a few signature industrial elements into the site design in partnership with the nonprofit corporation overseeing the Rivers of Steel National Heritage Area. On the other hand, the ongoing deterioration of the older central business district, which was separated from the Waterfront by active railroad lines, along with questions about what to do with the hulking Carrie Furnaces, revealed continuing struggles to control the region's physical and symbolic landscapes. Consequently, there is perhaps no better place than Homestead to encapsulate the fraught nature of metropolitan Pittsburgh's identity at the beginning of the twenty-first century.[35]

The story of Homestead's post-steel transformation began in 1983, even before the closure of the Homestead Works, with Park's purchase of the bankrupt Mesta Machinery in West Homestead for $9 million. According to the company's history, President Ray Park was approached by a Mesta bookkeeper during his initial stroll through the property and asked what he wanted to do about a number of unfilled orders. Park looked at the equipment, decided to turn everything on, and, after those orders were completed, kept the machines running. While portions of the site were put to other uses, most notably for the construction of a large waterpark, over the next few years Park acquired seven other industrial firms from around the Midwest and grouped them together to form West Homestead Engineering and Machine Company, a global supplier of heavy industrial components. As a result, when Park executives met with local leaders in July 1988 to discuss their recent acquisition of the much larger U.S. Steel site, many residents and unemployed steel workers expressed "a very high interest in reopening part of the Homestead Works." However, a subsequent study found that of the region's disused large mill sites, only the electric arc furnaces at LTV's South Side Works could be operated profitably as a standalone steel producer. As a result, despite some attempts by Park and others to restart parts of the mill over the next few years, by 1990 it was clear that the site's future would not primarily be one of reindustrialization.[36]

Other attendees at the meeting in July 1988 had a different vision for the site and advocated for the creation of a heritage park showcasing the region's "proud and nationally significant" industrial history. Earlier that year, Earl James of the Pittsburgh History and Landmarks Foundation had initiated the creation of a Steel Industry Heritage Task Force (SIHTF) that included historians, preservationists and the Allegheny Conference as well as community organizers and local leaders in the Monongahela Valley. In September, a preliminary report supported by the Pennsylvania Historical and Museum Commission recommended the creation of a heritage park that would include the Carrie Furnaces on the north side of the Monongahela, the Hot Metal Bridge across the river, and several buildings of the Homestead Works, including the Pump House and water tower that marked the landing site of the Pinkerton detectives at the beginning of the 1892 labor battle. Over the next few years, proponents expanded this vision to a series of interpretative sites throughout southwestern Pennsylvania that would "conserve and enhance this region's resources and, more importantly, create new economic development opportunities."[37]

As in Wheeling, however, the costs associated with transforming the riverfront brownfield site dwarfed the available resources as proponents looked to state and federal agencies for funding. In September 1988, David Bergholz, assistant executive director of the Allegheny Conference and chair of the SIHTF, urged state Commerce Secretary Ray Christman, who had formerly held positions with both URAP and the Allegheny Conference, to consider a "heritage park-related economic development agenda." "It's a very political process," Bergholz declared. "The only way this project is going to fly is with public support." The next year, Pennsylvania initiated a state Heritage Areas program, creating a bureaucratic and funding framework on which local heritage proponents would build. With backing from Pittsburgh foundations, in 1990 the SIHTF hired August Carlino, a Pittsburgh native from a politically connected family who had previously served in a number of political and lobbying positions in Washington, D.C., as executive director. As with Byrd in Wheeling, museum backers found a strong supporter in Senator John Heinz, who, before his sudden death in 1991, introduced a series of measures that helped fund National Park Service planning studies. The SIHTF reorganized as the Steel Industry Heritage Corporation (SIHC) the next year and took possession of their first property, the Bost Building in Homestead, which they hoped to restore as an archive, museum, and visitor's center. In April 1996, Rivers of Steel was designated as the state's eighth "heritage park" and later that year President Clinton signed the bill designating the region a National Heritage Area.[38]

Despite these political victories, events on the ground threatened to overtake heritage advocates as they negotiated the purchase of key properties from the Park Corporation and faced increasing impatience from community leaders desperate to create new jobs. Finding few options for either restarting the Homestead Works or selling properties to industrial firms, by the end of 1988 the company had already begun demolition of the site. While the SIHC and Park were able to compromise on some issues, including the dismantling and storage of a 200-ton rolling mill, tensions increased over the next two years as the company continued its demolition and advocates struggled to raise the funds necessary to purchase key buildings. "We don't want something to sit there for years and years with nothing done with it," Ray Park declared. "We don't believe they can do it. We don't believe it's feasible." Instead of trying to preserve the enormous Carrie Furnaces and large mill buildings, Park advocated a smaller museum focused on the Pump House and adjacent water tower where the Pinkerton guards landed by boat in 1892. For Jo DeBolt, who had replaced Bergholz as task force chair, however, "fixing up two little buildings" would not give the site the "size and kind of development" necessary for a National Park site.[39]

Following a series of tense public meetings, Park officials informed task force members and state legislators in spring 1990 that the company had "irrevocably" decided that it would not sell any of the property to museum backers, including the thirty-two acres of the Carrie Furnace site deemed essential for a potential national park. While the company subsequently backed off its hardline position, over the next four years it demolished virtually every building on the south side of the river except for the Pump House and water tower, which it suggested should be renovated and preserved as part of a "minimalist interpretive program for the site." Further, had there been a better market for scrap metal in the 1990s or the Carrie Furnaces located in a more easily accessible location, they, too, probably would have been dismantled and the site put up for sale. However, under

Carlino's leadership, museum backers slowly gained legitimacy and raised funds for their vision of the site, and in June 1992 Park agreed to sell seventy-seven acres of the Carrie Furnaces site to the SIHC for about $1.5 million. The Howard Heinz Endowment agreed to fund the purchase, but the whole project was contingent on obtaining designation as a national historic park site and a funding commitment from state officials and the National Park Service, which remained hesitant about the financial liability of maintaining the enormous complex. As a result, even before work began on the Waterfront in 1997, it was clear that the early concept of a comprehensive industrial museum that would drive economic development in Homestead would not come to fruition.[40]

As negotiations for the Carrie Furnaces dragged on, advocates began to reevaluate their strategy in terms of both regional development and community empowerment. First, Carlino focused on the more modest renovation of the Bost Building along Eighth Avenue in downtown Homestead, which SIHC researchers discovered was the headquarters for striking unionists in 1892, to house an archive and a small museum. "This building was abandoned and dilapidated, and the cost of renovation was far more than any business would put into it," Carlino later recalled. "We're talking about a small struggling task force at that point in time," and I said to Jo Debolt, "how are we ever going to convince Park Corporation or any political official that we can do something on the scale of Homestead and Carrie if we don't save this building?'" The project ended up taking ten years to complete even after they bought it at sheriff's sale for $2,000, paid $48,000 in back taxes with a foundation grant, and persuaded Mellon Bank to negotiate a $250,000 lien on the property. "We boarded up the windows and put a new roof on it," Carlino continued, which "bought us time to conduct the architectural designs, get a National Historic Landmark designation, [and] buy some of the adjacent lots for the necessary parking."[41]

By the time the Bost Building unveiled its first exhibit, titled "Century of Steel—Homestead Steel Works: 1881–1986," the public and private fundraising required to raise the $4.5 million needed for renovation had mobilized SIHC to assemble a regional coalition, not an easy task considering the area's political fragmentation and the frequent skepticism of local officials who saw little economic advantage in pouring resources into fixing up dilapidated buildings. In what was called an "unprecedented cooperative venture," in September 1990, six counties, three state agencies, the National

FIGURE 16. View of the Carrie Furnaces, 2014. Built in 1907, the furnaces on the north side of the Monongahela River produced iron for the Homestead Works from 1907 to 1978. Allegheny County purchased the site from Park Corporation in 2005. Furnaces 6 and 7 were declared a National Historic Landmark in 2006. Courtesy of Amanda Dieterich-Ward.

Park Service and various other groups signed a memorandum of understanding with the SIHC to coordinate their efforts in planning for the heritage area. A modest number of grants from state and national heritage programs allowed the SIHC to identify and provide support services for a broader range of historic sites in southwestern Pennsylvania that could be linked within the emerging heritage area framework. Most important, SIHC's modest staff served as "a filter" for state heritage area officials, which allowed for "building up a constituency" of local groups applying for grants. Holding this diverse coalition of local governments and nonprofits together, not to mention supporting their efforts with the Bost Building and

Carrie Furnaces, also required Carlino and his staff to justify "Homestead's existence as a key central mill [within] this Pittsburgh industrial system," in which mines, mills, and corporate offices were "connected because they were all part of this huge conglomerate that was working in different ways."[42]

At this point, the process of building a regional political coalition intersected with the scholarship of historical geographer Edward K. "Ted" Muller, an early member of the SIHTF and vice chair of SIHC after its formation in 1992. Muller was also a founder of the Friends of the Riverfront, and during the late 1980s he began publishing a series of influential essays that both explored the "legacy of industrial rivers" and suggested a new framework for integrating the industrial history of the city of Pittsburgh with its broader metropolitan region. "Ted's research . . . showed how all of these river communities and their industries were connected," Carlino recalled. "It was an epiphany when he explained it and it helped build a regional coalition were communities didn't feel slighted or left out. They were part of the big picture." Based on early planning efforts funded by state and federal grants and supported by Muller's scholarship, the SIHC's 1995 Management Action Plan called for a series of "Regional Journeys": driving tours and water routes that told the Steel Valley's story from Connellsville's "Mountains of Fire" to the "Thunder of Protest" by organized labor in Aliquippa and Ambridge to the mills of "Big Steel" in Pittsburgh and Homestead. "We were the first ones that said this is all an integrated system," Carlino concluded. "From as far as you can trace in the counties we were allowed to work on, [from] Brady's Bend all the way to the state line on the Ohio River, all the way down, you know this is all an integrated, complex system connected by this whole waterway. And I don't think anyone ever looked at it that way."[43]

Rivers of Steel's geographical location coupled with Pennsylvania's proactive heritage areas program allowed Carlino and his staff to scale up their activities to a regional level, acting as a coordinating body between government agencies and private businesses within the emerging framework of neoliberal urbanism. Indeed, Jo Debolt, the driving force in transforming the SIHTF into the SIHC, was executive director of the Mon Valley Initiative, a coalition of ten CDCs set up by the Allegheny Conference in 1988 to "unite the communities" and "restore the economic vitality" in one of the areas hardest hit by the collapse of steel. "I learned very quickly," Muller recalled, "from Jo that she wasn't in there for any of the history. This was all about helping communities that had been stomped on and [left] without much identity and sense of self-worth. And I very quickly came to agree with her, to be quite honest." Staff members Randy Harris and Mike Bilcsik would "go as community organizers before we'd even get to a town," Carlino explained. "Our philosophy was that we weren't going to do the project; we had to find people in those communities that would come to the table willing to do it. We'd help, but we couldn't re-create paternalistic institutions." A key example of SIHC's work was in Brownsville, where the local CDC had its eye on the 1835 Flatiron Building that would have greeted Reuben Gold Thwaites when he set out from the community on his journey down the Monongahela River a century earlier. Brownsville was really struggling and "this was a key project of theirs," Carlino remembered, so we wanted to demonstrate what "the heritage area effort meant to a redevelopment strategy for a CDC and point to the fact that you could restore these buildings in ways that they have meaning and use afterward."[44]

This goal of building an authentic community identity by adapting the physical and social landscape formed the key link to the public-private partnership guiding Pittsburgh's high-tech transformation. No one represented this connection better than Ray Christman, who, after leaving his position as state commerce secretary in 1991, was named president of the Pittsburgh High Technology Council and soon thereafter also took over as SIHC chair. "No region in the world symbolized steel more than Pittsburgh," Christman declared. "This place literally defined industrial activity and manufacturing," and SIHC represented "a way to remember and commemorate that." At the urging of heritage backers, including former executive director Robert Pease, the Allegheny Conference identified Rivers of Steel as a major initiative in 1994, particularly because of its focus on riverfront development and themed attractions. For the SIHC and its supporters making a place for the industrial past in the post-industrial future was about more than attracting tourists. What we "were saying is that this region has a very unique, iconic image and it's one that no place else can claim," Carlino later explained. Nevertheless, questions about the costs and benefits of heritage development lingered and Pittsburgh boosters including Christman remained concerned about public perception of the city as "stuck with steel." "Strangely [we] had to do a huge battle with the Conference" because of the focus on "rebranding Pittsburgh," Carlino added. It seemed like regional marketers were "saying that our heritage and anyone that worked in mining or manufacturing or a job related to that wasn't important to the new Pittsburgh." Instead, our goal was to say "look who we were, look who we are," Muller explained. "We still are that way even though all of this deindustrialization occurred and that is to be proud of [and] built on."⁴⁵

As the connections linking former industrial sites throughout the region began to take shape in the early years of the twenty-first century, however, the ongoing impasse over the Carrie Furnaces remained a symbol of the difficulties faced by public-private partnerships in overcoming the political, economic, and environmental inheritance of the Steel Valley's industrial age. SIHC's allies in Congress continued to advocate for creation of a national park, the renovated Bost Building in Homestead opened in 2002 as an archives and museum, Continental Realty donated the Pump House, and the Union Railroad transferred ownership of the Hot Metal Bridge across the Monongahela River. But, the group still did not own the Carrie Furnaces nor did it have the funds to fully renovate and maintain them. Further, the site straddled the boroughs of Rankin, Swissvale, and Braddock just outside of the Pittsburgh's city limits, which complicated the type of public-private deal making trumpeted by Tom Murphy. "It is unsightly, in a way," Ray Park declared in March 2000. "We only held onto it because of the ongoing talks. We are sort of at the end of our line on that."⁴⁶

However, following the successful collaboration between city and county officials in remaking the South Side Works, in 1999 the Redevelopment Authority of Allegheny County began planning for the Carrie Furnaces site in consultation with local communities and the SIHC. Negotiations with Park Corporation again bogged down amid uncertainty about the level of environmental remediation required before the site could be used. Finally, after the company received a permit to demolish the furnaces, in 2005 county officials announced agreement on a plan to purchase the 137 acres north of the river for $5.75 million. The next year, with the Park Corporation out of the picture, the National Park Service finally declared the Carrie Furnaces a National Historic Landmark more than twenty-five years after advocates began working to create a great museum of Pittsburgh's steel industry. "This is a good day and this site will be developed in our lifetime," declared U.S. Representative Mike Doyle of Swissvale, whose grandfather worked at the Carrie Furnaces for forty years. "We're going to leave this better for our kids and grandkids." "We've got all of our hard work ahead of us now," Carlino added.[47]

In September 2003, the same year the Bost Building finally launched its first exhibition on the Homestead Works and the opening of The Highlands spelled the end of the Victorian Wheeling Outlets, more than 2,500 politicians, journalists, corporate executives, community organizers, and Pittsburgh residents gathered on the banks of the Allegheny River to celebrate the massive renovation of the $354 million David L. Lawrence Convention Center. For Tom Murphy, the opening represented "a milestone" for the city that symbolized its "economic and environmental transition from industry-driven to innovation-driven." The original facility, built in 1981, had only loading docks on the water's edge, but the reoriented complex sat proudly along the Three Rivers Heritage Trail and the catenary curves of its award winning architecture paid homage to Pittsburgh's bridges. The project and the nearby Heinz History Center, housed in the exquisitely restored Chautauqua Lake Ice Company Building, served to connect the theaters of the city's thriving Cultural District to the trendy shops, restaurants, and bars of the heritage-themed Strip District. Looking to the left out of enormous windows, guests could see the lights of the new PNC Park, another project backed by the city's public-private partnerships, where that night the Pirates beat the Chicago Cubs 8-2. Despite the fact that unemployment in Pittsburgh was at about the state average and significantly lower than that of Philadelphia at the time the convention center opened, just three months later the city was officially declared "financially distressed" and its finances placed under state control. The visionary and acerbic mayor's political career was soon over.[48]

Tom Murphy's dramatic fall from grace was emblematic of the difficulties that communities throughout metropolitan Pittsburgh faced in confronting urban decline. While a consensus around river-oriented and heritage-themed development gradually emerged among planners and policy makers, economic stagnation and declining revenues forced political leaders to make hard choices about where and how to spend revenues. "We made a fundamental decision," Murphy explained, "that we needed to get money in a flat broke city." He later paid the political price for moving funds from services to the URAP, but Pittsburgh's resources and strong mayor system allowed city officials to make the deals necessary for effective public-private partnerships during the 1990s in a way that smaller communities could not. On the other hand, SIHC's eventual success in saving the Carrie Furnaces suggests the potential, however fraught, of heritage preservation in creating powerful symbols around which diverse coalitions can be assembled within the market-driven framework of neoliberal urbanism. In any event, it seems clear that the fate of the Steel Valley, and the rest of America's older manufacturing regions, rests with integrating the industrial past into the symbolic and built landscapes of the future.[49]

Epilogue

As we return to the journey west along the Pennsylvania Turnpike with which the book started, it is clear that the story of metropolitan Pittsburgh is that of a contemporary America seeking to balance jobs and environment, and searching for community identity in shared landscapes. In New Stanton, over the Laurel and Chestnut Ridges from the Allegheny Mountain Tunnel, the Regional Industrial Development Corporation (RIDC) is finding tenants for the enormous, still mostly empty site to which massive public incentives drew Volkswagen in the 1970s to assemble Rabbits and Sony in the 1990s to make the last generation of cathode-ray television sets before closing in 2008. Here, travelers must make a choice whether to stay on the turnpike and head northeast to Pittsburgh or follow Interstate 70 west across the Monongahela Valley and then to Wheeling along the Ohio River. On the drive north, the area around the highway begins to shift from rural to suburban on the relatively higher elevation of the Appalachian Plateau. Exiting onto the Penn-Lincoln Parkway (I-376) at Monroeville, we pass through ten miles of research campuses, office buildings, and residential areas like similar tableaus in other parts of the country before beginning our descent into the city.[1]

A casual observer would not know it, but the last of the housing developments visible on the ridge to the left just before entering the Squirrel Hill Tunnel sits on the massive slag pile produced over the course of a century by the Carrie Furnaces as they supplied steel to the Homestead Works. Begun in 1997, Summerset at Frick Park is the largest residential project in the city since World War II, and its existence symbolizes the region's economic transformation every bit as much as does the campus of the Pittsburgh Technology Center built on the former site of J&L Steel's Pittsburgh Works ahead of us along the Monongahela River. While Oakland is out of sight on the plateau to the right, the post-industrial vision of the city's public-private partnership is readily visible in these and other high-tech and health-related projects as well as the many billboards advertising Pitt and Carnegie Mellon. I recommend getting off here in Hazelwood, parking, unloading your bicycle, and switching to the Three Rivers Heritage Trail running between the parkway and the river. After a half-mile or so, you can cross the Hot Metal Bridge that once carried 15 percent of America's steel-making capacity over the Monongahela River. From there, it is a pleasant ride through the shops, offices, hotels, and apartments of the new urbanist-style SouthSide Works, the South Shore Riverfront Park, and the lovingly restored neighborhood of East Carson Street. A little past the festival marketplace of Station Square, you can lock your bike and buy a $5.00 ticket on the Duquesne Incline for a trip up Mt. Washington and a fantastic view of the city, no longer smoky, that recalls my childhood memories coming through the Fort Pitt Tunnel just below you on the hillside.

I traveled this route to Pittsburgh many times in 2008 and 2009, which proved to be particularly eventful years for the city as it celebrated its two hundred and fiftieth anniversary with a series of concerts, parades, and other public spectacles. This image-making effort received an unexpected boost when the Obama administration announced that the community would host an upcoming G20 Summit in September 2009. Obama's emphasis on "the green economy" meshed perfectly with the booster narrative of Pittsburgh as "a great poster child" for economic transformation and gave the region's residents plenty to justify claims that they were moving beyond the rust of deindustrialization. However, the excitement at the time also stemmed from the promise of new "blue" jobs flowing from oil and gas extraction in the region's Marcellus and Utica shale formations. Technological innovations, especially horizontal drilling and hydraulic fracturing or "fracking," allowed the exploitation of reserves deep under the Appalachian Plateau and rapidly revived Pittsburgh's status as an energy capital. The number of extractive wells drilled in southwestern Pennsylvania alone climbed from 65 in 2008 to 428 in 2012, prompting "an industrial renaissance" that has resulted in both exhilaration and alarm, especially from those vested in the symbolism of environmental transformation.[2]

FIGURE 17. View of Downtown Pittsburgh, 2008. Photograph taken from the top of Mt. Washington with the Duquesne Incline visible at the bottom center. Note the coal barge at the mouth of the Monongahela River across from Point State Park. The sightseeing ship visible just to the left of the Fort Pitt Bridge is part of the Gateway Clipper Fleet based at Station Square. PNC Park is visible on the north shore of the Allegheny River. Courtesy of Amanda Dieterich-Ward.

In order to understand the tensions brought to the surface by the fracking boom, we need to return to the New Stanton interchange and travel on I-70 through metropolitan Pittsburgh's southern and western periphery. Passing over the Youghiogheny River and the Great Allegheny Passage Trail, the route descends sharply to the Monongahela, and the view from here is less rosy than that from the restored Hot Metal Bridge forty miles downstream. North of the interstate, the communities of Charleroi, Monessen, and Donora continue to struggle with high poverty and unemployment rates as well as ongoing population loss. Barges and a loading dock on the eastern bank share the panorama with the hulking mass of the Speers Railroad Bridge, over which the Wheeling and Lake Erie Railway still carries steel, coal, and other raw materials to and from five different mills. These days the company's trains are running more often because they are loaded with pipes, machinery, and a host of other goods for the drilling companies. Indeed, some of those pipes are now being produced upriver in the RIDC's Duquesne City Center, where Dura-Bond Industries opened a new coating facility for gas transmission lines in 2011.[3]

Over the next forty miles to the Pennsylvania line, I-70 passes through Washington County, which, at more than 800 active wells, is one of the state's top producers. The drill sites themselves are not generally visible from the highway, but their presence is everywhere in the new roadside businesses supplying equipment and repairing machinery, the billboards advertising discounts for oil and gas workers, the shiny new pickups (often with plates from Colorado, Texas, and Oklahoma), and the multitude of tanker trucks hauling fracking fluid and wastewater. Local officials in Wheeling and across the river in Ohio are banking on oil and gas royalties to pay for street repairs, the local community college has begun training natural gas pipe welders, and in the now rapidly filling county industrial park, under which one of Robert Murray's companies began longwall mining in 2011, you can see the new offices of Chesapeake Energy, the Ohio Valley's largest driller. If you know what you are seeing, you'll soon recognize the broken hills and scrub brush of the largely uninhabited expanse of what was once Consolidation Coal's Egypt Valley Mine. There is still a little surface mining going on in the area, but the real story is the dozen drill rigs rising within ten miles of Barnesville's municipal limits. One is so close to the hospital that its flare turned night into day, reminiscent of James Parton's famous description of Pittsburgh's iron furnaces. Visits to my childhood home now are filled with talk of royalty payments and oil pipelines and a new generation that just might find good paying work in the region.[4]

The Steel Valley has been in the vanguard of both rust and renaissance; its evolution over the course of the last century provides a key window into the future of America's industrial cities. During the 1990s, a steady stream of articles, editorials, and letters to the editor depicted a "golden crossroads" between a smoky, industrial past and an environmentally friendly, high-tech future. For the city's public-private partnership, the greatest obstacle to progress continued to be a "mill mentality" among some residents and a community image that was "stuck with steel." Twenty-five years later metropolitan Pittsburgh, like the rest of the so-called Rust Belt, is no longer at that crossroads, but neither has either future ever fully materialized. The city attracted international attention after the 2008 recession because it lost fewer jobs and created new positions faster than most regions and the United States as a whole. As a result, the conversation in the metropolitan core has largely shifted from how the area will continue its evolution to who will take credit for its sudden emergence after the G20 summit as "a post-industrial paragon of economic transformation." A wave of residential construction that builds on enormous investments by taxpayers and private groups reflects downtown's increasing status among the "creative class," leading some pundits to declare Pittsburgh "the next Portland" and even "the city that Portland wishes it could be," a reference to the latter's reputation as a hip place to live and work.[5]

As Pittsburgh's twentieth-century history demonstrated, however, the sustainability of economic growth depends as much on the hinterland as on what happens downtown. There, intra-regional competition and mistrust continued to hold such sway that consultants for the Benedum Foundation, hired in 1999 to create a development plan reaching across the Pennsylvania border, reportedly suggested they be fired because they could find no realistic basis for cooperation. Since then the notion that metropolitan regions are the driving forces in our national economy has become more widely recognized. In 2010 the Benedum Foundation with Allegheny Conference support again launched a regional initiative, dubbed the Power of 32 (P32) for the number of partnering counties, which for the first time in the Steel Valley's history is bringing civic leaders and local officials from southwestern Pennsylvania, northern West Virginia, and southeastern Ohio into the same room. Despite a promising start, it is of course too early to tell what the long-term impact of regional initiatives like this may be. However, the changes symbolized by P32 have only happened because decades of infrastructure development and the creative destruction of painful economic transitions had already prompted a cultural transformation in the way residents understood themselves as a part of a broader community. "We're within 30 minutes of three other states," concluded Allegheny Conference CEO Dennis Yablonsky during a 2012 business conference highlighting Pittsburgh as a national model for regional partnerships, "so a lot of what we're doing doesn't stop at those artificial boundaries. We've started to cross state lines."[6]

Like that in the 1950s, the new "Pittsburgh Story" is a tale of enlightened leadership and powerful public-private partnerships: this time within a framework of neoliberal urbanism that emphasizes market driven solutions and decentralized decision-making spread across a variety of stakeholders. Tom Murphy, who became a policy consultant at the Urban Land Institute after leaving the mayor's post in early 2006, has been a "very popular speaker" in recent years, according to CEO Patrick Phillips with "a story that we've discovered travels really well." From Toronto to Tel Aviv and Beijing to Salt Lake City, Murphy and other boosters have trumpeted the city's development model with its strong political administration "able to make deals" in partnership with business groups like the Allegheny Conference and a host of well-funded foundations and powerful nonprofits. In Murphy's telling, universities and hospitals especially have become "anchor institutions" in an "innovation economy [that] is sweeping away the old rules of city building." Further, Pittsburgh's strong neighborhood identities serve as the cultural foundation in this story for efficient, businesslike nonprofit community development corporations that can draw investment to otherwise marginalized areas. "We're a capitalist society," Stanley Lowe, former Manchester community organizer and Murphy's housing authority director, declared in 2013. "The neighborhoods have as much right to capitalization and good deals as anybody else."[7]

There are both costs and limits to Pittsburgh's success, however, that pose a cautionary tale to those attempting to recreate its neoliberal model. First, the city has remained in Pennsylvania's "temporary" distressed communities program, known as Act 47, since December 2003 in part due to decisions Murphy made, including diverting millions of dollars from the operating budget to a development fund. While city officials have had to endure oversight by state-appointed overseers, Act 47 has also allowed for novel taxing techniques that are not legally available to city otherwise. In 2014, this put the city's new mayor, Bill Peduto, in the remarkable position of opposing a recommendation that the state end the program on the grounds that the city would "struggle to pay for daily operations" while funding employee pensions and investing in infrastructure. That Pittsburgh can still be in "distress" despite its highly touted turnaround is due in no small part to the nonprofit corporations, particularly the powerful universities and hospitals at the heart of its post-industrial success. Forty percent of Pittsburgh's land area is now tax-exempt, a fact that has led to nearly three decades of tension, especially between city officials and health care giant UPMC, culminating in competing lawsuits over the company's status as a charity and a push at the state level for a constitutional amendment widely regarded as favorable to nonprofits.[8]

The final component of the new Pittsburgh Story brings us back to the working landscape and its people with which the book began. "Every city has a choice," Tom Murphy recently declared to a group of preservationists in Providence, Rhode Island, "to build on its assets, the architectural and natural resources, or ignore them." While "this old stuff is . . . what's making Pittsburgh so hot and attractive to the millennials," as one advocate put it, the market-oriented model of heritage development pioneered by the Pittsburgh History and Landmarks Foundation also requires enormous attention to deal making through public-private collaboration, state and federal tax credits, and innovative financing. Planning for the enormous Carrie Furnace site, which spans four smaller communities and the City of Pittsburgh, finally began in 2010 and provides a key example of this process, with the public Redevelopment Authority of Allegheny County partnering with local governments as well as the nonprofit Steel Industry Heritage Corporation to develop and market the mixed-use project area to for-profit investors. Heritage-based development in other communities continues to lag behind, however, with Wheeling officials reduced to using royalty money from gas drilling beneath municipal parks to demolish once-handsome Victorian buildings due to a lack of demand.[9]

In the end, the shale gas boom makes it clear that the industrial terrain of the Steel Valley, and of the Northeast and Midwest in general, has not disappeared, nor will it be fully displaced by a regional renaissance driven by robotics labs, "eds and meds" employment, or even brownfield and riverfront development that has not accounted for the loss of unionized, family-wage, blue collar jobs. I ended the book's introduction with a software engineer bicycling from work along the Monongahela River past Homestead's preserved 12,000-ton press as one symbol of metropolitan Pittsburgh at the onset of the twenty-first century, but that vision must also encompass U.S. Steel's Edgar Thomson Works still forging raw iron, coal, and limestone into the metal fabric of modernity just two miles downstream. Indeed, recent studies have pointed to the continued significance of manufacturing networks, such as the region's steel technology cluster, that are actually growing in importance as dense local nodes combining business services, industrial research programs, financial firms, and production facilities connect to global supply chains. If transformation has come to the region, it is because there is no longer one industry that defines the areas as steel once did. Amid anxiety balancing between brawn and brain, economy and environment, and change and continuity, the final lesson to be learned is that industrial America is more than just a snapshot of a long-past time. The Steel Valley has adapted and changed over its lifetime with new economic layers deposited on but never fully erasing the old. Its resources, both social and natural, make it a place that people care deeply about and in this love of community lies the heart of innovation.[10]

SOURCES

Abbreviations for Archival Sources

ACCD   MSS#285, Records of the Allegheny Conference on Community Development, Detre Library & Archives, Senator John Heinz History Center, Pittsburgh, Pennsylvania

DFW   RG-6, Records of the Department of Forests and Waters, Pennsylvania State Archives, Harrisburg, Pennsylvania

DTP   MG-404, Dick Thornburgh Papers, Pennsylvania State Archives, Harrisburg, Pennsylvania

GNP   MSS#122, Papers of Graham Netting, Detre Library & Archives, Senator John Heinz History Center, Pittsburgh, Pennsylvania

GRPC   RG-10, Records of the Office of Governor Robert P. Casey, Pennsylvania State Archives, Harrisburg, Pennsylvania

OCPL   Subject File, Ohio County Public Library, Wheeling, West Virginia

ODOD   Records of the Ohio Department of Development, Ohio Historical Society, Columbus, Ohio

PDC   RG-31, Records of the Department of Commerce, Pennsylvania State Archives, Harrisburg, Pennsylvania

PWPC   RG-25, Records of the Pennsylvania Post-War Planning Commission, Pennsylvania State Archives, Harrisburg, Pennsylvania

SPB   RG-10, Records of the Pennsylvania State Planning Board, Pennsylvania State Archives, Harrisburg, Pennsylvania

TMP   MG-444, Thomas J. Murphy Papers, Pennsylvania State Archives, Harrisburg, Pennsylvania

WAHD   Wheeling Area Historical Database, Ohio County Public Library, Wheeling, West Virginia, available at http://www.ohiocounty library.org/wheeling-history/wheeling-area-historical-database/ 4770#index

WPC   AIS#1999.13, Records of the Western Pennsylvania Conservancy, Archives Service Center, University of Pittsburgh, Pittsburgh, Pennsylvania

Oral History Interviews

Brenda Barrett, Carlisle, Pennsylvania, March 17, 2014.
Eric Bugaile, Harrisburg, Pennsylvania, April 13, 2006.
August Carlino, Homestead, Pennsylvania, June 4, 2014.
Dale Davis, Cadiz, Ohio, March 15, 2011.
Gary DuFour, Steubenville, Ohio, August 19, 2004.
Charles Flynn, Yuma, Arizona, May 7, 2014.
Hydie Friend, Wheeling, West Virginia, May 5, 2014.
Richard Garrett, Barnesville, Ohio, November 30, 2004.
John Goodman, St. Clairsville, Ohio, August 13, 2004.
Charles Julian, Wheeling, West Virginia, January 17, 2004.
William Hunkler, Barnesville, Ohio, November 19, 2004.
Frank Joanou, Wheeling, West Virginia, August 16, 2004.
Nicholas Kaschak, Steubenville, Ohio, July 28, 2004.
John Major, Flushing, Ohio, June 6 and June 21, 1998.
Edward Muller, Homestead, Pennsylvania, June 4, 2014.
Donald Myers, Martins Ferry, Ohio, July 29 and August 18, 2004.
Sam Nazzaro, Wheeling, West Virginia, August 13, 2004.
Betty "Snookie" Nutting, Wheeling, West Virginia, May 15, 2014.
G. Ogden Nutting, Wheeling, West Virginia, May 15, 2014.
Robert Philby, Wheeling, West Virginia, August 20, 2004.
Aida Rizzi, St. Clairsville, Ohio, December 4, 2004.
Frank Brooks Robinson, Sr., Pittsburgh, Pennsylvania, September 7, 2010.

Milton Ronsheim, Cadiz, Ohio, November 29 and December 5, 2004.
Nately Ronsheim, Cadiz, Ohio, December 5, 2004.
Janet Smith, Barnesville, Ohio, January 7 and January 28, 2000.
Sam Smith, Barnesville, Ohio, January 7 and January 28, 2000.
Charles Steele, Columbia, Maryland, July 16 and July 23, 2004.
Earl Stephens, Barnesville, Ohio, January 28, 2000.
June Stephens, Barnesville, Ohio, January 28, 2000.
Tom Sexton, Camp Hill, Pennsylvania, April 11, 2006.
Theodore Voneida, Kent, Ohio, December 10, 2004.
Kenneth Ward, Barnesville, Ohio, December 27, 1999.
Lloyd Ward, Barnesville, Ohio, January 8, 2000.
Susan Ward, Barnesville, Ohio, July 19, 2004.
Jack Waterhouse, Wheeling, West Virginia, August 10, 2004.
James Weaver, Wheeling, West Virginia, July 22 and July 27, 2004.
Andrew Wiese, San Diego, California, January 31, 2006.
Robert Wirgau, Weirton, West Virginia, July 14 and August 16, 2004.
Dolores Witherow, St. Clairsville, Ohio, December 15, 2000.

NOTES

INTRODUCTION

1. "Penn Announces Largest U.S. Wind-Energy Purchase," Press Release, University of Pennsylvania, October 24, 2001, http://www.upenn.edu/pennnews/news/penn-announces-largest-us-wind-energy-purchase; Mark Hand, "Energy Rivalries, Debates Turn Pa. Turnpike into Billboard Battleground," *SNL Energy Daily Coal Report* 7, 236 (December 11, 2013): 11–12.

2. The term post-industrial society was first popularized in Daniel Bell, *The Coming of Post-Industrial Society* (New York: Harper Colophon, 1974). While the term is problematic for a number of reasons, in Pittsburgh's case it is useful for understanding the material and symbolic decline of the manufacturing sector coupled with rise of the service sector in the regional economy. For a critical analysis of applying the term "post-industrial" to Pittsburgh, see Sabina Deitrick, "The Post Industrial Revitalization of Pittsburgh: Myths and Evidence," *Community Development Journal* 34 (January 1999): 4–12.

3. Unless otherwise noted, population statistics for the Pittsburgh Metropolitan Region include the combined totals of Belmont and Jefferson Counties in Ohio; Allegheny, Beaver, Butler, Washington, and Westmoreland Counties in Pennsylvania; and Brooke, Hancock, Marshall, and Ohio Counties in West Virginia. The population of the eleven counties increased from 728,192 to 2,141,075 between 1880 and 1920. The regional core of Allegheny County accounted for a little less than half the Steel Valley's population at the beginning of this period and a little more than half at the end. *Historical Census Browser*, 2004. Retrieved March 5, 2015, from the University of Virginia, Geospatial and Statistical Data Center: http://mapserver.lib.virginia.edu/.

4. U.S. Bureau of the Census and Inter-University Consortium for Political and Social Research, *County and City Data Book* (Ann Arbor, Mich.: ICPSR, 1947–1983); U.S. Bureau of the Census, *Statistical Abstract of the United States*, 117th ed. (Washington, D.C.: Government Printing Office, 1997).

5. On civil rights and environmental activism in Pittsburgh, see Joe W. Trotter and Jared N. Day, *Race and Renaissance: African Americans in Pittsburgh Since World War II* (Pittsburgh: University of Pittsburgh Press, 2010); James Longhurst, *Citizen Environmentalists* (Hanover N.H.: Tufts University Press, 2010).

6. The term "brownfield" was coined in the early 1990s to describe land previously used for industrial purposes that requires removal or containment of low concentrations of

hazardous waste or other pollution before being reused for another purpose. More generally, the term is applied to former or current industrial sites that have some level of environmental degradation and are to be cleaned up and used for other less intensive purposes. Justin B. Hollander, *Polluted and Dangerous: America's Worst Abandoned Properties and What Can Be Done About Them* (Burlington: University of Vermont Press, 2009), 2.

7. For examples of the regional model, see William Cronon, *Nature's Metropolis: Chicago and the Great West* (New York: Norton, 1991), Craig E. Colten, *An Unnatural Metropolis: Wresting New Orleans from Nature* (Baton Rouge: Louisiana State University Press, 2006); Lewis, *Chicago Made*. The classic urban history of a postwar American city is Thomas J. Sugrue, *The Origins of the Urban Crisis: Race and Inequality in Postwar Detroit* (Princeton, N.J.: Princeton University Press, 1996). A well-regarded monograph on the suburbs is Becky M. Nicolaides, *My Blue Heaven: Life and Politics in the Working-Class Suburbs of Los Angeles, 1920–1965* (Chicago: University of Chicago Press, 2002). On recent metropolitan-oriented works that incorporate cities and suburbs, see Robert Self, *American Babylon: Race and the Struggle for Postwar Oakland* (Princeton, N.J.: Princeton University Press, 2003); Matthew D. Lassiter, *The Silent Majority: Suburban Politics in the Sunbelt South* (Princeton, N.J.: Princeton University Press, 2006); Andrew Needham, *Power Lines: Phoenix and the Making of the Modern Southwest* (Princeton, N.J.: Princeton University Press, 2014); Andrew R. Highsmith, *Demolition Means Progress: Flint, Michigan, and the Fate of the American Metropolis* (Chicago: University of Chicago Press, 2015). For a more theoretical perspective, see Neil Brenner, ed., *Implosions/Explosions: Towards a Study of Planetary Urbanization* (Berlin: Jovis, 2013).

8. This argument is made at greater length in Andrew Needham and Allen Dieterich-Ward, "Beyond the Metropolis: Metropolitan Growth and Regional Transformation in Postwar America," *Journal of Urban History* 35, 7 (November 1, 2009): 943–69. A number of the books in the University of Pennsylvania Press Metropolitan Portraits series have adopted this basic approach, though their relatively short length and presentist perspective preclude a full articulation of the metropolitan regional framework. See Carl Abbott, *Greater Portland: Urban Life and Landscape in the Pacific Northwest* (Philadelphia: University of Pennsylvania Press, 2001), and Edward Relph, *Toronto: Transformations in a City and Its Region* (Philadelphia: University of Pennsylvania Press, 2013).

9. Edward Muller, "Industrial Suburbs and the Growth of Metropolitan Pittsburgh 1870–1920," *Journal of Historical Geography* 27, 1 (2001): 58–73. For comparative examples, see Robert D. Lewis, ed., *Manufacturing Suburbs: Building Work and Home on the Metropolitan Fringe* (Philadelphia: Temple University Press, 2004). Statistical evidence for the connections between the Upper Ohio Valley and Pittsburgh can be found in Regional Industrial Development Corporation, *A Community of Interest Between the Pittsburgh Metropolitan Area and the Upper Ohio Valley: A Preliminary Analysis* (Pittsburgh: RIDC, 1959).

10. On the origins of the decline of American industrial regions, see Barry Bluestone and Bennett Harrison, *The Deindustrialization of America: Plant Closings, Community Abandonment, and the Dismantling of Basic Industry* (New York: Basic, 1982); Jefferson Cowie, *Capital Moves: RCA's Seventy-Year Quest for Cheap Labor* (New York: New Press, 2001); Steven C. High, *Industrial Sunset: The Making of North America's Rust Belt, 1969–1984* (Toronto: University of Toronto Press, 2003).

11. On Boston's Route 128 Corridor, see Lily Geismer, *Don't Blame Us: Suburban Liberals and the Transformation of the Democratic Party* (Princeton, N.J.: Princeton University Press, 2015). Historical scholarship on metropolitan development in the "Sun Belt" of the American

South and Southwest includes Bruce J. Schulman, *From Cotton Belt to Sunbelt: Federal Policy, Economic Development, and the Transformation of the South, 1938–1980* (New York: Oxford University Press, 1991); Ann R. Markusen et al., *The Rise of the Gunbelt: The Military Remapping of Industrial America* (New York: Oxford University Press, 1991); Self, *American Babylon*; Elizabeth Tandy Shermer, *Sunbelt Capitalism: Phoenix and the Transformation of American Politics* (Philadelphia: University of Pennsylvania Press, 2013); Needham, *Power Lines*. On the importance of understanding the connection between jobs and urban renewal, see Guian A. McKee, *The Problem of Jobs: Liberalism, Race, and Deindustrialization in Philadelphia* (Chicago: University of Chicago Press, 2008).

12. Allen Dieterich-Ward, "From Satellite City to Burb of the 'Burgh: Deindustrialization and Community Identity in Steubenville, Ohio," in James Connolly, ed., *After the Factory: Reinventing America's Industrial Small Cities* (Lanham, Md.: Lexington, 2010). Recent examples of historical scholarship seeking to move beyond the trope of deindustrialization and push the story of metropolitan development through the 1980s and 1990s include Jefferson Cowie and Joseph Heathcott, eds., *Beyond the Ruins: The Meanings of Deindustrialization* (Ithaca, N.Y.: Cornell University Press, 2003); Howard Gillette, *Camden After the Fall: Decline and Renewal in a Post-Industrial City* (Philadelphia: University of Pennsylvania Press, 2005); Margaret E. Dewar and June Manning Thomas, *The City After Abandonment* (Philadelphia: University of Pennsylvania Press, 2013).

13. The academic use of the term "neoliberalism" is closely associated with the work of a number of scholars of the left, especially geographer David Harvey. In general, it refers to a revival of classical liberal thinking by economists such as Friedrich von Hayek and Milton Friedman adopted by politicians and business people on the right as a justification for dismantling the postwar government commitment to social programs. More recently theorists such as Neil Brenner, Jamie Peck, and Nik Theodore have explored the complex interplay between processes of neoliberalization and the lived reality of preexisting social, cultural and political contexts at the urban scale. While perhaps overused as an ambiguous catchall by critics of policies deemed insufficiently progressive, "neoliberal urbanism" provides a useful framework for analyzing the complex origins, scope, and complicated outcomes of municipal growth strategies since the 1970s. David Harvey, *A Brief History of Neoliberalism* (New York: Oxford University Press, 2005); Mike Davis and Daniel Bertrand Monk, eds., *Evil Paradises: Dreamworlds of Neoliberalism* (New York: New Press, 2007); Jamie Peck, Nik Theodore, and Neil Brenner, "Neoliberal Urbanism: Models, Moments, Mutations," *SAIS Review* 19, 1 (Winter–Spring 2009): 49–66; Sarah Glynn, ed., *Where the Other Half Lives: Lower Income Housing in a Neoliberal World* (New York: Pluto Press, 2009); Jamie Peck, Nik Theodore, and Neil Brenner, "Neoliberal Urbanism Redux?: Debates and Developments," *International Journal of Urban and Regional Research* 37, 3 (May 2013): 1091–99.

14. The most comprehensive analysis of the Allegheny Conference is Sherie R. Mershon, "Corporate Social Responsibility and Urban Revitalization: The Allegheny Conference on Community Development, 1943–1968" (Ph.D. dissertation, Carnegie Mellon University, 2004). On planning and Pittsburgh politics before World War II, see John Bauman and Edward Muller, *Before Renaissance: Planning in Pittsburgh, 1889–1943* (Pittsburgh: University of Pittsburgh Press, 2006). On Pittsburgh as a model for postwar public-private partnerships, see Jon C. Teaford, *The Rough Road to Renaissance: Urban Revitalization in America, 1940–1985* (Baltimore: Johns Hopkins University Press, 1990). Recent scholarship on urban renewal

includes Samuel Zipp, *Manhattan Projects: The Rise and Fall of Urban Renewal in Cold War New York* (New York: Oxford University Press, 2010); Christopher Klemek, *The Transatlantic Collapse of Urban Renewal: Postwar Urbanism from New York to Berlin* (Chicago: University of Chicago Press, 2011).

15. Self, *American Babylon*; Joseph Heathcott and Maire Agnes Murphy, "Corridors of Flight, Zones of Renewal: Industry, Planning, and Policy in the Making of Metropolitan St. Louis, 1940–1980," *Journal of Urban History* 31, 2 (January 2005): 151–89; Highsmith, *Destruction Means Progress*. This was also true for Toronto and other Canadian cities with a stronger tradition of centralized planning by federal and provincial governments. See Relph, *Toronto*, and Tracy Neumann, "Goodbye, Steeltown: The Politics of Space in Pittsburgh and Hamilton" (Ph.D. dissertation, New York University, 2011).

16. Dieterich-Ward, "From Satellite City to Burb of the 'Burgh."

17. On the evolution of the "technoburb," see Robert Fishman, *Bourgeois Utopias: The Rise and Fall of Suburbia* (New York: Basic, 1987). See also Patrick Vitale, "The Atomic Capital of the World: Suburbanization, Technoscience, and the Remaking of Pittsburgh During the Cold War" (Ph.D. dissertation, University of Toronto, 2013); Margaret Pugh O'Mara, *Cities of Knowledge: Cold War Science and the Search for the Next Silicon Valley* (Princeton, N.J.: Princeton University Press, 2004); Judith Rodin, *The University and Urban Revival: Out of the Ivory Tower and Into the Streets* (Philadelphia: University of Pennsylvania Press, 2007); Geismer, *Don't Blame Us*. On the role of hospitals in Pittsburgh's economic development, see Andrew T. Simpson, "Health and Renaissance: Academic Medicine and the Remaking of Modern Pittsburgh," *Journal of Urban History* 41, 1 (January 2015): 19–27.

18. Tracy Neumann, "Privatization, Devolution, and Jimmy Carter's National Urban Policy," *Journal of Urban History* 40 (March 2014): 283–300; Robert A. Beauregard, "Public-Private Partnerships as Historical Chameleons: The Case of the United States," in Jon Pierre, ed., *Partnerships in Urban Governance: European and American Experience* (New York: St. Martin's, 1998). On the role of Richard Scaife in regional and national politics, see "Obituary: Richard M. Scaife/Ideologue, philanthropist, newspaper publisher, July 3, 1932–July 4, 2014," *Pittsburgh Post-Gazette*, July 5, 2014. On the relationship between festival marketplaces and downtowns, see Michael Sorkin, ed., *Variations on a Theme Park: The New American City and the End of Public Space* (New York: Hill and Wang, 1992); Alison Isenberg, *Downtown America: A History of the Place and the People Who Made It* (Chicago: University of Chicago Press, 2004); James Michael Lindgren, *Preserving South Street Seaport: The Dream and Reality of a New York Urban Renewal District* (New York: NYU Press, 2014).

19. Neumann, "Goodbye, Steeltown"; Edward Muller, "Downtown Pittsburgh: Renaissance and Renewal," in Joseph Scarpaci and Kevin Patrick, eds., *Pittsburgh and the Appalachians: Cultural and Natural Resources in a Postindustrial Age* (Pittsburgh: University of Pittsburgh Press, 2006).

20. Urban geographer Jason Hackworth used the term "neoliberal city" as the title for a 2006 book that serves as a good introduction to the scholarship. Jason Hackworth, *The Neoliberal City: Governance, Ideology, and Development in American Urbanism* (Ithaca, N.Y.: Cornell University Press, 2006). See also, Howard Gillette, "Is this the Neoliberal Moment?" *Journal of Urban History* 36, 3 (May 2003): 393–97.

21. On the importance of rivers to regional identity in metropolitan Pittsburgh, see Edward K. Muller, "River City," in Joel A. Tarr, ed., *Devastation and Renewal: An Environmental History of Pittsburgh and Its Region* (Pittsburgh: University of Pittsburgh Press, 2003),

41–63. On the role of "space" in contemporary urban history, see Gyan Prakash, "Introduction," in Gyan Prakash and Kevin Kruse, eds., *The Spaces of the Modern City: Imaginaries, Politics, and Everyday Life* (Princeton, N.J.: Princeton University Press, 2008).

22. The term "imagined communities" is from Benedict Anderson, *Imagined Communities: Reflections on the Origin and Spread of Nationalism*, rev. ed. (New York: Verso, 2006). For examples, see David Blackbourn, *The Conquest of Nature: Water, Landscape, and the Making of Modern Germany* (New York: Norton, 2007); Matthew W. Klingle, *Emerald City; An Environmental History of Seattle* (New Haven, Conn.; Yale University Press, 2007); Michael Rawson, *Eden on the Charles; The Making of Boston* (Cambridge, Mass.; Harvard University Press, 2010).

23. John Bodnar, Roger Simon, and Michael Weber, *Lives of Their Own: Blacks, Italians, and Poles in Pittsburgh, 1900–1960* (Urbana: University of Illinois Press, 1981); William Serrin, *Homestead: The Glory and Tragedy of an American Steel Town* (New York: Times Books, 1992); John H. Hinshaw, *Steel and Steelworkers: Race and Class Struggle in Twentieth-Century Pittsburgh* (Albany: State University of New York Press, 2002); Edward Slavishak, *Bodies of Work: Civic Display and Labor in Industrial Pittsburgh* (Durham, N.C: Duke University Press, 2008). On the evolution of labor and industry in the Ohio and West Virginia portions of the region, see David Javersak, "The Ohio Valley Trades and Labor Assembly: The Formative Years, 1882–1915" (Ph.D. dissertation, West Virginia University, 1977); Elizabeth Fones-Wolf and Ken Fones-Wolf, "Cold War Americanism: Business, Pageantry, and Antiunionism in Weirton, West Virginia," *Business History Review* 77, 1 (Spring 2003): 61–91; Louis Martin, "Working for Independence: The Failure of New Deal Politics in a Rural Industrial Place" (Ph.D. dissertation, West Virginia University, 2008).

24. For overviews of metropolitan Pittsburgh's environmental history, see Tarr, ed., *Devastation and Renewal*; Joseph L. Scarpaci and Kevin J. Patrick, *Pittsburgh and the Appalachians: Cultural and Natural Resources in a Postindustrial Age* (Pittsburgh: University of Pittsburgh Press, 2006).

25. The term "sacrifice zone" is used most prominently with regard to rural areas by environmental law scholar Jedediah Purdy. Jedediah Purdy, "Afterword: An American Sacrifice Zone," in Michele Morrone and Geoffrey Buckley, eds., *Mountains of Injustice: Social and Environmental Justice in Appalachia* (Athens: Ohio University Press, 2011), 182–83. For a critical analysis of the environmental legacy of the Pittsburgh Renaissance, see Samuel P. Hays, "Beyond Celebration: Pittsburgh and its Region in the Environmental Era—Notes by a Participant Observer," in Tarr, ed., *Devastation and Renewal*.

26. Richard L. Florida, *The Rise of the Creative Class: Revisited* (New York: Basic, 2012). Florida was actively engaged in regional planning in Pittsburgh while a faculty member at Carnegie Mellon University from 1987 to 2005. For an overview of the adaptive reuse of brownfield sites, see Niall Kirkwood, ed., *Manufactured Sites: Rethinking the Post-Industrial Landscape* (New York: Taylor & Francis, 2011). On the notion of "authenticity" in neighborhood renewal, see Sharon Zukin, *Naked City: The Death and Life of Authentic Urban Places* (New York: Oxford University Press, 2010), ix–xv. On the development of National Heritage Areas, see National Park Service, *Charting a Future for National Heritage Areas: A Report by the National Park System Advisory Board* (Washington, D.C.: BiblioGov, 2012).

27. For relevant examples of the growing literature on the uses of public history for economic and community development, see Andrew Hurley, *Beyond Preservation: Using Public History to Revitalize Inner Cities* (Philadelphia: Temple University Press, 2010); Ned Kaufman, *Place, Race, and Story: Essays on the Past and Future of Historic Preservation* (New York:

Routledge, 2009); Carolyn L. Kitch, *Pennsylvania in Public Memory: Reclaiming the Industrial Past* (University Park: Pennsylvania State University Press, 2012).

28. For the history of the 12,000-ton press through 1991, see William Serrin, *Homestead: The Glory and Tragedy of an American Steel Town* (New York: Times Books, 1992). See also Jefferson Cowie and Joseph Heathcott, "Introduction: The Meanings of Deindustrialization," in Cowie and Heathcott, eds., *Beyond the Ruins*, 2–3.

PART I: INTRODUCTION

1. Reuben Gold Thwaites, *Afloat on the Ohio: An Historical Pilgrimage of a Thousand Miles in a Skiff from Redstone to Cairo* (New York: Doubleday & McClure, 1900, c1897), Preface, Chapters 1–5 (Darlington Digital Library). See also Reuben Gold Thwaites, Robert L. Reid, and Dan Hughes Fuller, *Pilgrims on the Ohio: The River Journey & Photographs of Reuben Gold Thwaites, 1894* (Indianapolis: Indiana Historical Society, 1997).

2. W. T. Stead, "Incidents of Labor War in America," *Contemporary Review* (July 1894): 67–69.

CHAPTER 1. BUILDING THE REGION

1. Victor G. Reuther, *The Brothers Reuther and the Story of the UAW* (Boston: Houghton Mifflin, 1976), 10–13.

2. Reuther, *The Brothers Reuther*, 33.

3. Kim M. Gruenwald, *River of Enterprise: The Commercial Origins of Regional Identity in the Ohio Valley, 1790–1850* (Bloomington: Indiana University Press, 2002).

4. Richard White, *The Middle Ground: Indians, Empires, and Republics in the Great Lakes Region, 1650–1815* (New York: Cambridge University Press, 1991); Fred Anderson, *Crucible of War: The Seven Years' War and the Fate of Empire in British North America, 1754–1766* (London: Faber, 2000).

5. John Alexander Williams, *West Virginia: A History* (Morgantown: West Virginia University Press, 2001), 49–68.

6. "Steubenville, Ohio," *New Jersey Journal*, May 6, 1817; Eugene R. Harper, "Town Development in Early Western Pennsylvania," *Western Pennsylvania Historical Magazine* 71, 1 (January 1988); Marci Lynn McGuinness and Bill Sohonage, *The Explorer's Guide to the Youghiogheny River Region, Ohiopyle and S.W. Pennsylvania's Villages* (Ohiopyle, Pa.: Backwoods Books, 2000).

7. Christy Collins, "Kirkwood Township, Belmont County, Ohio," n.d (manuscript in the author's possession); Harper, "Town Development in Early Western Pennsylvania," 24.

8. John Lauritz Larson, *Internal Improvement: National Public Works and the Promise of Popular Government in the Early United States* (Chapel Hill: University of North Carolina Press, 2001); F. F. Crall, "A Half Century of Rivalry Between Pittsburgh and Wheeling," *Western Pennsylvania Historical Magazine* 13 (October 1930).

9. Diane Barnes, "Urban Rivalry in the Upper Ohio Valley: Wheeling and Pittsburgh in the Nineteenth Century," *Pennsylvania Magazine of History and Biography* 123, 3 (July 1999); Catherine Reiser, *Pittsburgh's Commercial Development, 1800–1850* (Harrisburg: Pennsylvania Historical and Museum Commission, 1951), 142–43.

10. *Wheeling Gazette*, November 17, 1849, quoted in Elizabeth B. Monroe, "Spanning the Commerce Clause: The Wheeling Bridge Case, 1850–1856," *American Journal of Legal History* 32, 3 (July, 1988); "The Wheeling Bridge Case," *New York Times*, May 22, 1852; Elizabeth Monroe, *The Wheeling Bridge Case: Its Significance in American Law and Technology*

(Boston: Northeastern University Press, 1992). On the material and symbolic importance of bridges, see Blackbourn, *The Conquest of Nature*.

11. Reiser, *Pittsburgh's Commercial Development*, 152.

12. "Opening of the Baltimore and Ohio Railroad." *New York Daily Times*, January 11, 1853; John Stover, *History of the Baltimore and Ohio Railroad* (West Lafayette, Ind.: Purdue University Press, 1995), 72; Edward K. Muller and Joel A. Tarr, "The Interaction of Natural and Built Environments in the Pittsburgh Landscape," in Tarr, ed., *Devastation and Renewal*, 18.

13. W. F. Switzler, Report on the Internal Commerce of the United States: Part II of Commerce and Navigation, Special Report on the Commerce of the Mississippi, Ohio, and Other Rivers, and of the Bridges Which Cross Them (Washington, D.C.: GPO, 1888), 421; Williams, *Appalachia*, 130; Douglas L. Crowell, *History of the Coal Mining Industry in Ohio* (Columbus: Ohio Division of Geologic Survey, 1995), 175–85.

14. H. D. Scott, *Iron and Steel in Wheeling* (Toledo, Ohio: Caslon, 1929), 40; Louis Martin, "Causes and Consequences of the 1909–1910 Steel Strike in the Wheeling District" (Master's thesis, West Virginia University, 1999), 4.

15. Williams, *Appalachia*, 128; Robert B. Gordon, *American Iron, 1607–1900* (Baltimore: Johns Hopkins University Press, 1996); Harold C. Livesay, *Andrew Carnegie and the Rise of Big Business*, 3rd ed. (New York: Pearson Longman, 2007), 87–94; John N. Ingham, *Making Iron and Steel: Independent Mills in Pittsburgh, 1820–1920* (Columbus: Ohio State University Press, 1991).

16. JoAnne Yates, *Control through Communication: The Rise of System in American Management* (Baltimore: Johns Hopkins University Press, 1989)

17. Ingham, *Making Iron*, 53; David Nasaw, *Andrew Carnegie* (New York: Penguin Press, 2006).

18. Hugh P. Meese, "Edgar Thomson Steel Works" in *The Unwritten History of Braddock's Field (Pennsylvania)* (Pittsburgh: Nicholson, 1917), 49–57; Ingham, *Making Iron*, 48.

19. Livesay, *Andrew Carnegie*, 127, 161–83. As a percentage of GDP, Carnegie Steel's profit would be more than $28 billion in 2010 dollars.

20. Livesay, *Andrew Carnegie*, 125–28; D. H. Aldcroft, "The Entrepreneur and the British Economy, 1870–1914," *Economic History Review* 17, 1 (1964): 113–34; Frank Thistlethwaite, *The Great Experiment: An Introduction to the History of the American People* (New York: Cambridge University Press, 1955), 211–12.

21. Edward Slavishak, *Bodies of Work: Civic Display and Labor in Industrial Pittsburgh* (Durham, N.C.: Duke University Press, 2008); Jill Jonnes, *Empires of Light: Edison, Tesla, Westinghouse, and the Race to Electrify the World* (New York: Random House, 2003); University of Virginia, *Historical Census Browser*.

22. *Wheeling Daily Intelligencer*, September 14, 1886; Livesay, *Andrew Carnegie*, 104–7. "LaBelle Iron Works Celebrating Seventieth Birthday," *Wheeling Register*, February 5, 1922.

23. Gibson L Cranmer, *History of Wheeling City and Ohio County, West Virginia and Representative Citizens* (Chicago: Biographical Pub., 1902); University of Virginia, *Historical Census Browser*; Nelson C. Hubbard to Andrew Carnegie, "Letter," May 12, 1899 (copy in author's possession); "LaBelle Iron Works."

24. Cranmer, *History of Wheeling City*.

25. Paul Kellogg, "The Pittsburgh Survey," *Charities and the Commons* 21 (1909): 519.

26. As historical geographer Edward K. Muller has observed, "neither Kellogg nor his team ever precisely defined their conception of the metropolitan geography. What, after all,

was the 'community' or the 'much larger territory' which they wanted to study?" Edward Muller, "The Pittsburgh Survey and 'Greater Pittsburgh': A Muddled Metropolitan Geography," in Maurine Greenwald and Margo Anderson, eds., *Pittsburgh Surveyed: Social Science and Social Reform in the Early Twentieth Century* (Pittsburgh: University of Pittsburgh Press, 1996), 70–71.

27. Joel A Tarr, *Transportation Innovation and Changing Spatial Patterns in Pittsburgh, 1850–1934* (Chicago: Public Works Historical Society, 1978).

28. According to a 1930 Official Guide to the Railways, travel time via Pennsylvania Railroad from Pittsburgh to Steubenville was one hour and twenty minutes for express trains. Scott Becker, Executive Director of the Pennsylvania Trolley Museum, email to author, January 16, 2010.

29. Angela Gugliotti, "'Hell with the Lid Taken Off': A Cultural History of Air Pollution—Pittsburgh" (Ph.D. dissertation, University of Notre Dame, 2004); Lynne Page Snyder, "Death-Dealing Smog over Donora, Pennsylvania: Industrial Air Pollution, Public Health, and Federal Policy, 1915–1963" (Ph.D. dissertation, University of Pennsylvania, 1994); John B. Hunter II, *Marine Memories*, interview by Carrie Noble-Kline and Steven W. Franklin, June 7, 1994, WAHD.

30. Dempsey O. Sheppard, *The Story of Barnesville, Ohio, 1808–1940* (Barnesville, Ohio., 1942; reprinted by Belmont County Chapter of the Ohio Genealogical Society; Freeport, Ohio: Freeport Press, 1983); Tim Palmer, *Youghiogheny: Appalachian River* (Pittsburgh: University of Pittsburgh Press, 1984); Lowry, *Portrait of a Region*.

31. Williams, *Appalachia*, 125–26; Stephen L. Stover, "Early Sheep Husbandry in Ohio," *Agricultural History* 36, 2 (April 1962), 105–6; Stephen L. Stover, "Ohio's Sheep Year: 1868," *Agricultural History* 38, 2 (April 1964): 102–7.

32. Brian Black, *Petrolia: The Landscape of America's First Oil Boom*, Creating the North American Landscape Series (Baltimore: Johns Hopkins University Press, 2000); John Williams, *West Virginia and the Captains of Industry* (Morgantown: West Virginia University Library, 1976); David A. Waples, *The Natural Gas Industry in Appalachia: A History from the First Discovery to the Maturity of the Industry* (Jefferson, N.C.: McFarland, 2005).

33. Thwaites, *Afloat on the Ohio*, 7; Davitt McAteer, *Monongah: The Tragic Story of the Worst Industrial Accident in U.S. History* (Morgantown: West Virginia University Press, 2007); Williams, *Appalachia*; Reuther, *The Brothers Reuther*, 19–24.

34. Muller, "Industrial Suburbs"; David Demarest and Eugene Levy, "Touring the Coke Region," *Pittsburgh History* 74, 3 (Fall 1991): 100–113.

35. Les Standiford, *Meet You in Hell: Andrew Carnegie, Henry Clay Frick, and the Bitter Partnership That Changed America* (New York: Crown, 2005); Serrin, *Homestead*, 46–51.

36. "Rivers of Steel, http://www.riversofsteel.com," *CRM Journal* 2, 1 (Winter 2005): 126; Muller, "Industrial Suburbs"; Casner, "Acid Mine Drainage"; Chad Montrie, *To Save the Land and People: A History of Opposition to Surface Coal Mining in Appalachia* (Chapel Hill: University of North Carolina Press, 2003), 34; Muriel Earley Sheppard, *Cloud by Day: The Story of Coal and Coke and People* (1947; Pittsburgh: University of Pittsburgh Press, 1991), 1.

37. Hubbard, "Letter," 1899.

CHAPTER 2. MINES AND MILLS

1. Tinning is the process of thinly coating sheets of steel with tin to prevent rust. Louis C. Martin, "Working for Independence: The Failure of New Deal Politics in a Rural Industrial

Notes to Page 46–54

Place" (Ph.D. dissertation, West Virginia University, 2008), 42; David T. Javersak, *History of Weirton, West Virginia* (Virginia Beach: Donning, 1999), 67–140.

2. "Community Attitude Survey: Steubenville," February 19, 1972, Binder "Second Progress Report," Box 55526, series 1857, ODOD; John Bauman and Edward Muller, *Before Renaissance: Planning in Pittsburgh, 1889–1943* (Pittsburgh: University of Pittsburgh Press, 2009), 9.

3. Serrin, *Homestead*, 56; Raymond A. Washlaski, "Leith Shaft Mine & Coke Works, Leith, South Uniontown, South Union Twp., Fayette County, Pennsylvania, U.S.A," http://patheoldminer.rootsweb.ancestry.com/fayleith.html.

4. Carmen DiCiccio, *Coal and Coke in Pennsylvania* (Harrisburg: Pennsylvania Historical and Museum Commission, 1996), 106. On the engineering of underground spaces for mass production, see Timothy LeCain, *Mass Destruction: The Men and Giant Mines that Wired America and Scarred the Planet* (New Brunswick, N.J.: Rutgers University Press, 2009).

5. Livesay, *Andrew Carnegie*, 56–57. U.S. Steel controlled plentiful limestone deposits through a subsidiary that operated quarries in Blair County, near Altoona, and at Wick in Butler County north of Pittsburgh. American Iron and Steel Institute, *Directory of Iron and Steel Works of the United States and Canada* (New York: The Institute, 1902), 12.

6. Serrin, *Homestead*, 57.

7. Serrin, *Homestead*, 58–60.

8. It was not uncommon for the Monongahela River at Pittsburgh to record a pH of 3, a level that immediately killed most organisms. Nicholas Casner, "Acid Water: A History of Coal Mine Pollution in Western Pennsylvania, 1880–1950" (Ph.D. dissertation, Carnegie Mellon University, 1994); Nicholas Casner, "Acid Mine Drainage and Pittsburgh Water Quality," in Joel A. Tarr, ed., *Devastation and Renewal: An Environmental History of Pittsburgh and Its Region* (Pittsburgh: University of Pittsburgh Press, 2003), 23; J. A. Mohr, "Acid in Monongahela River Water," *Proceedings of the Engineers Society of Western Pennsylvania* 17 (1901): 237–40.

9. Sheppard, *Cloud by Day*, 1.

10. DiCiccio, *Coal and Coke in Pennsylvania*; James Longhurst, *Citizen Environmentalists* (Medford, Mass.: Tufts University Press, 2010), 98.

11. Muller and Tarr, "The Interaction of Natural and Built Environments in the Pittsburgh Landscape," 18; Frederick Law Olmsted, Jr., *Pittsburgh Main Thoroughfares and the Down Town District: Improvements Necessary to Meet the City's Present and Future Needs; A Report* (Pittsburgh: Pittsburgh Civic Commission, 1911), 109.

12. Livesay, *Andrew Carnegie*, 123–24; J. Varga, Jr., and H. W. Lownie, Jr., "Final Technological Report on a System Analysis Study of the Integrated Iron and Steel Industry," Battelle Memorial Institute, May 15, 1969; Andrew Hurley, *Environmental Inequalities: Class, Race, and Industrial Pollution in Gary, Indiana, 1945–1980* (Chapel Hill: University of North Carolina Press, 1995), 20–21.

13. Hurley, *Environmental Inequalities*, 23; Serrin, *Homestead*, 62; John Fitch, *The Steel Workers* (New York: Russell Sage, 1910), 183.

14. Edward Muller, "Ash Pile or Steel City?: H. L. Mencken Helps Mold an Image," *Pittsburgh History* 74, 2 (Summer 1991); Slavishak, *Bodies of Work: Civic*, 3; Thwaites, *Afloat on the Ohio*, 7–8, 45.

15. James Parton, "Pittsburg," *Atlantic Monthly*, January 1868, 21; Lincoln Steffens, *The Shame of the Cities* (Mineola, N.Y.: Dover, 2004), 102.

16. Olmsted, Jr., *Pittsburgh Main Thoroughfares*, 93; University of Virginia, Geospatial and Statistical Data Center, *Historical Census Browser* (2004); John Bodnar, Roger Simon and

Michael Weber, *Lives of Their Own: Blacks, Italians, and Poles in Pittsburgh, 1900–1960* (Urbana: University of Illinois Press, 1982).

17. Richard Oestreicher, "Working-Class Development, Formation and Consciousness in Pittsburgh, 1790–1960," and Michael Weber, "Community-Building and Occupational Mobility in Pittsburgh, 1880–1960," both in Samuel P. Hays, ed., *City at the Point: Essays on the Social History of Pittsburgh* (Pittsburgh: University of Pittsburgh Press, 1989).

18. Oestreicher, "Working-Class Development"; John H. Hinshaw, *Steel and Steelworkers: Race and Class Struggle in Twentieth-Century Pittsburgh* (Albany: State University of New York Press, 2002), 18–23

19. Hinshaw, *Steel and Steelworkers*, 25–26.

20. Paul Krause, *The Battle for Homestead, 1880–1892: Politics, Culture, and Steel* (Pittsburgh: University of Pittsburgh Press, 1992), 4; Thwaites, *Afloat on the Ohio*, 18; Slavishak, *Bodies of Work*, 86–87; Richard Oestreicher, "The Spirit of '92: Popular Opposition in Homestead's Politics and Culture, 1892–1937," in Maurine W. Greenwald and Margo Anderson, eds., *Pittsburgh Surveyed: Social Science and Social Reform in the Early Twentieth Century* (Pittsburgh: University of Pittsburgh Press, 1996), 193.

21. Martin, "Causes and Consequences," 13; Len Boselovic, "Steel Standing: U.S. Steel Celebrates 100 Years," *Pittsburgh Post-Gazette*, February 25, 2001.

22. Martin, "Causes and Consequences, 26–35, 31.

23. Matthew Magda, *Monessen: Industrial Boomtown and Steel Community, 1898–1980* (Harrisburg, Pa.: Pennsylvania Historical and Museum Commission, 1985). Oestreicher, "The Spirit of '92"; L. C. Gardner, "Community Athletic Recreation for Employees and Their Families" (Carnegie Steel Co., Munhall, Pa., typeset, n.d.), quoted in Rob Ruck, *Sandlot Seasons: Sport in Black Pittsburgh* (Urbana: University of Illinois Press, 1993), 25; Javersak, *History of Weirton*.

24. Ernest T. Weir, "Some Aspects of Our Personal History," February 24, 1955, quoted in Ernest Dale, "Ernest Tener Weir: Iconoclast of Management," *California Management Review* 1 (Spring 1959); Author's Interview with Robert Wirgau, August 16, 2004; Sharon Zukin, *Landscapes of Power: From Detroit to Disney World* (Berkeley: University of California Press, 1991), 59–102

25. Martine Goldberg, "The Jewel of the Valley: The Carnegie Library of Homestead," *Pennsylvania History* 70, 2 (Spring 2003), 158; Curtis Miner, "The 'Deserted Parthenon': Class, Culture, and the Carnegie Library of Homestead, 1898–1937," *Pennsylvania History* 57, 2 (1990): 112.

26. Nelson C. Hubbard to Andrew Carnegie, "Letter," Wheeling, May 12, 1899 (copy in author's possession); *Wheeling Daily Intelligencer*, December 24, 1903, quoted in Reuther, *The Brothers Reuther*, 25.

27. Goldberg, "The Jewel of the Valley"; Reuther, *The Brothers Reuther*, 25–26; Hubbard, "Letter," 1899.

28. Charles Wingerter, *History of Greater Wheeling and Vicinity* (Chicago: Lewis Publishing, 1912), 520–22; Ken Fones-Wolf, *Glass Towns: Industry, Labor and Political Economy in Appalachia, 1980–1930s* (Urbana: University of Illinois Press, 2007), 59–74

29. Bill Hogan, *Wheeling's Wide Open Days*, interview by Michael Kline and Carrie Noble-Kline, July 5, 1994, WAHD; David W. Rose, "The Committee of One Hundred: A Social Reform Movement in Turn of the Century Wheeling," *Upper Ohio Valley Historical Review* 15 (1985): 2–22; David W. Rose, "The Trial of Alice Bradford: A Study in the Politics

of Prostitution in Wheeling, W. Va," *Upper Ohio Valley Historical Review* 16 (Autumn–Winter, 1986): 6–22; Norman Nygaard, *Twelve Against the Underworld* (New York: Hobson, 1947), 3–4; "Community Attitude Survey: Steubenville."

30. Bauman and Muller, *Before Renaissance*, 22; Hinshaw, *Steel and Steelworkers*, 23–26.

31. Bauman and Muller, *Before Renaissance*, 21–23.

32. Franklin Toker, *Pittsburgh: A New Portrait* (Pittsburgh: University of Pittsburgh Press, 2009), 40–93; John Holmes, *Remembering Steubenville: From Frontier Fort to Steel Valley* (Charleston, S.C.: History Press, 2009), 92–97; *Annual Report of the Department of Public Works, City of Pittsburgh, 1890* (Pittsburgh: 1890), 130.

33. H. L. Mencken, "The Libido for the Ugly," in *Prejudices: Sixth Series* (New York: Knopf, 1927), 187; Hinshaw, *Steel and Steelworkers*, 22–35; Michael Weber, *Don't Call Me Boss: David L. Lawrence, Pittsburgh's Renaissance Mayor* (Pittsburgh: University of Pittsburgh Press, 1988), 3–21; *The Majority*, January 29, 1914, quoted in David T. Javersak, "The Ohio Valley Trades and Labor Assembly: The Formative Years, 1882–1915" (Ph.D. dissertation, West Virginia University, 1977), 148.

34. Edward T. Devine, "Pittsburgh: The Year of the Survey," in Paul Kellogg, ed., *The Pittsburgh District: Civic Frontage* (New York: Survey Associates, 1914), 5–6; Clinton Rogers Woodruff, "Guthrie of Pittsburgh," *World Today* 17 (July–December, 1919): 1171–73; Bauman and Muller, *Before Renaissance*, 65–86.

35. Geo. H. Anderson, "Address on Economic Situation of Pittsburgh," June 30, 1902, in *Year Book and Directory of the Chamber of Commerce of Pittsburgh, Pa.* (Pittsburgh, 1903), http://digital.library.pitt.edu.

36. "Some Interesting Data About Wheeling and Vicinity, Compliments of Wheeling Corrugating Company," Wheeling, c. 1914, http://wheeling.weirton.lib.wv.us/history/General_History/.

37. City of Pittsburgh, Annual Reports of the Executive Departments For the Year Ending January 31, 1912 (Pittsburgh: 1912), quoted in Roy Lubove, *Twentieth-Century Pittsburgh*, vol. 1, *Government, Business, and Environmental Change* (Pittsburgh: University of Pittsburgh Press, 1996), 55; Roger W. Haigh, *Wheeling, West Virginia: A Community Profile* (Wheeling: Center for Wheeling Area Studies, 1969), 95.

38. "Names City Planning Commission," *Pittsburgh Press*, November 19, 1911; "City Engineers Will Examine Tunnel Plans," *Pittsburgh Press*, January 6, 1911; *Wheeling Intelligencer*, January 4, 1900, quoted in Rose, "The Committee of One Hundred," 4.

39. David Lonich, "Metropolitanism and the Genesis of Municipal Anxiety in Allegheny County," *Pittsburgh History* 76, 2 (Summer 1993): 79–88; "Some Interesting Data About Wheeling and Vicinity."

40. Thwaites, *Afloat on the Ohio*, 13, 23, 40.

41. Clayton Koppes and William Norris, "Ethnicity, Class and Mortality in the Industrial City: A Case Study of Typhoid Fever in Pittsburgh, 1890–1910," *Journal of Urban History* 11 (May 1985): 259–79.

CHAPTER 3. THE PITTSBURGH STORY

1. Lynne Page Snyder, "Revisiting Donora, Pennsylvania's 1948 Air Pollution Disaster," in Tarr, ed., *Devastation and Renewal*, 126–44; Don Hopey, "Museum Remembers Donora's Deadly 1948 Smog," *Pittsburgh Post-Gazette*, October 21, 2008; "Steel Company Pays $235,000 to Settle $4,643,000 in Donora Smog Death Suits," *New York Times*, April 18, 1951, 33.

2. John T. Holdsworth, *Report of the Economic Survey of Pittsburgh*, City of Pittsburgh, May 15, 1912; Weber, *Don't Call Me Boss*, 229; Karl Schriftgiesser, "The Pittsburgh Story," *Atlantic Monthly*, May 1951.

3. "The Smoke Law Passes Its Hardest Test," *Pittsburgh Press*, November 2, 1948, 10.

4. Reuther, *The Brothers Reuther*, 41–48.

5. Wilbert G. Fritz, "Long-Time Trend of Production in the Pittsburgh District," *Pittsburgh Business Review* 4 (November 1934): 17–22; Hinshaw, *Steel and Steelworkers*, 39; Pittsburgh Regional Planning Association, *Economic Study of the Pittsburgh Region*, vol. 1, *Region in Transition* (Pittsburgh: University of Pittsburgh Press, 1963).

6. Ira S. Lowry, *Economic Study of the Pittsburgh Region*, vol. 2, *Portrait of a Region* (Pittsburgh: University of Pittsburgh Press, 1963), 60; Javersak, *History of Weirton*, 150; House Committee on Investigation of United States Steel Corporation, *United States Steel Corporation: Hearings before the Committee on Investigation of United States Steel Corporation*, vol. 8 (Washington, D.C.: GPO, 1912), 68; Serrin, *Homestead*, 129–45; University of Virginia, *Historical Census Browser* (2004).

7. Keith Dix, *What's a Coal Miner to Do? The Mechanization of Coal Mining* (Pittsburgh: University of Pittsburgh Press, 1988), 61; Crowell, *History*, 5, 17–29.

8. Hinshaw, *Steel and Steelworkers*, 41–44; Melvyn Dubofsky and Warren Van Tine, *John L. Lewis: A Biography* (Urbana: University of Illinois Press, 1986), 162–204.

9. Foster Rhea Dulles and Melvyn Dubofsky, *Labor in America: A History* (Wheeling, Ill.: Harlan Davidson, 1993), 259; Serrin, *Homestead*, 190–214.

10. Hinshaw, *Steel and Steelworkers*, 41; Javersak, *History of Weirton*, 115–16.

11. Weber, *Don't Call Me Boss*, 37; Bruce Stave, *The New Deal and the Last Hurrah: Pittsburgh Machine Politics* (Pittsburgh: University of Pittsburgh Press, 1970), 182.

12. University of Virginia, *Historical Census Browser*; Bauman and Muller, *Before Renaissance*, 67–86, 250–60; Olmsted, *Pittsburgh Main*, xv; Robert Moses, *Arterial Plan for Pittsburgh* (Pittsburgh: Pittsburgh Regional Planning Association, 1939).

13. H. W. Prentis, Jr., "Post-War Planning in Pennsylvania," October 6, 1944, box 1, folder "Minutes, July 20–December 27, 1944," PWPC; Robert E. Doherty, "Statement Presented by Dr. Robert E. Doherty at the Organization Meeting of the Citizens Sponsoring Committee Leading to the Creation of the Allegheny Conference on Post-War Community Planning," May 24, 1943, cited in Mershon, "Corporate Social Responsibility," 169.

14. Wallace Richards, "A Fifty-Seven Million Dollar Program," *Allegheny Conference Digest*, December 1945, box 129, folder 5, ACCD; Mershon, "Corporate Social Responsibility," 19–24; Heathcott and Murphy, "Corridors of Flight"; Leland Hazard, *Attorney for the Situation* (Pittsburgh: Carnegie-Mellon University Press, 1975), 235.

15. Shelby Stewman and Joel A. Tarr, "Four Decades of Public-Private Partnerships in Pittsburgh" in R. Scott Fosler and Renee A. Berger, eds., *Public-Private Partnership in American Cities: Seven Case Studies* (Lexington, Mass.: Heath, 1982), 66; "City Target of Architect," *Pittsburgh Post-Gazette*, July 1, 1935, 28; Stefan Lorant, ed., *Pittsburgh: The Story of an American City* (Pittsburgh: Esselmont Books, 1964, rev. and expanded 1975, 1980, 1988, 1999), 373–74.

16. "Flood Commission's Report," *Pittsburgh Press*, November 5, 1911, 12; Holdsworth, *Report of the Economic Survey of Pittsburgh*, 10; David Lawrence, "Rebirth," in Lorant, ed., *Pittsburgh*, 373.

17. Parton, "Pittsburg"; Holdsworth, *Economic Survey of Pittsburgh*, 10; Angela Gugliotta, "How, When and for Whom Was Smoke a Problem in Pittsburgh?" in Tarr, ed., *Devastation and Renewal*, 110–25.

18. Gugliotta, "How, When and for Whom," 117–22; "Progress Against Smoke," *Pittsburgh Post-Gazette*, January 16, 1934, 10; Sherie Mershon and Joel Tarr, "Strategies for Clean Air: The Pittsburgh and Allegheny County Smoke Control Movements, 1940–1960," in Tarr, ed. *Devastation and Renewal*, 145–73.

19. Weber, *Don't Call Me Boss*, 201; Lawrence, "Rebirth," 399.

20. Lawrence, "Rebirth," 402; Allegheny Conference on Community Development, *Allegheny Conference Presents* (Pittsburgh: The Conference, 1956), 18; Mershon and Tarr, "Strategies for Clean Air," 145–73.

21. "Editorial," *Pittsburgh* Press, Mar. 22, 1947, 7; Lawrence, "Rebirth," 392–397; Mershon and Tarr, "Strategies for Clean Air," 165–66.

22. Longhurst, *Citizen Environmentalists*; Wheeling Area Conference on Community Development, "Air Pollution Control," *Highlights on Community Progress*, April 1956, 1, folder "Wheeling City Planning," OCPL; William K. Stevens, "Ohio Is Crucial Testing Ground in U.S. Pollution Fight," *New York Times*, February 10, 1976, 39.

23. Roland M. Smith, "The Politics of Pittsburgh Flood Control, 1908–1936," *Pennsylvania History* 42, 1 (January 1975); Roland Smith, "The Politics of Pittsburgh Flood Control, 1936–1960,"*Pennsylvania History* 44, 1 (January 1977); Flood Commission of Pittsburgh, "Safeguarding Pittsburgh from Floods," 1911; "Flood Commission's Report."

24. "Build These Dams!" *Pittsburgh Press*, June 13, 1943, Second Section, 1; Palmer, *Youghiogheny*, 83, 92; "Gigantic Youghiogheny Dam at Confluence Completed," *Pittsburgh Press*, December 29, 1943.

25. Palmer, *Youghiogheny*, 86, 91; Hal Jenkins, *A Valley Renewed: The History of the Muskingum Watershed Conservancy District* (Kent, Ohio: Kent State University Press, 1976); W. H. McWilliams, "Conservancy Authority to Provide Relief for Victim of Piedmont Dam," *Martins Fairy Daily Times*, March, d.u, 1941 (copy in author's possession); Author's Interviews with John Major, June 1998.

26. Olmsted, *Pittsburgh Main Thoroughfares*, 29; Robert C. Alberts, *The Shaping of the Point, Pittsburgh's Renaissance Park* (Pittsburgh: University of Pittsburgh Press, 1980), 63.

27. Alberts, *Shaping of the Point*, 70; James A. Kell to Robert Doherty, telegram, October 29, 1945, box 129, folder 5, ACCD; Lawrence, "Rebirth," 419.

28. Rachael Balliet Colker, "Gaining Gateway Center: Eminent Domain, Redevelopment, and Resistance," *Pittsburgh History* 78 (1995), 136–38.

29. Mershon, "Corporate Social Responsibility," 663–70; Vitale, "The Atomic Capital of the World," 66–115; Colker, "Gaining Gateway Center," 136–38; Hazard, *Attorney for the Situation*, i, 238.

30. Lubove, *Twentieth-Century Pittsburgh*, vol. 1, 130; Mallett, "The Lower Hill Renewal," 180, 182; Lawrence, "Rebirth," 436–47; Untitled Advertisement, *Los Angeles Times*, October 5, 1960, 30.

31. Michael A. Fuoco, "Return to Glory: Hill District Determined to Regain Lost Greatness," *Pittsburgh Post-Gazette*, April 11, 1999; "Federal Redevelopment Fund Reservation for the Commonwealth" and John P. Robin to Wallace Richards, "Letter," June 6, 1950, both in box 2, folder "Minutes and Agenda, 1950," SPB; Lawrence, "Rebirth," 437.

32. Pittsburgh Urban Redevelopment Authority, "Digest of the Urban Renewal Program," September 1967; Allegheny Conference on Community Development, "Report of

Working Committees of the Allegheny Conference on Community Development," 1944, box 377, folder 2, ACCD; Richards, "A Fifty-Seven Million Dollar Program"; untitled advertisement, *Los Angeles Times*, February 25, 1951, B10.

33. Park Martin, "Narrative of the Allegheny Conference on Community Development and the Pittsburgh Renaissance, 1943–1958," 1964, 4, box 308, folder 11, ACCD; Bob Prince, "A Network of Lakes for Pittsburgh and Vicinity," address delivered on Radio Station WJAS on Friday, December 17, 1943, and Samuel E. Phillips to Mark James, "Letter," May 22, 1944, box 4, folder "Aa–Al," PWPC; "Development of Recreational Resources in Pennsylvania," 1945, both in box 2, folder "Recreation Committee," PWPC; Ellwood Chapman to Hannah M. Durham, "Letter," December 16, 1946, box 3, folder "Durham, Hannah M," PWPC; Lester A. DeCoster, *The Legacy of Penn's Woods: A History of the Pennsylvania Bureau of Forestry* (Harrisburg: Pennsylvania Historical and Museum Commission and Pennsylvania Department of Conservation and Natural Resources, 1995).

34. Adolph W. Schmidt to Park H. Martin, "Letter," December 29, 1950, box 376, folder 5, ACCD; James McClain, "Colloquium on WHAT CAN THE PEOPLE DO ABOUT IT?," address to American Planning and Civic Association National Citizens Conference on Parks and Open Spaces for the American People, Washington, D.C., 22 May 1955, 4, box 376, folder 5, ACCD; M. Graham Netting, *50 Years of the Western Pennsylvania Conservancy: The Early Years* (Pittsburgh: Western Pennsylvania Conservancy, 1982), 84–87.

35. Charles F. Lewis and John R. Schell, "Impressive Growth and Achievements Recorded by Conservancy in Past Year (Annual Report)," *Water Land and Life* 9, 1 (April 1967); Adolph W. Schmidt to Charles F. Chubb, "Re: Prospectus for the Development of the Slippery Rock-Muddy Creek Drainage Area," July 5, 1951, box 2, folder 2, GNP; Netting, *50 Years*, 96

36. "Major Construction Work is Underway on Ohiopyle Sewer and Water System," *Water Land and Life* 9, 2 (July 1967), 6; "When We Brag About Our Area's Growth, We Mean White Oaks and Mountain Laurel, Too," *Wall Street Journal*, March 22, 1972.

37. Lawrence, "Rebirth," 374; Advertisement for *Pittsburgh: The Story of an American City, New York Times*, December 15, 1964, 62; Bob Hoover, "W. Eugene Smith," *Pittsburgh Post-Gazette*, December 9, 2001.

38. Southwestern Regional Planning Commission, *Issues in a Region of Contrasts*, 1968.

PART II INTRODUCTION

1. Ralph R. Widner, "The Regional City: An Approach to Planning Our Future Urban Growth, an Address to the Annual Meeting of the Allegheny Conference on Community Development," November 26, 1973, 1–25.

2. Lowry, *Economic Study of the Pittsburgh Region*, vol. 2, 98.

3. Southwestern Regional Planning Commission, *Issues in a Region of Contrasts*.

4. Pennsylvania State Planning Board, *Regional Development Reconnaissance: Region 12 [A Staff Working Paper]*, January 1966, 62.

CHAPTER 4. LIVE ON THE HILLS AND WORK IN THE CITY

1. Robert Levenson to Edward Magee, "Letter," November 12, 1959, box 166, folder 16, ACCD; Robert M. Rownd, "President's Report," *Highlights on Community Progress*, April 1957, 1, folder "Wheeling, City Planning," OCPL.

2. Francis Dodd McHugh, Proposed Plan for Future Land Use, 1957, 1; Wheeling Area Conference on Community Development, Inc.; "Enlarged Business District Seen Here," *Wheeling Intelligencer*, October 25, 1956, 1; "Now Plans are Begun to 'Open Up' the Hilltops," *Wheeling Intelligencer*, December 25, 1962; Rownd, "President's Report," 1, 2.

3. *County and City Data Book*. This was out of a total of 242 metropolitan areas in the U.S. Significant population loss in southeastern Ohio and the West Virginia Panhandle offset slight gains in southwestern Pennsylvania.

4. "New Plans Are Begun to 'Open Up' the Hilltops."

5. Virginia Ann Randolph Grottendieck, "Problems of Administration in a Bi-State Metropolitan Region" (Master's thesis, West Virginia University, 1970).

6. Author's Interview with Jack Waterhouse, August 2004; "New Ideas in Land Planning," *National Association of Homebuilders Journal*, May 1962, 93; Author's Interview with Frank Joanou, August 2004.

7. Edgar Hoover, "Pittsburgh Takes Stock of Itself, address delivered to the Economic Club of Pittsburgh," reprinted in "Summary Report of the Allegheny Seminar Conference, Oglebay Park, Wheeling West Virginia," September 20–22, 1964, 2; F. D. Hollinshead, "Locating Industry in the Pittsburgh Area, address to the Members of the Pittsburgh Junior Chamber of Commerce, June 14, 1946," reprinted in *Allegheny Conference Digest* 1, 4 (September 1946): 9–10, box 129, folder 4, ACCD; Author's Interview with Nicholas Kaschak, July 2004.

8. McKeesport City Planning Commission and Pittsburgh Regional Planning Association, "Master Plan, City of McKeesport: A Technical Report," 1964; Hal Maggied, "Report on Official Travel to Steubenville, OH," December 10, 1972, series 1857, box 55526, binder "Second Progress Report," ODOD.

9. Nygaard, *Twelve Against the Underworld*, 97–114; Francis F. Brown, *A History of the Roman Catholic Diocese of Steubenville, Ohio*, vol. 1 (Lewiston, N.Y.: Edwin Mellen, 1994), 56–60; Kaschak Interview.

10. "Editorially Speaking," *Highlights on Community Progress*, April 1956, 3, folder "Wheeling, City Planning," OCPL; Mary Chilton Chapman, "Anti-Smoke Law Studied by Wheeling," *Charleston Gazette*, January 14, 1955; "Enlarged Business District Seen Here"; "Wheeling Makes First Arrest on Pollution Charge," *Charleston Daily Mail*, July 18, 1956, 25.

11. "Redevelopment Plan Approval Awaited," "Planning Commission Takes Active Role in 'Forward Wheeling,'" and Wilbur S. Jones, "Past President's Report," all in *Highlights on Community Progress*, April 1957, folder "Wheeling, City Planning," OCPL.

12. "Fact Sheet on Center Wheeling Redevelopment Project," 1, folder "Wheeling, City Planning," OCPL; "Light Industrial District Urged for Center Wheeling," *Wheeling News Register*, January 2, 1957, 1.

13. Thomas Michaud, "The Legacy of WJU and Community Economic Development: The Work of Fr. Wheeling-Pitts F. Troy, S.J.," February 4, 2005; "Wheeling Is Concerned by Drop in Population," *Morgantown Post*, May 18, 1960, 6; "Around West Virginia" (reprint from *Wheeling News-Register*), *Morgantown Post*, September 28, 1959, 10.

14. Joanou Interview.

15. "Live on the Hills and Work in the City"; "Around West Virginia" (reprint from *Wheeling News-Register*), *Morgantown Post*, August 2, 1960, 10.

16. Mark Kauffman and John R. McDermott, "Rocky Cradle of Football," *Life* 53, 18, November 1962, 70–78; Steele Interview.

17. Martins Ferry Model Cities Department, "First Year Action Plan: To the Department of Housing and Urban Development," Model Cities Reports, OH 37 (1970), 15, 22.

18. David Reed, "Ohio Valley: America's Newest Industrial Empire," *Reader's Digest*, December 1963, 193.
19. Author's Interviews with Donald Myers, July and August 2004.
20. Myers Interview; Author's Interview with John Goodman, August 2004; "First Year Action Plan," 18; "Changes Made by W-P Steel," *Steubenville Herald Star*, March 16, 1976, 14.
21. Myers Interview; Author's Interview with James Weaver, July 2004.
22. Myers Interview; "Rt. 7 Job Set in Yorkville Area," *Steubenville Herald Star*, February 26, 1963, 1, 2.
23. Author's Interview with Charles Steele, July 2004; Myers Interview
24. "'Industry Hunter' Answer" (Reprinted from *Wheeling Intelligencer*), *Morgantown Post*, July 26, 1961, 6.
25. Steele Interview; Maxine S. Plummer, "Field Report Re: Laslo Rural Service Award Banquet," September 26, 1968,series 629, box 52035, folder "Belmont County," ODOD; John Laslo, "City Tour Features Projects, Buildings," *Model Cities Review*, August 1972, series 1857, box 55526, folder "Model Cities," ODOD.
26. Martins Ferry Model Cities Dept., "First Year Action Plan, " "Second Year Action Plan" (1971), and "Third Year Action Plan" (1972), series 1857, box 55526, folder "Model Cities," ODOD; Department of Housing and Urban Development Office of Demonstrations and Intergovernmental Relations, "Model Neighborhoods Under the Demonstration Cities Act" (Washington, D.C.: HUD, 1967); Myers Interview.
27. Martins Ferry Model Cities Dept., "First Year Action Plan," 56.
28. "Second Year Model Cities Program in Ferry Reviewed," *Model Cities Review*, June 1973, series 1857, box 55526, folder "Model Cities," ODOD; Martins Ferry Model Cities Dept., "First Year Action Plan," 56; Steele Interview.
29. "'Industry Hunter' Answer," 6; "Relocation of Route 250 Sought," *Steubenville Herald Star* Aug. 22, 1964, 3; Record Set in Hearing on Highway," *Steubenville Herald Star*, January 5, 1968, 1, 3; "Short Creek Plans Rejected for Relocation of Route 250," *Steubenville Herald Star*, June 25, 1968, 18.
30. Magda, *Monessen*; Redevelopment Authority of the City of Monessen, *Annual Report, 1968* (Monessen, Pa.: The Authority, 1969); Steele Interview.
31. Basic Oxygen Furnace Roars into Action Here," *Weirton Daily Times*, November 14, 1967, 1; Javersak, *History of Weirton*, 139, 163.
32. Curtis Miner and Paul Roberts, "Engineering an Industrial Diaspora: Homestead, 1941," *Pittsburgh History* 72 (1989); Zukin, *Landscapes of Power*, 62; William White, "Fabulous Steel Mill Town Holder of Top Liberty Title," first of 5-part series "Weirton—Where Freedom Rings," *Pittsburgh* Press, September 23, 1851, 25; Staughton Lynd, "Why We Opposed the Buyout at Weirton Steel," *Labor Research Review* 1, 6 (1985).
33. Elizabeth Fones-Wolf and Ken Fones-Wolf, "Cold War Americanism: Business, Pageantry, and Antiunionism in Weirton, West Virginia," *Business History Review* 77, 1 (Spring 2003): 67; DuFour Interview.
34. Fones-Wolf and Fones-Wolf, 68; Javersak, *History of Weirton*, 107–8.
35. "Weirton Pays Tribute to Millsop at Banquet," *Weirton Daily Times*, January 19, 1966, 1.
36. Javersak, *History of Weirton*, 110–11.
37. "Topics of the Times," *Weirton Daily Times*, June 29, 1955, 13; "Ralph Barone, Realty Developer, Dies at 75," *Weirton Daily Times*, September 26, 1974, 1; "Power Company Buys $180,000 Site for Building," *Weirton Daily Times*, September 18, 1967, 1.

Notes to Page 119–127   311

38. "Varied Reaction Noted in Sub-Division Talks," *Weirton Daily Times*, December 8, 1960, 1, 2; "Subdivision Law Passed by City," *Weirton Daily Times*, April 11, 1961, 1, 2; "Board Approves Housing Project of Barone Firm," *Weirton Daily Times*, June 8, 1961, 1, 2; Earle V. Wittpenn, "Topics of the Times," *Weirton Daily Times*, June 13, 1961, 11; Barone Outlines Housing Plan," *Weirton Daily Times*, February 19, 1962, 1.

39. "Another Record Year," *Weirton Daily Times*, April 28, 1965, 17; "National Steel Expands Capital Spending Plans in Report by Stinson," *Weirton Daily Times*, January 14, 1965, 1, 2.

40. "Fast Work on Roadway," editorial, *Weirton Daily Times*, March 4, 1967, 4; "Area Newsmen Inspect Oxygen Steel Making," *Weirton Daily Times*, March 5, 1965, 1, 2; Earle V. Wittpenn, "Favors Experts," *Weirton Daily Times*, April 3, 1965, 4; Earle V. Wittpenn, "Basic Oxygen," *Weirton Daily Times*, March 12, 1965, 4.

41. "Great Changes in Steel," editorial, *Weirton Daily Times*, December 13, 1966, 4; Vaclav Smil, *Transforming the Twentieth Century: Technical Innovations and Their Consequences* (New York: Oxford University Press, 2006), 99; "National Steel Expands Capital Spending Plans in Report by Stinson"; "Voting Is an Obligation," editorial, *Weirton Daily Times*, June 5, 1967, 4; "Council, Chamber Act," *Weirton Daily Times*, September 23, 1967, 4.

42. "Producers Agree on Symbol to Appear on Products; Steel Industry Opens Campaign," *New York Times*, January 14, 1960, 45; "Future of Steel Brighter Than Ever, Stinson Assures," *Weirton Daily Times*, May 17, 1967, 1.

43. "Council, Chamber Act"; "New Year Resolutions," *Weirton Daily Times*, December 31, 1969, 4.

CHAPTER 5. WE'RE APPALACHIA, BUT WE DON'T NEED TO BE

1. Robert Gaitens, "Ohiopyle Dedicates New Vacationland," *Pittsburgh Press*, July 8, 1962, 2; Netting, *50 Years of the Western Pennsylvania Conservancy*.

2. Consolidation Coal Company, *Egypt Valley . . . Today and Tomorrow*, 1967 (in author's possession); "Hanna Moves into Egypt Valley," *CONSOL News*, April 1967, 14.

3. Jedediah Purdy, "Afterword: An American Sacrifice Zone," in Morrone and Buckley, eds., *Mountains of Injustice*, 182–83; Author's Interviews with Milton Ronsheim, November and December 2004.

4. Widner, "The Regional City, 17; Candeub, Fleissig, and Associates, *Regional Comprehensive Plan for the Bel-O-Mar Area: Phase I, Basic Research, Surveys and Analysis* (Wheeling. W.V.: Bel-O-Mar Interstate Planning Commission, 1969), 33–41; Lowry, *Economic Study of the Pittsburgh Region*, vol. 2.

5. U.S. Bureau of the Census and Inter-University Consortium for Political and Social Research, *County and City Data Book* (Ann Arbor, Mich.: ICPSR, 1947, 1956, 1962, 1972, 1977, 1983); Nelson Vernon Frazier, "The Development of the Dairy Industry in Belmont County, Ohio" (Master's thesis, Ohio State University, 1959); Author's Interview with Sam and Janet Smith, January 2000.

6. "Hyslop Paints Prosperous Picture for Coal Industry," *Martins Ferry Times Leader*, January 7, 1946, 11; Martin B. Zimmerman, *The U.S. Coal Industry: The Economics of Policy Choice* (Cambridge, Mass.: MIT Press, 1981), 5–6; Joel A. Tarr, "Changing Fuel Use Behavior and Energy Transitions: The Pittsburgh Smoke Control Movement, 1940–1950—A Case Study in Historical Analogy," *Journal of Social History* 14, 4 (Summer 1981).

7. *County and City Data Book*; Ohio Department of Development, *Ohio Appalachian Development Plan* (Columbus: The Department, 1974); Author's Interview with Kenneth Ward, November 1999.

8. Ron Eller, *Uneven Ground: Appalachia since 1945* (Lexington: University Press of Kentucky, 2008), 40–41; John A. Andrew, *Lyndon Johnson and the Great Society* (Chicago: I.R. Dee, 1998); Ralph R. Widner, "Appalachian Development After 25 Years: An Assessment," *Economic Development Quarterly* 4, 4 (1990): 291–312; John Sweeney quoted in Eller, *Uneven Ground*, 181; Widner, "The Regional City."

9. Netting, *50 Years*, 96; Ohio Department of Development, *A Development Program for the Ohio Valley Region* (Columbus: The Department, 1964), 1.

10. Michael Sangiacomo, "Athens Area Awaits its Promised Highway," *Cleveland Plain Dealer*, March 6, 2000, 1B; Widner, "The Regional City"; DeCoster, *The Legacy of Penn's Woods*; Joseph S. Clark to William Scranton, Telegram, August 20, 1963, box 1, "Citizens Committee for Project 70 Files, 1961–1965," DFW.

11. Randy Ludlow, "Ohio's Lion in Winter," *Cincinnati Post*, September 11, 1999, 1A; John J. Gargan and James Guthrie Coke, *Political Behavior and Public Issues in Ohio* (Kent, Ohio: Kent State University Press, 1972), 39, 303.

12. Ronsheim Interviews. L. Milton Ronshseim is the father of Milton Ronsheim interviewed by the author. Both served as editor of the *Cadiz Republican*. Erving E. Beauregard, "L. Milton Ronsheim and Strip Coal Mining in Ohio," *Journal of Unconventional History* 9, 3 (1998): 16–33; Robert Vincent, "Strip Mining to 'Improve' Land: Ireland Testifies at State Hearing," *Martins Ferry Times Leader*, January 24, 1946, 1; Moore and Headington, *Agricultural and Land Use as Affected by Strip Mining*, 28.

13. Pennsylvania State Planning Board, "Twenty Years of State Planning: A Report to the Governor of the Commonwealth and to the General Assembly by the Pennsylvania State Planning Board," 1955, 7–10; Chad Montrie, *To Save the Land and People*, 43–59.

14. Pittsburgh Coal Company and Consolidation Coal Company merged to form the Pittsburgh Consolidation Coal Company (Consol) in 1945 and acquired the holdings of Cleveland-based Hanna Coal Company in 1946. The M. A. Hanna Company became Consol's largest shareholder, while the new company retained the Hanna Coal name for its Ohio surface mines throughout the 1950s and 1960s. "Big Coal Merger Goes into Effect," *New York Times*, November 28, 1945, 27; "Pittsburgh Consolidation Gets Hanna Ohio Mines," *New York Times*, June 7, 1946, 37.

15. W. C. Bramble, "Strip Mining: Waste or Conservation?" *American Forests* (June 1949): 24–27; A. E. Flowers, "Harmon Creek Goals: Profitable Stripping," *Coal Age* (May 1955): 112–13; Daniel Jackson, "Strip Mining, Reclamation, and the Public," *Coal Age* (May 1963); "Strip Mining Heals its Own Scars," *Business Week*, November 13, 1965, 140–45; "Hillman Cited as Honorary Life Member," *Water, Land, and Life* (Spring 1969): 19–20.

16. Coopers & Lybrand Associates, "A Study of the Economic Impact on the Greater Wheeling Area if Local Coal Mines Are Closed," 1973; D. Reed, "Ohio Valley: America's Newest Industrial Empire," *Reader's Digest*, December 1963, 193.

17. Ohio Department of Development, *A Development Program for the Ohio Valley Region*, 2; Terry Flynn, "Leaders Start Work to Train 1,400 Miners: Federal Agencies to Assist Firms, UMW in Program," *Wheeling Intelligencer*, d.u., 1967; Terry Flynn, "Homes for 1,600: Coal Operators Seek Housing Aid for Miners," *Wheeling Intelligencer*, d.u., 1967, both in series 2319, box 3932, folder 6, ODOD; C. D. Keyser, "Ohio Mine Manpower Development

Project, Final Draft Report," July 16, 1970; Coopers & Lybrand, "A Study of the Economic Impact," 198.

18. Gaitens, "Ohiopyle Dedicates New Vacationland," 2. Lillian McCahan to Maurice Goddard, "Letter," July 3, 1962; Lillian McCahan to David Lawrence et al., "Letter," December 22, 1961; Lillian McCahan to Charles Chubb, "Letter," August 6, 1952, all in box 23, folders 3–5, WPC.

19. Netting, *50 Years*, 135; Franklin Toker, *Fallingwater Rising: Frank Lloyd Wright, E. J. Kaufmann, and America's Most Extraordinary House* (New York: Knopf, 2005).

20. Netting, *50 Years*, 140.

21. Netting, *50 Years*, 143.

22. Netting, *50 Years*, 143, 148–49. The Allegheny Conference and the Conservancy had a particularly close relationship with West Penn Power and its president, Streuby Drumm. In addition to his duties at the electric utility, Drumm also led the Allegheny Conference-affiliated Pittsburgh Regional Planning Association and oversaw the landmark *Economic Study of the Pittsburgh Region*.

23. *County and City Data Book*; D'Appolonia Consulting Engineers, Inc., "Final Report, Feasibility Investigation, Abatement of Mine Acid Drainage, Cucumber Run Watershed, Ohiopyle State Park, Fayette County, Pennsylvania," March 1975.

24. "Hit-and-Run Strip Miners Hit," *Water Land and Life* 3, 2 (Autumn 1961), 13; "Cucumber-Jonathan Strip Fight Won," *Water Land and Life* 4, 2 (Summer 1962): 10; Joseph A. Krivak, "Strip Mining by a Real Conservationist?" *Water Land and Life* 3, 1 (Spring 1961); "Strip Mining Heals Its Own Scars," *Business Week*, November 13, 1965, 140–45; "Hillman Cited as Honorary Life Member," *Water Land and Life* 11, 1 (Spring 1969).

25. Stripping Near McConnell's Mill Alerts State," *Water Land and Life* 4, 2 (Summer 1962): 19; Fred Jones, "Old Deep Pit Spills Acids Above Park Site," *Pittsburgh Press*, October 8, 1961, 1, 2.

26. Pennsylvania Department of Environmental Resources, Bureau of Water Quality Management, "Final Report of the Pennsylvania Sanitary Water Board, 1923–1971," May 1971; "Stripper Denied Pit on Ohiopyle Stream," *Pittsburgh Press*, October 26, 1961, 1, 6.

27. "Stripper Denied Pit on Ohiopyle Stream," 6; "Scenic Falls Facing New Strip Threat," *Pittsburgh Press*, December 28, 1961, 8; "Disaster at Ohiopyle," *Pittsburgh Press*, October 6, 1961, 26; "State Weighs Scenic Falls Fate," *Pittsburgh Press*, December 29, 1961, 1, 4; "Strong Strip Mining Legislation Urged by Federation Head," *Reading Eagle*, March 31, 1962, 6; McCahan to Lawrence, December 22, 1961.

28. Netting, *50 Years*; "Beautiful Valley at Ohiopyle Out-of-Bounds for Spoilation," *Connellsville Daily Courier*, July 13, 1962, 1; Joseph S. Clark to William Scranton, Telegram, August 20, 1963, Citizens Committee for Project 70 Files, DFW; "Project 70 Wins Smashing Victory," *Water Land and Life* 5, 4 (Spring 1964), 14.

29. "Lillian McCahan, Ohiopyle Resident in Story of the Town," *Uniontown Evening Standard*, October 30, 1961, 6; "EDA Ohiopyle Grant Sparks New Era; State's Forest and Waters Fund Help to Assure Sewage and Water Facilities," *Water, Land, and Life* 8, 2 (July 1966); "Major Construction Work is Underway on Ohiopyle Sewer and Water System," *Water, Land, and Life* 9, 2 (July 1967).

30. "Great Benefits for Rural Areas," *Water Land and Life* 6, 1 (August 1964), 8; Palmer, *Youghiogheny*, 180.

31. Netting, *50 Years*, 139, 153–55; Nina J. Webb, "Green' Legacy," letter to the editor, *Wall Street Journal*, March 3, 1965, 14; Howard M. Swartz, "Citizens and Conservation,"

letter to the editor, *Wall Street Journal*, March 24, 1965, 16; Donna Harvey Myers, ed., *By the Side of the Road: The Autobiography of Miss Lillian McCahan* (Dunbar, Pa.: Dunbar Historical Society, 2011), 88; Ed Jackson, quoted in Palmer, *Youghiogheny*, 178.

32. Netting, *50 Years*, 139, 153–55.

33. "Ohiopyle House Burns," *New York Times*, November 14, 1964, 16; Palmer, *Youghiogheny*, 180; Marci Lynn McGuinness, *Ohiopyle, Heaven on Water, A Colorful Past*, http://www.ohiopyle.info/Ohiopyle_History.html (accessed September 25, 2012).

34. Consol Energy Inc., http://www.consolenergy.com (accessed 01/10/2012); Crowell, *History*, 22–23; Eric O. Ortemann, *Giant Earth Moving Equipment* (Osceola: Motorbooks International, 1995); "Hanna Plans 100 Per Cent Output Hike," *Martins Ferry Times Leader*, d.u., 1967, series 2319, box 3932, folder 6, ODOD.

35. "Index to Deeds—Belmont County, Ohio," available at Belmont County Courthouse, St. Clairsville, Ohio; Author's Interview with Rex and Verna Kaiser, December 1999; Author's Interview with Earl and June Stephens. January 2000; "Hanna Moves into Egypt Valley," 12–14; Crowell, *History*. See also "Eastern Ohio Mining Operations, Active and Proposed" in Keyser, "Ohio Mine Manpower Development Project, Final Draft Report," 8.

36. Consolidation Coal Company, "Egypt Valley . . . Today and Tomorrow,"

37. Author's interview with Michael Schuster, November 2004; "Ohio to Shut Interstate a Day for Shovel Crossing," *New York Times*, January 1, 1973; Girard Krebs, "A Gem in Egypt? Part II," *Mountain Life and Work 48*, 18 (September 1972): 23–31, 39–40.

38. Author's Interview with Aida Rizzi, October 2004; Girard Krebs, "A GEM in Egypt?" *Mountain Life and Work 48*, 7 (August 1972): 14–20. David Sweet to Norma Shuster, "Letter," May 2, 1972; Andreis Preide, "Barnesville Community Planning," August 28, 1972; David Sweet, "Barnesville Community Attitude Survey 8/21/1972"; Carol Reed, "Another Ralph Hatch Story," 1972, all in series 1857, box 3723 folder 2, ODOD.

39. Author's Interview with Theodore Voneida, December 2004; Theodore Voneida, "Strip Mining in Ohio," *Kent Environmental Council Newsletter*, November/December 2004, 2–3; Montrie, *To Save the Land and People*, 127–55; Ben A. Franklin, "Strip-Mining Boom Leaves Wasteland in Its Wake," *New York Times*, December 15, 1970; "GEM Power Shovel Casts a Shadow over Barnesville," *Akron Beacon Journal*, April 2, 1972; JG Films and ABC News, *Echo of Anger* (1972). Governor Gilligan eventually appointed Voneida to the state's Reclamation Board of Review, but, despite Democratic control, the Ohio Senate overwhelmingly voted to reject his confirmation on the premise that his anti-strip mine views were too extreme.

40. "GEM Devastates Ohio Hillsides in Search for Coal"; Garrett Interview; Ben A. Franklin, "Giant Mine Shovels Finally Cross Road," *New York Times*, January 5, 1973; Richards, "Strip Miners' Move Alarms Ohio Town," *Washington Post*, January 4, 1973, A4; George Vecsey, "Strip Mining and an Ohio Town: Economy vs. the Environment," *New York Times*, September 4, 1972; "Suit Eyed to Stop GEM Move," *Martins Ferry Times Leader*, August 7, 1972, 1.

41. "The Area's Economic Problems," *Martins Ferry Times* Leader, January 6, 1973, 7; Doral Chenoweth, "Say Good-by to Hendrysburg," editorial, *New York Times*, January 3, 1972.

42. Ben A. Franklin, "Strip-Mining Boom Leaves Wasteland in Its Wake," *New York Times*, December 15, 1970, A1, 34; John S. Brecher, "A Stripper Threatens to Invade Ohio Town; Citizenry Is Divided," *Wall Street Journal*, August 16, 1972, 12.

43. Fred Jones, "Strip-Mine Alibis Repeated in Ohio," *Pittsburgh Press*, March 23, 1972, 22; "Current Ohio Coal Mining Law & Rules," https://ohiodnr.com/mineral/law/tabid/17728/Default.aspx; Arnold W. Reitze, Jr., "Old King Coal and the Merry Rapists of Appalachia," *Case Western Reserve Law Review 22* (1971), 64.

44. Rizzi Interview; "Greenbelt Ideas Extensively Aired by Planners and Coal Co. Officials," *Barnesville Enterprise*, January, 25, 1973; Barnesville Planning Commission and Hurley Schnaufer & Associates, "Greenbelt Plan—Barnesville, Ohio," May 1973; "Coal Officials Re-Affirm Concern and Cooperation for Town's Future," *Barnesville Enterprise*, February 15, 1973; William Richards, "Strip Miners' Move Alarms Ohio Town," *Washington Post*, January 4, 1973, A4.

45. JG Films and ABC News, *Echo of Anger*.

46. "Ohio to Shut Interstate a Day for Shovel Crossing"; "Citizens Organized to Defend the Environment v. Volpe," *Environmental Law Reporter* (1972), S.D. Ohio, 72–289; "Environmentalists Plan Protest to 'Mourn Land' as Shovels Move," *Martins Ferry Times Leader*, January 3, 1973; Author's Interview with William Hunkler, November 2004; William Hunkler, "A Plea for Concern and Understanding," Press Release, Barnesville, Ohio, January 4, 1973 (copy in author's possession).

47. Fred Jones, "Strip-Mine Alibis Repeated in Ohio," *Pittsburgh Press*, March 23, 1972, 22.

CHAPTER 6. THE NEW METROPOLIS OF THE PLATEAU

1. Eileen Foley, "For Monroeville the Bloom Is Not Off the 30-Year Boom," *Pittsburgh Post-Gazette*, March 20, 1980, East edition, 1, 3; "She Nurses Mall Through Birth as 'Girl Friday' for Developers, *Pittsburgh Press*, May 12, 1969, 103; "Don-Mark Realty Develops Mall," *Pittsburgh Press*, May 12, 1969, 55.

2. Widner, "The Regional City," 23; Pennsylvania State Planning Board, *Regional Development Reconnaissance: Region 12*, 62.

3. Tarr, *Transportation Innovation and Changing Spatial Patterns in Pittsburgh*; Hoffman, "The Saga of Pittsburgh's Liberty Tubes"; Edwin Beachler, *Growing Pains in the Suburbs: The Story of Metropolitan Pittsburgh's Building Boom* (Pittsburgh: Pittsburgh Press, 1951). See also Edwin Beachler, *The Story of Pittsburgh's No. 1 Headache* (Pittsburgh: Pittsburgh Press, 1952) and Kent MacIntyre James, "Public Policy and the Postwar Suburbanization of Pittsburgh, 1945–1990" (Ph.D. dissertation, Carnegie Mellon University, 2005).

4. Richards, "A Fifty-Seven-Million-Dollar Program"; Sherie R. Mershon, "Corporate Social Responsibility," 556. The name for the Penn-Lincoln Parkway came from its combination of the William Penn Highway (Route 22) and the Lincoln Highway (Route 30) through the city.

5. Mershon, "Corporate Social Responsibility," 559.

6. Mershon, "Corporate Social Responsibility," 560–66; Jefrey Kitsko, "Interstate 376," http://www.pahighways.com/interstates/I376.html (accessed March 8, 2015).

7. Beachler, *Growing Pains in the Suburbs*; Demarest and Levy, "Touring the Coke Region," 108.

8. Beachler, *Growing Pains in the Suburbs*.

9. "The Economic and Social Impact of Highways: A Progress Summary of the Monroeville Case Study," Pennsylvania State University, Agricultural Experiment Station, June 1960; Park H. Martin, "Transportation and Community Development," November 18, 1948; Pittsburgh Regional Planning Association, "A Policy Statement Regarding Future Activities of the

Pittsburgh Regional Planning Association," December 2, 1964; Allegheny Seminar, "Summary Report of Session of the Lakeview Conference, April 23–25, 1961," 1.

10. Lonich, "Metopolitanism," 79–88; Mershon," Corporate Social Responsibility," 594–645; Brian Kent Jensen, "Masters of Their Own Destiny: Allegheny County Government Reform Efforts, 1929–1998" (Ph.D. dissertation, Carnegie Mellon University, 2004), 137–69.

11. Zandy Dudiak, *Remembering Monroeville: From Frontier to Boomtown* (Charleston, S.C.: History Press, 2009), 13; Foley, "For Monroeville the Bloom Is Not Off the 30-Year Boom." For Casto's contribution to the history of the suburban shopping mall, see Steven E. Schoenherr, "Evolution of the Shopping Center," February 17, 2006, http://www.sunnycv.com/steve/soc/shoppingcenter.html (accessed February 26, 2012).

12. Chandler, 127; "Economic and Social Impact of Highways," 8; Arthur T. Moore, *Pennsylvania Turnpike System: Boon to Business and Industry* (Harrisburg: Pennsylvania Turnpike Commission, 1952).

13. "Economic and Social Impact of Highways," 4, 8–9.

14. Chandler, 71; Patricia Sabaini, "Russell P. Miller: Home Builder for More Than 40 Years," Sep. 11, 2003, A-13; Foley, "Bloom"; "Garden City Home Goes into National Exhibit," *Pittsburgh Post-Gazette*, Oct. 22, 1955, 26; "Sampsons Building in Six Locations," *Pittsburgh Press*, Mar. 3, 1957, Sec. 4, p. 11; "Orin Sampson, Murrysville Home Builder," *Pittsburgh Post-Gazette*, July 23, 1988, 12.

15. Foley, "Bloom"; "Garden City Home"; Chandler, 72.

16. Beachler, *Growing Pains in the Suburbs*; Lowry, *Portrait of a Region*, 92; Michael Baker, Jr., Inc., "Allegheny County: Overall Economic Development Plan," 91.

17. Donald Maloney, "Moon Township Office Parks," in Robert Jockers, ed., *Forgotten Past: The History of Moon Township, Allegheny County, Pennsylvania* (Philadelphia: XLibris, 2006), 210, 118–32; "Beachler, *Growing Pains in the Suburbs*.

18. Ronald Potter, "Greater Pittsburgh International Airport," in Jockers, ed., *Forgotten Past*, 202; Edward R. Weidlein, "Allegheny Conference Progress," *Allegheny Conference Digest*, June 1947; Beachler, *Growing Pains in the Suburbs*.

19. Bruce S. Cridelbaugh, "Fort Pitt Tunnel," September 10, 2001, http://pghbridges.com (accessed March 24, 2013); Lowry, *Portrait of a Region*, 92–98, 98; Dudiak, *Remembering Monroeville*, 78–82.

20. Potter, "Greater Pittsburgh International Airport," 203–5; Hollinshead, "Locating Industry in the Pittsburgh area," 9–10.

21. Hollinshead, "Locating Industry in the Pittsburgh Area"; "Toward a New Pittsburgh," *Pennsylvania Plans* 1, 7 (October 1951): 31–36, SPB; Marshall Kaplan, Gans, and Kahn, "The First Action Year of the Model Cities Program in Allegheny County, Pennsylvania: A Case Study," 1972; Robert Lewis, "Planned Industrial Districts in Chicago: Firms, Networks, and Boundaries," *Journal of Planning History* 3, 1 (February 2004): 29–49; Weber, *Don't Call Me Boss*, 263.

22. Mershon, "Corporate Social Responsibility," 490–99.

23. Pennsylvania Economy League Inc.—Western Division, "A More Effective Industrial Development Program for the Pittsburgh Region," November 1, 1954; Mel Seidenberg, "New Non-Profit Development Group Is Formed: Board of 20 Members Composed of Top Level Business, Labor and Local Government Leaders," *Pittsburgh Post-Gazette*, June 19, 1955; Mershon, "Corporate Social Responsibility," 690–92; Regional Industrial Development Corporation, *A Community of Interest*.

24. Mershon, "Corporate Social Responsibility," 693–94; "Regional Industrial Development Corporation," *Breaking Ground*, January/February 2010, 30; Mel Seidenberg, "Labor, Two Counties Join PRIDC Program," *Pittsburgh Post-Gazette*, January 11, 1962; "Former RIDC President Robert Ryan," *Pittsburgh Press*, November 8, 1988, C4; William Allan, "Plan to Gain Industry Told by RIDC Chief," *Pittsburgh Press*, February 15, 1962.

25. Chenghua Guan, "Boston Route 128's Past and Present," *The Color of Innovation*, September 9, 2012, https://blogs.law.harvard.edu/cguan/2012/09/09/route-128-past-and-present/; William Pade, "$50 Million Industry Park at Workhouse Gets Okay: County Gives O'Hara Plan Green Light," *Pittsburgh Press*, October 11, 1962; Jack Markowitz, "RIDC Park: Believe It," *Pittsburgh Post-Gazette*, April 22, 1968; "RIDC Park Makes Jobs for 4,000: More Plants for O'Hara Twp. on Plan Board," *Pittsburgh Post-Gazette*, January 3, 1969; Joe Grata, "RIDC Attractive Industrial Proposition," *Pittsburgh Press*, January 29, 1979.

26. Mershon, "Corporate Social Responsibility," 692–93; Pennsylvania Economy League, "A More Effective Industrial Development Program"; William H. Wylie, "RIDC Runs 3 Years Ahead of Job, Tax Goals at Park," *Pittsburgh Press*, October 4, 1970, Sec. 3, 9, Allan, "Plan to Gain Industry."

27. Hollinshead, "Locating Industry in the Pittsburgh Area"; Regional Industrial Development Corporation of Southwestern Pennsylvania, *The Southwestern Pennsylvania Region Is on the Move!*, 1964. On the relationship between nuclear energy, suburbanization and the Pittsburgh Renaissance, see Vitale, "The Atomic Capital of the World."

28. Allegheny Conference on Community Development, "Allegheny Conference on Community Development . . . Presents," 14.

29. "Center to Add Two Buildings," *Pittsburgh Press*, July 5, 1964; Mershon, "Corporate Social Responsibility," 392; "US Airways Introduces 'Throwback VistaJet' with Allegheny Airlines Aircraft," press release, June 29, 2006; Thomas J. Porter, Jr., "RIDC West Park Gets Office, Lab Complex," *Pittsburgh Post-Gazette*, October 24, 1979; Author's interview with Frank Brooks Robinson, Sr., September, 2010; Joe Grata, "RIDC Doing a Job by Helping Many Keep Theirs," *Pittsburgh Press*, January 22, 1980; "RIDC Good Economic Tonic for District," *Pittsburgh Press*, January 18, 1982.

30. Joe Grata, "Sept. 16 Opening of Last Link to End 40-Year I-279 Odyssey," *Pittsburgh Press*, September 5, 1979, 1, 6; Abby Mendelson, "A Tale of Two Cities," *Pittsburgh* (February 1988), 31–32; Cassandra Burrell, "Interstate Link Opens Near Pittsburgh," *Altoona Mirror*, September 17, 1989, 1; Thomas J. Murphy to Paul M. Gladden, "Letter," December 6, 1990, TMP.

31. Edmund Arthur, *The Country Rambler: A Collection of Out-Door Essays* (Pittsburgh: Audubon Society of Western Pennsylvania, 1934).

32. Beachler, *Growing Pains*; "Township Opens Court Battle on New Homes," *Altoona Mirror*, February 4, 1958, 4.

33. Hayes, *Cranberry Township*; Southwestern Pennsylvania Regional Planning Commission, *Issues in a Region of Contrasts* (Pittsburgh: The Commission, 1968), 5

34. "Industrial Park Work Under Way," *Kittanning Leader-Times*, November 10, 1970, 14; Thomas Snyder, "New Industrial Hub Headed for County," *Pittsburgh Press*, March 4, 1969, 1, 12

35. Lowry, *Economic Study of the Pittsburgh Region*, vol. 2, 25; Butler County Planning Commission, *The Comprehensive Plan for Butler County. Report 5* (Butler, Pa.: The Commission, 1965); United States General Accounting Office, "History and Status of the East Street

Valley Expressway, Interstate Highway 279, Pittsburgh, Pennsylvania: Report of the Comptroller General of the United States," 1976; Pittsburgh City Planning Commission and Pittsburgh Regional Planning Association, *North Side Study*, April 1954.

36. Weber, *Don't Call Me Boss*, 395; Regional Industrial Development Corporation of Southwestern Pennsylvania, *The Southwestern Pennsylvania Region is on the Move!*; Dan Fitzpatrick, "A Story of Urban Renewal," *Pittsburgh Post-Gazette*, May 21, 2000; Aaron B Cowan, "A Nice Place to Visit: Tourism, Urban Revitalization, and the Transformation of Postwar American Cities" (Ph.D. dissertation, University of Cincinnati, 2007), 173.

37. "What About it Pete?" editorial, *North Hills News Record*, June 14, 1972, 4; "East Street Roadway Holds Key to Future," *North Hills News Record*, August 23, 1972, 1.

38. United States General Accounting Office, "History and Status of the East Street Valley Expressway," 2–4; "I-79 Moratorium," *New Castle News*, February 10, 1972, 2; "East Street Valley: Slope Residents are Being Forced to Play a Waiting Game," *North Hills News Record*, February 8, 1975, 17; "Interstate 79: From West Virginia to Erie . . . Almost," *Indiana Evening Gazette*, June 18, 1971, 13.

39. "What About it Pete?" 4; "Officials Reach Agreement on East Street Expressway," *Kittanning Leader Times*, June 4, 1975, 1; United States General Accounting Office, "History and Status of the East Street Valley Expressway," 7; Tom Pettit, "State Committee Approves $540 Million Highway Plan," *Indiana Gazette*, June 23, 1981, 6; Grata, "Sept. 16 Opening."

40. Bob Dvorchak, "Pittsburgh Ground-Breaking Ends 30-Year Highway Delay," *Indiana Gazette*, June 17, 1982, 9.

41. Richard Stouffer, "Wexford: Pittsburgh Link Spurs Building," *New York Times*, June 18, 1989, 21.

42. Stouffer, "Wexford," 21; Chriss Swaney, "An Oasis of Development in the Suburbs," *New York Times*, November 11, 1992, R5.

43. Tom Barnes, "RIDC Chief Answers Critics," *Pittsburgh Post-Gazette*, February 22, 1991, 7; "RIDC Good Economic Tonic for District," "Office, Warehouse Center is Key Feature of Creative Realty's Cranberry Twp. Complex," *Butler Eagle*, September 25, 1984; "Boom Development Anticipated in Cranberry Township This Year," *Butler Eagle*, January 28, 1986, 1.

44. Johanna Pro and David Guo, "Rezoning Changes Spark Suits, Probe," *Pittsburgh Post-Gazette*, July 7, 1990; Carroll V. Hill & Associates, "Comprehensive Plan for Cranberry Township in Butler County, Pennsylvania and Bradford Woods Borough, Franklin Park Borough, Marshall Township, Ohio Township, Pine Township, in Allegheny County, Pennsylvania: Report 2" (Pittsburgh: Carroll V. Hill & Associates, 1962); Toker, *Pittsburgh*, 463

45. Ellen M. Perlmutter, "Officials Critical of RIDC Practices: Question Use of Public Funds," *Pittsburgh Press*, February 7, 1991; Select Committee on Pennsylvania's Industrial Development Corporations, *Sharing the Wealth: A Report on Pennsylvania's Industrial Development Corporations* (Harrisburg: Pennsylvania House of Representatives, 1992); Barnes, "RIDC Chief Answers Critics," 7.

CHAPTER 7. NO DEVELOPMENT BEYOND THIS POINT

1. Joe Trotter and Jared Day, *Race and Renaissance: African Americans in Pittsburgh Since World War II* (Pittsburgh: University of Pittsburgh Press, 2010), 55–56; "The Line Drawn, a Place to Stand," *Pittsburgh Post-Gazette*, April 5, 1998, B1.

2. Jane Jacobs, "Downtown Is for People," in William H. Whyte, Jr., ed., *The Exploding Metropolis* (Berkeley: University of California Press, 1993), 159.

3. Mershon, "Corporate Social Responsibility," 709–22.

4. John Williamson, "Federal Aid to Roads and Highways Since the 18th Century: A Legislative History," Congressional Research Service, January 6, 2012; Kaschak Interview; Grottendieck, "Problems of Administration."

5. Longhurst, *Citizen Environmentalists*; Mershon, "Corporate Social Responsibility," 734–40; "Smoke Control Is 'Good Investment,'" *Beaver Valley Times*, April 21, 1959

6. Lubove, *Twentieth-Century Pittsburgh*, vol. 1, 144–55; Allegheny Conference on Community Development and Pennsylvania Economy League Inc.—Western Division, "Allegheny Council to Improve Our Neighborhoods-Housing: An Action Program for Meeting the Housing Problems of Western Pennsylvania," February 1957, ACTION-Housing, *Report to the Board of Directors*, September 11, 1962, 18 (cited in Lubove, 154).

7. Brown, *A History of the Roman Catholic Diocese of Steubenville, Ohio*, 328; Daniel Greene, "Steubenville's Black Ghetto," *National Observer*, April 1, 1968; "Segregation Builds Slums On Hill Ruins," *Pittsburgh Press*, February 2, 1958; Trotter and Day, *Race and Renaissance*, 91–103, 103.

8. Lubove, *Twentieth-Century Pittsburgh*, vol. 1, 154–55.

9. "Fabulous Night Spots Pep Renaissance of City: Is Pittsburgh Entertainment Capital of the United States?" *Pittsburgh Courier* (National edition), February 13, 1960, 23; Toki Schalk Johnson, "Pittsburgh Neighborhood Units Coping with Urban Renewal Migrations," *Pittsburgh Courier*, November 29, 1958, B1.

10. Lubove, *Twentieth-Century Pittsburgh*, vol. 1, 160; Mershon, "Corporate Social Responsibility," 746.

11. "City Mum on Planning for 'Upper Hill' Area," *Pittsburgh Courier*, April 6, 1963; "New Hill Will Have New Faces," *Pittsburgh Courier*, April 13, 1963; "New Hill Will Erase Landmarks," *Pittsburgh Courier*, April 20, 1963; "Harlem Fallout: Some Big Cities Fear the Spread of Race Rioting; Others Are Unworried," *Wall Street Journal*, July 27, 1964, 1; "11 Arrested in Pittsburgh," *New York Times*, August 19, 1965, 4; "Alcoa May Not Finish Hill Area Apartments," *Pittsburgh Post-Gazette*, February 4, 1965.

12. Roy Lubove, *Twentieth-Century Pittsburgh*, vol. 2, *The Post Steel Era*, 86–88; Louise Ann Jezierski, "Neighborhoods and Public-Private Partnerships in Pittsburgh," *Urban Affairs Quarterly* 26 (1990): 217–49; "Hill Committee Sets First Public Meeting," *Pittsburgh Courier*, March 30, 1963, 3; "Human Element a Moving Force on Hill," editorial, *Pittsburgh Press*, July 15, 1964.

13. Andrew Carnegie, "The Gospel of Wealth," 1889; Lubove, *Twentieth-Century Pittsburgh*, vol. 1, 153–67; Pittsburgh Foundation, *Building the Community's Foundation* (Pittsburgh: The Foundation, 1996), 13.

14. Lubove, *Twentieth-Century Pittsburgh*, vol. 1, 160–63; William J. Mallett, "Redevelopment and Response: The Lower Hill Renewal and Pittsburgh's Cultural District," *Pittsburgh History* 75, 4 (Winter 1992), 186–87; "Hope for the Hill," editorial, *Pittsburgh Post-Gazette*, July 14, 1988, 8.

15. Margalit Fox, "Peter Flaherty, 80, Politician and Former Pittsburgh Mayor, Dies," *New York Times*, April 21, 2005; Stewman and Tarr. "Four Decades," 89–90; Lorant, *Pittsburgh*, 449–63; Lubove, *Twentieth-Century Pittsburgh*, vol. 2, 58–61, 103–4.

16. In 1961, Ritchey had been named "Man of the Year in Architecture" by the Pittsburgh Chamber of Commerce for his work in Oakland and the Golden Triangle. James D.

Van Trump, "A Document of the New Urban Order," *Charette, Pennsylvania Journal of Architecture* 46, 8 (August 1966): 10–14.

17. Walter C. Kidney, *A Past Still Alive: The Pittsburgh History and Landmarks Foundation Celebrates Twenty-Five Years* (Pittsburgh: Pittsburgh History & Landmarks Foundation, 1989), 121; Arthur P. Ziegler, Jr., "Observations," *Charette, Pennsylvania Journal of Architecture* 46, 8 (August 1966), 4; "Hear! Hear!" *PHLF News* 1, 2 (August 1966), 2.

18. Urban Redevelopment Authority of Pittsburgh, *Allegheny Center: From a Rich History, a New Way of Life*, 1961.

19. Pittsburgh Regional Planning Association and Pittsburgh City Planning Commission, *North Side Study*, April 1954; William R. Schmidt, "North Side Boosted for Stadium Site," Letters to the Editor, *Pittsburgh Post-Gazette*, September 23, 1957, 7. The original editorial in which this quote appeared also identified disadvantages with the North Side stadium site.

20. Pittsburgh Regional Planning Association and Pittsburgh City Planning Commission, *North Side Study*.

21. Urban Redevelopment Authority of Pittsburgh, *Allegheny Center: Final Project Report*, March 1, 1961, 2; Urban Redevelopment Authority of Pittsburgh, *Allegheny Center: From a Rich History*, 8; Joseph Drexler, "The Political Economy of Neighborhood Revitalization: A Case Study of Pittsburgh's North Side Neighborhood" (Ph.D. dissertation, University of Pittsburgh, 1981), 105–6.

22. Pittsburgh Urban Redevelopment Authority and Pittsburgh City Planning Commission, *Redevelopment Area Report—1961*, 1961.

23. James D. Van Trump, *1300–1335 Liverpool Street, Manchester, Old Allegheny, Pittsburgh* (Pittsburgh: PHLF, c. 1965), 5, 20.

24. Van Trump, *1300–1335 Liverpool Street*, 5.

25. James D. Van Trump and Arthur P. Ziegler, Jr., *Landmark Architecture of Allegheny County Pennsylvania* (Pittsburgh: PHLF, 1967); Kidney, *A Past Still Alive*, 124; Charles Covert Aresenberg, "Foreword," in Van Trump and Ziegler, *Landmark Architecture*, vii.

26. Michael Wallace, *Mickey Mouse History and Other Essays on American Memory* (Philadelphia: Temple University Press, 1996), 196; Kidney, *A Past Still Alive*, 122.

27. Van Trump, *1300–1335 Liverpool Street*, 5–6; Kidney, *A Past Still Alive*, 122–25.

28. U.S. General Accounting Office, *History and Status of the East Street Valley Expressway, Interstate Highway 279, Pittsburgh, Pennsylvania: Report of the Comptroller General of the United States*, 1976; Drexler, *Political Economy*, 98–99; Norman Tyler, Ted Liqibel, and Irene Tyler, *Historic Preservation: An Introduction to Its History, Principles, and Practice*, 2nd ed. (New York: Norton, 2009), 46–48; Kidney, *A Past Still Alive*, 55, 123.

29. U.S. General Accounting Office, *History and Status of the East Street Valley Expressway*; Toker, *Pittsburgh*, 141.

30. U.S. General Accounting Office, *History and Status of the East Street Valley Expressway*; Drexler, "Political Economy,"106; Joe Grata, 'Residents Again Reject I-279," *Pittsburgh Press*, June 5, 1972, 2; U.S. General Accounting Office, "History and Status," 9; Edwina Rankin, "Save St. Boniface Drive Renewed," *Pittsburgh Press*, December 8, 1975; David Lehrer, "St. Boniface Gets Boost from U.S.," June 16, 1977.

31. "Renewal Agency Dying in Wheeling," *Wheeling Intelligencer*, September 2, 1973.

32. Roger Haigh, *Wheeling, West Virginia*, 34–36; Joanou Interview; "Our Hats Are Off," editorial reprinted from the *Wheeling News-Register*, *Morgantown Post*, August 13, 1960, 6; Urban Renewal Authority of Wheeling, "Land for Sale . . . For Light Industrial Use Located near Business District," advertisement, *Charleston Gazette-Mail*, June 9, 1963, 10C.

33. American Hospital Association, *American Hospital Association Guide to the Healthcare Field* (Chicago: The Association, 1945–); Congressional Budget Office, *Tax Subsidies for Medical Care: Current Policies and Possible Alternatives*, January 1980, 50; Author's Interview with Susan Ward, June 2004; Filby Interview; Author's Interview with Sam Nazzaro, August 2004.

34. Joanou Interview; "Keeping Weirton in Step," editorial, *Weirton Daily Times*, December 4, 1965, 4.

35. "Sketches of a Proposed Northern Gateway Area," *Wheeling News-Register*, October 28, 1962, 14; Wheeling Municipal Auditorium Board, "Progress Is a Civic Center, Vote 'Yes,'" 1971, folder "Wheeling Civic Center," OCPL.

36. "Wheeling URA Members Quit in Dispute," *Weirton Daily Times*, July 26, 1969, 2; "Wheeling Mayor Names Planners," *Weirton Daily Times*, August 27, 1969, 9; Author's Interview with Charles Steele, July 2004.

37. Author's Interview with G. Ogden Nutting, May 2014; Steele Interview; Wheeling Municipal Auditorium Board, "Progress Is a Civic Center"; Wheeling City Council and Wheeling Urban Renewal Authority, *Fort Henry Mall: Wheeling, West Virginia* (Wheeling: the Authority, 1971); "Wheeling Civic Center Bond Issue Approved, *Charleston Daily Mail*, November 3, 1971, 17;

38. Wheeling Urban Renewal Authority, "Fort Henry Mall"; "Urban Renewal Land for Sale . . . Fort Henry Mall Program," *Steubenville Herald Star*, June 9, 1972, 5; Michelle Blum, "Mall Disintegrated with Urban Renewal Rejection," *Wheeling Intelligencer*, April 10, 2004; Joanou Interview.

39. Steele Interview; C. J. Kaiser, *Hubris*, paper presented to Blue Pencil Club, Wheeling, March 30, 1999 (copy in author's possession), 8.

40. Kaiser, *Hubris*; "Sue to Block Shopper Mall," *Charleston Gazette*, October 26, 1972, 11B; "Businessmen Seek to Halt Wheeling Mall Development," *Charleston Daily Mail*, October 26, 1972, 7C; G. Ogden Nutting Interview.

41. Haigh, *Wheeling, West Virginia: A Community Profile*; "Fort Henry Mall No No No," bumper sticker, 1973, Box 3, Robert Levenson Papers, OCP.

42. "Wheeling Civic Center Opposed," *Weirton Daily Times*, December 27, 1972; "Wheeling Group Wants Council to Abolish URA," April 17, 1973; "URA Upheld," *Charleston Gazette*, April 14, 1973; "Petition Asks URA Ouster in Wheeling," *Charleston Gazette*, May 10, 1973; "Urban Renewal Plan Rejected," *Weirton Daily Times*, August 23, 1973; "Renewal Agency Dying in Wheeling."

43. Kaiser, *Hubris*; "Competition Called Survival Key," *Wheeling Intelligencer*, January 3, 1978; Hunter, *Marine Memories*.

44. Lawrence, "Rebirth," in Lorant, *Pittsburgh*, 374; Arthur Ziegler, "An Introduction, Both Personal and Programmatic," in Van Trump and Ziegler, *Landmark Architecture*, 4.

PART III INTRODUCTION

1. Author's Interview with Andrew Wiese, January 2006; John P. Hoerr, *And the Wolf Finally Came: The Decline of the American Steel Industry* (Pittsburgh: University of Pittsburgh Press, 1988), 11.

2. Widner, "The Regional City," 23.

3. University of Virginia, *Historical Census Browser*.

4. Reuben Gold Thwaites, *Afloat on the Ohio*, 13.

5. H. John Heinz III quoted in Susan Milligan, "Carnegie-Mellon, Lehigh U. Win Defense Contract," *Allentown Morning Call*, November 5, 1984, A4.

CHAPTER 8. RUST BELT AND ROBOBURGH

1. William Serrin, "A Chapter of Industrial History Closes with the Homestead Steel Works," *New York Times*, July 27, 1986, 16; Taylor Davidson, "Better Protection Sought in Clairton Housing Projects," *Pittsburgh Press*, July 11, 1991, B7.

2. Mary Brignano, *Curating the District: How the Pittsburgh Cultural Trust Is Transforming the Quality of Urban Life* (Pittsburgh: Pittsburgh Cultural Trust, 2000); "Arts Center for Pittsburgh," *New York Times*, September 26, 1987, 9; "The Benedum Begins," *Pittsburgh Post-Gazette*, September 25, 1987.

3. Lorant, *Pittsburgh*, 619. J&L Steel's Hazelwood and South Side Works were part of an integrated mill system known collectively as the Pittsburgh Works. A hot metal bridge across the Monongahela River, which served the same function as U.S. Steel's bridge upriver in Homestead, connected the two parts of the facility. While LTV shuttered nearly all the Pittsburgh Works by the end of the 1980s, the company continued to operate a coal coking facility in Hazelwood until 1998.

4. Max Nurnberg, *Economic Study of the Pittsburgh Region*, vol. 3, *Region with a Future* (Pittsburgh: University of Pittsburgh Press, 1963). Mershon, "Corporate Social Responsibility," 673–74.

5. Nurnberg, *Economic Study of the Pittsburgh Region*, vol. 1, *Region in Transition*.

6. Regional Economic Analysis Policy Group, "Policy Statement Based on the Economic Study of the Pittsburgh Region," January 14, 1964, 5, 7.

7. Nurnberg, *Economic Study of the Pittsburgh Region*, vol. 3, 268.

8. Charles J. Blankenship, "The State Role in Urban Economic Development: A Task Force Report Executive Summary," November 1974; Mershon, "Corporate Social Responsibility," 694–97; Pennsylvania State Planning Board," *Regional Development Reconnaissance: Region 12*, 34–36.

9. Allan, "Plan to Gain Industry."

10. Lubove, *Twentieth-Century Pittsburgh*, vol. 2, 61–66, 297 n15.

11. Lubove, *Twentieth-Century Pittsburgh*, vol. 2, 71–74, 303 n 48.

12. Toker, *Pittsburgh*, 54–58; Lubove, *Twentieth-Century Pittsburgh*, vol. 2, 73–74, 304 n 50; "Plan in Pittsburgh on Building Fought," *New York Times*, July 3, 1979, 51.

13. Peck, Theodore, and Brenner, "Neoliberal Urbanism Redux"; Roger S. Ahlbrandt, Jr., and Morton Coleman, "The Limits of Corporate Civic Responsibility," *Economic Development Review* 6 (Spring 1988): 40–43; Joyce Gannon, "Foundations Are Credited with Resurrecting Pittsburgh's Economy After the 1980s' Collapse," *Pittsburgh Post-Gazette*, December 24, 2012; The Pittsburgh Foundation, *Building the Community's Foundation*, 23–25.

14. The Pittsburgh Foundation, *Building the Community's Foundation*; Lubove, *Twentieth-Century Pittsburgh*, vol. 2, 103, 109, 113, 153–54; "Practical Preservation For People in Urban Areas," *Preservation News* 10, 10, October 1, 1970, 4; Wallace, *Mickey Mouse*, 233, 25.

15. Ziegler made an exception for "remarkable buildings," such as the iconic Allegheny County Courthouse and Jail along the Monongahela River. Arthur Ziegler, "Preservation as

a Tool for Achieving Economic Vitality," August 31, 2012, http://www.phlf.org/ (accessed August 13, 2014).

16. Roberta Brandes Gratz, *The Living City: How America's Cities Are Being Revitalized by Thinking Small in a Big Way* (New York: Wiley, 1994), 286–28; Lubove, *Twentieth-Century Pittsburgh*, vol. 2, 218–23; Kidney, *A Past Still Alive*, 126–30; Joyce, "Rolling Down the River," *Pittsburgh Post-Gazette*, November 18, 1997.

17. Llewelyn-Davies Associates, *Penn/Liberty Urban Design Study*, Prepared for Allegheny Conference on Community Development, December 1979; *Strategy 21*, 1, 2B–C; Christine H. O'Toole, "Building Trust," *H Magazine*, Summer 2009, 16–17.

18. The advertisements are available bound in Penn's Southwest Association, *Dynamic Pittsburgh: It's a Vital, Vibrant, Historic, Sporting, Bright, Breakthrough, Resourceful Place to Live and Work* (Pittsburgh: The Association, 1981).

19. John Heinz quoted in Milligan, "Carnegie-Mellon," A4; Allegheny Conference on Community Development, "A Strategy for Growth: An Economic Development Program for the Pittsburgh Region," November 1984, 13, 27.

20. Alberts. *Pitt*; 340–43; Toker, *Pittsburgh*, 322–38; Pittsburgh City Planning Commission and Urban Redevelopment Authority of Pittsburgh, *Redevelopment Area Report—1961*; "Renaissance, Phase 2," *Time*, June 21, 1963, 68; Alberts, *Pitt*, 340–43.

21. Alberts, *Pitt*, 210–19, 432–43; Steve Levin, "Western Psych a Perfect Place to Start," *Pittsburgh Post-Gazette*, December 25, 2005; Steve Levin, "Empire Building: Starzl's Success a Model for Growth at UPMC," *Pittsburgh Post-Gazette*, December 26, 2005.

22. "Carnegie Mellon University History," last updated November 18, 2009, 1. Available from http://www.cmu.edu/about/history/ (accessed July 17, 2013); Vitale, "The Atomic Capital of the World"; Allegheny Conference on Community Development, *The Allegheny Conference Presents*, 34; Mary Niederberger, "Cyert Engineered Carnegie Mellon's Rise in Prominence," *Pittsburgh Press*, May 13, 1990.

23. Widner, "The Regional City," 24; Regional Industrial Development Corporation of Southwestern Pennsylvania, "Pittsburgh's New Dimension in Advanced Technology," 1985, 6 (CDB). "Penn's Southwest, The New Neighborhood," *Wall Street Journal*, September 26, 1973, 12.

24. Kiley, *Getting the Bugs Out*, 131–39, 151; "PA Plans $100 Million in Aid for New VW Plant," *New York Times*, June 2, 1976, 53, 61; State Planning Board, *Choices for Pennsylvanians: Final Report*, September 1981, 1; Michael Osborne, *Economic Competitiveness: The States Take the Lead* (Washington D.C., Economic Policy Institute, 1987), 25–26.

25. Richard Thornburgh, *Advanced Technology Policies for the Commonwealth of Pennsylvania*, August 5, 1982, 1; Governor's Press Office, "Press Release," October 8, 1983, box 245, DTP; Jim Gallagher, "Posvar, The Man Who 'Rescued' Talks About the Past—And Future," *Pittsburgh Post-Gazette*, October 21, 1986, 10–11; Lubove, *Twentieth-Century Pittsburgh*, vol. 2, 45.

26. In a letter to Mayor Caliguiri and an Allegheny County commissioner, Murphy complained about the "apparent lack of coordination" in funding requests. Thomas J. Murphy to Richard Caliguiri and Thomas Foerster, "Letter re: Economic Development Activities in Allegheny County," January 14, 1985, TMP; Morton Coleman, "Public/Private Cooperative Response Patterns to Regional Structural Change in the Pittsburgh Region," in *Regional Structural Change and Industrial Policy in International Perspective: United States, Great Britain,*

France, Federal Republic of Germany, ed. Joachim Jens Hesse (Baden-Baden: Nomos, 1988); City of Pittsburgh, County of Allegheny, University of Pittsburgh, Carnegie-Mellon University, "Strategy 21: Pittsburgh/Allegheny Economic Development Strategy to Begin the 21st Century," June 1985, 1.

27. Western Pennsylvania Brownfields Center, "Pittsburgh Technology Center (LTV)," Summer 2007, http://www.cmu.edu/steinbrenner/brownfields/ (accessed July 30, 2013); Bob Dvorchak, "Reviving Steel City with a New Image," *Philadelphia Inquirer*, September 14, 1986, B3.

28. James Colker, "Transformation of an Industrial City: High Tech Comes to Pittsburgh," *Managment Review* 74, 5 (May 1985): 52; City of Pittsburgh et al., *Strategy 21*, 3B; City of Pittsburgh et al., "Strategy 21 Update: Progress Report and Proposed Amendments," January 1988, 4, 7, 9; Dvorchak, "Reviving Steel City."

29. City of Pittsburgh et al., *Strategy 21*, 3B; City of Pittsburgh et al., "Strategy 21 Update," 7; Western Pennsylvania Brownfields Center, "Pittsburgh Technology Center (LTV)"; Ellen M. Perlmutter, "State Oks Tech Center Despite Toxins," *Pittsburgh Press*, August 10, 1990, D1; Jon Schmitz and Mary Niederberger, "Troubled Pittsburgh Tech Center Gets Boosts from State, CMU," *Pittsburgh Press*, November 27, 1990, A1; "High-Promise High-Tech," editorial, *Pittsburgh Post-Gazette*, November 28, 1990, C2.

30. "High-Promise High-Tech," C2; Deitrick, "The Post Industrial Revitalization of Pittsburgh", 4; Lubove, *Twentieth-Century Pittsburgh*, vol. 2, 47; Carnegie-Mellon Gets Pentagon's Contract for Software Institute," *Wall Street Journal*, November 15, 1984, 54; "Pittsburgh and Atlanta in Billboard War," *New York Times*, April 9, 1985, A12.

31. Dan Kara, "All Signs Point to RoboBurgh," *Pittsburgh Post-Gazette*, June 20, 2006; Donald Miller, "Building the Future on the Past," *Pittsburgh Post-Gazette*, Mar. 2, 1993, D1; Working Together Consortium, "The Greater Pittsburgh Region: Working Together to Compete Globally," November 1994.

32. Penn's Southwest Association, *Dynamic Pittsburgh*; Doron P. Levin, "Big New Buildings Going Up in Pittsburgh Raise Fears of Another Office-Space Glut," *Wall Street Journal*, February 25, 1982, 29; Dan Fitzpatrick, "Stuck with Steel," *Pittsburgh Post-Gazette*, November 3, 2002, D1.

33. Hoerr, *And the Wolf Finally Came*, 11; Jonathan P. Hicks, "Bankruptcy Helps a Steelmaker," *New York Times*, July 19, 1990; David McDermott, "Coal Mining in the U.S. West: Price and Employment Trends," *Monthly Labor Review*, August 1997, 18–23; Scott Powers, "Coal Cutback Could Close Mine," *Columbus Dispatch*, July 2, 1994.

34. *County and City Data* Book; Denny Trombulak, "Steelworkers Lament from Beaver County," in *Overtime: Punchin' out with the Mill Hunk Herald, Worker Writer Anthology, 1979–1989* (Homestead: Piece of the Hunk Publishers, 1990), 44–45.

35. Michael J. Landini, *Understanding Federal Training and Employment Programs* (Washington, D.C.: National Commission for Employment Policy, 1995); Dale Russakoff, "Brawn Forged into Brain," *Washington Post*, April 12, 1987, A1.

36. Leon L. Haley and Ralph L. Bangs, "Policies to Improve African American Economic Conditions in Pittsburgh and Allegheny County" in University Center for Social and Urban Research, *The State of the Region Report* (Pittsburgh: UCSUR, 1999), 141–52; Ann Belser, "When Pittsburgh Men Lost Jobs in the '80s, Women Stepped in to Save Economy," *Pittsburgh Post-Gazette*, December 27, 2012; Ervin Dyer, "Pursuing the Dream," *Pittsburgh Post-Gazette*, Jan. 20, 2003, B5–6.

37. Deitrick, "The Post Industrial Revitalization of Pittsburgh," 4–12; Trombulak, "Steelworkers Lament," 44–45.

38. Javersak, *History of Weirton*; Jonathan Prude, "ESOPs Fable: How Workers Bought a Steel Mill in Weirton, West Virginia, and What Good It Did Them," *Socialist Review* 14 (1984); Zukin, *Landscapes of Power*, 59–102.

39. Staughton Lynd, "The Genesis of the Idea of a Community Right to Industrial Property in Youngstown and Pittsburgh, 1977–1987," *Journal of American History* 74, 3 (1987): 926–58; Lynd, "Why We Opposed the Buyout at Weirton Steel," 52–53; "In Strife-Torn Valley, a Quiet Effort to Save Jobs," *Philadelphia Inquirer*, January 8, 1985, B2; Mike Stout, "Reindustrialization from Below: The Steel Valley Authority," *Labor Research Review* 1, 9 (1986), 25; Marty Willis, "Jackson Seeks 'New Formula,'" *New Pittsburgh Courier*, February 2, 1985, 1, 3. For a detailed discussion of labor activism in Pittsburgh during the period, see Dale A. Hathaway, *Can Workers Have a Voice? The Politics of Deindustrialization in Pittsburgh* (University Park: Pennsylvania State University Press, 1993).

40. Stout, "Reindustrialization From Below," 27.

41. Robert A. Beauregard, Paul Lawless, and Sabina Deitrick, "Collaborative Strategies for Reindustrialization: Sheffield and Pittsburgh," *Economic Development Quarterly* 6, 3 (1992): 418–30; Allegheny County Department of Planning and Arthur D. Little, Inc., *Project Report: Steel Retention Study*, 1988; "LTV Mill Worth Reopening, Study Says," *Dallas Morning News*, Jan. 29, 1988, 4D; Stout, "Reindustrialization From Below," 31.

42. Mary Kane, "Steel Valley Panel Facing Tough Road in Plant Takeover," *Pittsburgh Press*, December 13, 1987, A8; Thomas Buell, Jr., "Steel Venture's Chances of Success Dim with Time," *Pittsburgh Press*, August 19, 1990, D18.

43. Ellen M. Perlmutter, "Housing, Marinas Planned at LTV's S. Side Site," *Pittsburgh Press*, July 3, 1991; Longhurst, *Citizen Environmentalists*, 160–70; Catherine Becker Lanni, "A Stench in the Air," Editorial, *Pittsburgh Press*, May 21, 1991.

44. Fitzpatrick, "Stuck with Steel," D1; "Rust Belt Cities are Trading in Old Economies," *Philadelphia Inquirer*, November 26, 1987, J1; Michael Drayton, "A New Ballgame," *Tampa Tribune*, December 14, 1992, 1; Christopher H. Marquis, "Radical Ministers Make Waves Over Joblessness in Pittsburgh," *Christian Science Monitor*, September 30, 1985, 1.

Robert Erikson, "Stealing Our Future from Blight," letter to the editor, *Pittsburgh Post-Gazette*, June 23, 1991, 4; Jim McKay, "Rescue Squad: A Look at the Men Behind the Campaign to Save Dorothy Six," *Pittsburgh Post-Gazette*, March 12, 1985, 19–20.

45. Neumann, "Goodbye, Steeltown," 405–11; Jim McKay, "Strike 3, and SVA Was Out," *Pittsburgh Post-Gazette*, July 3, 1991; "Developing the LTV Site," *Pittsburgh Press*, Editorial, July 3, 1991, B2; Kevin Guggenheim, "South Siders Present New Uses for LTV Mill Site," *Pittsburgh Press*, July 7, 1991; Perlmutter, "Housing, Marinas Planned."

46. Peter Miller, "Pittsburgh: Stronger Than Steel," *National Geographic* (December 1991): 125–45.

47. Gary Rotstein, "'Eds and Meds' Still Growing in Pittsburgh Region," *Pittsburgh Post-Gazette*, December 6, 2012; Deitrick, "The Post Industrial Revitalization of Pittsburgh"; Robert Gleeson and Jerry Paytas, "Pittsburgh: Economic Restructuring and Regional Development, 1880–2000," in *Sunbelt/Frostbelt: Public Policies and Market Forces in Metropolitan Development*, ed. Janet Rothenberg Pack (Washington, D.C.: Brookings Institution Press,

2005); Len Boselovic, "Still Churning After All These Years," *Pittsburgh Post-Gazette*, August 22, 2000.

CHAPTER 9. BURB OF THE 'BURGH

1. David Javersak, *A Historical Perspective*, recorded on December 15, 1994, WAHD (http://wheeling.weirton.lib.wv.us/history/wahp/wahp.htm); Brendan Sager, "Steubenville's Alliance 2000 Targets Pittsburgh," *Pittsburgh Post-Gazette*, November 20, 1998, D-8; Author's Interview with Gary DuFour, August 2004; "Steubenville: Coal and Steel Town Sees Rebirth," *Expansion Magazine Online*, January 1, 1998, http://www.expansionmanagement.com/.

2. Michael Marriott, "Pittsburgh Airport of Future Being Built," *New York Times*, November 12, 1991, A16; Tom Foerster, Pete Flaherty, and Lawrence W. Dunn, "The Allegheny County Commissioners Welcome You to the Airport of the Future," Special Supplement, *Beaver County Times*, September 13, 1992, 1

3. Allegheny Conference on Community Development, *Allegheny Conference on Community Development . . . Presents*, 1956, 14; "Pittsburgh's Airport Has Come a Long Way, Baby," Special Supplement, *Beaver County Times*, September 13, 1992; "Robinson Eyes Borough Status," *Pittsburgh Post-Gazette*, June 7, 1977; Lowry, *Economic Study of the Pittsburgh Region*, vol. 2, 92.

4. City of Pittsburgh et al., *Strategy 21: Pittsburgh/Allegheny Economic Development Strategy to Begin the 21st Century. A Proposal to the Commonwealth of Pennsylvania*, June 1985, 1–2; Sam Spatter, "Small Industries Taking over Steel's Role Here," *Pittsburgh Press*, July 8, 1982; Thomas J. Porter, Jr., "RIDC West Park Gets Office, Lab Complex," *Pittsburgh Post-Gazette*, October 24, 1979. "Hi-Tech Sites Give Realtors a Boost in Industrial Sales," *Pittsburgh Press*, November 28, 1982.

5. Tasso Katselas Associates Inc., *Greater Pittsburgh International Airport Expansion Program, New Terminal Complex, Concept Development Phase: Final Report*, 1981; City of Pittsburgh et al., *Strategy 21*, 1–2; Foerster, Flaherty, and Dunn, "Airport of the Future."

6. Richard Stouffer, "A $500 Million Suburban Mix," *New York Times*, October 16, 1988; Debra Utterback, "Outlook Optimistic, Colafella Says," *Beaver County Times*, February 3, 1986; John Barker, "Beaver County Economic Position a Matter of Outsider Perception," *Beaver County Times*, October 14, 1988.

7. DuFour Interview.

8. DuFour Interview.

9. Patty Tascarella, "Steubenville, Ohio, Casts Itself as New, Cheap Pittsburgh Suburb," *Pittsburgh Business Times*, May 21, 1999; "If Pittsburgh Site Doesn't Work, Steubenville Ready for Heinz," *Associated Press State & Local Wire*, July 30, 1999.

10. DuFour Interview; John Brown, "Brownfields Reform Towns," *Steubenville Herald-Star*, August 22, 2010.

11. Joe Grata, "RIDC Doing a Job by Helping Many Keep Theirs," *Pittsburgh Press*, January 22, 1980; Ellen M Perlmutter, "Officials Critical of RIDC Practices"; Select Committee on Pennsylvania's Industrial Development Corporations, *Sharing the Wealth*.

12. Thomas Murphy to Thomas Foerster, "Letter," June 24, 1992, box 11, TMP.

13. Teresa F. Lindeman, "Wal-Mart Distribution Center in Wintersville, Ohio, Covers a Lot of Ground," *Pittsburgh Post-Gazette*, July 16, 2003; "Hundreds of Jobs Coming to W.Va," *Titusville Herald*, June 12, 1999, 3; Suzanne Elliott, "Airport Area Balancing Boom, Bust, Home Builders Lag Commercial Developers," *Pittsburgh Business Times*, May 19, 2000; "Still

Waiting for Takeoff: Why Has Development on County-Owned Land Surrounding Pittsburgh International Airport Been So Slow?" *Pittsburgh Post-Gazette*, August 27, 2000.

14. Marriott, "Pittsburgh Airport of Future Being Built"; Alex Smith, "Strategy 21: Public and Private Cooperation in 21st Century Pittsburgh," Carnegie Mellon University, 2012, available from http://pittsburghmovingforward.org/library/; Mark Belko, "Silence Is Deafening in Airport Concourses," *Pittsburgh Post-Gazette*, November 11, 2007; Jim Ritchie, "Quiet Airport Corridor May See Activity," *Pittsburgh Tribune-Review*, June 6, 1999, sec. A1, 15; Sandra Fischione Donovan, "Landing Development, Airport Area Waits to Realize the Benefits," *Beaver County Times*, February 6, 1996; Paul Giannamore, "Progress Alliance Exec Establishes Ground Rules of Future," *Steubenville Herald-Star*, July 23, 2006, D1.

15. William Chesson, "Making the Case for Steubenville," *Pittsburgh Business Times*, December 28, 2001.

16. Ron Basescu, "Casey Breaks Ground for Expressway," *Uniontown Herald-Standard*, January 21, 1989, 1

17. Thornburgh, *Advanced Technology*, 1; Governor's Press Office, "Press Release," October 8, 1983, DTP; Coleman, "Public/Private Cooperative Response Patterns."

18. "Remarks by James Colker, President of the Pittsburgh High Technology Council at the SPIRC Check Presentation by Governor Casey," August 24, 1988, box 3, PDC; David Ranii, "High-Tech Council Expanding with Youthful Gusto," *Pittsburgh Press*, August 21, 1988, D18; Rick Teaff, "SPIRC Blending Manufacturing, High Technology," *Pittsburgh Business Times*, July 18, 1988; Commonwealth News Bureau, "Press Release Re: SPIRC," August 24, 1988, box 3, PDC; Gary Tuma, "Christman's Future in Cabinet Unknown," *Pittsburgh Post-Gazette*, January 12, 1991; Vince Gagetta, *Southwestern Pennsylvania: Land of Opportunity* (Montgomery, Ala.: Community Communications, 1999).

19. Ray Christman to Paul Brophy, "Letter," August 1, 1988; Ray Christman, "Inter-Office Memorandum," October 18, 1988; Ray Christman, to Paul Brophy, "Letter," July 10, 1989, all in box 73, PDC; Barbara W. Stack, "Technical Firms Are Hope for Economy," *Pittsburgh Post-Gazette*, July 28, 1982; "High Technology Unit Linked to Universities," *Pittsburgh Post-Gazette*, October 9, 1982; Barnes, "RIDC Chief Answers Critics," *Pittsburgh Post-Gazette*, February 22, 1991; Author's Interview with Frank Brooks Robinson, Sr., September 2010.

20. Richard Stouffer, "Big Mill Sites Go Public," *New York Times*, September 18, 1988, R25; Jim McKay, "RIDC Will Spend $20 Million to Revamp Westinghouse Plant," *Pittsburgh Post-Gazette*, January 19, 1989; Robinson Interview.

21. Sam Spatter, "Creating Jobs: Old Plant Sites Attract New Manufacturers," *Pittsburgh Press*, March 15, 1992, F7; Eleanor Chute, "Keystone Commons at Five Years," *Pittsburgh Post-Gazette*, April 7, 1994; Linda Wilson Fuoco, "Ghost of Past, Future Vision Seen in Tour of Steel Valley," *Pittsburgh Post-Gazette*, July 2, 1997.

22. Charles Bartsch, *Analysis of Pennsylvania's Brownfields Program*, Northeast Midwest Institute, December 2003, 10–13; Dan Fitzpatrick, "The Mon Valley—Haves and Have Nots with a Mix of Envy and Frustration," *Pittsburgh Post-Gazette*, October 14, 2001; Dan Fitzpatrick, "The ReDevelopment of RIDC," *Pittsburgh Post-Gazette*, August 22, 1999; Robinson Interview.

23. Ralph L. Bangs, Vijai P. Singh, and University Center for Social and Urban Research, *The State of the Region: Economic, Demographic and Social Trends in Southwestern Pennsylvania*, April 1988, 98; Robert C. Watson to Robert Casey, "Letter," July 12, 1990, box 172, folder

11, GRPC; Jeffrey J. Kitsko, "PA Turnpike 43, Mon-Fayette Expressway," updated January 4, 2014, http://www.pahighways.com/toll/PATurnpike43.html.

24. James B. Wilson," Letter to Readers," *Beltway Review*, Winter 1993, 1; Greater Uniontown Area Chamber of Commerce to Robert Casey, "The Mon Valley/Fayette Expressway Must Be Built Without Delay [Letter]," July 24, 1990, box 172, folder 11, GRPC.

25. Richard Caliguiri to James B. Wilson, "Letter," October 9, 1987 as cited in Kitsko, "PA Turnpike 43"; Tom Murphy, "Headline on Mon-Fayette Expressway Didn't Do Me Justice," *Pittsburgh Post-Gazette*, Letters to the editor, February 26, 1994, D2; Norma Dearfield to Gov. Robert Casey, "Letter," May, 26 1988, box 172, folder 11, GRPC.

26. Penn Future, *The Citizens' Plan: An Alternative to the Pennsylvania Turnpike Commission's Plan to Complete the Mon-Fayette Toll Road*, August 27, 2002, 10, 14; Joe Kirk, "Completion of the Mon/Fayette Expressway is Essential for Our Future," *Hotline*, Fall 2001, http://gasp-pgh.org/; Dave Kerr, "Not the Way to Go," Letters to the Editor, *Pittsburgh Post-Gazette*, October 14, 2001.

27. Tony Denslow, "Egypt Valley Looks like a Gem," *Elyria Chronicle Telegram*, February 26, 1995.

28. Mark Hofmann, "Preparing for Tourists," *Connellsville Daily Courier*, May 11, 2006; "Regular Meeting of the Board of Commissioners of Belmont County Ohio, St. Clairsville Ohio," January 30, 2002.

29. Southwestern Pennsylvania Commission, "Total Population by Municipality in Fayette County, 1930–2000," compiled May 2003, http://www.spcregion.org/data_datalib.shtml; Betty J. Pokas, ed., *Belmont County Bicentennial, 1801–2001* (Martins Ferry, Ohio: Times Leader, 2000).

30. Robert Gaitens, "Ohiopyle Dedicates New Vacationland," *Pittsburgh Press*, July 8, 1962, 2; "Conservancy to Transfer 9,300-Acre Wilderness Tract to State," *News Release*, September 6, 1973; Palmer, *Youghiogheny*, 215–19; Dave Lester, "There's Money in White Water Fun," *Altoona Mirror*, August 8, 1981, 28.

31. Edward K. Muller, ed., *An Uncommon Passage: Traveling Through History on the Great Allegheny Passage Trail* (Pittsburgh: University of Pittsburgh Press, 2009), 224, 245–57; McCahan, *By the Side of the Road*; Molly Gilmore, "Sportsmen and Cyclists in Harmony," *Altoona Mirror*, April 2, 1989, A1; Rails-to-Trails Conservancy, *Railbanking and Rail-Trails: A Legacy for the Future* (Washington, D.C.: The Conservancy, 2005); Rita Ariyoshi, "The World's Best Walks," *Travel & Leisure*, October 1994.

32. Don Wolf, "Rails-To-Trails Effort Likely on Fast Track," *Pittsburgh Press*, December 11, 1990, B1; Bob Batz, Jr, "Blazing a New Trail," *Pittsburgh Post-Gazette*, April 30, 1993, E4; "Mon/Yough Trail Council Application/Brochure," brochure, 1992, TMP; Hofmann, "Preparing for Tourists."

33. Author's Interview with Eric Bugaile, April 2006; Hofmann, "Preparing for Tourists"; Linda Wilson Fuoco, "Group Combines Forces to Raise $200,000 to Create Steel Valley Trail," *Pittsburgh Post-Gazette*, October 28, 1998, E8.

34. "Rails to Trails," http://www.barnesvilleohio.com/rails.htm, accessed August 4, 2014; "Rails to Trails Being Developed in Barnesville Despite Funding Turndown by ODOT," (*Cambridge, Ohio*) *Daily Jeffersonian*, November 10, 2005.

35. Edward Marotta, *Washington County: The Second One Hundred Years* (Washington, Pa.: Washington County Historical Publication Committee, 1980), 97–99; David Templeton,

"It's Official: Maple Creek Mine To Reopen This Year," *Pittsburgh Post-Gazette*, January 15, 1995, W1.

36. Don Hopey, "Mine Acid Curbs Life in the Yough," *Pittsburgh Post-Gazette*, December 19, 1994, A13; "Fish Endangered, Study Claims Acid Rain Killed Laurel Hill Trout," *Indiana Gazette*, April 6, 1984, 11; "Team Studies Threat of Old Mines," *Akron Beacon Journal*, September 23, 1996, B4.

37. "Coal Officials Re-Affirm Concern and Cooperation for Town's Future," *Barnesville Enterprise*, Feb. 15, 1973; Barnesville Planning Commission and Hurley Schnaufer & Associates, "Greenbelt Plan—Barnesville, Ohio," May 1973; "Council Pledges Support to Greenbelt Advocates," *Barnesville Enterprise*, October 21, 1987; "R&F Coal Will Move Dragline," *Barnesville Enterprise*, June 19, 1988.

38. David Jacobs, "Barnesville Hopes Replicas of Homes Attract Tourists and Bail Out Economy," *Columbus Dispatch*, August 10, 1991, 6C; "Village to Appeal Greenbelt Denial," *Barnesville Enterprise*, May 23, 2002; Rich Gibson, "ODNR Rejects Barnesville Petition," *Martins Ferry Times Leader*, February 18, 2005.

39. Schmid & Company, Inc. and Citizens Coal Council, *The Increasing Damage from Underground Coal Mining in Pennsylvania: A Review and Analysis of the PADEP's Third Act 54 Report* (Bridgeville, Pa., April 17, 2011); Beth Hope-Cushey, "Old Permits for New Mines Criticized," *Pittsburgh Post-Gazette*, October 5, 1997, Washington edition, W5.

40. "Township Residents Settle Mining Lawsuit," *Cleveland Plain Dealer*, August 15, 1991, 1C; Zachary Gooch, "ODNR Restricts Mining under Dysart Woods: Both Sides Unhappy with Ruling," *Martins Ferry Times Leader*, December 1, 1998; Myers Interview.

41. Myers Interview; "Regular Meeting of the Board of Commissioners of Belmont County Ohio."

42. Office of Management and Budget, *Revised Delineations of Metropolitan Statistical Areas, Micropolitan Statistical Areas, and Combined Statistical Areas, and Guidance on Uses Of the Delineations of These Areas* (Washington, D.C., February 28, 2013); Paul J. Gough, "Plans Envision Pittsburgh Airport of Future," *Pittsburgh Business Times*, June 14, 2011; Tim Schooley, "Developers Move Forward Despite Uncertainty Surrounding Mon-Fayette Expressway Plans," *Pittsburgh Business Times*, June 7, 2013.

43. "Murray Energy Corporation Confirms the Purchase of Consolidation Coal Company From CONSOL Energy, Inc.," *Press Release*, October 28, 2013, http://www.murrayenergy.net/pdf/10_28_13.pdf; Ann Besler, "Coal's Power: Pittsburgh Region Hosts Cutting-Edge Coal Research," *Pittsburgh Post-Gazette*, December 28, 2011; "Sunday Sit-Down: Murray Energy CEO Robert Murray," *Wheeling News-Register*, January 1, 2012.

CHAPTER 10: RIVERS OF STEEL

1. "Wheeling Site Among Heritage Areas," *Charleston Gazette*, October 6, 1994, 6C; George Hohmann, "A Downtown Turnaround," *Charleston Daily Mail*, December 4, 1998, D1; Richard Rabinowitz, "Interpreting Wheeling's Cityscape," in Lane Frenchman and Associates et al., "Summary of the Wheeling Interpretive Master Plan," February 1995, i–iv.

2. Harry Hamm, *Wheeling 2000*, 1989 (OCPL); Florida, *The Rise of the Creative Class*; "Editorial—Renaissance III," *Pittsburgh Post-Gazette*, March 27, 1998; Tom Barnes, "City URA Chief Quits Parallel County Job," *Pittsburgh Post-Gazette*, July 20, 2000.

3. "Editorial—Renaissance III"; Author's Interview with August Carlino and Edward K. Muller, June 4, 2014.

4. South Side Local Development Company, *"The South Side Works" A Community-Based Planning Evaluation: LTV Steel's South Side Mill Site Pittsburgh, Pennsylvania* (Pittsburgh: SSLDC, April 15, 1992); Jon Schmitz, "Golden Crossroads," *Pittsburgh Post-Gazette,* August 2, 1995, A1; James P. DeAngelis and Sabina Deitrick, *The Regional Economic Development Bibliography and Data Base (TRED/Biblio),* December 1994.

5. Neumann, "Goodbye, Steeltown," 342; Crowley, *The Politics of Place,* 103–4; Earl James, "Preserving Our History in Park," *Pittsburgh Post-Gazette,* editorial, September 10, 1988, 9.

6. Pittsburgh Cultural Trust, *The Cultural District Means Business: It's More Than You Imagine and More Than Meets the Eye,* 1993; Lubove, *Twentieth-Century Pittsburgh,* vol. 2, 196–97; Tom Murphy to David Abrams, "Letter," April 18, 1991, box 13, TMP.

7. Patricia Lowry, "Park Utilizes Native Amenities," *Pittsburgh Post-Gazette,* November 30, 1998; David Moffat, "Allegheny Riverfront Park, Pittsburgh, Pennsylvania," *Places* 15, 1 (2002): 10–13.

8. Carmen J. Lee, "Riverside Path for Hiking and Cycling Proposed," *Pittsburgh Post-Gazette,* December 6, 1990, 1, 6; Don Hopey, "Bike Trail Rolls $14 Million into Local Economies," *Pittsburgh Post-Gazette,* February 23, 1999; Forging Connections Book Committee, *Forging Connections: Friends of the Riverfront, Twenty Years of Building the Three Rivers Heritage Trail, 1991–2011* (Pittsburgh: Friends of the Riverfront, 2011); Tom Murphy, "Essay," n.d., TMP.

9. Tom Murphy et al., "The Pittsburgh Story" (Remaking Cities Congress, Pittsburgh, October 15, 2013), https://www.youtube.com/channel/UC6hrVs96jVkvZF8BUzM_xsg; "County Coup Targets Dunn," *Pittsburgh Post-Gazette,* August 14, 1997; "Tom Barnes, "City URA Chief Quits."

10. David M. Brown, "Masloff, 90, Recalls a Life Less Ordinary," *Pittsburgh Tribune-Review,* December 23, 2007.

11. "Stafford to Retire as CEO of Allegheny Conference," *Pittsburgh Business Times,* December 20, 2002; Tom Murphy et al., "The Pittsburgh Story"; Tom Murphy to Richard Stafford, "Letter," March 24, 1993, TMP; Metzger, "Reinventing Housing."

12. Lynn Ermann, "On Top of Mt. Slag, Homes Sprout," *New York Times,* March 6, 2003; Neumann, *Goodbye Steel Town,* 408–20; Nancy Perkins, "A Tale of Two Brownfield Sites: Making the Best of Times from the Worst of Times in Western Pennsylvania's Steel Valley," *Boston College Environmental Affairs Law Review* 34, 3 (2007): 503–32. The city's first casino, Rivers Casino, did not open until August 2009 on the North Side adjacent to the Carnegie Science Center. Mark Belko, "After 5 Years, Rivers Casino Seen as Good Neighbor," *Pittsburgh Post-Gazette,* August 9, 2014.

13. Ron Daparma, "Flora Leaving Green Building Alliance for Job in D.C.," *Pittsburgh Tribune-Review,* December 1, 2008; Diana Nelson Jones, "South Side Real Estate Board says Mission Accomplished," *Pittsburgh Post-Gazette,* November 1, 2010; South Side Local Development Company, "Farewell and Thank You," 2012, available from http://www.southsidepgh.com/

14. Crowley, *Politics of Place,* 112–39; Dan Fitzpatrick, "Developer Signs Fifth and Forbes Retail Deal," *Pittsburgh Business Times,* September 15, 1997.

15. Ziegler quote cited in Crowley, *The Politics of Place,* 113; "GroundZero Action Network," uploaded March 22, 2004, http://moncon.greenmuseum.org/papers/groundzero.pdf (accessed 9/1/2014); Crowley, *The Politics of Place,* 131; Tim Schooley, "Feelings Linger Over Battle for Fifth and Forbes," *Pittsburgh Business Times,* May 24, 2010.

16. Crowley, *Politics of Place*, 112–39; Bob Bauder, "City of Pittsburgh a Partner in Preservation," *Pittsburgh Tribune-Review*, August 9, 2012.

17. Ron Cook, "Plan B Flawed; Option Is Worse," *Pittsburgh Post-Gazette*, June 22, 1998; Tom Barnes, "Resurrecting the River's Edge," *Pittsburgh Post-Gazette*, July 11, 1999; Toker, *Pittsburgh*, 152–57; J. Brady McCullough, "Playoff Baseball to Give Nation a Glimpse of PNC Park Gem," *Pittsburgh Post*-Gazette, October 1, 2013; Tom Murphy, "They Took Political Risks that Paid Off for the Region," Letters to the Editor, *Pittsburgh Post*-Gazette, October 20, 2013.

18. Dennis B. Roddy, "Former Mayor Tom Murphy Heads into the Record Books (with an *)," *Pittsburgh Post-Gazette*, July 4, 2006.

19. "A Mayor for Pittsburgh," editorial, *Pittsburgh Post-Gazette*, May 2, 2001; Tom Barnes, "Analysis: Murphy's Triumphs, Failures a Test in Urban Realities," *Pittsburgh Post-Gazette*, January 17, 2004; Tim Schooley, "Tom Murphy Years Visionary, Vexing," *Pittsburgh Business Times*, May 10, 2013.

20. Kaiser, *Hubris*, 1999 (copy in author's possession); Hunter, *Marine Memories*; "Employment on the Decline," *Wheeling News-Register*, March 22, 1981; Rich Crofton, "Thomas Recalls Earlier Downtown Mall Plan," *Wheeling Intelligencer*, September 6, 1991, 13.

21. Author's Interview with Betty J. Nutting, May 2014; Susan Spencer-Smith, "Old and New In West Virginia," *Philadelphia Inquirer*, April 10, 1988, R1; Linda Comins, "Custom House Marks 150 Years, Historian Honored," *Wheeling Intelligencer*, November 1, 2009.

22. Hamm, *Wheeling 2000*; Margaret Beltz, "Lipphardt Presents 'History' Report on Downtown," *Wheeling News-Register*, April 23, 2000; Spencer-Smith, "Old and New In West Virginia"; Lisa Hechesky, "Return to Main Street: An Assessment of the Main Street Revitalization Program" (Master's thesis, Marshall University, 2005), 43, 46; McKinley Engineering Company, *Wheeling Waterfront Development Plan*, October 1983.

23. Torsten Ove, "Record-Setter to Push a New Future for Wheeling," *Pittsburgh Press*, July 5, 1987, A12.

24. Beltz, "Lipphardt Presents"; Spencer-Smith, "Old and New In West Virginia"; Wheeling National Heritage Area Task Force and Lane, Frenchman and Associates, Inc., *Plan for the Wheeling National Heritage Area* (August 1992); Author's Interview with Charles Flynn, May 2014.

25. Flynn Interview; Byrd, *Robert C. Byrd*, 499, 525, 540–41, 564, 710–11; Jake Thompson and Jeff Taylor, "Congress Leaves Fingerprints All Over Park Projects," *Hendersonville (North Carolina) Times-News*, November 21, 1993, D2–3.

26. "Wheeling Site Among Heritage Areas," *Charleston Gazette*, October 6, 1994: George Hohmann, "A Downtown Turnaround," *Charleston Daily Mail*, December 14, 1998, D1; ICON Architects, Inc., *Management Plan for the Wheeling National Heritage Area*, May 2004, B1; Ian Hicks, "WNHAC's Master Plan, 20 Years Later," *Wheeling Intelligencer*, May 28, 2012; Byrd, *Robert C. Byrd*, 499, 525, 540–41, 564, 710–11.

27. Author's Interview with Hydie Friend, May 2014; Centre Market Steering Committee et al., *Centre Market Action Program, Wheeling, West Virginia*, January 1983; "Biography," http://mckinley.house.gov/about-david/ (accessed 9/1/2014).

28. Milan Simonich, "37 Towns Join Fight to Create More Jobs," *Pittsburgh Post*-Gazette, October 14, 2001, B1; Regional Economic Development Partnership, "Orrick Global Operations Center Case Study," http://www.slideshare.net/REDPWV/orrick-global-operations-center-case-study (accessed 9/1/2014); Joyce Gannon, "Law Firm's Operations Center Helps

Restore an Old Building, Revitalizes West Virginia Mill Town," *Pittsburgh Post-Gazette*, August 13, 2012.

29. George Hohmann, "What's Next for Wheeling?" *Charleston Daily Mail*, July 15, 2003; Beltz, "Lipphardt Presents"; Thompson and Taylor, "Congress Leaves Fingerprints"; Friend Interview; Flynn Interview.

30. Hamm, *Wheeling 2000*; Kay Masters, "Council Studies Model Park Operations Concept," *St. Petersburg, Florida Evening Independent*, January 29, 1979; Terry Hazlett, "'Festival of Lights' Turned City Around," *Washington Observer-Reporter*, June 5, 1988, F1; Don Herschell, "People Who Work in Glass Houses," *Washington Observer-Reporter*, August 6, 1993, B1; Flynn Interview.

31. Flynn Interview; Friend Interview.

32. Beltz, "Lipphardt Presents"; Blum, "Mall Disintegrated with Urban Renewal Rejection," *Wheeling Intelligencer*, April 10, 2004; John McCabe, "Project Meant as Business District Revival"; Michelle Blum, "Heritage Group Reveals Choices," *Wheeling Intelligencer*, January 30, 2003.

33. *County and City Data Book*.

34. John McCabe, "Industrial Park Expected to Be Ready by Next Fall," *Wheeling Intelligencer*, October 13, 1997; Carley Amico, "Too Many Hurdles in Way for Outlets," *Wheeling Intelligencer*, January 10, 2004; Andy Stamp, "Downtown's Heyday Fades into Memory," *Wheeling Intelligencer*, April 10, 2004; Joselyn King, "Gallagher Retiring from Crones," *Wheeling Intelligencer*, October 1, 2007.

35. Donna Seiling, "Merging Town and Mall into a New Alloy, Town Center Design Comes to Pittsburgh in Homestead Project," *Pittsburgh Business Times*, October 2, 1998; "Homecoming? Homestead Tries to Make a Comeback," editorial, *Pittsburgh Business Times*, October 22, 1998; Suzanne Elliott, "Homestead Set to Benefit from the Promise of Waterfront Development," *Pittsburgh Business Times*, July 15, 2001.

36. *International Directory of Company Histories*, vol. 22 (Detroit: St. James Press, 1998), 414–16; Linda Wilson, "Ex-Steel Workers Would Return to Homestead Shop," *Pittsburgh Post-Gazette*, July 28, 1988; Allegheny County Department of Planning and Arthur D. Little, Inc, *Project Report*; Ray Christman to Ivan Tylawsky, memorandum, "Homestead Industrial Park Regional Opportunity," November 29, 1989, box 73, PDC.

37. James, "Preserving Our History in Park," 9; "Historical Society of Western Pennsylvania, *Preliminary Report on Steel Historic Site Evaluation to the Steel Heritage Task Force*, 1988; Michael Newman, "Rivers of Steel Six-County Area is Designated as Heritage Park," *Pittsburgh Post-Gazette*, April 30, 1996, B1.

38. Bill Steigerwald, "Mill-Site Museum Backed by Heinz," *Pittsburgh Post-Gazette*, June 29, 1989; David Bergholz to Raymond Christman, "Letter," September 14, 1988, box 73, PDC; "Group Saves Bost Building," *Pittsburgh Post-Gazette*, August 1, 1991; Newman, "Rivers of Steel"; "Clinton Signs Measure Designating Region a National Heritage Area," November 14, 1996.

39. "Historic Ruins on the Mon," *Pittsburgh Post-Gazette*, August 3, 1988; Christine Vorce, "Homestead Historic Park Dispute Growing After Talks," *Pittsburgh Press*, June 24, 1990.

40. Vorce, "Homestead Historic Park"; Christine Vorce, "It's History Now, Homestead Roll Shop Comes Down Despite Museum Plans," *Pittsburgh Press*, June 30, 1990, B1; Carlino and Muller Interview; Linda Wilson Fuoco, "Historic Steel Strike Site to be Preserved,

Restored," *Pittsburgh Post-Gazette,* October 26, 1994, B1; "Parking a Project, It's Time to Move a Steel-Heritage Museum Forward," editorial, *Pittsburgh Post-Gazette,* February 4, 1994, B2; Jan Ackerman, "Doyle Bill Makes Museum Chronicling Steel Industry Less of a Long Shot Here," *Pittsburgh Post-Gazette,* August 22, 2000, C5.

41. Carlino and Muller Interview; Linda Wilson Fuocco, "Bost Building Has Its First Official Exhibit," *Pittsburgh Post-Gazette,* April 9, 2003.

42. Carlino and Muller Interview; Monica L. Haynes, "Steel-Heritage Plan Signed in Mon Valley," *Pittsburgh Post-Gazette,* September 6, 1990, 2; Steel Industry Heritage Corporation, *Rivers of Steel Management Action Plan,* December 1995.

43. Carlino and Muller Interview; Edward K. Muller, *Pittsburgh's Waterfront Lands: A Final Report for the Urban Redevelopment Authority of Pittsburgh* (Pittsburgh: The Authority, 1983); Edward K. Muller, "The Legacy of Industrial Rivers," *Pittsburgh History* 72 (Summer 1989); Edward K. Muller, "Metropolis and Region: A Framework for Enquiry into Western Pennsylvania," in Hays, ed., *City at the Point:* 181–211; Muller, "Industrial Suburbs," reprinted and expanded in Lewis, *Manufacturing Suburbs,* 124–42.

44. Mon Valley Initiative, *Building on Our Strengths: A Community-Based Strategy for the Mon Valley Initiative,* April 1993; Carlino and Muller Interview; Scott Beveridge, "Light Shines Brightly on Brownsville's Historic Flatiron Building, Especially During the Holidays," *Washington Observer-Reporter,* December 11, 1998. See also Edward K. Muller, "Industrial Preservation: Connecting People, Place, and History," Sixth Annual Frederic M. Miller Memorial Lecture, Washington, D.C., 2004.

45. Tom Barnes, "Steel Museum Gets New Funding Push," *Pittsburgh Post-Gazette,* March 27, 1996; "Rivers of Steel: A Bold Plan to Commemorate Our Industrial Heritage," editorial, *Pittsburgh Post-Gazette,* March 31, 1996; Steve Massey, "Manufacturing Change," *Pittsburgh Post-Gazette,* February 16, 1997; Robert Mehrabian et al., *The Greater Pittsburgh Region: Working Together to Compete Globally,* Regional Economic Revitalization Initiative, November 1994; Fitzpatrick, "Stuck with Steel"; Carlino and Muller Interview

46. Jan Ackerman, "Pittsburgh Will Settle for Steel Industry's Past," *Pittsburgh Post-Gazette,* March 12, 2000.

47. Ackerman, "Doyle Bill"; Ann Belser, "Vote Set on Carrie Furnace Site," *Pittsburgh Post-Gazette,* September 19, 2001; Ann Belser, "Owner Has Permit to Demolish Carrie Furnace," *Pittsburgh Post-Gazette,* October 13, 2004, EZ1; Ann Belser, "Forging the Future," *Pittsburgh Post-Gazette,* June 16, 2005, EZ1.

48. "The Newest Jewel in the Skyline," *Pittsburgh Post-Gazette,* September 22, 2003; Toker, *Pittsburgh,* 90–91; "2003 Pittsburgh Pirates Schedule," http://www.baseball-almanac.com/; Rich Lord, "Murphy Looks Back at His 12 Rocky Years, Three Terms Spanned Trouble with Police to City's Financial Woes," *Pittsburgh Post-Gazette,* December 25, 2005.

49. Murphy et al., "The Pittsburgh Story."

EPILOGUE

1. Joe Napsha, "Former Sony Corp. Plant Near New Stanton Auditions for New Tenant," *Pittsburgh Tribune-Review,* June 23, 2010.

2. "Pittsburgh 250 Blows Out Birthday Candles on Year-Long Celebration," Press Release, Allegheny Conference on Community Development, December 18, 2008; "G-20 Summit Coming to Pittsburgh in September," *Pittsburgh Business Times,* May 28, 2009; "Pennsylvania Counties with Active Wells," StateImpact Pennsylvania, http://stateimpact.npr.org/

pennsylvania/drilling/; Evan Pattak, "An Industrial Renaissance," *Pittsburgh Quarterly* (Summer 2012).

3. "Wheeling and Lake Erie Railway," http://www.wlerwy.com; Dave Whipkey, "Dura-Bond's New Facility Will Bring Jobs," *Pittsburgh Post-Gazette*, December 16, 2010.

4. Ohio Department of Natural Resources, "Ohio Oil & Gas Wells," https://gis.ohiodnr.gov/website/dog/oilgasviewer/.

5. Jon Schmitz, "Golden Crossroads," *Pittsburgh Post-Gazette*, July 30, 1995; Michael Janofsky, "Pittsburgh at Progress Crossroads," *New York Times*, September 21, 1997; James E. Rohr, "We Can Rise to the Challenge," editorial, *Pittsburgh Post-Gazette*, December 6, 1998, B1; Christopher Briem, "Parsing the 'New Pittsburgh' Narrative," editorial, *Pittsburgh Post-Gazette*, March 1, 2015, D1; Niv Elis, "Puzzling Pittsburgh," *Jerusalem Post*, January 2, 2015, 14; Michael Anderson, "Pittsburgh Is (in Many Ways) the City That Portland Wants to Become," *BikePortland.org*, September 17, 2014, http://bikeportland.org/2014/09/17/pittsburgh-is-basically-the-city-that-portland-wants-to-become-110941.

6. *Vision to Action: 2012 Annual Report* (Pittsburgh: Claude Worthington Benedum Foundation, 2013); Patty Tascarella, "Power of 32 Raises $43M, Aims to Attract Businesses to Region," *Pittsburgh Business Times*, January 2, 2015; Sam Kusic, "Power of 32 Meeting Sets Stage for Regional Plan," *Pittsburgh Business Times*, December 19, 2014; Tracie Mauriello, "City Touted as Role Model for Job Creation: U.S. Chamber Takes Notice of Innovation, Networking Here," *Pittsburgh Post-Gazette*, June 14, 2012, A9. For a more critical view, see Colin McNickle, "Where Did the Power of 32 Go?" editorial, *Pittsburgh Tribune Review*, April 1, 2012.

7. Brian O'Neill, "Why Downtown Keeps Getting Better, Bit by Bit," *Pittsburgh Post-Gazette*, February 12, 2015, A2; Elis, "Puzzling Pittsburgh"; Adam Radwanski, "The Rising: With the Drop in Oil Prices, Ontario Is Being Touted Again for Its Economic Potential," *Globe and Mail*, January 17, 2015, F1; Tim Schooley, "Former Mayor Tells City's Story Worldwide with Urban Land Institute," *Pittsburgh Business Times*, May 10, 2013; Tom Murphy, *Building on Innovation The Significance of Anchor Institutions in a New Era of City Building* (Washington, D.C.: Urban Land Institute, 2011); Murphy et al., "The Pittsburgh Story." For a recent high profile example of the role of community development corporations in Pittsburgh, see Mark Belko, "Penguins, City, Hill Leaders Clear Way for U.S. Steel Plan," *Pittsburgh Post-Gazette*, January 20, 2015, B1.

8. Murphy et al., "The Pittsburgh Story"; Tim Schooley, "Tom Murphy Years Visionary, Vexing," *Pittsburgh Business Times*, May 10, 2013; Public Financial Management, Inc. and Eckert Seamans Cherin & Mellott, LLC, *Municipalities Financial Recovery Act Amended Recovery Plan: City of Pittsburgh Allegheny County, Pennsylvania* (Pennsylvania Department of Community and Economic Development, June 24, 2014); Kate Giammarise, "Sweeping Changes to Act 47 Proposed in Harrisburg," *Pittsburgh Post-Gazette*, August 31, 2014; Brian O'Neill, "Mayors' Finance Statements Can't All Add Up," *Pittsburgh Post-Gazette*, May 14, 2014; Brian O'Neill, "Tough Scrutiny Ought to Be the Cost of Tax-Exempt Status," *Pittsburgh Post-Gazette*, February 22, 2015.

9. Tom Murphy, "Six Pittsburgh Lessons for Providence," *The Providence Journal*, February 15, 2015, 1; Carlino Interview; Eric Slagle, "Flyover Ramp to Open Development of Carrie Furnace Site," *Pittsburgh Tribune-Review*, May 24, 2014; Ian Hicks, "Dilapidated Houses to Be Torn Down," *Wheeling Intelligencer*, January 14, 2015.

10. Carey Durkin Treado, *Sustaining Pittsburgh's Steel Technology Cluster* (Center for Industry Studies, University of Pittsburgh, September 2008).

INDEX

ACTION-Housing, 173, 175–77, 179, 197
Aetna Insurance, 158, 233
African Americans, 5, 9, 54, 105, 212, 236; discrimination against, 175–77; opposition to urban renewal, 172, 178–79
Agriculture, 1, 27, 30, 37, 39, 41–42, 165, 184; decline of, 70–71, 126–28; and surface mining, 141–42
Air pollution, 2, 10, 21, 41, 51, 68, 120, 175; acid rain, 67, 223, 250; and environmentalism, 79, 175, 228, 254; and smoke control movement, 75–80, 104; as symbol of industrial power, 37
Airport Corridor, 156–64, 232–40
Aldridge, Jay, 220, 228, 235, 241
Aliquippa, 203, 223, 278
Allegheny Airlines, 163. See also US Airways
Allegheny Center, 167, 182–87, 212, 262. See also North Side
Allegheny City, 40, 64, 184
Allegheny Conference on Community Development, 3–5, 9, 11–12, 21; declining influence of, 181–82; formation of, 74–77; regional vision of, 68, 84, 140, 149; Strategic Investment Fund, 260. See also Golden Triangle; Pittsburgh Renaissance; Public-private partnerships
Allegheny County, 10, 38, 54, 70, 73, 153, 169, 224–25, 227; commissioners, 161, 174, 214, 233–34, 238, 258, 264; Regional Asset District, 260–63. See also Foerster, Tom; Dawida, Michael
Allegheny County Sportsmen's League, 86, 130

Allegheny Foundation. *See* Scaife foundations
Allegheny Mountains, 1, 13–14, 29–30, 38–41, 44, 95, 142, 207, 215, 207–8, 278
Allegheny River Valley, 1, 40–41, 64, 166, 174, 181–85, 219, 258, 263, 281
Allegheny Trail Alliance, 248–49
Amalgamated Association of Iron and Steel Workers, 54–56
Ambridge, 202–3, 278
Appalachia, 29–32; crisis in, 125, 127; Pittsburgh as, 94–95
Appalachian Mountains. *See* Allegheny Mountains
Appalachian Plateau, 29; suburban development on, 123, 151–52, 283
Appalachian Regional Commission, 93, 95, 127, 129, 132, 209
Arlen Inner-Cities Industries, 193–94
Army Corps of Engineers, 80, 112
Atomic energy, 147, 163, 223. *See also* Bettis Atomic Research Laboratory
A. W. Mellon Educational and Charitable Trust. *See* Mellon foundations

Baltimore, 29–30, 31, 152
Baltimore & Ohio Railroad, 30–33, 38, 48, 104, 151–52
Barnesville, 41, 81, 247, 286; Greenbelt, 143, 146, 250–51; and post-industrial transition, 249–50; surface mining near, 124–29, 131, 140–47
Barone, Ralph, 115, 118–19, 122
Barr, Joseph, 174, 179

Beachler, Edwin, 151, 156–57
Beaver County, 150–51, 160; and Pittsburgh International Airport, 234–35; unemployment in, 224–25
Beaver River Valley, 8, 24, 241
Beaver Valley Expressway, 235
Belmont County, 33, 196, 246–47; commissioners, 252–53
Ben Franklin Technology Partners, 218–20, 240–41
Benedum Center for the Performing Arts, 205–6, 214, 258, 265
Benedum Foundation, 214, 265–66, 287
Bergholz, David, 274–75
Bettis Atomic Research Laboratory, 11, 217
Birru, Mulugetta, 259, 261
Boggs & Buhl Department Store, 184
Bost Building, 275–77, 280–81
Boston, 8, 11, 94, 161–62, 208, 218, 296n11
Braddock, 245, 253
Braddock Road, 21, 29–30, 41
Brown, Carol, 205, 230. *See also* Pittsburgh Cultural Trust
Brownfields, 5, 15, 221, 236, 243, 245, 261, 273–74, 295n6; compared to greenfield development, 161, 208, 242
Brownsville, 21–22, 279
Buhl Foundation, 138, 179, 216
Butler County, 87, 151, 162, 165–66, 224
Byrd, Robert C., 267–70, 274

Caliguiri, Richard, 12, 168, 206, 209–11, 214, 227–28, 241, 244–45
Carlino, August, 274, 276, 278–79, 281
Carnegie, Andrew, 1, 11, 34–38, 43–45, 54–55, 70; and philanthropy, 58–59, 179
Carnegie Institute of Technology. *See* Carnegie Mellon University
Carnegie Mellon University, 11, 76, 215–21, 240–42; Software Engineering Institute, 217, 220–21, 241
Carnegie Science Center, 1, 263
Carnegie Steel Company, 36–38, 48, 51, 55–56. *See also* U.S. Steel
Carrie Furnaces, 49, 273–78, 280, 282–83, 289
Carter administration, 11, 181, 209
Casey, Robert, 164, 239–41
Catholic churches, 168, 188–89; and institution building, 104, 190–91, 216; religious tensions, 60, 103–5, 109

Center for the Arts, 84, 172, 177, 180–81, 213
Center Wheeling, 105–7, 190–91, 194, 268–69
Centre Market, 234, 265, 268, 272
Charleston, 59, 190, 236
Chicago, 47–48, 70, 94, 160
Christman, Ray, 241, 274, 279
Churchill, 159
Cincinnati, 29, 32, 37, 76
Citizens Committee for Hill District Renewal, 179–80
Citizens Organized to Defend the Environment, 144, 146–47
Civic Arena, 84, 172, 177–78, 181
Clairton, 201, 205, 223
Clairton Works, 51, 209, 224, 230. *See also* U.S. Steel
Clean Air Act, 175, 223, 250
Cleveland, 70, 94, 112, 236
Coal mining, 2, 7, 14, 22, 28, 33, 42, 48; automation in, 71; and coke production, 34–35, 43, 49–51; and electrical power production, 131–32; longwall method, 250, 286; opposition to, 135–38, 143–48, 153, 252; regulation of, 129–31, 251; surface mining, 4–5, 14, 44, 71, 80–81, 87–88, 124–30; unemployment in, 78, 126–27
Community development corporations, 12–13, 178, 211, 278–79. *See also names of individual organizations*
Connellsville, 134–35, 137, 248
Consolidation Coal Company, vii, 45, 119, 223, 246, 253, 312n14; Hanna Coal Division, 124–26, 130–32, 140–48; and Pittsburgh Renaissance, 77, 88
Continental Realty, 273, 280
Cranberry Township, 150, 164–66, 169–70, 224
Cranmer, Bob, 259
Creative class, 262, 272, 287; and Richard Florida, 15, 256
Cultural District, 181, 205, 213, 257–59, 265, 281. *See also* Pittsburgh Cultural Trust
Cyert, Richard, 217, 219–20

David Lawrence Convention Center, 210, 281
Dawida, Michael, 259, 263
DeBolt, Jo, 275–76, 278

Democratic Party, 2–3, 9, 11, 62; in Martins Ferry, 109–11, 129, 143, 152; in Pittsburgh, 61, 68, 72–73, 170, 181, 259; and state politics, 129, 143, 152, 174, 267; in Wheeling, 267. *See also* Republican Party
Denominational Ministry Strategy, 229
Detroit, 8, 10, 46, 69–70, 113, 119
Doherty, Robert, 74, 82
Donora, 285; air pollution in, 67–68, 79, 88,
Downtown Wheeling Associates, 106, 190, 194–95
Doyle, Mike, 280
Dravo Corporation, 215
DuFour, Gary, 116, 231, 235–36
Duquesne, 223, 242, 245
Duquesne Works, 35, 201, 227; and City Center of Duquesne, 242–43, 286
Dynamic Pittsburgh, 215, 222–23. *See also* Penn's Southwest Association

East Carson Street Historic District, 257, 260–61, 284
East End, 61, 64, 153, 176
East Liberty, 177, 260
Economic Study of the Pittsburgh Region, 161, 206–9
Edgar Thomson Works, 35–37, 51, 55, 57, 230, 289. *See also* U.S. Steel
Education, 8, 203, 216; and economic development, 76, 121, 161, 208, 218, 221, 230, 244, 266; as key to jobs, 224–25; low levels of, 127, 176. *See also names of individual universities*; Post-industrial economy
Egypt Valley, vii–viii, 30, 81, 126–28; Mine, 7, 124–25, 140–48, 246, 251; and Piedmont Lake, 128; Wildlife Area, 246, 249
Eliza Furnace, 34, 220
Employee Stock Ownership Plan, 226
Environment, 7, 13–14, 46, 62, 76, 85, 215, 284; degradation of, 23, 50–52, 67, 71, 221; and extractionist ethic, 2, 23, 37, 130, 253–54; and environmentalism, 5, 15, 144–48, 175, 187, 228, 245, 250, 258.
Esper, Betty, 273
Ethnicity, 47, 54–55, 60, 102, 105, 109, 117, 154, 178

Fairless, Benjamin, 79, 88
Fallingwater, 75, 128, 133–34

Farms. *See* Agriculture
Fayette County, 87, 153, 247–48
Federal government, 9, 11–12, 29, 73, 80–81; cuts in aid to cities, 11, 181–82; and highways, 102, 152, 189; and hospitals, 190–91; and park creation, 86, 267–68, 270, 272, 275; and urban renewal, 112, 132, 135, 152, 181, 227, 251, 267. *See also* Appalachian Regional Commission; *names of individual politicians*
Ferncliff Peninsula, 133–36, 138–39, 247. *See also* Ohiopyle
Fetterman, John, 253
Fifth and Forbes, 261–62, 271. *See also* Murphy, Tom
Flaherty, Peter, 168, 173, 188–89, 197, 209–11, 213; fiscal populism, 11–12, 181; support for neighborhood planning, 181, 211
Flinn, William, 47, 60, 62, 66
Floods, 30, 63, 67, 75, 79, 81, 93, 126; and dam construction, 4, 10, 21, 68, 75, 80–81, 100
Flynn, Charles, 255, 266–67, 271
Foerster, Tom, 168, 238, 242
Ford Foundation, 179, 211
Fort Duquesne, 82; bridge, 184
Fort Pitt, 82, 84; bridge, 285; tunnel, 1, 158, 284
Fort Henry Industrial and Commerce Park, 272
Fort Henry Mall, 192–97, 264, 266, 271
Foundations, role in urban development, 12, 133, 179, 186, 211–14, 216, 245, 249, 276. *See also* Community development corporations; *names of individual organizations*
Fox Commerce Park, 247–48, 252–53
Frick, Helen Clay, 186
Frick, Henry Clay, 1, 43–45, 48, 55, 61, 76, 257, 283
Frick Coke Company, 43, 48
Friedman, Milton, 211, 297n13
Friend, Hydie, 268, 270
Friends of the Riverfront, 258–59, 278
Friends of Wheeling, 197, 265, 268
Fulton Theater, 258. *See also* Pittsburgh Cultural Trust

Garrett, Richard, 144, 147
Gateway Center, 83–84, 172

General Electric, 158, 233
Gentrification, 187, 202, 258. See also Heritage preservation
Giant Earth Mover of Egypt, 125, 140–47
Gilligan, John, 129, 143, 146, 250, 314n39
Glass industry, 8, 33, 66, 69–70, 109, 207. See also Pittsburgh Plate Glass
Goddard, Maurice, 86, 124, 128–29, 137–39
Golden Triangle, 4, 8–10, 13–14, 81–85, 172–73. See also Pittsburgh Renaissance; the Point
Great Allegheny Passage, 249, 285
Great Depression, 71–76, 81, 151, 157, 216
GroundZero Action Network, 262
Group Against Smog and Pollution, 228, 245
Grove, John J., 64, 83
Gulf Oil Company, 217, 221
Guthrie, George, 62–64

Hamm, Harry, 105, 107, 265–67
Harmon Creek Coal Company, 131
Hatch, Ralph, 125, 145–46, 148
Hays, Wayne L., 110, 112, 114, 174–75
Hazard, Leland, 75, 83
Hazelwood, 160, 284
Hazelwood Works, 206, 220, 228. See also Jones and Laughlin Steel Company; Pittsburgh Technology Center
Healthcare industry, 4, 16, 104, 107, 190–91, 203, 209, 217; in post-industrial era, 224–25, 230, 264. See also names of individual hospitals; University of Pittsburgh
H. J. Heinz Company, 223
Heinz, H. J., 80
Heinz, Howard, 73
Heinz, H. J. II "Jack," 213
Heinz, H. John III, senator, 214–15, 275. See also John Heinz History Center
Heinz Endowments, 180, 211, 245, 258, 276
Heinz Hall, 181, 205, 213–14, 258. See also Cultural District
Heritage preservation, 12, 15–16; and authenticity, 5, 15, 186, 189, 256, 279; and economic development, 245, 248–49, 256–58; 266, 268, 270–72, 274; and housing rehabilitation, 173, 179, 188, 197, 211–12. See also National Trust for Historic Preservation; Pittsburgh History and Landmarks Foundation; Rivers of Steel: Wheeling National Heritage Area

The Highlands, 272, 281
Highway Emergency and Relocation Team, 168, 188
Hill District, 9, 78, 84–85, 172, 176–78, 185, 213; Community Council, 179–80
Hillman, Henry, 186
Hillman, James, 131, 136, 140
Hollinshead, F. D., 102, 158–60, 162
Homestead, 14–15, 22, 95, 115; post-steel era, 239–40, 248, 255–56, 275–76
Homestead Works, 16–17, 48–50, 57, 153; expansion of, 35, 37, 40, 43, 115; closure of, 201, 205–6, 223, 273, 275; 1892 strike, 22, 55–56, 58, 71; preservation of, 274, 277–81. See also Carrie Furnaces; Rivers of Steel; U.S. Steel.
Homewood-Brushton, 61, 177, 179
Hubbard, Nelson, 44–45, 58–59
Hunter, John, II, 41, 196

Independent Steelworkers Union, 116, 226
Industrial corporations, 2, 7, 45, 66, 68, 217, 228; relationship with communities, 57–58, 61–62; relationship with workers, 54–56, 59, 71–72, 116–17; and vertical integration, 34–35, 37–38, 43, 56, 63. See also names of individual companies
Industrial economy, 7, 45, 58–59, 69, 223; based on heavy industry, 16, 28, 27, 109, 230; deindustrialization, 8, 10, 78, 88, 126, 150, 101, 208, 214, 239, 224–25, 232, 246, 280; diversification of, 4, 56, 68, 76, 131, 146, 162–63, 166, 208, 219–20, 233, 252; reindustrialization of, 203, 206, 218–20, 226–29, 240, 260, 273–74. See also Coal mining; Post-industrial economy; Railroads; Steel Industry
Irvin Works, 158, 230

Jacobs, Jane, 173
James, Earl, 258, 274
Joanou, Frank, 102, 107, 191
John Heinz History Center, 257, 281
Johnson administration, 112, 179
Jones and Laughlin Steel Company, 33–35, 43, 159–60, 203; part of LTV Steel, 220, 223, 225, 241. See also Hazelwood Works; Pittsburgh Works; South Side Works
Joy Mining Machinery, 71, 223

Index

Kaufmann, Edgar, 75, 87, 133–34, 138, 140
Kellogg, Paul, 39, 62, 301n26
Kennywood, 57
Kittanning, 41

LaBelle Iron Works, 35, 37–38
Labor unions, 14, 22, 54–58, 62, 71–72, 161, 207, 251, 264. *See also* Industrial corporations; *names of individual unions*
Laslo, John, 100, 108–14, 119, 193, 252
Laurel Highlands, 1, 124, 133–34, 232, 247–50, 283
Lawrence, David, 9, 11–12; and Pittsburgh Renaissance, 68, 73–77, 82–85, 88, 158–60; as Pennsylvania governor, 128, 135, 137, 173
Leith Mine and Coke Works, 48, 50
Levenson, Robert, 99, 105, 107, 190, 192, 194–96
Lewis, Charles, 132, 137
Lewis, John L., 71–72
Lorant, Stefan, 88, 196, 214
Love, George H., 88
Lowe, Stanley, 212, 288
LTV Steel. *See* Jones and Laughlin Steel Company

Magee, Christopher, 47, 60–64, 66
Magee, Edward, 99, 174
Manchester, 177; historic preservation in, 183, 185, 257, 288; industrial development in, 160, 185; and Manchester Citizens Corporation, 187, 212
Maple Creek Mine, 250–52. *See also* Murray, Robert E.
Marietta, Bob, 134, 247
Market Auditorium (Wheeling), 192–96
Market Square, 256, 262. *See also* Fifth and Forbes
Marland Heights, 117–18
Martin, George C., 82, 151
Martin, Park, 134, 156–57, 173–74
Martins Ferry, 2, 6, 95, 100, 108–15, 122–23, 144
Masloff, Sophie, 230, 260
McCahan, Lillian, 133–34, 137–40, 143, 247
McClain, James, 134, 140
McConnells Mill, 87
McCoy, James, 172

McKeesport, 103, 154, 201, 223–24, 248–49; Industrial Center of, 242–43
Mellon, Andrew, 60–61
Mellon, Richard King, 9, 12, 68, 73–79, 87, 106, 138, 153, 174
Mellon, Thomas, 43
Mellon Bank, 211, 225, 276
Mellon foundations, 87, 135, 138, 176, 216–17
Mellon Institute. *See* Carnegie Mellon University
Mesta Machine Company, 226; purchase by Park Corporation, 273
Mexican War Streets, 183, 187, 257
Midfield Terminal. *See* Pittsburgh International Airport
Millsop, Thomas, 116–19
Mon-Fayette Expressway, 232, 243–45, 247
Mon Valley Initiative, 278
Mon Valley Progress Council, 245
Mon-Yough Conference on Community Planning, 103
Monessen, 10, 40, 46, 114, 285
Monongahela River Valley, 1, 8, 16; deindustrialization of, 201, 223, 227; development of, 21–22, 29–30, 32, 34–35, 39–40
Monroeville, 149, 152–56, 158, 162, 170, 217, 233, 240, 244, 283
Moon Township, 157, 238
Moore, Arch, 174–75
Moses, Robert, 73, 151
Mt. Washington, 283–84
The Mountaineer, 140, 147
Muller, Edward K., 278, 280
Murphy, Tom, 15, 288–89; as Pittsburgh mayor, 245, 256, 259–64, 281; as state representative, 170–71, 219, 230, 234, 236–38, 248
Murray, Robert, 224, 249–54, 286
Mussio, John King, 103–4
Myers, Donald, 108–12, 252

National Association for the Advancement of Colored People, 172, 180
National Heritage Areas. *See* Rivers of Steel; Wheeling National Heritage Area
National Park Service, 86, 130, 266–68, 275–76, 280
National Register of Historic Places, 187–89, 197; and historic districts, 212, 257–58; and historic landmarks, 276–77, 280

National Steel Corporation, 119, 215, 222, 226. *See also* Weirton Steel Corporation
National Technology Transfer Center, 267
National Tube Company, 56, 242
National Trust for Historic Preservation, 212; Main Street program, 257–58, 265–66, 270
Neoliberal urbanism, 9, 12–13, 15, 297n13; development of, 173, 179, 183, 187–91, 257; limits of, 196–97, 243, 288; and Renaissance II, 203, 211–15, 220; and Renaissance III, 257–61
New Stanton, 218, 241, 283, 285
Netting, H. Graham, 87, 133–34, 139
New Deal, 73, 75
North Carolina Research Triangle, 8, 11, 218
North Hills, 164–69, 183–84. *See also* Cranberry Township; Parkway North
North Side, 78, 164–71, 174, 177, 181–89, 201, 218–19, 257, 259, 263, 285. *See also* Allegheny Center; Murphy, Tom; Parkway North; Three Rivers Stadium
Nutting, Betty, 265
Nutting, G. Ogden, 192, 265

Oakland, 61–62, 216, 284; and Pittsburgh Renaissance, 47, 93, 217; and Renaissance II, 211, 240–41. *See also* Carnegie Mellon University; University of Pittsburgh
Oakland Community Council, 245
Oglebay Park, 270–71
Ohio, state government, 6–10, 59, 110, 114, 128–29, 143, 236
Ohio River Valley, 2, 7–10, 13, 21; deindustrialization of, 223–24, 235–36, 239; development of, 28–33, 36, 38, 43, 45
Ohio Valley Medical Center, 107, 190–91, 194, 268, 272
Ohiopyle, 30, 41, 80, 125, 128, 143, 148, 215, 232; burning of Ohiopyle House, 140; and recreation industry, 1, 246–48; state park in, 7, 87, 124, 129, 133–41
Oil and gas industry, 8, 39, 42, 46, 48, 70, 76–77, 157, 223; and fracking, 284–86
Olmsted, Frederick Law, Jr., 51, 53, 63–64, 73, 82
Orrick, Herrington & Sutcliffe, LLP, 268–69

Pace, Frankie, 172
Parton, James, 53, 76, 286

Patton Township, 149, 154. *See also* Monroeville
Pease, Robert, 219, 279
Peduto, Bill, 264, 288
PennFuture. *See* Citizens for Pennsylvania's Future
Penn-Lincoln Parkway, 85, 149, 220, 233–34, 283; construction of, 151–58
Penn's Southwest Association, 215, 218, 220–22, 235, 241
Pennsylvania: state government, 59, 61, 74, 79, 128, 152, 174, 264; Department of Forests and Waters, 82, 86, 124, 128, 135, 138; Historical and Museum Commission, 274; Industrial Development Authority, 209, 218–19, 241; Post-War Planning Commission, 74, 86
Pennsylvania Railroad, 1, 32, 34, 51, 60; and Pittsburgh Renaissance, 79, 88, 136
Pennsylvania Turnpike, 85, 94, 149–51, 154–56, 162, 164–66, 233, 283
Philadelphia, 29, 31, 83, 281
Phipps, Henry, 51, 61
Pinchot, Gifford, 71
Pinkerton Detective Agency, 22, 55, 274
Public Interest Research Group (Ohio), 144
Pittsburgh and Lake Erie Railroad, 212–13, 248
Pittsburgh Chamber of Commerce, 63, 75, 80, 168, 239, 257
Pittsburgh Civic Commission, 63
Pittsburgh City Council, 61, 73, 184, 210, 227, 229
Pittsburgh Courier, 177–78
Pittsburgh Cultural Trust, 214, 230. *See also* Cultural District; Fulton Theater; Stanley Theater
Pittsburgh High Technology Council, 220, 228, 279
Pittsburgh History and Landmarks Foundation, 12, 168, 173, 229, 257–59, 274, 289; formation of, 182–83, 185; and housing rehabilitation, 186–89. *See also* Earl, James; Station Square; Van Trump, James; Ziegler, Arthur, Jr.
Pittsburgh International Airport, 11; and Airport of the Future, 219, 232–35, 244; and Pittsburgh Renaissance, 85, 94, 151, 156–58. *See also* Airport Corridor; Strategy 21

Index

Pittsburgh Partnership for Neighborhood Development, 211
Pittsburgh Pirates, 108, 168, 263, 281
Pittsburgh Plate Glass, 158, 210–11
Pittsburgh Post-Gazette, 61, 162, 184, 206, 221, 256
Pittsburgh Press, 80, 83, 137, 147, 151, 156, 229
Pittsburgh Regional Planning Association, 74, 153, 155, 166, 183, 206
Pittsburgh Renaissance, 4, 9–10, 81–89; as model for urban renewal, 4, 15, 68, 88; Renaissance II, 209–14, 219–23; Renaissance III, 256–64; revolt against, 164, 173–82. *See also* Allegheny Conference on Community Development; Golden Triangle; Lawrence, David
Pittsburgh: The Story of an American City, 88, 196, 214
Pittsburgh Steelers, 236, 263
Pittsburgh Survey, 39, 62, 76
Pittsburgh Symphony, 180, 214
Pittsburgh Technology Center, 219–21, 227, 229, 241, 258, 261, 284
Pittsburgh Works, 223, 322n3
PNC Park, 281, 285. *See also* Three Rivers Stadium
The Point, 1, 82–83, 151–52; Point State Park, 85, 104, 172, 181, 285. *See also* Golden Triangle
Pollution. *See* Air pollution; Water pollution
Post-industrial economy, 2, 4, 8–9, 16, 295n2; development of, 206–7, 219, 223, 247–48, 252–53, 256, 265, 284, 287–88; distribution of wealth in, 176, 225–26; opposition to, 203, 229–30; symbolism of, 215, 221, 235, 279
Posvar, Wesley, 218–19
Power of 32, 287
Power plants, 79, 131–32, 207, 223, 250
Powhatan Mine, 250–52. *See also* Murray, Robert
Prisbylla, Larry, 224–25
Progress Alliance, 231, 235–38, 244, 253
Project 70, 129, 138–39. *See also* Goddard, Maurice; Ohiopyle
Public-private partnerships, 2, 4–5, 9–12, 86–88, 99–100, 104–7, 209–11, 259–60; difficulty in maintaining, 79, 181–82, 194–96. *See also* Allegheny Conference on

Community Development; Wheeling Area Conference on Community Development

Railroads, 2, 28, 32–35, 40, 42, 44, 49–52, 60–61; decline of, 93, 122, 134, 247–49. *See also names of individual railroad companies*
Rail-Trails, 5, 15, 232; difficulty in developing, 249; as post-industrial symbols, 255–56; and public-private partnerships, 248–49; and riverfront revitalization, 258–59, 267, 281, 284. *See also names of individual trails*
Rails-to-Trails Conservancy, 249, 259
Rankin, 49, 201, 223, 280
Regional Industrial Development Corporation, 160–61; criticism of, 170–71, 236–37, 243; Industrial Development Fund, 162, 208–9; O'Hara Township, 161–62; Park West, 50, 157, 164, 233–34; redevelopment of mill sites, 219–20, 240–43, 283, 286; suburban focus of, 162–64, 172, 253; Thorn Hill, 150, 162, 166, 170, 241
Regional Renaissance Initiative, 263
Republican Party, 2, 62; in Martins Ferry, 109–10; in Pittsburgh, 60, 67, 72–74, 82–83, 181, 259, 264; and state politics, 71, 129, 143, 159, 174, 240; in Wheeling, 59, 267. *See also* Democratic Party
Reuther, Valentine, 27, 37, 58, 62, 69
Reuther, Victor, 27, 69, 72
Reuther, Walter, 69, 72
Rhodes, James, 110, 114, 129, 143
Richards, Wallace, 74
Rivers, 13–5; and industrialization, 22–23, 40, 49–51; and recreation, 85, 132–39, 215, 242, 250, 258–59, 267; and riverine society, 16, 21, 27–28, 33. *See also* Friends of the Riverfront; *names of individual rivers*; Water pollution
Rivers of Steel, 15, 255–56, 263–64, 273; designation as National Heritage Area, 275; regional vision of, 278–79. *See also* Carrie Furnaces; Homestead Works; Steel Industry Heritage Corporation
Riverside Ironworks, 27, 37
Rizzi, Aida, 143, 146
Robert C. Byrd Intermodal Transportation Center, 268–69

Robin, John P., 83–84, 210
Robinson, Frank Brooks, Sr., 164, 171, 241–43
Robinson Township, 157, 234
Ronsheim, Milton, 125, 129, 312n12
Roosevelt, Franklin D., 71, 73
Rust Belt, 8, 10, 206, 223, 225, 227, 229
Ryan, Robert H., 161–64, 208–9, 218

Sacrifice zones, 14, 125
St. Clairsville, 109
St. Louis, 10, 47, 74, 76, 83
Salk, Jonas, 216
Sanitary Water Board, 137–38
Scaife, Richard Mellon, 12, 187, 262, 298n18
Scaife foundations, 186–87, 212–13, 216
Schmidt, Adolph, 87, 134, 140, 186
Schuster, Norma, 143, 146
Scranton, William, 128–29, 139
Sewickley, 157, 165
Shadyside, 61
Shapp, Milton, 167, 214
Silicon Valley, 8, 11
Silver Spade, 140, 142
Sinclair, Dohrman, 61
Skybus, 181
Smoke control. *See* Air pollution
Smithfield Mining Company, 136–38
Soffer Organization, 261
Somerset, 1; rail-trails in, 248
Sony Corporation, 241, 283
South Hills, 85, 151, 157, 176
South Side, 40, 64, 176, 212, 256–57; Local Development Corporation, 257, 260–61. *See also* South Side Works
South Side Works, 227–29; redevelopment of, 256, 260–61, 274. *See also* Jones and Laughlin Steel Company
Southern Beltway, 233, 240, 244–45, 253
Southwestern Pennsylvania Industrial Resource Center, 241
Squirrel Hill Tunnel, 152, 283
Stafford, Richard, 259–60
Stanley Theater, 206, 265. *See also* Pittsburgh Cultural Trust
Station Square, 12, 212–15, 256–57, 284–85. *See also* Pittsburgh History and Landmarks Foundation
Steel industry, 8, 12, 16, 32–36, 55, 72, 119; decline of, 122, 169, 202, 223–24; representations of, 52–53, 228–29, 279; steelmaking process, 47–51, 54–56, 119, 121; Steelmark campaign, 121; steelworkers, 116, 161, 172, 225–26, 229, 247. *See also names of individual companies*; Industrial economy; United Steelworkers of America
Steel Industry Heritage Corporation, 275–80, 282, 289; formation of task force, 274–75, 278. *See also* Rivers of Steel
Steel Valley, as describing Pittsburgh metropolitan region, 2, 6–8, 21–23, 45, 295n3
Steel Valley Authority, 227–29, 260
Steel Valley Trail Council, 248
Steele, Charles, 110–15, 193
Stone & Thomas, Inc., 194, 271
Stout, Mike, 227
Strategy 21, 219–21, 229, 233–34, 237–38, 240, 257, 259, 266
Strip District, 257, 281
Summerset at Frick Park, 283
Steubenville, 6–7, 9–10, 253; during industrial era, 56–60; early development, 30–33, 37–42; economic and urban decline of, 103–4, 174. *See also* Progress Alliance
Sun Belt, 8, 118, 150, 221
Swissvale, 151, 280

Thornburgh, Richard, 168–69, 214, 218, 240–41
Three Rivers Stadium, 181, 202; replacement of, 259, 263; and urban renewal, 167–68, 174, 181, 183, 185, 320n19
Three Rivers Task Force, 258
Thwaites, Reuben Gold, 21–23, 42, 53, 55, 65, 93, 201–3, 279
Tax increment financing, 12, 257, 260–61, 263
Turtle Creek, 154, 160, 208, 242

Union Switch and Signal, 221
Uniontown, 22, 43, 50
US Airways, 163, 238. *See also* Allegheny Airlines
United Mine Workers of America, 54–55, 71, 130, 250
United Negro Protest Committee, 172, 176, 178
United Steelworkers of America, 71–72, 116, 161, 172, 226–27

Index

University of Pittsburgh, 1, 11, 82, 84, 158, 215–21, 229, 284–85; Cathedral of Learning, 78, 216; Medical Center, 217, 288
Upper Ohio Valley. *See* Ohio River Valley; Steel Valley
U.S. Route 22, 118–19, 122, 154, 157, 231, 236–39; Byrd Expressway, 235; Findlay Connector, 239, 244; Veterans Memorial Bridge, 237
U.S. Steel, 16, 45–46, 244, 289; and Century III Mall, 244; decline of, 201, 205, 223, 230, 240, 244, 273; and environmental problems, 228, 260; growth of, 48, 56–57, 70–72; and Pittsburgh Renaissance, 67–68, 79, 84, 88, 158, 217
Urban Redevelopment Authority of Pittsburgh, 9, 12, 83–85, 159. *See also* Allegheny Center; Caliguiri, Richard; Flaherty, Peter; Heritage preservation; Lawrence, David; Murphy, Tom; Pittsburgh Renaissance
Urban Renewal Authority of Wheeling, 189–97

Van Buskirk, Arthur, 74–75, 83, 152
Van Trump, James D., 182, 185–87, 189, 197, 212
Victorian Wheeling, 264–65, 271; proposed outlets, 281
Volkswagen, 218, 241, 283
Voneida, Theodore, 128, 143–44, 314n39

Washington (Pa.), 30, 41, 156
Washington County, 86, 151, 160, 234, 244, 286,
Washington's Landing, 261
Water pollution, 51–52, 62, 65, 80, 165, 201, 221; acid mine drainage, 44, 50, 80, 137, 156, 250
The Waterfront, 16, 273, 276
Waterhouse, Jack, 102, 192
Weir, Ernest, 46, 57, 72–73, 115, 117. *See also* Weirton Steel Corporation
Weirton, 2, 6, 40, 57–58, 60, 100, 115–16, 118–20, 122; Chamber of Commerce, 121; reorientation toward Pittsburgh, 235–36, 238, 253
Weirton Steel Corporation, 45–47, 70, 121, 226; and antiunion efforts, 72, 116–17. *See*

also Weir, Ernest; Independent Steelworkers Union
West Penn Power, 134, 138, 313n22
West Virginia, state government of, 32–33, 59, 63, 104–5, 236, 267
West Virginia Independence Hall, 197, 265, 272
West Virginia Northern Community College, 268
Western Maryland Railway, 133, 247
Western Pennsylvania Conservancy, 86–87, 124–25, 128, 131–41, 148, 186, 246–49
Westinghouse Electric Corporation, 11, 37, 45, 85, 137, 158–60, 163, 215, 217–18, 226, 242
Westmoreland County, 150–51, 160, 218, 248
Wharf garage, 104–6, 255, 268–69
Wheeling & Lake Erie Railway, 285
Wheeling: City Council, 101, 105–6, 189, 192–96; competition with Pittsburgh, 29–38, 44–45; 265–66, 269; Planning Commission, 105, 193
Wheeling Area Conference on Community Development, 10, 83, 99, 99–100, 189–92, 104–7, 112, 191–97, 265; absorbed into Chamber of Commerce, 189
Wheeling Civic Center, 192, 195–96, 264, 269
Wheeling College, 105, 192, 216
Wheeling Corrugating Company, 63, 69, 193. *See also* Wheeling-Pittsburgh Steel
Wheeling National Heritage Area, 255, 266–71; Artisan Center, 267–72
Wheeling-Pittsburgh Steel, 109–10, 223
Wheeling Suspension Bridge, 31, 265–66
White Oak, 154
White water rafting, 1, 128, 247
Whorls, Randy, 267, 270–71
Widner, Ralph, 93–95, 99, 125, 127–29, 148, 150, 201, 218
Wiese, Andrew, 201–3, 258
Wright, Frank Lloyd, 75, 133. *See also* Fallingwater

Yablonsky, Dennis, 287
Youghiogheny River, 30, 41, 50, 135, 137, 248, 250, 285

Ziegler, Arthur, Jr., 182–83, 185, 187, 189, 196–97, 212, 262

ACKNOWLEDGMENTS

I had the good fortune to cast down my bucket at Shippensburg University, where I have found incredibly supportive colleagues, respectful administrators, engaged students, and the financial support that has made this project possible. With regard to the latter, I first want to thank donors to the Shippensburg University Foundation who have provided research and travel funds through the Center for Faculty Excellence in Scholarship and Teaching. Jim Mike's leadership as dean of the College of Arts and Sciences resulted in a number of faculty-student collaborative research grants from which I have benefited greatly. I am grateful to the Pennsylvania State System of Higher Education and my tuition-paying students for a two-course research reassignment in Fall 2009 and a sabbatical in Spring 2014. Among my wonderful colleagues in the History and Philosophy Department, I owe a particular debt to Steve Burg for covering many service responsibilities during my sabbatical. I would also like to acknowledge the many research assistants that have toiled for me over the years, especially Makenzie Diehl for her work on Pittsburgh's North Side and Chad Crumrine for his research on coal mining near Ohiopyle State Park.

During the course of research and writing this book, I have made many friends among Pittsburgh residents and scholars. First among these is Ted Muller, whose kindness, cheerfully given criticism, and expansive knowledge gathered during more than three decades as an activist-scholar have made him a mentor to a generation of researchers. Joel Tarr has also been exceptionally generous with his time and consistently supportive of my project since its inception. I have appreciated the feedback and support from attendees of the Pittsburgh History Roundtable held periodically at the Heinz History Center, especially Alexis Macklin, John McCarthy,

Michael Glass, Patrick Vitale, Jared Day, and Vagel Keller, as well as Sherie Mershon, whose encyclopedic dissertation on the Allegheny Conference on Community Development is the go-to guide for scholars of postwar Pittsburgh. Similarly, conversations with Ken and Liz Fones-Wolf, Lou Martin, Charles Julian, David Javersak, Augie Carlino, and Jeremy Morris greatly enhanced my understanding of Wheeling, Weirton, Homestead and Steubenville. I also want to thank participants in a double session on the Pittsburgh Renaissance at the 2013 conference of the Society for American City and Regional Planning History; those not already mentioned include Laura Grantmyre, Mariel Isaacson, Andrew Simpson, Jon Teaford and Tracy Neumann. Over the past few years, Tracy and I have become writing buddies and I am deeply appreciative of her own top-notch research on Pittsburgh's political history from which I have drawn liberally as well as her insightful comments on the preliminary version of this manuscript.

This project would not have been possible without the willingness of many residents of metropolitan Pittsburgh to share their stories with me. A list of oral history interviews conducted over the past fifteen years is included at the beginning of the notes. In particular, I would like to pay my respects to Don Myers, who passed away suddenly in 2008. A devoted public official who served in a number of roles throughout his lifetime, Don was an unabashed champion of his hometown of Martins Ferry and the Upper Ohio Valley in general. I also relied heavily on the staffs of numerous archives ranging in size from the Ohio Historical Society and Pennsylvania State Archives down to the tiniest reading areas at local libraries. David Grinnell at the Heinz History Center and more recently the University of Pittsburgh Archives Service Center has been a good friend and provided great leads over the years.

Bob Lockhart at the University of Pennsylvania Press has been an unfailing champion of this project. He provided just the right combination of patience, gentle pressure and unfailingly good advice that I needed to complete the book in a form with which we could both be pleased. In my opinion, widely shared among those who know him, Bob is the best in the business. Thank you to Tom Sugrue who advocated on my behalf as well as the editorial board and staff at the press. David Stradling and Andrew Hurley provided exceptionally good reader's reviews that significantly enhanced the final product. Jim Hodges has been a steadfast mentor ever since my time at the College of Wooster, while Matt Lassiter continues to be a trusted advisor long after I left his care at the University of Michigan.

Acknowledgments

Thanks also to Andrew Wiese, whose canoe trip down the Ohio River in 1987 is recounted in the introduction to Part III.

Finally, thank you to my parents, Marsha and David Ward, aunts, uncles, grandparents, and great grandparents who provided the motivation for this project as well as a number of key interviews. My in-laws, Sally and David Dieterich, have been enthusiastic cheerleaders as well as welcoming hosts during yearly retreats to their lake house. Though she has long since moved out from Pittsburgh's suburbs to the rural hinterland, my inspirational grandmother, Dot Witherow, still tells stories of hopping on the streetcar to see the Pirates (and twice the Homestead Grays) at Forbes Field and how she was in the stands when Clemente hit an RBI in Game 5 of the 1971 World Series. Thank you also to Montana and Eli, who remind me that keyboards are occasionally better suited to sitting on and fingers used for chin scratches than for typing. My greatest thanks go to my wife, Amanda, who makes work worth stopping and the present much more appealing than anything the past can offer.